Lecture Notes in Computer Science   3640

Commenced Publication in 1973
Founding and Former Series Editors:
Gerhard Goos, Juris Hartmanis, and Jan van Leeuwen

T0218634

Miguel Castro   Robbert van Renesse (Eds.)

Peer-to-Peer Systems IV

4th International Workshop, IPTPS 2005
Ithaca, NY, USA, February 24-25, 2005
Revised Selected Papers

 Springer

Volume Editors

Miguel Castro
Microsoft Research
7 JJ Thomson Avenue, Cambridge CB3 0FB, UK
E-mail: mcastro@microsoft.com

Robbert van Renesse
Cornell University, Department of Computer Science
Ithaca, NY 14853, USA
E-mail: rvr@cs.cornell.edu

Library of Congress Control Number: 2005936069

CR Subject Classification (1998): C.2.4, C.2, H.3, H.4, D.4, F.2.2, E.1, D.2

ISSN   0302-9743
ISBN-10   3-540-29068-0 Springer Berlin Heidelberg New York
ISBN-13   978-3-540-29068-1 Springer Berlin Heidelberg New York

Springer is a part of Springer Science+Business Media

springeronline.com

© Springer-Verlag Berlin Heidelberg 2005
Printed in Germany

Typesetting: Camera-ready by author, data conversion by Scientific Publishing Services, Chennai, India
Printed on acid-free paper   SPIN: 11558989   06/3142   5 4 3 2 1 0

Preface

The 4th International Workshop on Peer-to-Peer Systems was held at Cornell on February 24th and 25th 2005. The IPTPS workshop continued to bring together researchers and practitioners from a variety of disciplines, including networking, theory, databases, security, and scientific computing. They described experimental findings, discussed challenges, and presented novel techniques.

We received 123 submissions. Submissions were limited to 6 pages, one page more than in previous years. The submissions were reviewed by a Program Committee consisting of 18 international experts from academia and industry. After a bidding process, each committee member was assigned 20 papers to review, generating 3 reviews for each paper. Controversial papers were assigned additional reviewers. The papers were then ranked based on originality, technical merit, and topical relevance, as well as the likelihood that the ideas expressed would lead to insightful technical discussions at the workshop. The program chairs suggested a program which was extensively discussed and revised by the entire committee to produce the final program.

We accepted 24 papers, which were organized into 8 sessions: Security and Incentives, Search, Multicast, Overlay Algorithms, Empirical Studies, and Network Locality, and two sessions on miscellaneous topics. Authors revised their submissions for a preproceedings distributed at the workshop. After the workshop, the authors revised their papers once more for the proceedings before you.

In order to focus discussions, attendance was restricted to Program Committee and to Steering Committee members and to at most two authors per paper. This resulted in 55 attendees from 9 countries at the workshop. Each session included 3 talks (20 minutes presentation and 5 minutes for questions), and a discussion panel (15 minutes). This format stimulated lively interaction between the participants of the workshop, and resulted in interesting and insightful discussions. The workshop was webcast, and followed by approximately 50 additional attendees from 10 countries.

The organization of the workshop involved many people. We thank the Program Committee for their hard work and for selecting an excellent program. Bill Hogan did an outstanding job with all of the local arrangements and maintaining the web server. Wenjie Wang and Sugih Jamin provided the live webcast. Twelve student scribes kept notes for the workshop report included in this proceedings. The Steering Committee provided guidance behind the scenes. Microsoft provided generous support. But, most of all, we wish to thank all participants of IPTPS 2005 for making this workshop a success.

July 2005   Miguel Castro and Robbert van Renesse

Organization

Workshop Co-chairs

Miguel Castro	Microsoft Research
Robbert van Renesse	Cornell University

IPTPS Steering Committee

Peter Druschel	Rice University
Frans Kaashoek	MIT
Antony Rowstron	Microsoft Research
Scott Shenker	UC Berkeley
Ion Stoica	UC Berkeley

Program Committee

Karl Aberer	EPFL
Mary Baker	HP Labs
Hari Balakrishnan	MIT
Bobby Bhattacharjee	Maryland
Miguel Castro	Microsoft Research
Peter Druschel	Rice
Hector Garcia-Molina	Stanford
Anne-Marie Kermarrec	INRIA
Barbara Liskov	MIT
Dahlia Malkhi	HUJI, Microsoft Research
Timothy Roscoe	Intel Research
Emin Gun Sirer	Cornell
Alex Snoeren	UC San Diego
Ion Stoica	UC Berkeley
Robbert van Renesse	Cornell
Maarten van Steen	VU Amsterdam
Helen Wang	Microsoft Research
Ben Zhao	UC Santa Barbara

Administrative Assistant

Bill Hogan	Cornell

Sponsoring Institution

Microsoft Corporation

Table of Contents

Multicast

Overlay Algorithms

Empirical Studies

Miscellaneous

Exploiting Network Locality

Workshop Report

Mahesh Balakrishnan[1], Maya Haridasan[1], Prakash Linga[1], Hongzhou Liu[1],
Venu Ramasubramanian[1], Sean Rhea[2], Manpreet Singh[1],
Vidhyashankar Venkatraman[1], Vivek Vishnumurthy[1], Kevin Walsh[1],
Bernard Wong[1], and Ming Zhong[3]

[1] Cornell University
[2] University of California Berkeley
[3] University of Rochester

Session 1: Security and Incentives

A Self-Repairing Peer-to-Peer System Resistant to Dynamic Adversarial Churn. Presented by Stefan Schmid.

Q: Is d (the dimensionality of the hypercube) constant? Does it scale? **A:** Yes, it scales. d is logarithmic in the number of peers in the system.

Q: Presumably in some cases you need to copy data between the core and periphery of nodes. Do you have any analysis? **A:** When a new peer joins the core, it needs to copy data, but when a peer becomes a core peer, it never becomes peripheral again unless there is a dimension change. I don't have an analysis of how often this happens.

Q: What happens to locality properties in the system? **A:** Locality is not a prime issue in our system. However, there is often a peer in the neighboring node that is geographically close. So this could be one heuristic to take locality into account.

Q: All routes are going to pass through core nodes. Could that be a problem? **A:** Yes, that is true. To address that, one optimization would be to distribute the cores' load into the peripheral peers.

A First Look at Peer-to-Peer Worms: Threats and Defenses. Presented by Lidong Zhou.

Q: Have you looked into imposing some structure on guardian placement? **A:** We haven't looked at it. Under our current model, having guardian nodes at strategic locations will improve the containment results. However, a worm might be able to infer those locations and change its path of infection. It is not clear in the end whether strategic placement helps.

Q: You consider that it takes zero time to generate an alert. How realistic is that assumption? **A:** We have some data based on our more recent work on alert generation mechanisms. It certainly varies with worms, but is under 1 second for some existing worms we have looked at.

Q: It seems like you are picking regular peers to become guardian peers. How do you know you can trust them? **A:** The alerts are verifiable and must be verified before they are accepted. Otherwise, they can be used to launch attacks on the receiving nodes. Fake alerts generated by malicious nodes will be dropped. This helps reduce the level of trust on guardian nodes.

Q: Patches to remove vulnerabilities may require human intervention and considerable time, even though detecting a signature for particular worms may be easier. Have

M. Castro and R. van Renesse (Eds.): IPTPS 2005, LNCS 3640, pp. 1–12, 2005.
© Springer-Verlag Berlin Heidelberg 2005

you thought about the impact of this? **A:** Human intervention is not suited for containing p2p worms, which could spread very quickly. We are working on automating the process of generating and applying patches.

Q: How effective can guardians be? We could have a hybrid propagation mode where worms propagate also through links other than the peer-to-peer links. **A:** Hybrid worms require a combination of defense mechanisms. We haven't yet studied how those hybrid worms propagate and how effective our mechanism would be for those attacks.

Q: What if the guardian nodes are connected? **A:** We actually have a graph that shows what happens if we connect all the guardian nodes. It shows a visible but limited effect.

Kill the Messenger: A Taxonomy of Rational Attacks. Presented by Seth Nielson.

Q: Sometimes systems relax strict behavioral requirements from the nodes in order to handle exigencies. For example, tit-for-tat is relaxed when nodes join a p2p network after a failure. How would you classify attacks that exploit this? **A:** We classified those attacks under the excuses category but they certainly would also be policy attacks.

Q: Attacks are possible in systems, for example BitTorrent, where mechanisms (incentives) are good but the implementation is wrong. How do you classify these attacks? **A:** There may be attacks due to implementation faults, for example, a manufactured evidence attack can happen in BitTorrent. But, despite that, incentives in BitTorrent work well.

Q: BitTorrent is successful because payoff is low. If payoff is high, can the behavior change? **A:** Yes.

Q: Is tit-for-tat in BitTorrent beneficial? **A:** There would be more rational manipulation without tit-for-tat.

Q: Is BitTorrent the first system to implement rational incentives? **A:** Other systems have tried to apply incentive techniques as well, for example, Kazaa, but they were easily subverted. It is hard to build incentive mechanisms in a distributed manner. BitTorrent does pretty well.

Panel Discussion

Q: (For Lidong) You did not mention existing worms in Gnutella. **A:** I would not call them worms in the same sense, but rather viruses. They require users' actions to propagate and therefore their propagation is slow and can be relatively easily stopped.

Q: (For Seth) How does rational behavior work at the overlay routing layer? **A:** It would depend on the user's view of cost/benefit. We would need a cooperation model to tackle it.

Q: (For Lidong) Can worm propagation be mitigated by having different systems connected to each other as neighbors, for example, a Windows system with a Linux system? **A:** Diversity at one hop may yield better containment results under our current worm model. But, p2p worms can find two-hop neighbors and infect those directly. So diversity just among neighbors does not solve the problem completely.

Q: (For Seth) Do attacks go away if we can reason about client protocols? For example, we could get a certificate that all Gnutella nodes use the same Gnutella library. **A:** It could make it worse. If all the nodes are running the same software, then they are all vulnerable to the same attacks. However, it will eliminate rational attacks.

Session 2: Search

Brushwood: Distributed Trees in Peer-to-Peer Systems. Presented by Chi Zhang.

Q: One of your slides shows a distributed KD-tree built with Brushwood which allows nearest neighbor selection in an n-dimensional virtual coordinate space. Can you use this nearest neighbor selection scheme in the tree construction to make it proximity-aware, to allow for low latency/stretch routing? **A:** No, proximity neighbor selection is handled by the underlying skip graph. The skip graph performs proximity neighbor selection by selecting close neighbors for the large hops.

Q: What is the latency stretch of Brushwood? **A:** Similar to the stretch of Pastry.

Q: How does Brushwood perform node deletion? **A:** When a node leaves, its tree fragments are merged with a neighbor node.

Arpeggio: Metadata Searching and Content Sharing with Chord. Presented by Dan Ports.

Q: Do you know the average number of keywords in Gnutella queries? **A:** I don't have the exact number for you, but I can imagine it's something similar to web queries, where the average number is about 2.5.

Q: Instead of introducing Index Gateways to decide if metadata is already in the network, can you just query for the metadata to decide if it already exists? **A:** The Index Gateway has other advantages related to some things I didn't present in this talk. For example, since the availability of a file changes constantly, we expire the metadata on a regular basis. The metadata needs to be refreshed periodically to prevent expiration. The gateway knows when metadata will expire and is responsible for renewing it on all the index nodes.

Q: Since you have the sub-rings, can you just assign a specific node, like the last node, of the sub-ring to do that? **A:** That's one possibility, but our design is intended to keep the indexing system and the content distribution system independent.

Q: Suppose a node shares a lot of files. Does that mean it needs to join lots of sub-rings? What's the cost of that? **A:** The cost of joining a sub-ring is $O(\log N)$ communications, while the storage cost is constant.

Q: By "constant," do you mean per sub-ring? **A:** Per node in the sub-ring. **Q:** Suppose you are a member of K sub-rings. Does that mean you have storage cost proportional to K? **A:** Yes, but the cost is only a few bytes per sub-ring, as compared to many megabytes for the actual file data. It's negligible.

Q: I think Overnet is a deployed file sharing system that allows for keyword search using heuristic methods. **A:** I believe Overnet uses an inverted index table with some index side filtering. We are adding keyword sets that improve the distribution of load across nodes in the network.

Q: The idea of keyword-set indexing is trading storage for lookup time, but the storage overhead seems too high to me. Suppose there are 10 keywords per metadata and a query contains 3 keywords on average. The overhead will be a ratio of 1000. Isn't this too high? **A:** We are looking at files with a small amount of metadata. The FreeDB analysis shows that constructing the index requires an increase of only a factor of ten.

Q: Suppose you have only 10 keywords in a metadata block, why don't you just use a 10-dimension DHT? In this way, you can find the metadata simply by DHT lookup? **A:** We don't believe this would work. It's not clear how to perform a multi-keyword search with this scheme.

Q: For FreeDB, how much storage space do you need? **A:** The total requires about one and a half billion index entries, but each index entry is very small, since it only needs to store the file metadata. For comparison, the total amount of audio data indexed by FreeDB is hundreds of terabytes.

Q: How would you do sub-string search? **A:** We don't provide support for sub-string search.

Q: It seems to me you are underestimating the size of the query because a query for Gnutella, unlike the web case, usually contains more than 3 keywords. **A:** Even if this is true, it isn't a problem if queries are larger. Suppose you have a query of size 6 and the maximum keyword-subset has a size of 3. You can still select a random three-keyword subset, and send the query to the index responsible. Because we're using index-side filtering, this still requires only transmitting relevant results.

Q: Have you thought about locality when choosing a node that's storing a file? **A:** The sub-ring lookups will give you a list of nodes that are sharing a file. You can choose one that's nearby. **Q:** By pinging each of them? **A:** Yes.

Overcite: A Cooperative Digital Research Library. Presented by Jeremy Stribling.

Q: Do you have the numbers for the search and storage costs of Google scholar? Do you think services supported by Google will obviate the need for Citeseer? **A:** We do not have any numbers on that but I don't think it will obviate the need for Citeseer. Google's services are free but there cannot be community control over them. For example, you will not be able to support new features that the community wants.

Q: How are you replicating the documents? **A:** Using the DHT. **Q:** What is the replication factor? **A:** Two. **Q:** How do you know that is enough? **A:** We feel this is good enough since nodes donated by universities can be assumed to be relatively stable. Even if it is not sufficient, we can alter the replication factor.

Q: You should be looking for volunteers. How can universities contribute resources to this system? **A:** The system is not completed. Once it is, we will make a formal announcement.

Q: You were talking about using one-hop DHTs. Instead, it makes a lot of sense if we can use existing, deployed DHTs such as OpenDHT or eDonkey. Have you ever thought of it? **A:** I don't think OpenDHT can support 760GB of data. **C:** This seems a perfect application for OpenDHT.

Q: There are certain things offered by centralized solutions that are very difficult to apply in the distributed case, such as spam filtering, correcting bad entries, and other administrative support. How do you plan to address them? **A:** First of all, Citeseer doesn't provide support for these features currently. But that is an interesting question and we have to think about it.

Q: Have you thought about security implications of distributing this system over the wide area. Potentially there are incentives for people to manipulate indices, the ranking and so on. **A:** Good point. We haven't thought about it yet.

Q: Aren't there copyright issues if you are going to replicate these documents? **A:** Legal issues may crop up. At present, Citeseer does not have any special agreements with the authors and it works well without them.

Q: Do you think a decentralized system is necessary at all? **A:** Let's see after we build it. I think it makes sense to try. **C:** I think Google scholar will need a lot of machines and bandwidth to make their system scalable. The p2p solution offers a simpler and cheaper way to do this. There is a technical and social side to the management issue and your system solves the technical side to these management issues.

Panel Discussion

Q: (For Jeremy) Ignoring non-computer science issues like copyrights, how would you compare using DHTs against regular mirroring or CDNs like Akamai? Even if you use DHTs, certain things have to be done in a centralized way as others have pointed out. Even if you want to extend features, a centralized authority (a committee of some form) may have to agree as to whether to do it or not. So issues against Citeseer may turn against Overcite as well. But leaving that aside, I am trying to think of the advantages that a pure distributed system would give when compared to the other alternatives. **A:** We do not know the exact answer, since we have not deployed our system yet. **C:** Leveraging Google-like solutions may require high bandwidth. Costs will definitely decrease if p2p is used. **C:** But why can't you mirror then? I can't seem to find a convincing answer as to why a p2p solution should be used. **C:** Never mind using p2p or mirroring. Finding an alternative to Citeseer is important and this work is a significant step in that direction.

Session 3: Miscellaneous 1

Peering Peer-to-Peer Providers. Presented by Michael Walfish.

Q: The benefit of DHTs is that you can run one per application—they could be decoupled. **A:** I'm not advocating coupling.

Q: Do you really expect people to run DSPs, and if so, what would their motivation be? **A:** That's what happened when NSF-Net turned into a bunch of Internet service providers, so there is some precedent.

NetProfiler: Profiling Wide-Area Networks using Peer Cooperation Presented by Venkata Padmanabhan

Q: Blame assignment may cause pushback; Can you certify diagnoses? **A:** It's hard for one client to prove a problem. It's easier to prove you *can* get to a website than that you *can't*. Our tool gives a better diagnosis for rational ISPs, which want to fix the problems identified in order to retain users.

Q: If you want to deploy the system on a large scale, and you are interested in diagnosing long-term failures, how do you handle churn in P2P systems? **A:** This is an interesting issue that we haven't yet looked into. But we already replicate data in P2P systems; we could replicate failure information. Also failure information may not need to be as fault-tolerant.

A Statistical Theory of Chord under Churn. Presented by Supriya Krishnamurthy.

Q: Is it easy to extend this analysis to consider latency distributions? **A:** Yes, I think so.

Panel Discussion

Q: (For Venkata) Can NetProfiler be used to detect DDoS attacks? **A:** We can use it to detect new virus outbreaks, and the initial steps (causality) involved in a DDoS attack.

Q: (For Michael) About the forest of DSPs model: does put/get scale like BGP, which uses aggregation? **A:** We're only talking about small multiplicative factors; people using the service can absorb that cost.

Q: (For Michael) I'm not aware of any peering storage services at present. **A:** What kind of peering services do you have in mind? **C:** The non-existence of peered storage services indicates a problem for you. **C:** Inktomi web cache peering is a good example.

Q: (For Michael) Can you think of particular examples that might benefit from DSPs? **A:** HIP. Keys identify hosts, values identify IP addresses. For music sharing, the "bring your own infrastructure" model works fine.

Session 4: Multicast

The Impact of Heterogeneous Bandwidth Constraints on DHT-Based Multicast Protocols. Presented by Sanjay Rao.

Q: I don't quite see what you mean about the multi-tree approach not being useful. **A:** If you have constant degree, the multi-tree approach is useful. But with varying degrees, you want the higher degree nodes higher in the tree in order to minimize depth, and multi-trees do not accomplish this.

Q: It seems that the issues you raise are not fundamental. I can think of some simple fixes that might work. For example, it is possible to remove the in-degree skew in Pastry. It would also help to make the degree proportional to the capacity of the node. You can do this by changing the way proximity neighbor selection works to bias it towards nodes with higher degree. **A:** Maybe you are right but I am pointing out these issues that have not been solved yet.

Q: Does SplitStream address these issues? **A:** (Miguel) I think it does! (Sanjay) I think it does not!

Chainsaw: Eliminating Trees from Overlay Multicast. Presented by Vinay Pai.

Q: What is the difference between BitTorrent and your multicast streams, really? **A:** BitTorrent distributes files, not live content. **Q:** But they both stream. Is it just your sliding window? **A:** Yes, it may be just the sliding window.

Q: You mention that your SplitStream implementation has problems with recovery. Did you try the version from Rice, which has more functionality? **A:** No, we didn't, because we thought that using the Macedon version would be fairer, since the others were implemented in Macedon. But Macedon's implementation of SplitStream is not complete.

Q: Did SplitStream use erasure coding to recover from errors in your experiments? **A:** No. I don't think that is implemented in Macedon.

Q: You mention for the DVD example that you use 8KB packets. How do you deal with the 1500 byte packet limit? **A:** Our implementation is over TCP. **Q:** Do you have a breakdown of costs and overheads. Say, the costs relative to the bandwidth of the stream, versus costs that are constant regardless of the size of the data, etc.? **A:** No, I don't have those numbers. We haven't looked at it.

FeedTree: Sharing Web Micronews with Peer-to-Peer Event Notification. Presented by Dan Sandler.

Q: It seems that this might already be solved. Can't Akamai and others do this? There is a lot of work on cooperative caching. **A:** This is very different because the data set is very volatile. I am a big fan of Akamai and CDNs but it seems that multicast is just a very natural fit for micronews.

Panel Discussion

Q: Why do multicast and not just file distribution with buffering? File distribution gives you time shifting like TiVo and people love it. **A:** There are lectures and video conferencing where you need low delay for real-time interaction.

Q: (For Vinay) Is the delay such that you can't get it with file distribution with buffering? With multicast, if you don't get the bits in time, they just go away forever, but with file distribution with buffering, you can still get all the bits. **A:** No, the bits don't have to go away permanently. As long as seeds still have the bits, they can be recovered. Also, you might have the availability window in Chainsaw spanning GBytes to allow time shifting. **C:** Trees might have better delay than Chainsaw. **C:** But Chainsaw might be more resistant to failures.

Session 5: Overlay Algorithms

Hybrid Overlay Structure Based on Random Walk. Presented by Xiong Yongqiang.

Q: You compute coordinates for nodes in an n-dimensional space using GNP and then map them to a one-dimensional space to enable DHT lookups. Two nodes that are close in the n-dimensional space map to close location numbers in the one-dimensional space but what about the converse property? **A:** It is possible that two nodes close together in the one-dimensional space are actually far apart in the n-dimensional space. So when a node joins, it gets the list of clusters that have location numbers that are close to its own. Then the new node needs to measure the latencies between the different clusters and decide which cluster to join.

Quickly routing searches without having to move content. Presented by Brian Cooper.

Q: With the two optimizations you proposed, every step of the route becomes deterministic. With high network churn, many walks are likely to fail because the target neighbor is down. **A:** If you worry about churn, you can combine these techniques with random walks. At some steps, you choose the next hop by document count and at others, you choose it randomly. An alternative is to perform two walks simultaneously: one based on document counts and a pure random walk.

Q: Did you try random walks biased by node degree in the power law network? **A:** Yes, we did try that. We looked at previous work that performs random walks biased by node degree. This works with the assumption that the node knows the data stored by its neighbors, which requires content movement. If we perform random walks biased by degree without content information, the result is roughly the same as a pure random walk. That's the reason we didn't bias by degree but by document count.

Q: When you use a square root topology, what does the CDF of node degrees look like compared to power law networks? **A:** The peers with the largest degrees have significantly lower degree than in power law networks. The skew is significantly smaller than in power law networks.

Practical Locality-Awareness for Large Scale Information Sharing. Presented by Dahlia Malkhi.

Q: I am worried about coloring and vicinity balls. You assume that a node's vicinity ball has at least a node from each color but that's not guaranteed. **A:** When we get to probability 2^{-80}, that's good enough. If you are still concerned that with churn we cannot find a node of the desired color, that's not a problem. We just go to another neighbor. **Q:** Can you take those extra local hops and still be within the routing stretch of 2? **A:** Our experimental cumulative stretch graph shows stretch above 2 for about 5% of the nodes. That's the difference between the system and the formal algorithm.

Q: Have you done a worst case analysis of node degree? **A:** Yes, it's $\sqrt{n} \cdot \log n$.

Q: What happens when the number of nodes grows or shrinks? **A:** Obviously we need to estimate $\sqrt{n}$, but it does not have to be accurate. This is pretty easy: as the network grows all the red nodes will realize the network is growing and split into two different shades of red. When the network shrinks that's even easier: for example, the red and blue nodes decide to have the same color.

Panel Discussion

Q: We regularly see new routing protocols being proposed. Have we reached a point where instead of proposing new protocols, we should be evaluating how existing protocols serve specific applications? **A:** You are right. I agree that we should tweak the knobs inside each algorithm, instead of trying to engineer a new algorithm.

Q: It's interesting to note that Brian and Dahlia's papers have taken very different approaches: Dahlia's paper talks of 2-hop routes by keeping a lot of state, whereas Brian's paper throws away state but has routes with average hop-lengths of about 8000. **A:** (Brian Cooper) Yes, there are tradeoffs involved but it is difficult to maintain invariants when there is churn if the degree is large. **C:** (Dahlia Malkhi) But without large enough degree, the network will be partitioned under churn.

Session 6: Empirical Studies

An Empirical Study of Free-Riding Behavior in the Maze P2P File Sharing System. Presented by Zheng Zhang.

Q: Is free-riding a real problem? Do free-riders consume that many resources that we need to figure out a way to make them stop? **A:** Yes, free-riding is a problem. The system performance can be improved by getting a better utilization of free-rider's resources. **C:** A brand new user starts with more points than a user that consumes some files. You could consider a version of the system where the user starts at the bottom of the hierarchy, with no points to use, as a way to reduce whitewashing.

Q: Should you set a bottom limit on the point system? **A:** We haven't thought about it. It's a good suggestion. **C:** Once you get past a certain point, it doesn't matter how low your points get. There's only an upper bound on bandwidth. **Q:** But it affects your position in the queue, which is the log of points. **A:** Yes, that's true.

Q: I'd like to ask about attacks where people cheat to get more points. For the fake file attack or colluding attack, maybe some reputation mechanism can be adopted, for example, Pagerank or EigenTrust. **A:** Absolutely. We have an algorithm to detect that. There's another related problem that happens in Maze. Sometimes a student transfers a file from his office to his dorm, and ends up getting points for that transfer.

Q: Does altruism really exist in Maze? From the graphs, it seems like there are a couple of users that upload a few terabytes? Do they offset the free-riders? **A:** Yes. Our top 10 list motivates people to upload to gain recognition.

Q: What are the typical types of data you found on Maze? **A:** Interesting images, Hollywood DVDs, software.

Clustering in P2P exchanges and consequences on performances. Not presented.

The BitTorrent P2P File Sharing System: Measurement and Analysis. Presented by Johan Pouwelse and Pawel Garbacki.

Q: When the tracker crashes everything stops. Why doesn't the RIAA DoS trackers? **A:** It's not true that everything stops when the tracker fails. What happens is that no new peers can join the system, but the joined peers can continue. The peer selection mechanism is done locally. When the tracker fails, it's not possible to detect the newcomers, but a peer can continue downloading. One of the things we're trying to do now is to distribute the tracker's functionality, for example, having the peers gossip the IP addresses of peers in the system. **Q:** And who runs the trackers now? **A:** Web sites like Supernova run big trackers.

Q: How do you measure the peer uptime? **A:** We just contact the peers and ask them for some random pieces to check whether they are up or not. We do this once every few minutes.

Q: Is there any data downloaded that is not copyrighted material? Have you collected any statistics to check whether there is different behavior of users for copyrighted and not copyrighted material? **A:** It depends on the tracker list. There are basically three types of users. The first group consists of the Linux Open Source population, which shows altruistic behavior and has high performance. The second group consists of regular users, sharing illegal content, and which have no sharing ratio requirements. And the last consists of a membership-based community, that enforces a strict sharing ratio to further stimulate the performance of the network.

Q: How well does tit-for-tat work in BitTorrent? Do we need additional mechanisms? **A:** Tit-for-tat outperforms the queuing mechanism in EDonkey or the aggressive seed-jumping policy used by Pirate Bay.

Panel Discussion

C: You have been talking about altruism in file sharing systems. But it is not really altruism, it is just contributing your idle CPU time and unused bandwidth capacity for stealing copyrighted material.

Q: (For Zheng Zhang) Is it easy to collude or manipulate your point system? **A:** We can detect some cheaters but we may not ban them since that may lead to population shrinkage.

Q: (For Zheng Zhang) Will high-end users be willing to give their resources? Is there a penalty for users with slow links? **A:** There is a built-in natural selection mechanism.

Session 7: Miscellaneous 2

Dynamic Load Balancing in DHTs. Presented by Miroslaw Korzeniowski.

Q: You are trying to achieve uniform load balancing. What about heterogeneous load balancing when nodes have different capacities? **A:** This is hard. We may be able to do this within a constant factor, but I am not sure. **C:** One of our algorithms [Karger and Ruhl, SPAA 2004] could do this. I think the $O(\log \log N)$ moves guarantee would still hold but we might need additional assumptions like constant skew in capacity.

Q: If nodes leave, do they need to do so politely to help rebalance? **A:** We don't react to joins and leaves. We run the algorithm continuously.

Q: How about using a virtual node approach to do heterogeneous load balancing? **A:** I don't like virtual nodes because you need to keep track of more state. **C:** Virtual nodes also add more links that you have to maintain. **C:** Right, and they don't work well for fractional load balancing. To have one node with 10% more load than another, we must have at least 11 virtual nodes in one node and 10 in the other.

Q: How do you prevent people from claiming arbitrary node identifiers to attack the DHT? **A:** Preventing people from migrating is not sufficient for security. **C:** No, but it's still necessary. It is the first step. **C:** One solution is to allow each node to choose from a small set of ids for its virtual nodes. $\log N$ ids to choose from does not give the attacker too much power.

High Availability in DHTs: Erasure Coding vs. Replication. Presented by Rodrigo Rodrigues.

Q: Can better coding techniques increase the usefulness of coding relative to replication? **A:** Currently, we use IDA with 14 fragments, 7 of which are needed to reconstruct. I'm not sure if other techniques could help.

Q: Is there an advantage to erasure coding for updates? **A:** Writes are faster using coding since less data must be copied into the DHT but this comes at some additional CPU cost. **C:** But you can't do sub-block updates as easily with erasure coding because you must reconstruct, update, and then re-encode.

Conservation vs. Consensus in Peer-to-Peer Preservation Systems. Presented by Prashanth Bungale.

Q: How is bit-rot defined? In particular, are bit insertion and deletion included in your definition of bit-rot? **A:** Corruption, insertion, and deletion of bits are all included in the definition of bit-rot.

Q: Do coordinated attacks make the consensus-based scheme more vulnerable? **A:** Yes, we have an analysis of coordinated attacks is in the paper.

Q: If a library's reputation is damaged, it cannot join the system again because of black-listing. **A:** It is not a problem because the black-listing can be removed using out-of-band channels.

Q: Since objects in this system are immutable, why can't you use digital signatures to verify integrity? **A:** We do not use digital signatures because the public key would have to be remembered for a long time. **C:** The arguments against using hashing schemes and digital signatures for checking bit-rot are not convincing, and these issues are not discussed in the paper. **C:** Using signatures will simply shift the preservation problem to preserving the public key. **C:** But the problem of preserving the public key also exists in remembering the name of the document being preserved.

Panel Discussion

Q: (For Prashanth Bungale) Is there a role for erasure codes in digital archival? **A:** No. There isn't much need for coding because replicas already exist in the digital archival case. **C:** But coding might be useful because it alters the nature of bit-rot. **C:** (Rodrigo Rodrigues) Indeed, coding would make bit-rot more noticeable, and it might also make insertion attacks less likely.

Session 8: Exploiting Network Locality

Locality Prediction for Oblivious Clients. Presented by Kevin Shanahan.

Q: Why not use IP anycast? **A:** I am not familiar with IP anycast.

Q: I'm confused about the problem you saw with Vivaldi coordinates Do you have an intuition about what's going wrong? **A:** It is just due to the local errors in the estimates. 20% can be attributed to misbehaving PlanetLab nodes.

Q: Have you thought about using something other than latency? **A:** Certainly, we could use other metrics, such as server reliability.

Impact of Neighbor Selection on Performance and Resilience of Structured P2P Networks. Presented by Byung-Gon Chun.

Q: How does the CDF of latencies for the transit-stub model compare to the one on PlanetLab? **A:** It's almost a normal distribution. **Q:** Which is not what PlanetLab looks like at all. **A:** Yes, maybe.

Q: You show that adding random links adds resilience. Did you look at taking a random first hop after noticing a failure? **A:** I think in this case it may not help but in other cases it might.

Evaluating DHT-Based Service Placement for Stream-Based Overlays. Presented by Jeff Schneidman.

Q: How planar is the transit-stub graph? **A:** It's planar. **C:** So this is an optimistic case for network coordinates. You could use the King data set, which is non-planar. I think you can also manipulate the transit-stub generator to make it non-planar. PlanetLab is very non-planar.

Q: Could you have more than one join operator? **A:** Yes.

Q: Did you do this on real DHTs or is it all simulated? **A:** What I've shown you is all simulated.

Panel Discussion

C: It would be great if we had an alternative to the transit-stub model. We have good all-pairs latency sets but not a good topology model. **C:** You can use the Mercator router-level topology. **C:** But it does not have latency annotations.

C: (Peter Druschel) Eugene Ng and I started a project a few months ago to replicate the properties of the King data set. One thing we already know is that the statistical properties of the King data set are very different from what we see in the transit-stub model.

C: One reason I used the transit-stub model is because it has nice hierarchical properties that make it easier to compute routes. We can compute routes inside a domain, then compute the routes between domains. I tried power-law networks, but it is too much computation.

C: Our experience with Vivaldi on PlanetLab was terrible. We put lots of effort into it, for example, reducing scheduling delays. We're not entirely sure what's the cause but it may be just due to congestion and utilization.

A Self-repairing Peer-to-Peer System Resilient to Dynamic Adversarial Churn*

Fabian Kuhn, Stefan Schmid, and Roger Wattenhofer

Computer Engineering and Networks Laboratory,
ETH Zurich, 8092 Zurich, Switzerland

Abstract. We present a dynamic distributed hash table where peers may join and leave at any time. Our system tolerates a powerful adversary which has complete visibility of the entire state of the system and can continuously add and remove peers. Our system provides worst-case fault-tolerance, maintaining desirable properties such as a low peer degree and a low network diameter.

1 Introduction

Storing and handling data in an efficient way lie at the heart of any data-driven computing system. Compared to a traditional client/server approach, decentralized peer-to-peer (P2P) systems have the advantage to be more reliable, available, and efficient. P2P systems are based on common desktop machines ("peers"), distributed over a large-scale network such as the Internet. These peers share data (as well as the management of the data) that is conventionally stored on a central server. Usually, peers are under control of individual users who turn their machines on or off at any time. Such peers join and leave the P2P system at high rates ("churn"), a problem that is not existent in orthodox distributed systems. In other words, a P2P system consists of unreliable components only. Nevertheless, the P2P system should provide a reliable and efficient service.

Most P2P systems in the literature are analyzed against an adversary who can crash a functionally bounded number of random peers. After crashing a few peers the system is given sufficient time to recover again. The scheme described in this paper significantly differs from this in two major aspects. First, we assume that joins and leaves occur in a worst-case manner. We think of an adversary which can remove and add a bounded number of peers. The adversary cannot be fooled by any kind of randomness. It can choose which peers to crash and how peers join.[1] Note that we use the term "adversary" to model worst-case behavior. We do not consider Byzantine faults. Second, the adversary does not have to wait until the system is recovered before it crashes the next batch of peers.

---

* Research (in part) supported by the Hasler Stiftung and the Swiss National Science Foundation.

[1] We assume that a joining peer knows a peer which already belongs to the system. This is known as the *bootstrap* problem.

M. Castro and R. van Renesse (Eds.): IPTPS 2005, LNCS 3640, pp. 13–23, 2005.

Instead, the adversary can constantly crash peers while the system is trying to stay alive. Indeed, our system is *never fully repaired* but *always fully functional*. In particular, our system is resilient against an adversary which continuously attacks the "weakest part" of the system. Such an adversary could for example insert a crawler into the P2P system, learn the topology of the system, and then repeatedly crash selected peers, in an attempt to partition the P2P network. Our system counters such an adversary by continuously moving the remaining or newly joining peers towards the sparse areas.

Clearly, we cannot allow our adversary to have unbounded capabilities. In particular, in any constant time interval, the adversary can at most add and/or remove $O(\log n)$ peers, n being the total number of peers currently in the system. This model covers an adversary which repeatedly takes down machines by a distributed denial of service attack, however only a logarithmic number of machines at each point in time. Our algorithm relies on messages being delivered timely, in at most constant time between any pair of operational peers. In distributed computing such a system is called *synchronous*. Note that if nodes are synchronized locally, our algorithm also runs in an asynchronous environment. In this case, the propagation delay of the slowest message defines the notion of time which is needed for the adversarial model.

The basic structure of our P2P system is a hypercube. Each peer is part of a distinct hypercube node; each hypercube node consists of $\Theta(\log n)$ peers. Peers have connections to other peers of their hypercube node and to peers of the neighboring hypercube nodes. In the case of joins or leaves, some of the peers have to change to another hypercube node such that up to constant factors, all hypercube nodes own the same number of peers at all times. If the total number of peers grows or shrinks above or below a certain threshold, the dimension of the hypercube is increased or decreased by one, respectively.

The balancing of peers among the hypercube nodes can be seen as a dynamic token distribution problem [1] on the hypercube. Each node of a graph (hypercube) has a certain number of tokens, the goal is to distribute the tokens along the edges of the graph such that all nodes end up with the same or almost the same number of tokens. While tokens are moved around, an adversary constantly inserts and deletes tokens. Our P2P system builds on two basic components: i) an algorithm which performs the described dynamic token distribution and ii) an information aggregation algorithm which is used to estimate the number of peers in the system and to adapt the dimension accordingly.

Based on the described structure, we get a fully scalable, efficient P2P system which tolerates $O(\log n)$ worst-case joins and/or crashes per constant time interval. As in other P2P systems, peers have $O(\log n)$ neighbors, and the usual operations (e.g. search) take time $O(\log n)$. In our view a main contribution of the paper, however, is to propose and study a model which allows for dynamic adversarial churn. We believe that our basic algorithms (dynamic token distribution and information aggregation) can be applied to other P2P topologies, such as butterflies, skip graphs, chordal rings, etc. It can even be used for P2P systems that go beyond distributed hash tables (DHT).

The paper is organized as follows. In Section 2 we discuss relevant related work. Section 3 gives a short description of the model. A detailed discussion of our P2P system is given in Sections 4 and 5. Section 6 concludes our work.

2   Related Work

A plethora of different overlay networks with various interesting technical properties have been proposed over the last years (e.g. [2][3][4][5][6][7][8][9][10][11][12]). Due to the nature of P2P systems, fault-tolerance has been a prime issue from the beginning. The systems usually tolerate a large number of random faults. However after crashing a few peers the systems are given sufficient time to recover again. From an experimental point of view, churn has been studied in [13], where practical design tradeoffs in the implementation of existing P2P networks are considered.

Resilience to worst-case failures has been studied by Fiat, Saia et al. in [14][15]. They propose a system where, w.h.p., $(1 - \varepsilon)$-fractions of peers and data survive the adversarial deletion of up to half of all nodes. In contrast to our work the failure model is static. Moreover, if the total number of peers changes by a constant factor, the whole structure has to be rebuilt from scratch.

Scalability and resilience to worst-case joins and leaves has been addressed by Abraham et al. in [16]. The focus lies on maintaining a balanced network rather than on fault-tolerance in the presence of concurrent faults. In contrast to our paper, whenever a join or leave happens, the network has some time to adapt.

The only paper which explicitly treats arbitrarily concurrent worst-case joins and leaves is by Li et al. [17]. In contrast to our work, Li et al. consider a completely asynchronous model where messages can be arbitrarily delayed. The stronger communication model is compensated by a weaker failure model. It is assumed that peers do not crash. Leaving peers execute an appropriate "exit" protocol and do not leave before the system allows this; crashes are not allowed.

3   Model

We consider the *synchronous message passing model*. In each round, each peer can send a message to all its neighbors. Additionally, we have an adversary $\mathcal{A}(J, L, \lambda)$ which may perform J arbitrary joins and and L arbitrary leaves (crashes) in each interval of λ rounds.

We assume that a joining peer π_1 contacts an arbitrary peer π_2 which already belongs to the system; π_2 then triggers the necessary actions for π_1's integration. A peer may be contacted by several joining peers simultaneously. In contrast to other systems where peers have to do some finalizing operations before leaving, we consider the more general case where peers depart or crash without notice.

4   Algorithm

In this section, we describe the maintenance algorithm which maintains the simulated hypercube in the presence of an adversary which constantly adds and removes peers. The goal of the maintenance algorithm is twofold. It guarantees that each node always contains at least one peer which stores the node's data. Further, it adapts the hypercube dimension to the total number of peers in the system.

This is achieved by two basic components. First, we present a dynamic token distribution algorithm for the hypercube. Second, we describe an information aggregation scheme which allows the nodes to simultaneously change the dimension of the hypercube.

4.1   Dynamic Token Distribution

The problem of distributing peers uniformly throughout a hypercube is a special instance of a *token distribution problem*, first introduced by Peleg and Upfal [1]. The problem has its origins in the area of load balancing, where the workload is modelled by a number of *tokens* or jobs of unit size; the main objective is to distribute the total load equally among the processors. Such load balancing problems arise in a number of parallel and distributed applications including job scheduling in operating systems, packet routing, large-scale differential equations and parallel finite element methods. More applications can be found in [18].

Formally, the goal of a token distribution algorithm is to minimize the maximum difference of tokens at any two nodes, denoted by the *discrepancy* ϕ. This problem has been studied intensively; however, most of the research is about the *static variant* of the problem, where given an arbitrary initial token distribution, the goal is to redistribute these tokens uniformly. In the *dynamic variant* on the other hand, the load is dynamic, that is, tokens may arrive and depart *during* the execution of the token distribution algorithm. In our case, peers may join and leave the simulated hypercube at arbitrary times, so the emphasis lies on the dynamic token distribution problem on a d-dimensional hypercube topology.

We use two variants of the token distribution problem: In the *fractional token distribution*, tokens are arbitrarily divisible, whereas in the *integer token distribution* tokens can only move as a whole. In our case, tokens represent peers and are inherently integer. However, it turns out that the study of the fractional model is useful for the analysis of the integer model.

We use a token distribution algorithm which is based on the *dimension exchange method* [19][20]. Basically, the algorithm cycles continuously over the d dimensions of the hypercube. In step s, where $i = s \bmod d$, every node $u := \beta_0...\beta_i...\beta_{d-1}$ having a tokens balances its tokens with its adjacent node in dimension i, $v := \beta_0...\overline{\beta_i}...\beta_{d-1}$, having b tokens, such that both nodes end up with $\frac{a+b}{2}$ tokens in the fractional token distribution. On the other hand, if the tokens are integer, one node is assigned $\lceil \frac{a+b}{2} \rceil$ tokens and the other one gets $\lfloor \frac{a+b}{2} \rfloor$ tokens.

It has been pointed out in [19] that the described algorithm yields a perfect discrepancy $\phi = 0$ after d steps for the static fractional token distribution. In [20], it has been shown that in the worst case, $\phi = d$ after d steps in the static integer token distribution. We can show that if the decision to which node to assign $\lceil \frac{a+b}{2} \rceil$ and to which node to assign $\lfloor \frac{a+b}{2} \rfloor$ tokens is made randomly, the final discrepancy is constant in expectation. However, we do not make use of this because it has no influence on our asymptotic results.

In the following, the dynamic integer token distribution problem is studied, where a "token adversary" $\mathcal{A}(J, L, 1)$ adds at most J and removes at most L tokens at the beginning of each step. In particular, we will show that if the initial distribution is perfect, i.e., $\phi = 0$, our algorithm maintains the invariant $\phi \leq 2J + 2L + d$ at every moment of time.

For the dynamic fractional token distribution, the tokens inserted and deleted at different times can be treated independently and be superposed. Therefore, the following lemma holds.

Lemma 1. *For the dynamic fractional token distribution, the number of tokens at a node depends only on the token insertions and deletions of the last d steps and on the total number of tokens in the system.*

Proof. Assume that a total amount of T tokens are distributed in two different ways on the d-dimensional hypercube. According to [19], each node has exactly $\frac{T}{2^d}$ tokens after d steps in the absence of an adversary. On the other hand, the token insertions and removals of the adversary that happen in-between can be treated as an independent superposition, as the corresponding operations are all linear. ∎

We can now bound the discrepancy of the integer token distribution algorithm by comparing it with the fractional problem.

Lemma 2. *Let v be a node of the hypercube. Let $\tau_v(t)$ and $\tau_{v,f}(t)$ denote the number of tokens at v for the integer and fractional token distribution algorithms at time t, respectively. We have $\forall t : |\tau_v(t) - \tau_{v,f}(t)| \leq \frac{d}{2}$.*

Proof. For $t = 0$, we have $\tau_v(t) = \tau_{v,f}(t)$. For symmetry reasons, it is sufficient to show the upper bound $\tau_v(t) \leq \tau_{v,f}(t) + \frac{d}{2}$. We first prove by induction that $\tau_v(t) \leq \tau_{v,f}(t) + \frac{t}{2}$ at time t.

For the induction step, we consider two neighbors u and v which exchange tokens. We have

$$\tau_v(t+1) \leq \left\lceil \frac{\tau_v(t) + \tau_u(t)}{2} \right\rceil$$

$$\leq \left\lceil \frac{\lfloor \tau_{v,f}(t) + \frac{t}{2} \rfloor + \lfloor \tau_{u,f}(t) + \frac{t}{2} \rfloor}{2} \right\rceil$$

$$\leq \frac{\lfloor \tau_{v,f}(t) + \frac{t}{2} \rfloor + \lfloor \tau_{u,f}(t) + \frac{t}{2} \rfloor}{2} + \frac{1}{2}$$

$$\leq \tau_{v,f}(t+1) + \frac{t+1}{2}.$$

The second inequality follows from the induction hypothesis and the fact that $\tau_v(t)$ and $\tau_u(t)$ are integers. Note that adding or removing tokens has no influence on the difference between τ_v and $\tau_{v,f}$ because it modifies τ_v and $\tau_{v,f}$ in the same way.

So far, we have seen that the number of integer tokens can deviate from the number of fractional tokens by at most $\frac{d}{2}$ after the first d steps. In order to show that this holds for all times t, we consider a fractional token distribution problem $\hat{\tau}_{v,f}$ for which $\hat{\tau}_{v,f}(t-d) = \tau_v(t-d)$. Using the above argument, we have $\tau_v(t-d) \leq \hat{\tau}_{v,f}(t)$ and by Lemma 1, we get $\hat{\tau}_{v,f}(t) = \tau_{v,f}(t)$. This concludes the proof.

Lemma 3. *In the presence of an adversary $\mathcal{A}(J, L, 1)$, it always holds that the integer discrepancy $\phi \leq 2J + 2L + d$.*

Proof. We show that the *fractional* discrepancy ϕ_f is bounded by $2J+2L$. Since Lemma 2 implies that for the integer discrepancy ϕ_i it holds that $\phi_i - \phi_f \leq d$, the claim follows. Let $J_t \leq J$ and $L_t \leq L$ be the insertions and deletions that happen at the beginning of step t. First, we consider the case of joins only, i.e., $L_t = 0$. Assume that all J_t tokens are inserted at node $v = \beta_0...\beta_i...\beta_{d-1}$ where $i := t \bmod d$. In the upcoming paragraph, all indices are implicitly modulo d. In step t, according to the token distribution algorithm, v keeps $J_t/2$ tokens and sends $J_t/2$ to node $u = \beta_0...\overline{\beta_i}...\beta_{d-1}$. In step $t+1$, $J_t/4$ are sent to nodes $\beta_0...\beta_i\overline{\beta_{i+1}}...\beta_{d-1}$ and $\beta_0...\overline{\beta_i}\overline{\beta_{i+1}}...\beta_{d-1}$, and so on. Thus, after step $t+d-1$, every node in the d-dimensional hypercube has the same share of $\frac{J_t}{2^d}$ tokens from that insertion. We conclude that a node can have at most all insertions of this step, half of the insertions of the last step, a quarter of all insertions two steps ago and so on:

$$\underbrace{J_t + \frac{J_{t-1}}{2} + \frac{J_{t-2}}{4} + ... + \frac{J_{t-(d-1)}}{2^{d-1}}}_{< 2J} + \underbrace{\frac{J_{t-d}}{2^d} + \frac{J_{t-(d+1)}}{2^d} + \frac{J_{t-(d+2)}}{2^d} + ...}_{\text{shared by all nodes}}$$

Since $J_{t-i} \leq J$ for $i = 0, 1, 2, ...$, we have $\phi_f \leq 2J$. For the case of only token deletions, the same argument can be applied, yielding a discrepancy of at most $2L$. Finally, if there are both insertions and deletions which do not cancel out each other, we have $\phi_f \leq 2J + 2L$.

4.2   Information Aggregation

When the total number of peers in the d-dimensional hypercube system exceeds a certain threshold, all nodes $\beta_0 ... \beta_{d-1}$ have to split into two new nodes $\beta_0 ... \beta_{d-1}0$ and $\beta_0 ... \beta_{d-1}1$, yielding a $(d+1)$-dimensional hypercube. Analogously, if the number of peers falls beyond a certain threshold, nodes $\beta_0 ... \beta_{d-2}0$ and $\beta_0 ... \beta_{d-2}1$ have to merge their peers into a single node $\beta_0 ... \beta_{d-2}$, yielding a $(d-1)$-dimensional hypercube. Based on ideas also used in [21][22][23], we present an algorithm which provides the same estimated number of peers in the system to all nodes in every step allowing all nodes to split or merge synchronously, that is, in the same step. The description is again made in terms of *tokens* rather than peers.

Assume that in order to compute the total number of tokens in a d-dimensional hypercube, each node $v = \beta_0...\beta_{d-1}$ maintains an array $\Gamma_v[0...d]$, where $\Gamma_v[i]$ for $i \in [0, d]$ stores the estimated number of tokens in the sub-cube consisting of the nodes sharing v's prefix $\beta_0...\beta_{d-1-i}$. Further, assume that at the beginning of each step, an adversary inserts and removes an arbitrary number of tokens at arbitrary nodes. Each node $v = \beta_0...\beta_{d-1-i}...\beta_{d-1}$ then calculates the new array $\Gamma_v'[0...d]$. For this, v sends $\Gamma_v[i]$ to its adjacent node $u = \beta_0...\overline{\beta_{d-1-i}}...\beta_{d-1}$, for $i \in [0, d-1]$. Then, $\Gamma_v'[0]$ is set to the new number of tokens at v which is the only node with prefix $\beta_0...\beta_{d-1}$. For $i \in [1, d]$, the new estimated number of tokens in the prefix domain $\beta_0...\beta_{d-1-(i+1)}$ is given by the total number of tokens in the domain $\beta_0...\beta_{d-1-i}$ plus the total number of tokens in domain $\beta_0...\overline{\beta_{d-1-i}}$ provided by node u, that is, $\Gamma_v'[i+1] := \Gamma_v[i] + \Gamma_u[i]$.

Lemma 4. *Consider two arbitrary nodes v_1 and v_2 of the d-dimensional hypercube. Our algorithm guarantees that $\Gamma_{v_1}[d] = \Gamma_{v_2}[d]$ at all times t. Moreover, it holds that this value is the correct total number of tokens in the system at time $t - d$.*

Proof. We prove by induction that at time $t + k$, all nodes sharing the prefix $\beta_0...\beta_{d-1-k}$ for $k \in [0, d]$ store the same value $\Gamma_v[k]$ which represents the correct state of that sub-domain in step t.

$k = 0$: There is only one node having the prefix $\beta_0...\beta_{d-1}$, so the claim trivially holds.

$k \rightarrow k+1$: By the induction hypothesis, all nodes v with prefix $\beta_0...\beta_{d-1-(k+1)}$ β_{d-1-k} share the same value $\Gamma_v[k]$ which corresponds to the state of the system k steps earlier, and the same holds for all nodes u with prefix $\beta_0...\beta_{d-1-(k+1)}$ $\overline{\beta_{d-1-k}}$. In step $k + 1$, all these nodes having the same prefix $\beta_0...\beta_{d-1-(k+1)}$ obviously store the same value $\Gamma_v'[k+1] = \Gamma_u'[k+1] = \Gamma_v[k] + \Gamma_u[k]$.

5 Simulated Hypercube

Based on the components presented in the previous sections, both the topology and the maintenance algorithm are now described in detail. In particular, we show that, given an adversary $\mathcal{A}(d + 1, d + 1, 6)$ which inserts and removes at most $d+1$ peers in any time interval of 6 rounds, 1) the out-degree of every peer is bounded by $\Theta(\log^2 n)$ where n is the total number of peers in the system, 2) the network diameter is bounded by $\Theta(\log n)$, and 3) every node of the simulated hypercube has always at least one peer which stores its data items, so no data item will ever be lost.

5.1 Topology

We start with a description of the overlay topology. As already mentioned, the peers are organized to simulate a d-dimensional hypercube, where the hypercube's nodes are represented by a group of peers. A data item with identifier id is stored at the node whose identifier matches the first d bits of the hash-value of id.

The peers of each node v are divided into a *core* $\mathcal{C}_v$ of at most $2d+3$ peers and a *periphery* $\mathcal{P}_v$ consisting of the remaining peers; all peers within the same node are completely connected (*intra-connections*). Moreover, every peer is connected to all *core* peers of the neighboring nodes (*inter-connections*). Figure 1 shows an example for $d = 2$.

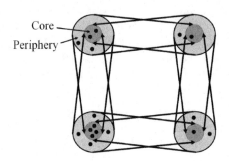

Fig. 1. A simulated 2-dimensional hypercube with four nodes, each consisting of a core and a periphery. All peers within the same node are completely connected to each other, and additionally, all peers of a node are connected to all core peers of the neighboring nodes. Only the core peers store data items, while the peripheral peers may move between the nodes to balance biased adversarial changes.

The data items belonging to node v are replicated on all core peers, while the peripheral peers are used for the balancing between the nodes according to the peer distribution algorithm and do not store any data items. The partition into core and periphery has the advantage that the peers which move between nodes do not have to replace the data of the old node by the data of the new nodes in most cases.

5.2   6-Round (Maintenance) Algorithm

The *6-round (maintenance) algorithm* maintains the simulated hypercube topology described in the previous section given an adversary $\mathcal{A}(d + 1, d + 1, 6)$. In particular, it ensures that 1) every node has at least one core peer all the times and hence no data is lost; 2) each node always has between $3d + 10$ and $45d + 86$ peers; 3) only peripheral peers are moved between nodes, thus the unnecessary copying of data is avoided.

In the following, we refer to a complete execution of all six rounds of the maintenance algorithm as a *phase*. Basically, the 6-round algorithm balances the peers across one dimension in every phase according to the token distribution algorithm as described in Section 4.1; additionally, the total number of peers in the system is computed with respect to an earlier state of the system by the information aggregation algorithm of Section 4.2 to expand or shrink the hypercube if the total number of peers exceeds or falls below a certain threshold. In our system, we use the lower threshold $LT := 8d + 16$ and the upper threshold $UT := 40d + 80$ for the total number of peers *per node on average*.[2]

While peers may join and leave the system at arbitrary times, the 6-round algorithm considers the (accumulated) changes only once per phase. That is, a snapshot of the system is made in round 1; rounds 2 – 6 then ignore the changes that might have happened in the meantime and depend solely on the snapshot at the beginning of the phase.

Round 1: Each node v makes the snapshot of the currently active peers. For this, each peer in v sends a packet with its own ID and the (potentially empty) ID set of its joiners to all adjacent peers *within* v.

Round 2: Based on the snapshot, the core peers of a node v know the total number of peers in the node and send this information to the neighboring core with which they have to balance in this phase (cf. Section 4.1). The cores also exchange the new estimated total number of peers in their domains with the corresponding adjacent cores (cf. Section 4.2). Finally, each peer informs its joiners about the snapshot.

Round 3: Given the snapshot, every peer within a node v can compute the new periphery (snapshot minus old core). This round also prepares the transfer for the peer distribution algorithm across dimension i: The smaller of the two nodes determines the peripheral peers that have to move and sends these IDs to the neighboring core.

Round 4: In this round, the peer distribution algorithm is continued: The core which received the IDs of the new peers sends this information to the periphery. Additionally, it informs the new peers about the neighboring cores, etc.

The dimension reduction is prepared if necessary: If the estimated total number of peers in the system is beyond the threshold, the core peers of a node which will be reduced send their data items plus the identifiers of all their peripheral peers (with respect to the situation *after* the transfer) to the core of their adjacent node in the largest dimension.

Round 5: This round finishes the peer distribution, establishes the new peripheries, and prepares the building of a new core. If the hypercube has to grow in this phase, the nodes start to split, and vice versa if the hypercube is going to shrink.

Given the number of transferred peers, all peers can now compute the new peripheries. Moreover, they can compute the new core: It consists of the peers of the old core which have still been alive in Round 1, plus the $2d + 3 - |\mathcal{C}|$ smallest IDs in the new periphery, where $\mathcal{C}$ is the set of the old core peers which have still been alive in Round 1. The old core then informs all its neighboring nodes (i.e., their old cores) about the new core.

---

[2] Note that since we consider the threshold *on average*, and since these values are provided with a delay of d phases in a d-dimensional hypercube (see Lemma 4), the number of peers at an individual node may lie outside $[LT, UT]$.

If the hypercube has to grow in this phase, the smallest $2d+3$ peers in the new periphery of the node that has to be split become the new core of the expanded node, and half of the remaining peripheral peers build its periphery. Moreover, the necessary data items are sent to the core of the expanded node, and the neighboring (old) cores are informed about the IDs of the expanded core.

If the hypercube is about to shrink, all old cores in the lower half of the hypercube (the surviving sub-cube) inform their periphery about the peers arriving from the expanded node and the peers in the expanded node about the new core and its periphery. The data items are copied to the peers as necessary.

Round 6: In this round, the new cores are finally built: The old core forwards the information about the new neighboring cores to the peers joining the core.

Moreover, if the hypercube has been reduced, every peer can now compute the new periphery. If the hypercube has grown, the old core forwards the expanded cores of its neighbors to *all* peers in its expanded node.

6   Conclusion

We presented a first distributed hash table which provably tolerates dynamic worst-case joins and leaves. Our techniques can also be used to create robust P2P systems based on other topologies having different properties. For example in [24], we present a system based on the pancake graph with peer degree $O(\frac{\log n}{\log \log n})$ and network diameter $O(\frac{\log n}{\log \log n})$, tolerating an adversary that may join and crash $\Theta(\frac{\log n}{\log \log n})$ many peers per communication round.

We believe that our approach opens several exciting P2P research challenges. For example: How well perform classic P2P proposals when studied with a dynamic failure model or what is the adversary/efficiency tradeoff when studying dynamic models?

References

1. Peleg, D., Upfal, E.: The Token Distribution Problem. SIAM J. on Computing **287(2)** (1989) 229–243
2. Aberer, K.: P-Grid: A Self-Organizing Access Structure for P2P Information Systems. In Proc. 9th Int. Conference on Cooperative Information Systems (CoopIS) (2001) 179–194
3. Abraham, I., Dobzinski, O., Malkhi, D.: LAND: Stretch $(1 + \varepsilon)$ Locality-Aware Networks for DHTs. Proc. 15th Ann. ACM-SIAM Symp. on Discrete Algorithms (SODA) (2004) 550–559
4. Aspnes, J., Shah, G.: Skip Graphs. In Proc. 14th Ann. ACM-SIAM Symp. on Discrete Algorithms (SODA) (2003) 384–393
5. Awerbuch, B., Scheideler, Ch.: The Hyperring: A Low-Congestion Deterministic Data Structure for Distributed Environments. In Proc. 15th Ann. ACM-SIAM Symp. on Discrete Algorithms (SODA) (2004)
6. Harvey, N., Jones, M., Saroiu, S., Theimer, M., Wolman, A.: SkipNet: A Scalable Overlay Network with Practical Locality Properties. In Proc. 4th USENIX Symp. on Internet Technologies and Systems (USITS) (2003)

7. Bindel, D., Chen, Y., Eaton, P., Geels, D., Gummadi, Kubiatowicz, J., R., Rhea, S., Weatherspoon, H., Weimer, W., Wells, Ch., Zhao, B.: OceanStore: An Architecture for Global-scale Persistent Storage. In Proc. of ACM ASPLOS (2000)
8. Malkhi, D., Naor, M., Ratajczak, D.: Viceroy: A Scalable and Dynamic Emulation of the Butterfly. In Proc. 21st Ann. Symp. on Principles of Distributed Computing (PODC) (2002) 183–192
9. Plaxton, G., Rajaraman, R., Richa, A.: Accessing Nearby Copies of Replicated Objects in a Distributed Environment. In Proc. 9th Ann. ACM Symp. on Parallel Algorithms and Architectures (SPAA) (1997) 311–320
10. Francis, P., Handley, Karp, R., M., Ratnasamy, S., Shenker, S.: A Scalable Content Addressable Network. In Proc. of ACM SIGCOMM 2001
11. Balakrishnan, H., Kaashoek, F., Karger, D., Morris, R., Stoica, I.: Chord: A Scalable Peer-to-peer Lookup Service for Internet Applications. In Proc. ACM SIGCOMM Conference (2001)
12. Joseph, A., Huang, L., Kubiatowicz, J., Stribling, J., Zhao, B.: Tapestry: A Resilient Global-scale Overlay for Service Deployment. IEEE Journal on Selected Areas in Communications **22** (2004)
13. Geels, D., Kubiatovicz, J., Rhea, S., Roscoe, T.: Handling Churn in a DHT. In Proc. USENIX Ann. Technical Conference (2004)
14. Fiat, A., Saia, J.: Censorship Resistant Peer-to-Peer Content Addressable Networks. In Proc. 13th Symp. on Discrete Algorithms (SODA) (2002)
15. Gribble, S., Fiat, A., Karlin, A., Saia, J., Saroiu, S.: Dynamically Fault-Tolerant Content Addressable Networks. In Proc. 1st Int. Workshop on Peer-to-Peer Systems (IPTPS) (2002)
16. Abraham, I., Awerbuch, B., Azar, Y., Bartal, Y., Malkhi, D., Pavlov, E.: A Generic Scheme for Building Overlay Networks in Adversarial Scenarios. In Proc. 17th Int. Symp. on Parallel and Distributed Processing (IPDPS) (2003)
17. Li, X., Misra, J., Plaxton, G.: Active and Concurrent Topology Maintenance. In Proc. 18th Ann. Conference on Distributed Computing (DISC) (2004)
18. Hurson, Kavi, K., A., Shirazi, B.: Scheduling and Load Balancing in Parallel and Distributed Systems. IEEE Computer Science Press (1995)
19. Cybenko, G: Dynamic Load Balancing for Distributed Memory Multiprocessors. Journal on Parallel Distributed Computing **7** (1989) 279–301
20. Plaxton, G.: Load Balancing, Selection and Sorting on the Hypercube. In Proc. 1st Ann. ACM Symp. on Parallel Algorithms and Architectures (SPAA) (1989) 64–73
21. Albrecht, K., Arnold, R., Gähwiler, M., Wattenhofer, R.: Aggregating Information in Peer-to-Peer Systems for Improved Join and Leave. 4th IEEE Int. Conference on Peer-to-Peer Computing (P2P) (2004)
22. Birman, P., van Renesse, R., Vogels, W.: Astrolabe: A Robust and Scalable Technology for Distributed System Monitoring, Management, and Data Mining. ACM Transactions on Computing Systems **21(2)** (2003) 164–206
23. Bozdog, A., van Renesse, R.: Willow: DHT, Aggregation, and Publish/Subscribe in One Protocol. In Proc. 3rd Int. Workshop on Peer-To-Peer Systems (IPTPS) (2004)
24. Kuhn, F., Schmid, S., Smit, J., Wattenhofer, R.: Constructing Robust Dynamic Peer-to-Peer Systems. TIK Report 216, ETH Zurich, http://www.tik.ee.ethz.ch (2005)

A First Look at Peer-to-Peer Worms:
Threats and Defenses

Lidong Zhou[1], Lintao Zhang[1], Frank McSherry[1], Nicole Immorlica[2,*],
Manuel Costa[3], and Steve Chien[1]

[1] Microsoft Research Silicon Valley
{lidongz, lintaoz, mcsherry, schien}@microsoft.com
[2] Laboratory for Computer Science, MIT
nickle@theory.lcs.mit.edu
[3] Microsoft Research Cambridge and University of Cambridge
manuelc@microsoft.com

Abstract. Peer-to-peer (P2P) worms exploit common vulnerabilities in member hosts of a P2P network and spread topologically in the P2P network, a potentially more effective strategy than random scanning for locating victims. This paper describes the danger posed by P2P worms and initiates the study of possible mitigation mechanisms. In particular, the paper explores the feasibility of a self-defense infrastructure inside a P2P network, outlines the challenges, evaluates how well this defense mechanism contains P2P worms, and reveals correlations between containment and the overlay topology of a P2P network. Our experiments suggest a number of design directions to improve the resilience of P2P networks to worm attacks.

1 Introduction

Peer-to-peer (P2P) overlay networks enjoy enormous and ever increasing popularity both in real-life deployment (e.g., Gnutella and KaZaA) and in the research community (e.g., Chord [18], CAN [13], Pastry [14], and Tapestry [24]). While security issues for P2P networks have received attention, the main focus remains on ensuring correct operations within a P2P network in the face of failures and malicious participants. Examples include maintaining the internal structure of a P2P network (e.g., [2]) and fair sharing of resources (e.g., [5]). The threats that a large-scale P2P network deployment poses to Internet security have largely been ignored.

In this paper, we argue that P2P networks provide an ideal venue for new types of worms that prey on common vulnerabilities on the hosts in a P2P network. These worms identify new victims simply by following P2P neighbor information on infected hosts. They are different from the currently popular *scanning worms*, which probe addresses randomly for new victims, in three important ways. First, they spread much faster, since they do not waste time probing unused IP addresses. Second, they do not generate high rates of failed connections. Finally, they can blend into the normal traffic patterns of the P2P network. The lack of abnormal network behavior makes P2P worms a potentially more deadly threat because most existing defense mechanisms against scanning

---

* Work done during internship at Microsoft Research Silicon Valley.

M. Castro and R. van Renesse (Eds.): IPTPS 2005, LNCS 3640, pp. 24–35, 2005.

worms are no longer effective. Because the number of subscribers to a P2P network such as KaZaA is estimated to be in the millions, P2P worms have the potential to compromise a significant fraction of the Internet population.   We therefore study the feasibility of constructing a self-defense infrastructure within a P2P network for containing P2P worms. The infrastructure imposes new and challenging requirements for worm-defense mechanisms, while the evaluation of the proposed infrastructure, both analytically and through simulation, reveals interesting correlations between worm containment in a P2P network and the overlay topology of the network. Furthermore, our experiments suggest a number of design directions to improve the resilience of P2P networks to worm attacks.

The rest of the paper is organized as follows. Section 2 elaborates on the imminent threat of P2P worms and makes a case for new defense mechanisms. Section 3 explores possible countermeasures against P2P worms, outlines a self-defense infrastructure, and presents a containment model. The evaluation of the self-defense infrastructure through both theoretical analysis and simulations appears in Section 4. We conclude in Section 5.

2   Imminent Threat of P2P Worms

Popular P2P clients such as KaZaA already have a high penetration into the Internet population. Any vulnerability in such a P2P client can put all those hosts at risk. The likelihood of having an exploitable vulnerability in these pieces of software is alarmingly high. A buffer overflow bug in the FastTrack network core, the underlying network for KaZaA and several others, was discovered and disclosed recently [12]. To make things worse, many P2P clients are bundled with spyware, further increasing the chances of introducing intentional or unintentional backdoors into hosts in P2P networks. For example, Saroiu et al. [15] found vulnerabilities in two wide-spread spyware programs due to lack of authentication in their auto-update processes.

Proof-of-concept viruses, such as Gnuman, VBS.Gnutella, and Fizzer [20], which propagate through Gnutella or KaZaA were released in the wild as early as 2000. The impact of these viruses was limited largely because their propagation relied heavily on certain user actions. In contrast, a P2P worm can infect vulnerable hosts automatically by exploiting the same types of vulnerabilities that led to notorious scanning worms such as CodeRed and Slammer. Whereas these random-scanning worms search for new vulnerable hosts by probing "randomly" generated IP addresses, a P2P worm can quickly identify new vulnerable hosts by following the list of neighbors in the overlay topology.

As a form of topological worm [21], P2P worms do not exhibit easily detectable anomalies in network traffic as scanning worms do. A scanning worm has no information on the locations of vulnerable hosts and thus is error-prone in choosing targets; it has to rely on both a reasonable density of vulnerable hosts in the entire IP address space and on the ability to probe different hosts at a high rate. It is these characteristics that lead to schemes for containing scanning worms (e.g., [23,26,7,22]) by detecting and reacting to various network anomalies.

Although these proposed mechanisms show promise for fast detection and successful containment of scanning worms, they have limited power against P2P worms. The

P2P topology provides an accurate way for worms to find more vulnerable hosts without probing random ones; the vastly improved accuracy in identifying vulnerable hosts also eliminates the need to communicate with a large number of different hosts at a high rate. The attack traffic can thus easily blend into normal P2P traffic. Therefore, new defense mechanisms are needed.

3   Mitigating Threats of P2P Worms

P2P worms would not exist if we could eliminate vulnerabilities on P2P hosts or cut off a worm's propagation between neighboring P2P hosts. But neither is achievable in practice. To eliminate vulnerabilities, P2P client programs should be written in a type-safe language (e.g., Java or C#), so that it is free of buffer-overflow vulnerabilities. Unfortunately, this is not the case for most existing client programs. Furthermore, common vulnerabilities could exist on co-located software or even the underlying platform. Increased diversity in a P2P network reduces the likelihood of common vulnerabilities and makes it harder for a P2P worm to propagate through P2P neighbors. Further measures can be taken to protect the neighbor list from access by worms. But it is usually hard to distinguish valid accesses from invalid ones.

Given that P2P clients will unlikely be free of common exploitable vulnerabilities in the foreseeable future, an interesting research question is the feasibility of incorporating a self-defense infrastructure into a P2P network for the network itself to detect outbreaks of any unknown worm and contain its spread.

3.1   Automatic Detection of Worms

Automatic detection of P2P worms is a prerequisite to any worm containment infrastructure—human responses are simply too slow. Because P2P worms target only hosts in a P2P network, referred to as *nodes*, automatic detection mechanisms must be deployed within the P2P network. We call nodes with automatic worm detection capabilities *guardian nodes*.

Because P2P worms do not exhibit easily detectable anomalies in network behavior, guardian nodes must instead detect worms by identifying the infection process inside running applications. Such detectors can detect broad classes of vulnerabilities. One promising approach, pioneered by several independent research projects [19,4,6,11], is based on the observation that a majority of worms work by hijacking the control flow of a vulnerable program to execute malicious code injected from the network or to force a different execution of code that was already loaded by the program. By tracking how information from untrusted sources propagates its influence in memory during code execution, a worm can be detected when the control flow of the program is arbitrarily controlled by information from untrusted sources. However, the proposed detection mechanisms either require hardware modifications [19,6] or demand expensive binary rewriting/interpretation with significant performance degradation [4,11]. It is therefore reasonable to assume that such general guardian nodes constitute only a small fraction of a P2P population. Since the detection mechanism contains the vulnerable code in a sandboxed environment, we can assume the guardian nodes are invulnerable to worm attacks.

3.2 Alert Generation, Propagation, and Processing

With a small fraction of guardian nodes, it is crucial that, once a guardian node detects a worm, it promptly generates a message about the ongoing attack and informs other nodes in the P2P network. We refer to these messages as *alerts*. The purpose of alerts is for a recipient to learn enough information about the attack in order to take appropriate action to become immune to the attack.

Because alerts trigger actions by receiving nodes, an adversary could attack by disseminating bogus alerts. If the receiver of an alert responded by shutting down the vulnerable application, this would turn a worm attack into a denial-of-service attack. To avoid this problem, guardians can generate self-certifying alerts, as described in [4]. Self-certifying alerts are machine-verifiable proofs of vulnerability; they contain a description of the events that lead to a vulnerable behavior—for instance a sequence of network messages—and they can be independently and inexpensively verified by any host. Use of self-certifying alerts also implies that any host can independently decide to become a guardian, since guardians do not have to be trusted. This setting makes it difficult to mount targeted attacks on the guardians. Alternatively, alerts can be submitted to a trusted authority, who verifies the authenticity of the alert and signs the alert using the private key corresponding to a well-known public key. Such an infrastructure for distributing and verifying signed updates already exists in many pieces of software for securing automatic software updates. The trusted authority could be implemented using multiple servers [25] to withstand attacks to a fraction of the servers.

Upon verifying the authenticity of an alert, a host can take several actions to protect itself. For instance, it can stop the vulnerable application or install a new local firewall rule to block a worm "signature"[1]; this could be a simple byte pattern on network messages or a more elaborate signature that accesses network messages and application state. Ideally, a host should identify the vulnerability exploited by the detected attack and patch it automatically. Such patches can be generated locally by the hosts receiving an alert, avoiding the need to trust patches produced by the host that generated the alert. We are currently working towards this goal.

We assume alerts are propagated in the same P2P network as P2P worms. After all, any existing link used by alerts requires that the destination address be recorded on the source; such information is also available to attackers when the source is compromised. This assumption distinguishes our model from that in [4], which also explored the concept of alerts for containment of Internet worms; there, a special P2P network is used for fast and reliable alert dissemination.

3.3 A Basic Worm Containment Model

The previous discussions on a self-defense infrastructure yield the following basic model for the containment study. Variations of the basic model are investigated in Section 4.

---

[1] While several schemes ([16,9,8]) have been proposed for automatic detection of worms and automatic generation of worm signatures, the detection mechanisms rely heavily on the network anomalies that scanning worms exhibit.

Consider a P2P network and a worm that exploits a vulnerability in the nodes of the network. We consider node A a *neighbor* of node B if the address of A appears in node B's state as a P2P client. The topology of a P2P network can be modeled as a directed graph in which each vertex in the graph corresponds to a node in the P2P network and each edge is weighted by the latency of the corresponding link from a node to its neighbor.

Each node in the P2P network has an independent probability p of being a guardian node; otherwise, the node is *vulnerable*. A vulnerable node becomes *infected* when the worm probes this node. A worm starts at a uniformly random node and in each step probes all the neighbors of newly infected nodes. If a worm probes a guardian node, the guardian node will detect the worm, generate an alert, and immediately propagate the alert to its neighbors. A vulnerable node becomes *immune* upon receiving the alert and propagates the alert further to its neighbors. An infected node ignores the alert; it does not propagate it further. Immune nodes do not become infected even upon worm probing. For simplicity, we assume that the worm and the alert incur the same latency on each link, although different links may have different latencies. Furthermore, we ignore the dynamic changes in the P2P network and assume a static topology.

4   Analysis and Evaluation

The basic worm containment model characterizes a battle between worm propagation and alert propagation within the same P2P network. The following questions naturally arise.

- With only a small number of guardian nodes, can the self-defense infrastructure contain a P2P worm?
- With a P2P network serving as the battlefield, how can we design and deploy a P2P network to offer an advantage over P2P worms? What strategies can a P2P worm employ to gain advantage?

This section documents our initial efforts to answer these questions. In particular, we evaluate containment of worms as measured by the percentage of vulnerable nodes that are infected when the network reaches a stable state, where neither alerts nor the worm can propagate further. Note that the containment problem is entirely different from the seminal containment study by Moore et al. [10] because that study focused on random probing worms in the Internet.

4.1   P2P Network Topology and Worm Containment

Theoretical analysis. The topology of a P2P network dictates propagation of a P2P worm and its containment in our basic model. In the absence of guardian nodes, the diameter of the graph, defined to be the longest among the shortest distances between any pair of nodes in the graph, is the upper bound on the amount of time it takes for a worm to compromise the entire P2P network. Here, we show a simple theoretical analysis of worm containment in our basic model.

Suppose a P2P network contains n nodes in a graph of maximum degree d, where each node is a guardian node with independent probability p. Then for a uniformly random starting infection point, the expected fraction of nodes that become infected is bounded above by $O(n^{\log_d(1-p)})$.

To see this, let x be the starting point of the infection, and consider the shortest path tree from x in the network topology. The key observation is that another node y will become infected if and only if there is no guardian node on the shortest path from x to y. Thus the expected number of infected nodes is $\sum_{i=1}^{\ell} n_i(1 - p)^i$, where n_i is the number of nodes at depth i in the shortest path tree from x. Since the topology has maximum degree d, we have that $n_i < d^i$; in fact, it is not hard to see that the worst case occurs when the inequality is tight. A straightforward calculation then yields that the expected fraction of infected nodes in this case is $O(n^{\log_d(1-p)})$.

Although the theoretical analysis offers only a loose upper bound for worm containment in our basic model, it does indicate that the number of nodes in the network, the maximum degree of the graph, and the percentage of guardian nodes are likely the factors influencing the containment result. We use simulations to validate the trends predicated by the theoretical results.

Simulation setup. Our experiments were performed on P2P graphs generated using a P2P simulator. Among others, the simulator implements the protocols described in Gnutella 0.4, Gia [3], and Pastry. Nodes in those topologies are randomly placed in a 5050-router Internet topology generated using Georgia Tech's Transit-Stub Internet Topology generator [1] with distance between a pair of nodes computed accordingly.

We further developed an epidemic simulator. This simulator takes as input the P2P topology graph and the probability of a node being a guardian node. For each run, the simulator randomly selects a node in the graph as the initial entry point for the worm and picks a set of guardian nodes according to the specified probability. It then simulates the process of worm propagation and alert propagation (after guardian nodes are triggered.) Each of our experiments takes 500 runs, with different randomly chosen initial infection points and different randomly chosen sets of guardian nodes. We report the mean (over the 500 runs) of the infected fraction, measured as the percentage of infected nodes over the entire vulnerable population. (Note that guardian nodes are excluded from the vulnerable population.)

Simulation results. In this set of experiments, we look at Gnutella 0.4 graphs. A Gnutella topology can be modeled as an undirected graph because the neighbor relation is symmetric. (We assume that the weights on links are also symmetric.) When a node joins, it selects a seed node already in the P2P network and performs a random walk to find more nodes as potential neighbors. A node A might refuse to be the neighbor for the joining node if the resulting number of allowed connections for A exceeds the maximum degree allowed. The generated graph is the result of running the P2P simulator for n consecutive joins, where n is the specified number of nodes. No node failures or node leavings are modeled.

We generated a set of Gnutella 0.4 graphs with different settings for minimum/maximum node degrees and total number of nodes. The generated graphs have average degrees that are close to the maximum degrees, indicating that nodes tend to have the same degree. Figure 1 clearly indicates that the infected fraction increases when min/max degrees

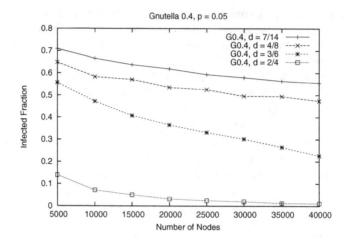

Fig. 1. Infected fraction as a function of number of nodes for Gnutella 0.4 graphs with different min/max-degree settings

increase, but decreases when the number of nodes increases, confirming the trends in the theoretical analysis. We want to point out that due to resource limitations, we can only simulate relatively small P2P networks. For real P2P networks with millions of nodes the infection fraction may be significantly lower than the simulation results suggest.

4.2   The Effects of Super Nodes

The notion of *super nodes* has been introduced to P2P networks for better scalability. Super nodes are nodes with sufficient resources and high-quality links to accommodate a large number of neighbors. Gia [3] is a proposal to introduce super nodes into Gnutella. In Gia, super nodes emerge as a result of dynamic topology adaptation based on the different capacities of the nodes. Adopting the setting in [3], we set the percentages of nodes at capacity levels 1, 10, 100, 1000, and 10000 at 20%, 45%, 30%, 4.9%, and 0.1%, respectively. Figure 2 shows the infected fraction for a Gia graph, with an average degree around 15 and min/max degrees of 3/128, compared to Gnutella 0.4 graphs with varying min/max degrees. We see a clear downtrend of the infected fraction when the probability of guardian nodes increases and that Gia exhibits the worst containment result.

Super nodes undoubtedly play a significant role in aiding the propagation of the worm due to their high connectivity. It seems that the defense mechanism would be more effective if the choice of guardian nodes were biased towards such high-degree nodes. This is confirmed by the result shown in Figure 3, where, in the case of biased choices of guardian nodes, the probability of a node being a guardian node is proportional to its degree. Note that, even if a worm knows about this strategy and tries to evade detection by biasing against high-degree nodes, the worm propagation will be at a significant disadvantage compared to alert propagation, which is able to exploit the powerful super nodes.

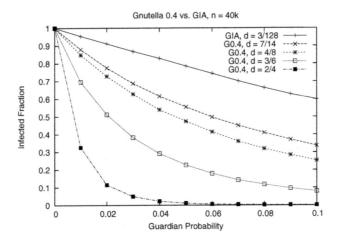

Fig. 2. Gnutella 0.4 vs. Gia, 40,000 nodes. Infected fraction as a function of probability of guardian nodes

4.3   Hit List and Secret Network of Guardian Nodes

For bootstrapping, P2P networks such as Gnutella and KaZaA offer an initial list of hosts in the network to serve as seed nodes for new nodes to join. An attacker can also collect a large number of addresses through crawling. A P2P worm can use those addresses as an initial hit list [17] instead of starting with a single node.

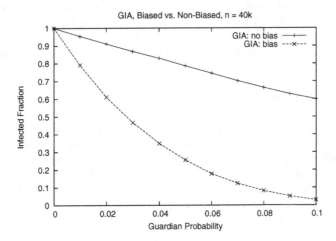

Fig. 3. Biased choices of guardian nodes vs. non-biased choices. Gia with 40,000 nodes. Infected fraction as a function of probability of guardian nodes.

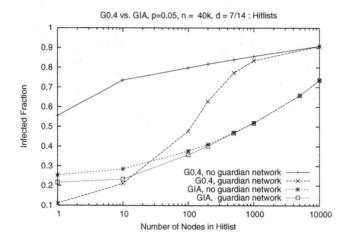

Fig. 4. Infected fraction, with and without a secret network of guardian nodes, as the function of number of nodes in the hit list (log scale). Gia with bias and Gnutella 0.4 with min/max degrees of 7/14, 40,000 nodes and 5% of guardian nodes.

In response, guardian nodes could be made aware of each other and form a secret network to tunnel alerts through directly.[2] For simplicity, we assume that this secret network is fully connected with direct links between any two guardian nodes with an average network delay.

Figure 4 shows how the infected fraction reacts to an increasing number of nodes on the hit list, as well as the effects of having a secret network of guardian nodes. Using a hit list seems to be an effective strategy for worms especially when the percentage of the nodes in the hit list becomes significant. Connecting all guardian nodes has a limited advantage in these cases. Define *worm diameter* to be the amount of time for a worm to reach the entire population of the network in the absence of guardian nodes. The effect of connecting the guardian nodes seems to diminish as the worm diameter decreases.

4.4 The Effects of Diversity

We have been assuming that the entire population (except for the guardian nodes) is vulnerable. This might not be the case in practice. In particular, P2P clients might use different implementations of the same protocol and run on different hardware/software platforms. Vulnerabilities in one particular implementation or on one particular platform may not affect the entire population due to diversity. The existence of the initially immune nodes works to our advantage because these nodes block worm propagation but pass alerts on to other nodes.

---

[2] It might seem that we are violating our assumption that the worm and the alerts are propagating in the same topology. This is not the case. In our model, links in the secret network cannot be exploited by worms because guardian nodes are never compromised.

Figure 5 shows the impact of having initially immune nodes in the network. We vary the percentage of the nodes that are initially immune from 0% to 60%. These nodes are chosen uniformly at random. Every node in the set of the non-immune nodes becomes a guardian node with 0.05 probability. The infected fraction shows the percentage of vulnerable nodes (i.e., excluding initially immune nodes and guardian nodes) that are infected. The results show a significant reduction in infected fraction as the immune proportion grows and suggest that diversity is an effective deterrence to P2P worms.

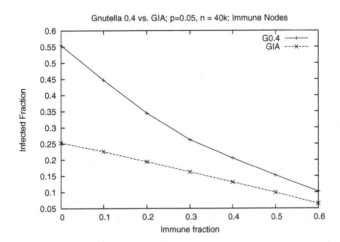

Fig. 5. Infected fraction as a function of percentage of immune nodes. Gia and Gnutella 0.4 (max/min degree of 7/14), with 40,000 nodes, 5% guardian nodes, and biased choice of guardian nodes for Gia.

4.5   Design Implications for P2P Networks

In summary, our experiments suggest a number of design directions over which P2P networks could evolve to increase their resilience to worm attacks. First, P2P protocols should bias their choice of neighbors to maximize diversity. Second, mechanisms should be included to make crawling the overlay more difficult or impossible. Otherwise, an attacker can gain a substantial advantage by building a large initial hit list to launch the worm. Finally, mechanisms should exist to deploy guardian nodes at flexible locations in the P2P network. As our preliminary results show, placement of these nodes has an important effect on containment.

5   Concluding Remarks

P2P worms constitute a potentially deadly threat to Internet security, a threat that we are not yet prepared for. This paper outlines a self-defense infrastructure to be built into a P2P network for containing P2P worms. The proposed infrastructure not only poses new challenges to worm-containment research, but also gives rise to an interesting phenomenon of competing epidemics (worm vs. worm-triggered alerts) in a P2P network.

The paper represents our initial study on containment of P2P worms with debatable assumptions. We plan to explore further the feasibility of the self-defense infrastructure, investigate more topologies and new strategies, and work towards a unifying theory that identifies the defining characteristics of the network topology on worm containment. Such a theory would help predict worm containment for a given topology and help develop strategies to improve defense against P2P worms, because applying those strategies can always translate into some network topology transformation.

Acknowledgements

The authors would like to thank Martín Abadi, Úlfar Erlingsson, Chandu Thekkath, and Ted Wobber, as well as the anonymous reviewers, for their helpful suggestions.

References

1. K. Calvert, M. Doar, and E. Zegura. Modeling Internet topology. *IEEE Communications Magazine*, June 1997.
2. M. Castro, P. Druschel, A. Ganesh, A. Rowstron, and S. S. Wallach. Secure routing for structured peer-to-peer overlay networks. In *Proceedings of the 5th Symposium on Operating Systems Design and Implementation (OSDI '02)*, pages 299–314, Boston, MA, USA, December 2002. USENIX.
3. Y. Chawathe, S. Ratnasamy, L. Breslau, N. Lanham, and S. Shenker. Making Gnutella-like p2p systems scalable. In *Proceedings of SIGCOMM'03*, pages 407–418, Karlsruhe, Germany, August 2003. ACM.
4. M. Costa, J. Crowcroft, M. Castro, and A. Rowstron. Can we contain Internet worms? In *Proceedings of the 3rd Workshop on Hot Topics in Networks (HotNets-III)*, November 2004.
5. L. P. Cox and B. D. Noble. Honor among thieves in peer-to-peer storage. In *Proceedings of the 19th ACM Symposium on Operating Systems Principles*, pages 120–132, Bolton Landing, NY, USA, November 2003. ACM SIGOPS, ACM Press.
6. J. R. Crandall and F. T. Chong. Minos: Control data attack prevention orthogonal to memory model. In *Proceedings of the 37th Annual IEEE/ACM International Symposium on Microarchitecture*. IEEE/ACM, December 2004.
7. J. Jung, V. Paxson, A. W. Berger, and H. Balakrishnan. Fast portscan detection using sequential hypothesis testing. In *Proc. 25th Symposium on Security and Privacy*. IEEE, May 2004.
8. H. Kim and B. Karp. Autograph: Toward automated, distributed worm signature detection. In *Proceedings of the 13th USENIX Security Symposium*, August 2004.
9. C. Kreibich and J. Crowcroft. Honeycomb—creating intrusion detection signatures using Honeypots. In *Proc. of the 2nd Workshop on Hot Topics in Networks (HotNets-II)*, November 2003.
10. D. Moore, C. Shannon, G. Voelker, and S. Savage. Internet quarantine: Requirements for containing self-propagating code. In *Proceedings of IEEE INFOCOM 2003*. IEEE, March 2003.
11. J. Newsome and D. Song. Dynamic taint analysis: Automatic detection and generation of software exploit attacks. In *Proceedings of the 12th Annual Network and Distributed System Security Symposium (NDSS 2005)*, Feb 2005. To Appear.

12. random nut.   The PACKET 0' DEATH FastTrack network vulnerability.   NET-SYS.COM Full Disclosure Mailing List Archives, May 2003. http://www.netsys.com/full-disclosure/2003/05/msg00351.html.

13. S. Ratnasamy, P. Francis, M. Handley, R. Karp, and S. Shenker.   A scalable content-addressable network. In *Proceedings of ACM SIGCOMM*, pages 161–172, San Diego, CA, USA, August 2001.

14. A. Rowstron and P. Druschel.   Pastry: Scalable, distributed object location and routing for large-scale peer-to-peer systems. In *Proc. IFIP/ACM Middleware 2001*, Heidelberg, Germany, Nov. 2001.

15. S. Saroiu, S. D. Gribble, and H. M. Levy. Measurement and analysis of spyware in a university environment. In *Proceedings of the 1st Symposium on Networked Systems Design and Implementation (NSDI)*, San Francisco, CA, March 2004.

16. S. Singh, C. Estan, G. Varghese, and S. Savage. The EarlyBird system for real-time detection of unknown worms. Technical Report CS2003-0761, UC San Diego, August 2003.

17. S. Staniford, V. Paxson, and N. Weaver. How to 0wn the Internet in your spare time. In *Proceedings of the 11th USENIX Security Symposium*, August 2002.

18. I. Stoica, R. Morris, D. Karger, M. F. Kaashoek, and H. Balakrishnan. Chord: A scalable peer-to-peer lookup service for Internet applications. In *Proc. ACM SIGCOMM*, pages 149–160, 2001.

19. G. E. Suh, J. Lee, and S. Devadas. Secure program execution via dynamic information flow tracking. In *Proceedings of ASPLOS XI*, pages 85–96, Boston, MA, USA, October 2004.

20. http://securityresponse.symantec.com/.

21. N. Weaver, V. Paxson, S. Staniford, and R. Cunningham. A taxonomy of computer worms. In *The First ACM Workshop on Rapid Malcode (WORM)*, 2003.

22. N. Weaver, S. Staniford, and V. Paxson. Very fast containment of scanning worms. In *Proceedings of the 13th USENIX Security Symposium*, August 2004.

23. M. M. Williamson. Throttling viruses: Restricting propagation to defeat malicious mobile code. In *Proc. 18th Annual Computer Security Applications Conference*, Las Vegas, NV, Dec. 2002.

24. B. Y. Zhao, L. Huang, S. C. Rhea, J. Stribling, A. D. Joseph, and J. D. Kubiatowicz. Tapestry: A global-scale overlay for rapid service deployment. *IEEE Journal on Selected Areas in Communications (J-SAC)*, 22(1):41–53, January 2004.

25. L. Zhou, F. B. Schneider, and R. van Renesse. COCA: A secure distributed on-line certification authority. *ACM Transactions on Computer Systems*, 20(4):329–368, November 2002.

26. C. Zou, L. Gao, W. Gong, and D. Towsley. Monitoring and early warning for Internet worms. In *Proc. of the 10th ACM Conference on Computer and Communication Security*, Oct. 2003.

A Taxonomy of Rational Attacks

Seth James Nielson, Scott A. Crosby, and Dan S. Wallach

Department of Computer Science, Rice University
{sethn, scrosby, dwallach}@cs.rice.edu

Abstract. For peer-to-peer services to be effective, participating nodes must cooperate, but in most scenarios a node represents a self-interested party and cooperation can neither be expected nor enforced. A reasonable assumption is that a large fraction of p2p nodes are *rational* and will attempt to maximize their consumption of system resources while minimizing the use of their own. If such behavior violates system policy then it constitutes an attack. In this paper we identify and create a taxonomy for *rational attacks* and then identify corresponding solutions if they exist. The most effective solutions directly incentivize cooperative behavior, but when this is not feasible the common alternative is to incentivize evidence of cooperation instead.

1 Introduction

A significant challenge in peer-to-peer (p2p) computing is the problem of cooperation. Unlike client-server systems, a p2p network's effectiveness in meeting design goals is directly correlated to the cooperation of the member nodes. For example, a p2p system might be designed for content distribution. To decrease the upload bandwidth burden on the original content server, only a small number of nodes directly contact it. The content is then propagated from these nodes to additional peers. This system can only scale if nodes are willing to pass on content to downstream peers. Unfortunately, a self-interested node may realize that it can save expensive upload bandwidth if it chooses not to share. If a large number of nodes are self-interested and refuse to contribute, the system may destabilize.

In most p2p systems, self-interested behavior at the expense of the system can be classified as a *rational manipulation* failure [1] or, from a different perspective, a *rational attack*[1]. Successful p2p systems must be designed to be robust against this class of failure. Ideally, a p2p system should be perfectly *faithful* to the designer's specification. In such a system, a self-interested, utility-maximizing node "will follow the default strategy because... there is no other strategy that yields a higher utility for this node" [2]. To achieve faithfulness, a system may employ various measures such as *problem partitioning, catch-and-punish,* and *incentives* [1]. Even when these techniques cannot make a system perfectly faithful, they may be enough to prevent destabilization.

---

[1] Our definition for rational follows the narrow definition provided by Shneidman et al [1]. For the purposes of our paper, rational participants are only interested in exploiting the resources and benefits of the system.

M. Castro and R. van Renesse (Eds.): IPTPS 2005, LNCS 3640, pp. 36–46, 2005.

An example of a viable p2p technology designed to be robust against rational manipulation failures is BitTorrent [3]. This technology first breaks large files into chunks that are downloaded individually and reassembled by the receiver. The receiving nodes contact one another and trade for chunks they do not yet possess. Each node employs an incremental exchange algorithm that leads it to upload chunks to cooperating nodes and not to share with selfish ones. These incentives encourage cooperative behavior in participating nodes [3]. While BitTorrent is not completely immune to rational manipulation, it is viable in practice [2].

In this paper, we identify, analyze, and create a taxonomy of rational attacks in p2p systems. We then examine this taxonomy to identify corresponding solutions. In the next two sections, we first provide a short background on the economics principles applicable to p2p systems and then specify our system model. The following two sections define our taxonomy of rational attacks and discuss solutions. The final section presents our conclusions.

2   Economics Background

Much of our analysis of p2p cooperation is based on economic models of game theory and mechanism design [4]. In this section, we briefly review some critical terms and concepts as they relate to p2p systems.

An economic *game* is a model of interaction between *players* in which the actions of any player influence the outcome of all other players. The *mechanism* in a game defines what legitimate actions the players can perform and the outcome of their behavior. These outcomes are assigned a numeric value called *utility*. Players that use an algorithm to determine behavior are said to follow a *strategy*

Players in the p2p world represent the nodes participating in the system. There are two types of nodes that do *not* strategize.

1. *Altruistic* or *obedient* nodes cooperate with the system irrespective of any other considerations.
2. *Faulty* nodes stop responding, drop messages, or act arbitrarily.

There are two types of nodes that do strategize.

1. *Rational* nodes strategize to achieve maximal utility and their actions are based on their current knowledge and understanding of the p2p system. Rational nodes will not attempt to disrupt routing, censor data, or otherwise corrupt the system unless such behavior increases the node's access to shared resources. These nodes are also described as *self-interested*.
2. *Irrational* nodes also strategize, but their strategies are either incomplete because they cannot understand the mechanism or they lie outside the economic mechanisms of the system. Denial of service or censorship attacks are examples of this second form of economically irrational behavior[2].

---

[2] Our goal is to design systems which are immune to manipulation by nodes seeking increased shared resources. Our definition of rational only includes nodes whose utility function is independent of utility payout to other nodes. Strategies, such as censorship strategies, that obtain benefit by denying utility to other nodes are considered irrational.

Mechanism design (MD) is the process of creating games where rational behavior by players leads to outcomes desired by the designer. Of course, such systems only affect the behavior of rational nodes. Mechanism design has no impact on faulty or irrational nodes and we exclude them from further discussion, though we recognize that any practical p2p system deployed "in the wild" must be resistant to their behavior. Of course, most p2p systems are robust against failure. The impact of irrational and malicious nodes is an open research problem that is discussed in Castro et al [5].

Distributed algorithmic mechanism design (DAMD) is a subclass of MD that is computationally tractable and operates without centralization. For this reason DAMD is well suited to systems like p2p networks [4]. DAMD assumes each node can independently reward the cooperation of other nodes or penalize their misbehavior but that each node has only limited information on the global state of the system.

3   Model

3.1   Incentives Capabilities

Incentives in p2p systems have some limitations. First, incentives are limited in the guarantees they can provide. While the use of incentives strengthens the p2p system against rational attacks, by themselves they do not guarantee that the system is faithful. To be guaranteed faithful, a mechanism must be validated by a formal proof, the construction of which is not trivial.

The second limitation is that they must be DAMD compatible. DAMD is limited to creating mechanisms that are are computationally tractable across distributed computing resources. Nodes are expected to reward cooperation and penalize misbehavior, but doing so is difficult when trusted global knowledge is unavailable.

With these two limitations in mind, we identify two types of incentives that may be used to create a faithful p2p system. The first type is *genuine incentives* and is characterized by directly incentivizing cooperation. A genuine incentive ties current behavior and future payoff together in some inseparable way. Genuine incentives are inherently robust against rational attacks and limit the strategies available to adversaries.

One example of genuine incentives is incremental exchanges as used in Bit-Torrent. Money could also be an effective genuine incentive but it would require very efficient micropayment schemes, where potentially every network packet transmission would require an associated payment. Unfortunately, the current generation of such systems (e.g., Millicent [6]) were never intended for such fine-grained commerce.

The second type of incentive is *artificial incentives*[3] which incentivize evidence of cooperation. Such incentives are weaker than their genuine counterparts

---

[3] Roussopoulos et al. suggests that highly valuable shared resources have inherent incentives while less valuable ones require an extrinsic or artificial incentives for cooperation [7]. Our concept of genuine and artificial incentives is similar, but focuses only on the mechanism and not the value of the resources or social network in which the resources are exchanged.

because, to be rewarded, a node only has to *appear* to cooperate. Nevertheless, artificial incentives are generally easier to create and deploy and may be necessary under circumstances where genuine incentives are not feasible.

Artificial incentives are often designed around an *auditing* process on top of which an enforcement mechanism is layered. In a decentralized system, auditing cannot be globally managed. Each node is aware of the system's policies, but is independently responsible for determining whether peers are in compliance. This can be done by requiring each node to publish assertions about its state which are audited by other nodes. An auditing policy of this type is consistent with DAMD; each node is capable of determining its behavior within the system. An auditing system, however, is subject to the vulnerabilities that we describe in Section 4.1.

3.2 Service Maturation

A p2p service provides some tangible benefit to participating nodes. New participants may obtain their payout spread over time, or they can obtain maximal benefit immediately in a lump sum. We have termed this service characteristic as *service maturation*. A service is mature when a node has obtained all of the benefit that the service can provide. Services that give out all possible benefit immediately have *instantaneous maturation* while services that distribute benefit over time have *progressive maturation*. Progressive maturation can be further classified as *bounded* or *unbounded* based on whether or not the service has a known, fixed termination of benefit pay-out. The relationship between the different classes of maturation is illustrated in Figure 1.

A content distribution service might have instantaneous or progressive maturation depending on policy. If a newly joined node can completely download its desired content before redistributing that content to peers, the service has instantaneous maturation. Conversely, BitTorrent has progressive maturation because it only allows nodes to obtain the full content through repeated interaction with the system. Because BitTorrent's pay-out of benefit ends when the file download is complete, its progressive maturation is bounded.

An example of a service with unbounded progressive maturation is a remote back-up service. In such a system, the benefit payout is distributed over time without a fixed point of termination.

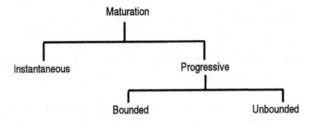

Fig. 1. Service maturation taxonomy

There is a correlation between instantaneous maturation to the Prisoner's Dilemma (PD) and progressive maturation to the Iterated Prisoner's Dilemma (IPD). In the single round PD, all of the utility that the game can pay out is disbursed in a single interaction. In IPD, the total utility is paid out to participants over some arbitrary number of interactions.

IPD also has an analog to the concept of bounded maturation. The game can be played with the players either aware or ignorant of the number of rounds that they will play. From the players' perspective, the game is bounded only if they know the number of rounds. An IPD game degenerates into a PD game if the number of rounds are known.

Game theoretic analysis has proven that it is not rational to cooperate in single round PD but that it is rational to cooperate in IPD [8]. Services with instantaneous maturation are extremely susceptable to the attacks described in Section 4.2.

3.3   System Model

For convenience, we define a constrained environment suitable to explore rational attacks. The p2p model characterized in this section has many features that are common to most p2p networks. In Section 5 we break some of these assumptions as possible solutions to rational attacks.

Our model is described by the following assumptions and limitations.

1. **Assumption: *Secure node ID's.*** Douceur [9] observes that if identity within the p2p system is not centrally controlled, any participant can simultaneously assume a plethora of electronic personae. With many identities at its disposal, a participant can subvert the entire network by subverting the routing primitive. We assume that the node ID's in our model are made secure in one of three ways:
   (a) **Trust.** Node ID creation and distribution is done through a centralized and mutually trusted agent.
   (b) **Expense.** Node ID creation has some arbitrary cost attached. A participant can replace its node ID infrequently and with some difficulty.
   (c) **Relevance.** Node ID creation is unrestricted because having multiple ID's cannot aid the rational attacker.
2. **Assumption: *There is no "trusted" software.*** A p2p system cannot guarantee that their members are using conforming software. Trusted computing technologies allow a node to attest that it is running a conforming application [10,11]. Enforcing a trusted software policy is not only technically challenging, but developing and deploying such a policy is undesirable to many groups for ethical or practical reasons [12].
3. **Assumption: *Nodes are computationally limited.*** We assume that any given node may have the same resources as the typical desktop PC. Nodes may subvert their machine to behave in arbitrary ways. However nodes are assumed to be incapable of breaking cryptographic primitives or taking global control of the underlying network.

Due to the potential size of p2p systems and because nodes are in mutually untrusting domains, we apply the following limitations to our model.

1. **Limitation:** *Each node maintains minimal state.* A node can only have firsthand observations about a small fraction of the nodes in the system. Similarly a node can only maintain state about a small number of the nodes in the system.
2. **Limitation:** *No second-hand information.* Nodes can only trust what they directly observe because there is no inherent reason to trust an assertion by any node about a third party. An accusation can only be trusted if the evidence is independently believable regardless of trust in the accuser. Such proofs usually require the cooperation of the accused to create.

4 Taxonomy of Rational Attacks

The motive for the attacks we consider are unfairly increased access to p2p shared resources. We identify two general classes of attack:

1. Unrecorded Misuse of Resources
2. Unpunished Misuse of Resources

Attacks can be made by a single node, or by several nodes colluding together for an advantage.

4.1 Unrecorded Misuse of Resources

If an attacker can obtain resources without producing a record of the misuse, the attacker is safe from any sanctions. Attacks of this kind exploit "holes" in auditing policies (*policy attacks*), or actively disrupt the auditing mechanism (*auditing attack*).

Policy Attacks. A rational node may exploit an auditing policy. We identify two examples.

1. **Excuses.** Any legitimate "excuse" for being unable to perform a service may be exploited. Such excuses may be needed to deal with edge conditions including crash recovery, network interruption, packet loss, etc. Consider a remote backup system like Samsara that requires every node to contribute as much space as it consumes [13]. If the system policy is overly generous to recovering nodes that recently crashed by not requiring them to prove they are maintaining their quota, a malicious node may exploit this by repeatedly claiming to have crashed.
2. **Picking on the newbie.** Some systems require that new nodes "pay their dues" by requiring them to give resources to the system for some period of time before they can consume any shared resources [14,15]. If this policy is not carefully designed, a veteran node could move from one newbie node to another, leeching resources without being required to give any resources back.

Auditing Attacks. Auditing attacks are designed to prevent the auditing system from identifying misbehavior. These attacks only apply to designs based around auditing using artificial incentives. Here are a number of examples of this type of attack:

1. **Fudged books.** Auditing relies on the accounting records being tamper-resistant and difficult to forge.
2. **Manufactured evidence.** In this scenario, an attacker who is in a state of non-compliance manages to produce "proof" of compliance deceptively.
3. **Accounting interruption (kill the auditor).** A node being audited can attempt to interfere with the auditing node. This might be accomplished by a denial-of-service attack, a worm, a virus, etc.
4. **Group deception, local honesty.** This attack is a type of manufactured evidence attack through collusion. Ngan, et al describes an accounting system where nodes publishing their debits and credits publicly in logs which are later audited by nodes' peers [16]. Debts on one node must match credits on another node, making it more difficult for a node to cook its books. However, it is possible for single node in debt to become locally honest for an audit by pushing its debt to a co-conspirator. As a group, the conspiring nodes' books are not balanced and they are in debt jointly. All colluding nodes reciprocate in sharing (or hiding) the debt.

4.2   Unpunished Misuse of Resources

An identified misbehaving node may attempt to avoid or mitigate punishment. Two such attacks are:

1. **Elusion.** The attacker leaves the system permanently before they can be sanctioned by the p2p system. This attack generally exploits short-maturation and high-value resources. In such a scenario, the attacker obtains the resources and leaves (e.g., join a content distribution service long enough to obtain an object and then disappear forever).
2. **Reincarnation.** Reincarnation is repeated elusion. The attacker avoids punishment for misbehavior by assuming a new node ID thus releasing them from any penalties associated with its old reputation. We note that this attack is a limited form of the Sybil attack [9] where multiple ID's are acquired and discarded over time rather than all at once.

This class of attacks operates almost entirely against p2p services with instantaneous maturation.

5   Solutions

As stated previously, an ideal p2p system is perfectly faithful, but creating such a mechanism and proving its validity is difficult. In some cases a perfectly faithful design may be impossible, but a p2p system need not be perfectly faithful to be viable. In this section, we describe defenses against rational attacks by self-interested nodes in descending order of theoretical effectiveness.

5.1   Eliminate Rationality as a Concern

Under certain circumstances, forcing all nodes to be obedient may be practical and desirable. We identify three options for coercing obedience.

1. **Out-of-band trust.** Obedience is enforced external to the p2p system. Such a scenario might be viable for a group of friends, or centrally administered machines within corporations, academic institutions, and government agencies.
2. **Partial centralization.** It may be possible to introduce some aspect of centralization that induces nodes to be obedient. For instance a central authority can be used to require secure node ID creation. BitTorrent uses a central authority to act as a rendezvous point where nodes can determine the addresses of their peers.
3. **Trusted software.** If a user is prevented from modifying their software, they must behave obediently. Many software applications are closed-source and difficult to modify. This may also be done with "trusted computing" technologies [17,11].

5.2   Design Genuine Incentives

Genuine incentives are always preferred to artificial incentives. Because they are often difficult to implement in a DAMD context, it may be tempting for a designer to overlook them. Not only do genuine incentives eliminate many of the attacks described in Section 4.1, but they are also simpler than artificial incentives because they require no additional enforcement mechanisms.

For example, consider a back-up system with a storage policy similar to Samsara where each node must provide as much disk-space as it consumes in backups. One artificial incentives approach proposed by Fuqua, et al is to require that all nodes publish what data they are storing locally and to prove that they actually have that data in their possession on audit [16]. The auditing mechanism may be vulnerable to one or more of the auditing attacks described in Section 4.1.

A genuine incentive for the remote back-up service is to require that all of a node's data that is stored on the network be tangled with the data it is supposed to be storing [14]. Nodes can then occasionally broadcast portions of the tangled data they are storing and ask for its owner to claim it or risk its deletion. Now the self-interested node must actually keep the data it claims to be storing or it cannot recognize claim-requests for its own data. However, to be useful, there must be a policy that allows a node to reclaim its data after a crash even if it has lost all local-storage. This policy may expose the mechanism to the excuses attack described in Section 4.1. Despite this weakness, however, this mechanism is more robust and significantly simpler than the auditing alternative.

5.3   Improving Artificial Incentives Design

Artificial incentives are a less desirable solution to rational attacks, but they may be the easiest to design into a service and are sometimes the only viable solution. Artificial incentives will generally entail having a well-defined auditing policy. A number of design decisions influence the effectiveness of these incentives.

Eliminating instantaneous maturation. A service which instantaneously matures is difficult to secure against rational attacks. Once a rational node has obtained the maximum benefit for a service, it has no incentive to continue participation. Thus, services that instantly mature are inherently vulnerable to elusion and reincarnation attacks. Also, because a node obtains its desired utility quickly, there is not much time for an auditing scheme to stop an attacker. Several techniques may help convert instantaneous to progressive maturation:

1. **Centralized ID Creation.** If node ID's are centrally created and distributed, a node will be forced to maintain its identity in all of its future interactions with the p2p system. In this case if a node steals from the system and leaves, it will face punishment when it returns.
2. **Security Deposit.** A node must contribute resources during a probationary period before it can benefit from the system's shared resources. Tangler is an example of system using this technique [14,15].

Limited number of peers. Changing a node's ID incurs a cost. If an auditing system can detect and kick out a misbehaving node sufficiently fast, then the cost of changing identity outweighs the benefit. In most p2p systems, a node can only access the network through a limited number of neighbors. Once an attacker has freeloaded on its neighbors, they will refuse to interact with it and it will be effectively removed from the system. This solution has been used for multicast and storage accounting [18,19,20].

Reputation. With perfect global knowledge of every peer's behavior, a node would be incentivized to cooperate because any time it cheated, that information would be immediately available to all of its peers. Unfortunately, perfect global knowledge is only possible through an oracle which is not available in a DAMD context such as p2p networks.

Distributed systems may try to recreate the notion of a global, trusted oracle using gossip protocols, rating schemes, or some other from of peer endorsements. Mojo Nation had a global reputation system and EigenTrust describes how such systems might be built [21].

Protecting an auditing infrastructure. Because artificial incentives require building and protecting an auditing infrastructure, these mechanisms have additional complexity that may be prone to design and implementation errors. We suggests three practices for building effective auditing mechanisms:

1. **Force the truth to be told.** Nodes can usually only believe what they observe for themselves. Secure history techniques [22], however, may be useful to generate authenticated records of misbehavior that are trustable by remote hosts.
2. **Double-entry bookkeeping.** A double-entry bookkeeping system as described earlier in Section 4.1.
3. **Create a global clock.** When multiple nodes are being audited, they may be able to pass debts around from one node to the next, such that any particular node, while it is being audited, appears to have its books balanced. If several nodes can be simultaneously audited at provably the same time,

this may defeat such attacks. Again, secure history techniques may provide an approximate solution to this problem.

6   Conclusions

In this paper we explored a number of rational attacks. While we used a narrow definition of "rational", we feel that this usage is justified by the unique nature of such attacks. From our analysis, we believe that designs that incorporate genuine incentives will generally be simpler and more robust that those with artificial incentives. Artificial incentives often require an auditing mechanism that is complicated and difficult to construct.

Unfortunately, given the difficulty of designing and implementing genuine incentives in a DAMD context such as p2p networks, artificial incentives will often be essential to incentivize cooperation for some parts of the system. When this is the case, avoiding instantaneous maturation eliminates unpunished misuse of resources attacks. A carefully designed policy and a robust auditing scheme are essential to mitigating unrecorded misuse of resources.

References

1. Shneidman, J., Parkes, D.C.: Specification faithfulness in networks with rational nodes. In: Proc. 23rd ACM Symp. on Principles of Distributed Computing (PODC'04), St. John's, Canada (2004)
2. Shneidman, J., Parkes, D.C., Massoulie, L.: Faithfulness in internet algorithms. In: Proc. SIGCOMM Workshop on Practice and Theory of Incentives and Game Theory in Networked Systems (PINS'04), Portland, OR, USA (2004)
3. Cohen, B.: Incentives build robustness in BitTorrent. In: 1st Internation Workshop on Economics of P2P Systems. (2003)
4. Shneidman, J., Parkes, D.: Rationality and self-interest in peer to peer networks. In: IPTPS '03, Berkeley, CA, USA (2003)
5. Castro, M., Druschel, P., Ganesh, A., Rowstron, A., Wallach, D.S.: Secure routing for structured peer-to-peer overlay networks. In: Proceedings of Operating System Design and Implementation, Boston, MA (2002)
6. Glassman, S., Manasse, M., Abadi, M., Gauthier, P., Sobalvarro, P.: The millicent protocol for inexpensive electronic commerce. World Wide Web Journal, Fourth International World Wide Web Conference Proceedings 1 (1996) 603–618
7. Roussopoulos, M., Baker, M., Rosenthal, D.S.H.: 2 p2p or not 2 p2p? In: IPTPS '04. (2004)
8. Axelrod, R., Hamilton, W.D.: The evolution of cooperation. Science 211 (1981) 1390–1396
9. Douceur, J.R.: The Sybil attack. In: Proceedings for the 1st International Workshop on Peer-to-Peer Systems (IPTPS '02), Cambridge, Massachusetts (2002)
10. Microsoft Corporation: Microsoft "Palladium": A business overview (2002)   http://www.microsoft.com/presspass/features/2002/jul02/0724 palladiumwp.asp.
11. TCPA: Building a foundation of trust in the PC. Technical report, Trusted Computing Platform Alliance (2000)
12. Anderson, R.: 'Trusted Computing' frequently asked questions (2003) http://www.cl.cam.ac.uk/~rja14/tcpa-faq.html.

13. Cox, L.P., Noble, B.D.: Samsara: Honor among thieves in peer-to-peer storage. In: SOSP '03: Proc. of the Nineteenth ACM Symposium on Operating Systems Principles, ACM Press (2003) 120–132

14. Waldman, M., Mazieres, D.: Tangler: a censorship-resistant publishing system based on document entanglements. In: Proc. of the 8th ACM Conference on Computer and Communications Security, ACM Press (2001) 126–135

15. Friedman, E.J., Resnick, P.: The social cost of cheap pseudonyms. Journal of Economics & Management Strategy **10** (2001) 173–199

16. Fuqua, A.C., Ngan, T.W.J., Wallach, D.S.: Economic behavior of peer-to-peer storage networks. In: Workshop on Economics of Peer-to-Peer Systems, Berkeley, CA (2003)

17. Arbaugh, W.A., Farber, D.J., Smith, J.M.: A secure and reliable bootstrap architecture. In: Proc. of the 1997 IEEE Symposium on Security and Privacy, San Diego, CA, USA, IEEE Computer Society (1997) 65

18. Ngan, T.W.J., Wallach, D.S., Druschel, P.: Incentives-compatible peer-to-peer multicast. In: 2nd Workshop on the Economics of Peer-to-Peer Systems, Cambridge, MA (2004)

19. Ngan, T.W.J., Nandi, A., Singh, A., Wallach, D.S., Druschel, P.: On designing incentives-compatible peer-to-peer systems. In: 2nd Bertinoro Workshop on Future Directions in Distributed Computing (FuDiCo II: S.O.S.), Bertinoro, Italy (2004)

20. Ngan, T.W.J., Wallach, D.S., Druschel, P.: Enforcing fair sharing of peer-to-peer resources. In: 2nd International Workshop on Peer-to-Peer Systems (IPTPS), LNCS 2735, Berkeley, CA (2003) 149–159

21. Kamvar, S.D., Schlosser, M.T., Garcia-Molina, H.: The eigentrust algorithm for reputation management in p2p networks. In: Proc. of the Twelfth International Conference on World Wide Web. (2003) 640–651

22. Maniatis, P., Baker, M.: Secure history preservation through timeline entanglement. In: Proc. of the 11th USENIX Security Symposium, USENIX Association (2002) 297–312

Brushwood: Distributed Trees in Peer-to-Peer Systems

Chi Zhang[1], Arvind Krishnamurthy[2,*], and Randolph Y. Wang[1,**]

[1] Princeton University
[2] Yale University

Abstract. There is an increasing demand for locality-preserving distribution of complex data structures in peer-to-peer systems. Current systems either do not preserve object locality or suffer from imbalances in data distribution, routing state, and/or query processing costs. In this position paper, we take a systematic approach that enables the deployment of searchable tree structures in p2p environments. We achieve distributed tree traversal with efficient routing distance and routing state. We show how to implement several p2p applications using distributed tree structures.

1 Introduction

In recent years, a group of Distributed Hash Table-based (DHT-based) peer-to-peer infrastructures, exemplified by Chord, Pastry, Tapestry, CAN, *etc.* [16,15,20,13], have received extensive attention. Such systems provide many attractive properties, including scalability, fault tolerance and network proximity. A number of applications have been built using DHTs, like distributed file systems and application level multicast. However, the original DHT schemes only provide searching in hashed key space, which is not sufficient to support applications with complex data structure and semantics [12,8]. To support such applications, some specific schemes have been proposed to enhance DHTs. For example, Space Filling Curves [1], Prefix Hash Tree [14], *etc.*, are used to support range queries, but these approaches are specific to their target problems. For many applications, it is not clear how to distribute existing data structures without destroying the intrinsic locality critical to performance. In this paper, we propose a general paradigm for distributing and searching tree data structures in peer-to-peer environments while preserving data locality.

1.1 Locality-Sensitive Applications

We target data-intensive applications that can benefit from locality-preserving distributions in one of two manners. On one hand, many of our target applications require support for queries that are more complex than exact lookups in a flat name space. For such applications, the data is typically organized in hierarchical search trees that enable them to perform similarity queries and updates. On the other hand, for some of our target applications, locality-preserving data organization is a critical performance issue. These applications often exhibit strong correlation among data accesses. For example, file system users frequently access a small set of files and directories. The logical

---

* Krishnamurthy is supported by NSF grants CCR-9985304, ANI-0207399 and CCR-0209122.
** Wang is supported by NSF grants CCR-9984790 and CCR-0313089.

M. Castro and R. van Renesse (Eds.): IPTPS 2005, LNCS 3640, pp. 47–57, 2005.

structure of a tree hierarchy is a good representation of the access locality in such applications. Centralized systems often benefit from access locality when the data structure is laid out appropriately on secondary storage. In a distributed peer-to-peer system, the high communication costs, which can be thought of as being analogous to the storage access latency and throughput limits of centralized systems, make locality-preserving distributions essential. These issues lead to the following question: can we implement these hierarchical tree data structures in peer-to-peer computing platforms while preserving the inherrent locality?

1.2   Challenges to Peer-to-Peer Systems

Besides common requirements like scalable peer state and efficient routing, a peer-to-peer searchable tree faces several other problems:

- **Tree lookups:** In some trees, the search key is given as a tree path. In more general cases, the path or ID of the destination node(s) is not known a priori, but discovered through top-down tree lookup for a data key. With high network communication costs, efficient lookup demands high locality in the mapping of nearby tree nodes and minimal routing steps when the nodes are apart. Some systems use DHTs to distribute individual tree nodes, possibly by hashing each node to a unique key. To search such trees, a DHT lookup is needed for every tree edge starting from the root, resulting in lookup costs that could be as high as $O(\log^2(n))$ [4] or $O(\log \log(n) \cdot \log(n))$ [14] for structures with balanced depth. This process can be even more inefficient if the tree has long branches. Besides, the root tends to become a bottleneck and a single point of failure.

- **Skewed data and load balancing:** DHTs depend on hashing to ensure uniform distribution of data among participating processors. However, hashing destroys data locality and is therefore not suitable in our application settings. Using unhashed data keys suffers from skewed data distribution. Some systems, such as [17], use sampling techniques to achieve asymptotic load balance. However, in case of dynamic load changes, reactive load balancing schemes are more desirable [11,6].

- **Tree maintenance:** Most practical tree structures are dynamic, as they are subject to online insertion, deletion and structural changes. While the maintenance is easy in centralized settings, it can affect many nodes in a distributed tree. For example, a distributed B-tree [10] replicates internal nodes to improve search efficiency. This optimization however requires the system to perform tree updates in a consistent manner, thereby requiring complex protocols for maintaining tree consistency.

In this paper, we propose a distributed tree scheme called Brushwood. We solve the problems of how to partition a tree while preserving locality and load balance and how to search the partitioned tree efficiently in peer-to-peer systems.

2   Design of Brushwood

Our solution is based on a linearization of the tree. The upper half of Figure 1 (a) illustrates a file system tree. The directories are drawn as circles. Edges labeled with

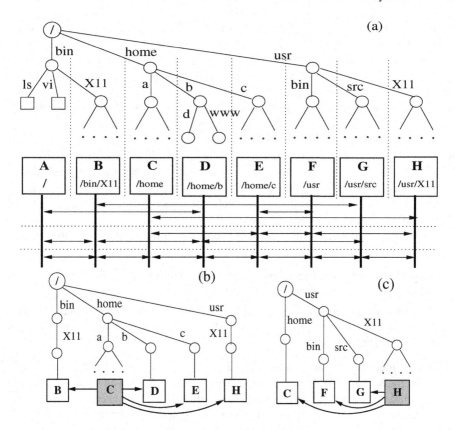

Fig. 1. Partitioning and Distribution of a File Tree

names represent directory entries. We linearize the tree nodes by pre-order traversal and then partition them into eight segments as shown by the dotted vertical bars. This partitioning method preserves locality since the low level subtrees are not split. The partitions are assigned to eight processors A - H, shown as the rectangles below the tree. We use the word "processor" to denote peer-to-peer nodes, in order to avoid confusion with tree nodes. Each processor is identified by its left boundary, which is the left-most tree node in the partition. The path name inside a processor box shows the left boundary of that partition.

To ensure system scalability, we limit the knowledge of individual processors about the tree and other peers. Each processor only knows $\log N$ peers and their partition boundaries in an N-processor system. A tree lookup can be done within $\log N$ steps regardless of the shape of the tree. We extend Skip Graphs/Nets [3,9] to achieve such an efficient lookup.

Conceptually, a processor in a Skip Graph maintains $\log N$ levels of peer pointers, pointing to exponentially farther peers in the linear ordering of N processors. The arrows under processor boxes in Figure 1 depict the three levels of peer pointers between the processors. Processors construct their local partial view of the tree from the boundaries of their peers. Figure 1 (b), (c) show the partial view of C and H, respectively.

Now we show how to perform object location in a distributed tree by illustrating the lookup of file /bin/X11/X from processor H. H uses its partial view to find the the peer that is farthest in the same direction as the target (given the pre-order linearization of tree nodes) without passing over the target. In this example, H determines that the target is to the left of peer C, which has a boundary of /home, and it forwards the request to C. C in turn uses its partial tree view, and determines that the peer that is closest to the target is peer B with a left boundary of /bin/X11. So it forwards the request to B. Tree lookup is therefore performed starting from any processor by "jumping" among the processors with each hop reducing the distance to the target, instead of traversing a tree path from the root to the target. The number of hops is therefore logarithmic in the number of processors, regardless of tree depth.

Generally, an application tree provides two pieces of information to enable the distributed lookup toward a target key:

- **A label l_{edge} on each tree edge.** There is a total order among the labels on edges out of a node, for example, the dictionary order for the entry names.

- **A comparison function f_{node} in each tree node.** This function compares a target key to the label of an edge of this node, telling whether it matches this edge, or falls to the left/right of it.

A node identifies its partition by a sequence of $\langle f_{node}, l_{edge} \rangle$ values from the root to its left boundary node. We define this sequence as the *Tree ID*. This ID is sent to peers so that a partial tree view can be constructed. The nature of the target key, f_{node}, and l_{edge} values are specific to the application. For example, in a file system tree, target keys are directory paths, each l_{edge} is a string, and f_{node} is simply string comparison. In more general trees, the target might not be specified explicitly by a tree path. For example, in a high dimensional index tree (see Section 3.1), each tree node corresponds to a region of space, the target key is simply a point coordinate or a range, and f_{node} encapsulates information regarding a *split plane* that can be used to decide which branch to follow.

For certain operations, such as a range query in high dimensional space (Section 3.1), the target objects are located by a generalization of the above process. The querying node may find that the target range is relevant to more than one branch, and it would therefore forward the request to multiple peers simultaneously, resulting in a "multicast" query.

Maintaining the partitioned tree in the above scheme is quite simple. Insertion and deletion of a branch only affects the processor whose boundaries enclose the target branch. For instance, insertion of /home/b1 affects only processor D.

Several optimizations are possible in Brushwood distributed tree. We provides data redundancy by allowing neighboring processors to maintain overlapping partitions. Besides added availability, it also improves locality, because the partitions now cover larger subtrees. The P-Table mechanism from Skip Nets provides proximity-aware routing similar to Pastry. It can be further enhanced by proximity-aware load balancing (Section 2.2).

2.1   Choice of Routing Substrate

Our tree routing depends on a linear ordering of partitions. In this sense, any linear space DHT routing facility can be used. We choose Skip Graphs for two reasons. First of all, Skip Graphs do not impose constraints on the nature and structure of keys. It can work with complex keys, like the variable-length Tree IDs, as long as there is a total ordering. Second, even if one can encode tree nodes into key values, such unhashed and often skewed keys can cause routing imbalance in some DHTs, as they use key values to decide peering relation. Skip Graphs do not suffer from this problem because its peering is decided by purely random membership vectors, even though the keys are unhashed.

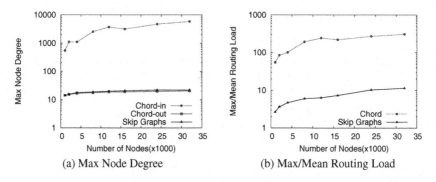

(a) Max Node Degree   (b) Max/Mean Routing Load

Fig. 2. Imbalance under Skewed Key Distribution

We simulated Chord and Skip Graphs with a skewed key distribution to show the imbalance in routing. Figure 2 (a) depicts the maximal processor degrees of Chord and Skip Graphs with 1K~32K processors. The processor keys are derived from a normal distribution with standard deviation 0.125 in the range $[0, 1]$. With such unhashed keys, Chord processors falling into the sparsely populated regions will manage larger portions of the keyspace, and are therefore likely to have a large number of in-bound peers. Furthermore, the imbalance in peer distribution also leads to imbalance in routing costs. We route 1000 messages between random pairs of nodes. Figure 2 (b) shows the imbalance as the ratio of maximal routing load to mean load.

2.2   Load Balancing

Balancing the assignment of tree nodes to processors is an important issue, because the distribution of items in the tree could be skewed and might also change with time. We propose a dynamic load balancing scheme that augments previous work [11,6,2].

Each processor maintains load information about the nodes in its partial tree. The load in an internal node is the aggregated load on all processors managing portions of this node. The root node therefore is associated with the global average load. Each processor periodically gets load information from its peers and does its aggregation from the bottom up the partial tree. Load information therefore propagates through the entire system via a combination of local aggregation steps and peer-to-peer exchanges. This process can be proved to converge after $O(\log N)$ steps.

There are two types of load balance operations, both taking advantage of the load information in the partial tree. When a processor joins, it navigates the tree to find a processor with high load, and partitions its data set. If a processor sustains significantly higher load than global average, it may navigate the tree to find an underloaded processor. This processor is forced to quit its current position and rejoin to take over half of the load from the overloaded processor. We favor a physically nearby processor in the above navigation, so that the data items may retain network proximity after the partition.

3   Applications

3.1   Multi-dimensional Indexing

The first application we build with Brushwood is a high dimensional index supporting complex queries. The data set being indexed are points in a D-dimensional Cartesian space. The typical queries are not exact point matches, but are searches for points falling in a certain range, or close to a given point. Such data sets are frequently found in multimedia databases, geographic information systems, data mining, decision support, pattern recognition, and even text document retrieval.

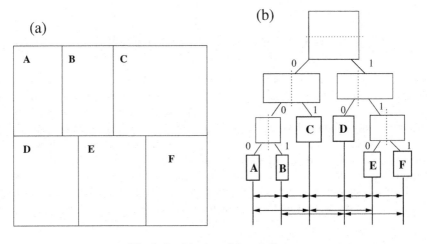

Fig. 3. Partitioning of Search Space

Partitioning K-D Tree. SkipIndex [19], our peer-to-peer high dimensional index, distributes a K-D tree [5] with Brushwood. K-D tree is a widely used index tree for high dimensional data. It hierarchically partitions the search space and data set into smaller and smaller regions. Each internal node specifies a partition dimension and a split position, and splits its region into two children. The data points are stored in leaf nodes. Figure 3 (a) illustrates partitioning of a 2-D search space to six processors, (b) shows the corresponding K-D tree and the skip graph routing tables.

Insertion and query operations in SkipIndex navigate the distributed tree to reach appropriate leaf nodes. The target is specified by a high-dimension point (insertion) or range (range query). To enable Brushwood tree lookup, SkipIndex defines the following elements:

- l_{edge} is 0 or 1, denoting left or right child.
- f_{node} compares the target point or range to the splitting plane of the node. For a point, it only returns one matching child branch. For a range, it may return both branches.

As we described before, the tree ID of a processor is given by the tree path from the root to the left boundary node of its partition. For each internal node along the path, it includes a tuple of $\langle dim_{split}, pos_{split}, 0/1 \rangle$, specifying the dimension and position of the split plane and the branch taken. A processor builds its routing state as a partial K-D tree containing the tree IDs of peers and itself.

When a processor joins, it locates a heavily loaded node (Section 2.2) and partitions its search space. A key benefit provided by Brushwood is the flexible choice of the split plane. We partition the most distinguishing dimension, so that the points in the two partitions are less similar, and the partitions are less likely to be involved together in a query. We split along the median of the items to balance the load.

Insertion and lookup of a point is straight-forward. At each hop, the processor navigates its partial tree by comparing the point to the split planes in tree nodes from root down, and it forwards the request to a peer that is maintaining a region that is closest to the target point.

Complex Queries. Range query in SkipIndex exploits another type of tree lookup. Now the target is a range in high dimensional space. While navigating the partial view, at each tree node, the target range is tested for intersection with the regions corresponding to its children. Each intersecting branch is further traversed until the traversal reaches the leaves of the partial tree. If the leaf is a remote region, a request is routed to the peer to search within the region. Otherwise, a local search is performed to find matching points.

Nearest neighbor search returns k points having the smallest Euclidean distances to a query point. While range query performs a parallel lookup of the K-D tree, our nearest neighbor search algorithm performs a sequence of lookups, gradually refining the results. At each lookup step, a search request is routed to a processor managing a search region close to the query point. Such regions are searched in the order of expanding distances from the query point. We can perform an exact search where we exhaust all processors that may contain a closer point. We also provide an approximate search that significantly reduces the search cost with controllable accuracy.

We evaluated SkipIndex with a 20-dimension image feature vector data set. This data set is highly skewed. We compare with pSearch [17] which uses unhashed CAN to index high dimensional vectors. Compared to CAN, SkipIndex allows more flexible partition of search space. Brushwood routing is also more stable in face of skewed data distribution. In Figure 4 (a), Brushwood routing in SkipIndex shows routing distances unaffected by data dimension, while CAN and pSearch suffer when data dimension is

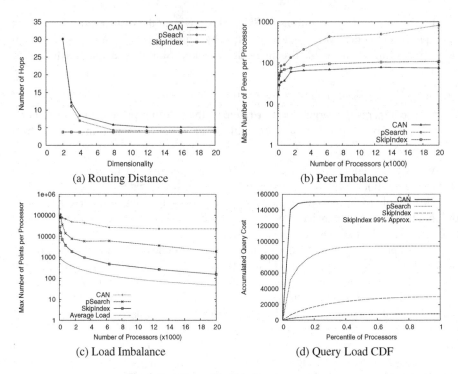

Fig. 4. Routing and load balance comparisons

low. Figure 4 (b) compares the maximal number of peers. Brushwood/SkipIndex routing exhibits more stable routing state, which confirms the analysis in Section 2.1. Under skewed data distribution, SkipIndex enjoys better load balance as shown in Figure 4 (c). Figure 5 compares the nearest neighbor search cost measured by the number of processors visited per query, averaged across 1000 queries. SkipIndex achieves lower exact search cost than pSearch thanks to the flexibility in space partitioning. Approximation further reduces the cost significantly. Note that this query span does not fully reflect the cost of search, because the load on the processors may be unequal. CAN achieves low query span as most of the data objects are maintained by a small number of high load processors. To better understand the search cost, Figure 4 (d) depicts the CDF of query load measured by the number of object distance calculations during the search. SkipIndex exhibits lower total cost and more balanced load distribution.

3.2 Distributed File Service

Now we go back to the example in Section 2 to review the potential for implementing a partitioned file service using Brushwood. It is well known that disk locality is critical to file system performance. In a distributed file service, locality of a file and its directory also impacts performance, since the lookup of objects costs network communication. By keeping related objects on the same processor, one can reduce the lookup overhead.

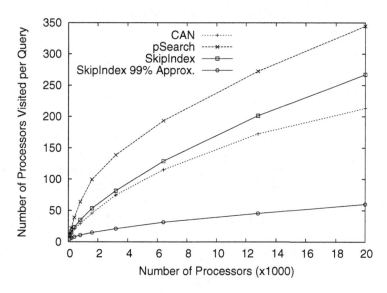

Fig. 5. Nearest Neighbor Search Cost

Availability is another reason to consider distribution locality. Accessing a large set of processors for a given task is more vulnerable to failures than accessing a few, if the redundancy level is the same.

We analyze an NFS trace from Harvard University [7] to confirm the above observations. The trace was collected on EECS department server running research workload. We use a week-long period of October 22 to 28, 2001. There are a total of 29 million requests involving 540K file handles. We reconstructed the file system tree from the trace. The tree is split into 1000 partitions using the load balancing process described in Section 2.2.

To measure the access locality, we identify the user "sessions" in the trace activities. A session is defined as a series of operations sent by the same user with intervals less than 5 minutes. The maximal length of a session is limited to 1 hour. There are a total of 6470 sessions in the period, with an average duration of 701.8 seconds. The user activity shows strong locality within a session. Table 1 gives the number of unique blocks/files/directories/partitions accessed during an average session. Tree partition appears to be the best granularity to exploit locality.

To evaluate availability, we replay the trace with Poisson failures. We set the mean-time-to-failure as 10 hours, and the mean-time-to-repair as 5 minutes to simulate a dynamic peer-to-peer environment. The file system is distributed to 1000 processors with four different schemes: hashing by block ID, hashing by file ID, hashing by directory ID, and tree partitioning. We randomly place two copies of each block/file/directory/partition on the processors. Only if both replicas fail, a request fails. The second row of Table 1 shows the number of sessions experiencing request failures under different distribution schemes. When data locality improves, a client depends on less number of servers to perform the same task. Therefore, better locality reduces the chance of encountering server failures.

Table 1. Trace Analysis Results

Distribution scheme	Block	File	Directory	Partition
Number of unique objects accessed per session	1594.14	117.28	21.26	6.01
Number of sessions seeing request failures	236	153	53	21

4   Related Work

As far as we know, our work is the first general scheme to efficiently distribute, maintain, and traverse search trees in peer-to-peer systems. Previous efforts on distributed search trees, like replicated B-tree [10], focus on parallelizing the operations and do not exploit the symmetric node capability of peer-to-peer systems. DHTs like CAN, Chord, Pastry and Tapestry achieve scalability and resilience by building self-organizing overlays to locate resources in peer-to-peer systems. But since these systems use hashing to achieve load-balance, they are not suitable for maintaining complex data structures. Several schemes [17,6] use unhashed DHTs for complex queries in flat key space, but it is not clear how to build a general search tree.

Our dynamic load balancing scheme is inspired by previous work [11,6]. However, instead of using random sampling, our scheme uses peer-wise gossiping to aggregate load information in the distributed tree, which directs reactive load adjustment operations. Similar aggregation schemes are used in previous systems like [18].

Multi-dimensional queries in peer-to-peer systems have been addressed in a few other systems. We had discussed pSearch earlier. Mercury [6] provides range query by indexing the data set along each individual attributes. It uses random sampling to ensure efficient routing ($O(\log^2 N)$ hops) under skewed data distribution. However, the per-attribute index makes Mercury inappropriate for nearest neighbor query which involves all dimensions.

5   Conclusions

In this paper, we propose a general scheme to efficiently distribute and navigate tree data structures in peer-to-peer systems. The approach is shown to be effective in several locality-sensitive applications. We believe that more applications will benefit from this system for maintaining complex data structures in peer-to-peer environments.

References

1. A. Andrzejak and Z. Xu. Scalable, efficient range queries for grid information services. In *Second IEEE International Conference on Peer-to-Peer Computing*, 2002.
2. J. Aspnes, J. Kirsch, and A. Krishnamurthy. Load balancking and locality in range-queriable data structures. In *Proc. of PODC*, 2004.
3. J. Aspnes and G. Shah. Skip Graphs. In *Proceedings of Symposium on Discrete Algorithms*, 2003.
4. B. Awerbuch and C. Scheideler. Peer-to-peer systems for Prefix Search. In *PODC*, 2003.

5. J. L. Bentley. Multidimensional binary search trees used for associative searching. *Commun. ACM*, 18(9), 1975.
6. A. R. Bharambe, M. Agrawal, and S. Seshan. Mercury: Supporting scalable multi-attribute range queries. In *SIGCOMM*, 2004.
7. D. Ellard, J. Ledlie, P. Malkani, and M. Seltzer. Passive NFS tracing email and research workloads. In *USENIX Conference on File and Storage Technologies*, 2003.
8. M. Harren, J. Hellerstein, R. Huebsch, B. Loo, S. Shenker, and I. Stoica. Complex queries in dht-based peer-to-peer networks. In *Proceedings of IPTPS02*, 2002.
9. N. J. A. Harvey, M. B. Jones, S. Saroiu, M. Theimer, and A. Wolman. SkipNet: A Scalable Overlay Network with Practical Locality Properties. In *USITS*, 2003.
10. T. Johnson and P. Krishna. Lazy updates for distributed search structures. In *Proceedings of ACM SIGMOD*, 1993.
11. D. R. Karger and M. Ruhl. Simple efficient load balancing algorithms for peer-to-peer systems. In *IPTPS*, 2004.
12. P. Keleher, B. Bhattacharjee, and B. Silaghi. Are virtualized overlay networks too much of a good thing. In *Proc. of IPTPS*, 2002.
13. S. Ratnasamy, P. Francis, M. Handley, R. Karp, and S. Shenker. A scalable content addressable network. In *Proceedings of ACM SIGCOMM*, 2001.
14. S. Ratnasamy, J. Hellerstein, and S. Shenker. Range Queries over DHTs. Technical Report IRB-TR-03-009, Intel Research, 2003.
15. A. Rowstron and P. Druschel. Pastry: Scalable, distributed object location and routing for large-scale peer-to-peer systems. In *ICDCS*, 2002.
16. I. Stoica, R. Morris, D. Karger, F. Kaashoek, and H. Balakrishnan. Chord: A scalable peer-to-peer lookup service for internet applications. In *SIGCOMM*, 2001.
17. C. Tang, Z. Xu, and S. Dwarkadas. Peer-to-peer information retrieval using self-organizing semantic overlay networks. In *Proceedings of SIGCOMM*, 2003.
18. R. van Renesse and K. P. Birman. Scalable management and data mining using astrolabe. In *IPTPS*, 2002.
19. C. Zhang, A. Krishnamurthy, and R. Y. Wang. Skipindex: Towards a scalable peer-to-peer index service for high dimensional data. Technical Report TR-703-04, Princeton Univ. CS, 2004, http://www.cs.princeton.edu/~chizhang/skipindex.pdf.
20. B. Y. Zhao, L. Huang, J. Stribling, S. C. Rhea, A. D. Joseph, and J. Kubiatowicz. Tapestry: A resilient global-scale overlay for service deployment. *IEEE Journal on Selected Areas in Communications*, 2004.

Arpeggio: Metadata Searching and Content Sharing with Chord

Austin T. Clements, Dan R.K. Ports, and David R. Karger*

MIT Computer Science and Artificial Intelligence Laboratory,
32 Vassar St., Cambridge MA 02139
{aclements, drkp, karger}@mit.edu

Abstract. Arpeggio is a peer-to-peer file-sharing network based on the
Chord lookup primitive. Queries for data whose metadata matches a
certain criterion are performed efficiently by using a *distributed keyword-
set index*, augmented with index-side filtering. We introduce *index gateways*, a technique for minimizing index maintenance overhead. Because
file data is large, *Arpeggio* employs subrings to track live source peers
without the cost of inserting the data itself into the network. Finally, we
introduce *postfetching*, a technique that uses information in the index to
improve the availability of rare files. The result is a system that provides
efficient query operations with the scalability and reliability advantages
of full decentralization, and a content distribution system tuned to the
requirements and capabilities of a peer-to-peer network.

1 Overview and Related Work

Peer-to-peer file sharing systems, which let users locate and obtain files shared
by other users, have many advantages: they operate more efficiently than the
traditional client-server model by utilizing peers' upload bandwidth, and can
be implemented without a central server. However, many current file sharing
systems trade-off scalability for correctness, resulting in systems that scale well
but sacrifice completeness of search results or vice-versa.

Distributed hash tables have become a standard for constructing peer-to-peer
systems because they overcome the difficulties of quickly and correctly locating
peers. However, the *lookup by name* DHT operation is not immediately sufficient
to perform complex *search by content* queries of the data stored in the network.
It is not clear how to perform searches without sacrificing scalability or query
completeness. Indeed, the obvious approaches to distributed full-text document
search scale poorly [9].

In this paper, however, we consider systems, such as file sharing, that search
only over a relatively small amount of *metadata* associated with each file, but
that have to support highly dynamic and unstable network topology, content,

---

* This research was conducted as part of the IRIS project
(http://project-iris.net/), supported by the National Science Foundation
under Cooperative Agreement No. ANI0225660.

M. Castro and R. van Renesse (Eds.): IPTPS 2005, LNCS 3640, pp. 58–68, 2005.

and sources. The relative sparsity of per-document information in such systems allows for techniques that do not apply in general document search. We present the design for *Arpeggio*, which uses the LOOKUP primitive of Chord [14] to support metadata search and file distribution. This design retains many advantages of a central index, such as completeness and speed of queries, while providing the scalability and other benefits of full decentralization. *Arpeggio* resolves queries with a constant number of Chord lookups. The system can consistently locate even rare files scattered throughout the network, thereby achieving near-perfect recall.

In addition to the search process, we consider the process of distributing content to those who want it, using subrings [8] to optimize distribution. Instead of using a DHT-like approach of storing content data directly in the network on peers that may not have originated the data, we use indirect storage in which the original data remains on the originating nodes, and small pointers to this data are managed in a DHT-like fashion. As in traditional file-sharing networks, files may only be intermittently available. We propose an architecture for resolving this problem by recording in the DHT requests for temporarily unavailable files, then actively increasing their future availability.

Like most file-sharing systems, *Arpeggio* includes two subsystems concerned with searching and with transferring content. Section 2 examines the problem of building and querying distributed keyword-set indexes. Section 3 examines how the indexes are maintained once they have been built. Section 4 turns to how the topology can be leveraged to improve the transfer and availability of files. Finally, Sect. 5 reviews the novel features of this design.

2 Searching

A content-sharing system must be able to translate a search query from a user into a list of files that fit the description and a method for obtaining them. Each file shared on the network has an associated set of metadata: the file name, its format, etc. For some types of data, such as text documents, metadata can be extracted manually or algorithmically. Some types of files have metadata built-in; for example, ID3 tags on MP3 music files.

Analysis based on required communications costs suggests that peer-to-peer keyword indexing of the Web is infeasible because of the size of the data set [9]. However, peer-to-peer indexing for metadata remains feasible, because the size of metadata is expected to be only a few keywords, much smaller than the full text of an average Web page.

2.1 Background

Structured overlay networks based on distributed hash tables show promise for simultaneously achieving the recall advantages of a centralized index and the scalability and resiliency attributes of decentralization. Distributed hash location services such as Chord [14] provide an efficient LOOKUP primitive that maps a key to the node responsible for its value. Chord uses at most $O(\log n)$ messages per lookup in an n-machine network, and minimal overhead for routing table maintenance. Building on this primitive, DHash [3] and other distributed hash tables provide a standard GET-BLOCK/PUT-BLOCK hash table abstraction. However, this interface alone is insufficient for efficient keyword-based search.

2.2   Distributed Indexing

A reasonable starting point is a *distributed inverted index*. In this scheme, the DHT maps each keyword to a list of all files whose metadata contains that keyword. To execute a query, a node performs a GET-BLOCK operation for each of the query keywords and intersects the resulting lists. The principal disadvantage is that the keyword index lists can become prohibitively long, particularly for very popular keywords, so retrieving the entire list may generate tremendous network traffic.

Performance of a keyword-based distributed inverted index can be improved by performing *index-side filtering* instead of joining at the querying node. Because our application postulates that metadata is small, the entire contents of each item's metadata can be kept in the index as a *metadata block*, along with information on how to obtain the file contents. To perform a query involving a keyword, we send the full query to the corresponding index node, and it performs the filtering and returns only relevant results. This dramatically reduces network traffic at query time, since only one index needs to be contacted and only results relevant to the full query are transmitted. This is similar to the search algorithm used by the Overnet network [12], which uses the Kademlia DHT [10]; it is also used by systems such as eSearch [15]. Note that index-side filtering breaks the standard DHT GET-BLOCK abstraction by adding network-side processing, demonstrating the utility of direct use of the underlying LOOKUP primitive.

2.3   Keyword-Set Indexing

While filtering reduces network usage, query load may be unfairly distributed, overloading nodes responsible for popular keywords. To overcome this problem, we propose to build inverted indexes not only on keywords but also on keyword *sets*. As before, each unique file has a corresponding metadata block that holds all of its metadata. Now, however, an identical copy of this metadata block is stored in an index corresponding to each subset of at most K metadata terms. The maximum set size K is a parameter of the network. This is the Keyword-Set Search system (KSS) introduced by Gnawali [6].

Essentially, this scheme allows us to precompute the full-index answer to all queries of up to K keywords. For queries of more than K keywords, the index for a randomly chosen K-keyword subset of the query can be filtered. This approach has the effect of querying smaller and more distributed indexes whenever possible, thus alleviating unfair query load caused by queries of more than one keyword.

Since the majority of searches contain multiple keywords [13], large indexes are no longer critical to result quality as most queries will be handled by smaller, more specific indexes. To reduce storage requirements, maximum index size can be limited, preferentially retaining entries that exist in fewest other indexes, i.e. those with fewest total keywords.

In *Arpeggio*, we combine KSS indexing with index-side filtering, as described above: indexes are built for keyword sets and results are filtered on the index nodes. We make a distinction between *keyword metadata*, which is easily enumerable and excludes stopwords, and therefore can be used to partition indexes with KSS, and *filterable metadata*, which can further constrain a search. Index-side filtering allows for more complex searches than KSS alone. A user may only be interested in files of size greater than 1 MB, files in `tar.gz` format, or MP3 files with a bitrate greater than 128 Kbps, for example. It is not practical to encode this information in keyword indexes, but the index obtained via a KSS query can easily be filtered by these criteria. The combination of KSS indexing and index-side filtering increases both query efficiency and precision.

2.4   Feasibility

Techniques such as KSS improve the distribution of indexing load, reducing the number of very large indexes — but they do so by creating more index entries. In order to show that this solution is feasible, we argue that the increase in total indexing cost is reasonable.

Using keyword set indexes rather than keyword indexes increases the number of index entries for a file with m metadata keywords from m to $I(m)$, where

$$I(m) = \sum_{i=1}^{K} \binom{m}{i} = \begin{cases} 2^m - 1 & \text{if } m \leq K \\ O(m^K) & \text{if } m > K \end{cases}$$

For files with many metadata keywords, $I(m)$ is polynomial in m. Furthermore, if m is small compared to K (as for files with few keywords), then $I(m)$ is no worse than exponential in m. The graph in Fig. 1 shows that $I(m)$ grows polynomially with respect to m, and its degree is determined by K. As discussed below, for many applications the desired value of K will be small (around 3 or 4), and so $I(m)$ will be a polynomial of low degree in m.

Example Application. To gain further insight into indexing costs, we analyzed the number of index entries that would be required to build an index of song metadata, using information from the FreeDB [4] database. This application[1] is well-suited for *Arpeggio*'s indexing because it consists of many files which have large (audio) content and only a few metadata keywords such as the song title

---

[1] Readers familiar with the FreeDB service will be aware that its primary application is to translate disc IDs to track names, not to perform metadata searches for songs. We do not propose *Arpeggio* as a *replacement* for FreeDB; we are merely using its database as an example corpus of the type of information that could be indexed by *Arpeggio*.

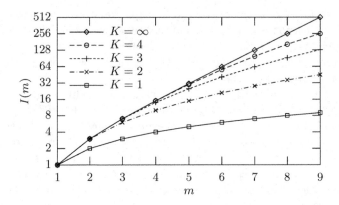

Fig. 1. Growth of $I(m)$ for various K

Table 1. Index size (FreeDB)

Number of songs	21,195,244
Total index entries $(K = 1)$	134,403,379
Index entries per song $(K = 1)$	6.274406
Total index entries $(K = 3)$	1,494,688,373
Index entries per song $(K = 3)$	66.078093

or artist. The database contains over 1.5 million discs, with a total of over 21 million songs. Each song has an average of 6.27 metadata keywords.

Table 1 compares the number of index entries required to create a KSS index over the metadata of discs in FreeDB for $K = 1$ and $K = 3$. The $K = 1$ case corresponds to a single index entry for each keyword in each song: a simple distributed inverted index. Increasing K to 3 allows KSS to be used effectively, better distributing the load throughout the network, but only increases the total indexing cost by an order of magnitude.

Choosing K. The effectiveness and feasibility of *Arpeggio*'s indexing system depend heavily on the chosen value of the maximum subset size parameter K. If K is too small, then the KSS technique will not be as effective: there will not be enough multiple-keyword indices to handle most queries, making long indexes necessary for result quality. If K is too large, then the number of index entries required grows exponentially, as in Fig. 2. Most of these index entries will be in many-keyword indices that will be used only rarely, if at all.

The optimum value for the parameter K depends on the application[2], since both the number of metadata keywords for each object and the number of search terms per query vary. The average number of search terms for web searches

---

[2] We are currently investigating the effectiveness of methods for splitting indexes into more specific indexes only when necessary (essentially, adapting K per index).

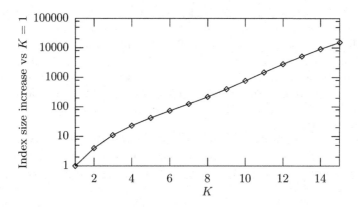

Fig. 2. Index size increase for varying K (FreeDB)

is approximately 2.53 [13], so assuming queries follow a similar distribution, a choice of $K = 3$ or $K = 4$ would allow most searches to be handled by specific indexes. Using the FreeDB data, this choice of K requires only an order of magnitude increase in total index size.

3 Index Maintenance

Peers are constantly joining and leaving the network. Thus, the search index must respond dynamically to the shifting availability of the data it is indexing and the nodes on which the index resides. Furthermore, certain changes in the network, such as nodes leaving without notification, may go unnoticed, and polling for these changing conditions is too costly, so the index must be maintained by passive means.

3.1 Metadata Expiration

Instead of polling for departures, or expecting nodes to notify us of them, we expire metadata on a regular basis so that long-absent files will not be returned by a search. Nevertheless, blocks may contain out-of-date references to files that are no longer accessible. Thus, a requesting peer must be able to gracefully handle failure to contact source peers. To counteract expiration, we *refresh* metadata that is still valid, thereby periodically resetting its expiration counter. We argue in Sect. 4.3 that there is value in long expiration times for metadata, as it not only allows for low refresh rates, but for tracking of attempts to access missing files in order to artificially replicate them to improve availability.

3.2 Index Gateways

If each node directly maintains its own files' metadata in the distributed index, the metadata block for each file will be inserted repeatedly. Consider a file F that has m metadata keywords and is shared by s nodes. Then each of the s nodes will attempt to insert the file's metadata block into the $I(m)$ indexes in which it belongs. The total cost for inserting the file is therefore $\Theta\left(sI(m)\right)$ messages. Since metadata blocks simply contain the keywords of a file, not information about which peers are sharing the file, each node will be inserting the *same* metadata block repeatedly. This is both expensive and redundant. Moreover, the cost is further increased by each node repeatedly renewing its insertions to prevent their expiration.

To minimize this redundancy, we introduce an *index gateway* node that aggregates index insertion. Index gateways are not required for correct index operation, but they increase the efficiency of index insertion. With gateways, rather than directly inserting a file's metadata blocks into the index, each peer sends a single copy of the block to the gateway responsible for the block (found via a LOOKUP of the block's hash). The gateway then inserts the metadata block into all of the appropriate indexes, but *only* if necessary. If the block already exists in the network and is not scheduled to expire soon, then there is no need to re-insert it into the network. A gateway only needs to refresh metadata blocks when the blocks in the network are due to expire soon, but the copy of the block held by the gateway has been more recently refreshed.

Gateways dramatically decrease the total cost for multiple nodes to insert the same file into the index. Using gateways, each source node sends only one metadata block to the gateway, which is no more costly than inserting into a centralized index. The index gateway only contacts the $I(m)$ index nodes once, thereby reducing the total cost from $\Theta\left(sI(m)\right)$ to $\Theta\left(s + I(m)\right)$.

3.3   Index Replication

In order to maintain the index despite node failure, index replication is also necessary. Because metadata blocks are small and reading from indexes must be low-latency, replication is used instead of erasure coding [3]. Furthermore, because replicated indexes are independent, any node in the index group can handle any request pertaining to the index (such as a query or insertion) without interacting with any other nodes. *Arpeggio* requires only *weak consistency* of indexes, so index insertions can be propagated periodically and in large batches as part of index replication. Expiration can be performed independently.

4   Content Distribution

The indexing system we describe above simply provides the ability to search for files that match certain criteria. It is independent of the file transfer mechanism. Thus, it is possible to use an existing content distribution network in conjunction with *Arpeggio*. A simple implementation might simply store a HTTP URL for the file in the metadata blocks, or a pointer into a content distribution network such as Coral [5]. A DHT can be used for direct storage of file contents, as in distributed storage systems like CFS [2]. For a file sharing network, direct storage

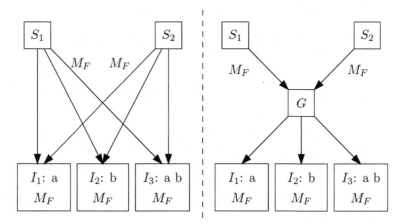

Fig. 3. Two source nodes $S_{1,2}$, inserting file metadata block M_F to three index nodes $I_{1,2,3}$, with (right) and without (left) a gateway node G

is impractical because the amount of churn [7] and the content size create high maintenance costs.

Instead, *Arpeggio* uses *indirect storage*: it maintains pointers to each peer that contains a certain file. Using these pointers, a peer can identify other peers that are sharing content it wishes to obtain. Because these pointers are small, they can easily be maintained by the network, even under high churn, while the large file content remains on its originating nodes. This indirection retains the distributed lookup abilities of direct storage, while still accommodating a highly dynamic network topology, but may sacrifice content availability.

4.1   Segmentation

For purposes of content distribution, we segment all files into a sequence of *chunks*. Rather than tracking which peers are sharing a certain file, *Arpeggio* tracks which chunks comprise each file, and which peers are currently sharing each chunk. This is implemented by storing in the DHT a *file block* for each file, which contains a list of *chunk IDs*, which can be used to locate the sources of that chunk, as in Table 2. File and chunk IDs are derived from the hash of their contents to ensure that file integrity can be verified.

The rationale for this design is twofold. First, peers that do not have an entire file are able to share the chunks they do have: a peer that is downloading part of a file can at the same time upload other parts to different peers. This makes efficient use of otherwise unused upload bandwidth. For example, Gnutella does not use chunking, requiring peers to complete downloads before sharing them. Second, multiple files may contain the same chunk. A peer can obtain part of a file from peers that do not have an exactly identical file, but merely a *similar* file.

Table 2. Layers of lookup indirection

Translation	Method
keywords → file IDs	keyword-set index search
file ID → chunk IDs	standard DHT lookup
chunk ID → sources	content-sharing subring

Though it seems unlikely that multiple files would share the same chunks, file sharing networks frequently contain multiple versions of the same file with largely similar content. For example, multiple versions of the same document may coexist on the network with most content shared between them. Similarly, users often have MP3 files with the same audio content but different ID3 metadata tags. Dividing the file into chunks allows the bulk of the data to be downloaded from any peer that shares it, rather than only the ones with the same version.

However, it is not sufficient to use a segmentation scheme that draws the boundaries between chunks at regular intervals. In the case of MP3 files, since ID3 tags are stored in a variable-length region of the file, a change in metadata may affect all of the chunks because the remainder of the file will now be "out of frame" with the original. Likewise, a more recent version of a document may contain insertions or deletions, which would cause the remainder of the document to be out of frame and negate some of the advantages of fixed-length chunking.

To solve this problem, we choose variable length chunks based on content, using a chunking algorithm derived from the LBFS file system [11]. Due to the way chunk boundaries are chosen, even if content is added or removed in the middle of the file, the remainder of the chunks will not change. While most recent networks, such as FastTrack, BitTorrent, and eDonkey, divide files into chunks, promoting the sharing of partial data between peers, *Arpeggio*'s segmentation algorithm additionally promotes sharing of data *between files*.

4.2   Content-Sharing Subrings

To download a chunk, a peer must discover one or more sources for this chunk. A simple solution for this problem is to maintain a list of peers that have the chunk available, which can be stored in the DHT or handled by a designated "tracker" node as in BitTorrent [1]. However, the node responsible for tracking the peers sharing a popular chunk represents a single point of failure that may become overloaded.

We instead use *subrings* to identify sources for each chunk, distributing the query load throughout the network. The Diminished Chord protocol [8] allows any subset of the nodes to form a named "subring" and allows LOOKUP operations that find nodes in that subring in $O(\log n)$ time, with constant storage overhead per node in the subring. We create a subring for each chunk, where the subring is identified by the chunk ID and consists of the nodes that are sharing that chunk. To obtain a chunk, a node performs a LOOKUP for a random Chord ID in the subring to discover the address of one of the sources. It then contacts that node and requests the chunk. If the contacted node is unavailable or overloaded, the requesting node may perform another LOOKUP to find a different source. When a node has finished downloading a chunk, it becomes a source and can join the subring. Content-sharing subrings offer a general mechanism for managing data that may be prohibitive to manage with regular DHTs.

4.3   Postfetching

To increase the availability of files, *Arpeggio* caches file chunks on nodes that would not otherwise be sharing the chunks. Cached chunks are indexed the same way as regular chunks, so they do not share the disadvantages of direct DHT storage with regards to having to maintain the chunks despite topology changes. Furthermore, this insertion symmetry makes caching transparent to the search system. Unlike in direct storage systems, caching is non-essential to the functioning of the network, and therefore each peer can place a reasonable upper bound on its cache storage size.

Postfetching provides a mechanism by which caching can increase the supply of rare files in response to demand. *Request blocks* are introduced to the network to capture requests for unavailable files. Due to the long expiration time of metadata blocks, peers can find files whose sources are temporarily unavailable. The peer can then insert a request block into the network for a particular unavailable file. When a source of that file rejoins the network it will find the request block and actively increase the supply of the requested file by sending the contents of the file chunks to the caches of randomly-selected nodes with available cache space. These in turn register as sources for those chunks, increasing their availability. Thus, the future supply of rare files is actively balanced out to meet their demand.

5   Conclusion

We have presented the key features of the *Arpeggio* content sharing system. *Arpeggio* differs from previous peer-to-peer file sharing systems in that it implements both a metadata indexing system and a content distribution system using a distributed lookup algorithm. We extend the standard DHT interface to support not only lookup by key but complex search queries. Keyword-set indexing and extensive network-side processing in the form of index-side filtering, index gateways, and expiration are used to address the scalability problems inherent in distributed document indexing. We introduce a content-distribution system based on indirect storage via subrings that uses chunking to leverage file similarity, and thereby optimize availability and transfer speed. Availability is further enhanced with postfetching, which uses cache space on other peers to replicate rare but demanded files. Together, these components result in a design that couples reliable searching with efficient content distribution to form a fully decentralized content sharing system.

References

1. BitTorrent protocol specification. http://bittorrent.com/protocol.html.
2. F. Dabek, M. F. Kaashoek, D. Karger, R. Morris, and I. Stoica. Wide-area cooperative storage with CFS. In *Proc. SOSP '01*, Oct. 2001.
3. F. Dabek, J. Li, E. Sit, J. Robertson, M. F. Kaashoek, and R. Morris. Designing a DHT for low latency and high throughput. In *Proc. NSDI '04*, Mar. 2004.
4. FreeDB. http://www.freedb.org.
5. M. J. Freedman, E. Freudenthal, and D. Mazières. Democratizing content publication with Coral. In *Proc. NSDI '04*, Mar. 2004.
6. O. Gnawali. A keyword set search system for peer-to-peer networks. Master's thesis, Massachusetts Institute of Technology, June 2002.
7. K. P. Gummadi, R. J. Dunn, S. Sariou, S. D. Gribble, H. M. Levy, and J. Zahorjan. Measurement, modeling, and analysis of a peer-to-peer file-sharing workload. In *Proc. SOSP '03*, Oct. 2003.
8. D. R. Karger and M. Ruhl. Diminished Chord: A protocol for heterogeneous subgroup formation in peer-to-peer networks. In *Proc. IPTPS '04*, Feb. 2004.
9. J. Li, B. T. Loo, J. M. Hellerstein, M. F. Kaashoek, D. Karger, and R. Morris. On the feasibility of peer-to-peer web indexing and search. In *Proc. IPTPS '03*, Feb. 2003.
10. P. Maymounkov and D. Mazières. Kademlia: A peer-to-peer information system based on the XOR metric. In *Proc. IPTPS '02*, Mar. 2002.
11. A. Muthitacharoen, B. Chen, and D. Mazières. A low-bandwidth network file system. In *Proc. SOSP '01*, Oct. 2001.
12. Overnet. http://www.overnet.com/.
13. P. Reynolds and A. Vahdat. Efficient peer-to-peer keyword searching. In *Proc. Middleware '03*, June 2003.
14. I. Stoica, R. Morris, D. Liben-Nowell, D. R. Karger, M. F. Kaashoek, F. Dabek, and H. Balakrishnan. Chord: a scalable peer-to-peer lookup protocol for internet applications. *IEEE/ACM Trans. Netw.*, 11(1):17–32, 2003.
15. C. Tang and S. Dworkadas. Hybrid local-global indexing for efficient peer-to-peer information retrieval. In *Proc. NSDI '04*, Mar. 2004.

OverCite: A Cooperative Digital Research Library[*]

Jeremy Stribling[1], Isaac G. Councill[2], Jinyang Li[1], M. Frans Kaashoek[1],
David R. Karger[1], Robert Morris[1], and Scott Shenker[3]

[1] MIT Computer Science and Artificial Intelligence Laboratory
{strib, jinyang, kaashoek, karger, rtm}@csail.mit.edu
[2] PSU School of Information Sciences and Technology
igc2@psu.edu
[3] UC Berkeley and ICSI
shenker@icsi.berkeley.edu

Abstract. CiteSeer is a well-known online resource for the computer science research community, allowing users to search and browse a large archive of research papers. Unfortunately, its current centralized incarnation is costly to run. Although members of the community would presumably be willing to donate hardware and bandwidth at their own sites to assist CiteSeer, the current architecture does not facilitate such distribution of resources. OverCite is a proposal for a new architecture for a distributed and cooperative research library based on a distributed hash table (DHT). The new architecture will harness resources at many sites, and thereby be able to support new features such as document alerts and scale to larger data sets.

1 Introduction

CiteSeer is a popular repository of scientific papers for the computer science community [12], supporting traditional keyword searches as well as navigation of the "web" of citations between papers. CiteSeer also ranks papers and authors in various ways, and can identify similarity among papers. Through these and other useful services, it has become a vital resource for the academic computer science community.

Despite its community value, the future of CiteSeer is uncertain without a sustainable model for community support. After an initial period of development and deployment at NEC, CiteSeer went mostly unmaintained until a volunteer research group at Pennsylvania State University recently took over the considerable task of running and maintaining the system (see Table 1).

If CiteSeer were required to support many more queries, implement new features, or significantly expand its document collection or its user base, the

---

[*] This research was conducted as part of the IRIS project (http://project-iris.net/), supported by the National Science Foundation under Cooperative Agreement No. ANI-0225660. Isaac G. Councill receives support from NSF SGER Grant IIS-0330783 and Microsoft Research.

M. Castro and R. van Renesse (Eds.): IPTPS 2005, LNCS 3640, pp. 69–79, 2005.

resources required would quickly outstrip what PSU, or any other single non-commercial institution, could easily provide. A commercially-managed system, such as Google Scholar, is one feasible solution; however, because of CiteSeer's value to the community, it is likely that many institutions would be willing to donate the use of machines and bandwidth at their sites in return for more control over its evolution. Thus, for CiteSeer to prosper and grow as a noncommercial enterprise, it must be adapted to run on a distributed set of donated nodes [11].

OverCite is a design that allows such an aggregation of distributed resources, using a DHT infrastructure. Our emphasis is not on the *novelty* of the design, but on its *benefits*. The DHT's role as a distributed storage layer, coupled with its robust and scalable models for data management and peer communication, allows the decentralization of the CiteSeer infrastructure and the inclusion of additional CPU and storage resources. Besides serving as a distributed, robust archive of data, the DHT simplifies the coordination of distributed activities, such as crawling. Finally, the DHT acts as a rendezvous point for producers and consumers of meta-data and documents.

By potentially aggregating many resources in this manner, CiteSeer could offer many more documents and features, enabling it to play an even more central role in the community. We are currently developing an OverCite prototype, and hope to make it available as a service to the community in the future.

2   CiteSeer Background

CiteSeer's major components interact as follows. A Web crawler visits a set of Web pages that are likely to contain links to PDF and PostScript files of research papers. If it sees a paper link it hasn't already fetched, CiteSeer fetches the file, parses it to extract text and citations, and checks whether the format looks like that of an academic paper. Then it applies heuristics to check if the document duplicates an existing document; if not, it adds meta-data about the document to its tables, and adds the document's words to an inverted index. The Web user interface accepts search terms, looks them up in the inverted index, and displays data about the resulting documents.

CiteSeer assigns a document ID (DID) to each document for which it has a PDF or Postscript file, and a citation ID (CID) to every bibliography entry within a document. CiteSeer also knows about the titles and authors of many papers for which it has no file, but to which it has seen citations. For this reason CiteSeer also assigns a "group ID" (GID) to each title/author pair for use in contexts where a file is not required.

CiteSeer uses the following tables:

1. The document meta-data table, indexed by DID, which records each document's authors, title, year, abstract, GID, CIDs of document's citations, number of citations to the document, etc.
2. The citation meta-data, indexed by CID, which records each citation's GID and citing document DID.

Table 1. Statistics for the PSU CiteSeer deployment

Property	Measurement
Number of papers (# of DIDs)	715,000
New documents per week	750
HTML pages visited	113,000
Total document storage	767 GB
Avg. document size	735 KB
Total meta-data storage	44 GB
Total inverted index size	18 GB
Hits per day	>1,000,000
Searches per day	250,000
Total traffic per day	34.4 GB
Document traffic per day	21 GB
Avg. number of active conns	68.4
Avg. load per CPU	66%

3. A table mapping each GID to the corresponding DID, if a DID exists.
4. A table mapping each GID to the list of CIDs that cite it.
5. An inverted index mapping each word to the DIDs of documents that contain that word.
6. A table indexed by the checksum of each fetched document file, used to decide if a file has already been processed.
7. A table indexed by the hash of every sentence CiteSeer has seen in a document, used to gauge document similarity.
8. A URL status table to keep track of which pages need to be crawled.
9. A table mapping paper titles and authors to the corresponding GID, used to find the target of citations observed in paper bibliographies.

Table 1 lists statistics for the current deployment of CiteSeer at PSU. CiteSeer uses two servers, each with two 2.8 GHz processors. Most of the CPU time is used to satisfy user searches. The main costs of searching are lookups in the inverted index, collecting and displaying meta-data about search results, and converting document files to user-requested formats. The primary costs of inserting new documents into CiteSeer are extracting words from newly found documents, and adding the words to the inverted index. It takes about ten seconds of CPU time to process each new document.

3   OverCite Design

The primary goal of OverCite is to spread the system's load over a few hundred volunteer servers. OverCite partitions the inverted index among many participating nodes, so that each node only indexes a fraction of the documents. This parallelizes the work of creating, updating, and searching the index. OverCite executes the user interface on many nodes, thus spreading the work of serving files and converting between file formats. OverCite stores the document files in a DHT, which spreads the burden of storing them. OverCite also stores its meta-data in the DHT for convenience, to make all data available to all nodes, and for reliability. The choice of a DHT as a shared storage medium ensures robust, scalable storage along with the efficient lookup and management of documents and meta-data. OverCite partitions its index by document, rather than keyword [13, 18, 21, 22], to avoid expensive joins on multi-keyword queries, and limit the communication necessary on document insertions.

3.1 Architecture

OverCite nodes have four active components: a DHT process, an index server, a web crawler, and a Web server that answers queries. Isolating the components in this manner allows us to treat each independently; for example, the inverted index is not tied any particular document storage solution. We describe each component in turn.

DHT process. OverCite nodes participate in a DHT. The DHT provides robust storage for documents and meta-data, and helps coordinate distributed activities such as crawling. Since OverCite is intended to run on a few hundred stable nodes, each DHT node can keep a full routing table and thus provide one hop lookups [9, 15, 14]. Because we expect failed nodes to return to the system with disks intact in most cases, and because all the data is soft state, the DHT can be lazy about re-replicating data stored on failed nodes.

Index server. To avoid broadcasting each query to every node, OverCite partitions the inverted index by document into k index partitions. Each document is indexed in just one partition. Each node maintains a copy of one index partition, so that if there are n nodes, there are n/k copies of each index partition. OverCite sends a copy of each query to one server in each partition, so that only k servers are involved in each query. Each of the k servers uses about $1/k$'th of the CPU time that would be required to search a single full-size inverted index. Each server returns only the DIDs of the m highest-ranked documents (by some specified criterion, such as citation count) in response to a query.

We can further reduce the query load by observing that many queries over the CiteSeer data will involve only paper titles or authors. In fact, analysis of an October 2004 trace of CiteSeer queries shows that 40% of answerable queries match the title or author list of at least one document. Furthermore, a complete index of just this meta-data for all CiteSeer papers is only 50 MB. Thus, an effective optimization may be to replicate this full meta-data index on all nodes, and keep it in memory, as a way to satisfy many queries quickly and locally. Another option is to replicate an index containing common search terms on all nodes. Moreover, if we would like to replicate the full text index on all nodes for even faster queries (*i.e.*, $k = 1$), we may be able to use differential updates to keep all nodes up-to-date on a periodic basis, saving computation at each node when updating the index.

In future work we plan to explore other possible optimizations for distributed search (*e.g.*, threshold aggregation algorithms [7]). If query scalability becomes

Table 2. The data structures OverCite stores in the DHT

Name	Key	Value
Docs	DID	FID, GID, CIDs, etc.
Cites	CID	DID, GID
Groups	GID	DID + CID list
Files	FID	Document file
Shins	hash(shingle)	list of DIDs
Crawl		list of page URLs
URLs	hash(doc URL)	date file last fetched
Titles	hash(Ti+Au)	GID

an issue, we plan to explore techniques from recent DHT search proposals [10, 8, 17, 19, 22, 1] or unstructured peer-to-peer search optimizations [23, 4].

Web crawler. The OverCite crawler design builds on several existing proposals for distributed crawling (*e.g.*, [5, 16, 3, 20]). Nodes coordinate the crawling effort via a list of to-be-crawled page URLs stored in the DHT. Each crawler process periodically chooses a random entry from the list and fetches the corresponding page. When the crawler finds a new document file, it extracts the document's text words and citations, and stores the document file, the extracted words, and the document's meta-data in the DHT. The node adds the document's words to its inverted index, and sends a message to each server in the same index partition telling it to fetch the document's words from the DHT and index them. A node keeps a cache of the meta-data for documents it has indexed, particularly the number of citations *to* the paper, in order to be able to rank search results locally. While many enhancements to this basic design (such as locality-based crawling and more intelligent URL partitioning) are both possible and desirable, we defer a more complete discussion of the OverCite crawler design to future work.

Web-based front-end. A subset of OverCite nodes run a Web user interface, using round-robin DNS to spread the client load. The front-end accepts query words from the user, sends them to inverted index servers, collects the results and ranks them, fetches meta-data from the DHT for the top-ranked results, and displays them to the user. The front-end also retrieves document files from the DHT, optionally converts them to a user-specified format, and sends them to the user.

3.2   Tables

Table 2 lists the data tables that OverCite stores in the DHT. The tables are not explicitly distinct entities in the DHT. Instead, OverCite uses the DHT as a single large key/value table; the system interprets values retrieved from the DHT based on the context in which the key was found. These tables are patterned after those of CiteSeer, but adapted to storage in the DHT. These are the main differences:

- The `Files` table holds a copy of each document PDF or PostScript file, keyed by the FID, a hash of the file contents.
- Rather than use sentence-level duplicate detection, which results in very large tables of sentences, OverCite instead uses *shingles* [2], a well-known and effective technique for duplicate detection. The `Shins` table is keyed by the hashes of shingles found in documents, and each value is a list of DIDs having that shingle.
- The `Crawl` key/value pair contains the list of URLs of pages known to contain document file URLs, in a single DHT block with a well-known key.
- The `URLs` table indicates when each document file URL was last fetched. This allows crawlers to periodically re-fetch a document file to check whether it has changed.

In addition to the tables stored in the DHT, each node stores its partition of the inverted index locally. The index is sufficiently annotated so that it can satisfy queries over both documents and citations, just as in the current CiteSeer.

4   Calculations

OverCite requires more communication resources than CiteSeer in order to manage the distribution of work, but as a result each server has less work to do. This section calculates the resources consumed by OverCite, comparing them to the costs of CiteSeer.

4.1   Maintenance Resources

Crawling and fetching new documents will take approximately three times more bandwidth than CiteSeer uses in total, spread out over all the servers. For each link to a Postscript or PDF file a node finds, it performs a lookup in `URLs` to see whether it should download the file. After the download, the crawler process checks whether this is a duplicate document. This requires (1) looking up the FID of the file in `Files`; (2) searching for an existing document with the same title and authors using `Titles`; and (3) verifying that, at a shingle level, the document sufficiently differs from others. These lookups are constant per document and inexpensive relative to downloading the document. Steps (2) and (3) occur after the process parses the document, converts it into text, and extracts the meta-data.

If the document is not a duplicate, the crawler process inserts the document into `Files` as Postscript or PDF, which costs as much as downloading the file, times the overhead f due to storage redundancy in the DHT [6]. The node also inserts the text version of the document into `Files` and updates `Docs`, `Cites`, `Groups`, and `Titles` to reflect this document and its meta-data.

Next, the node must add this document to its local inverted index partition (which is stored a total of n/k nodes). However, each additional node in the same index partition need only fetch the *text* version of the file from `Files`, which is on average a tenth the size of the original file. Each of these n/k nodes then indexes the document, incurring some cost in CPU time.

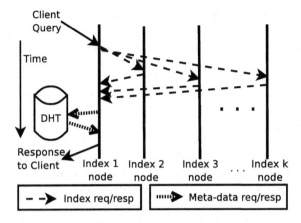

Fig. 1. The timeline of a query in OverCite, and the steps involved. Each vertical bar represents a node with a different index partition.

The additional system bandwidth required by OverCite to crawl and insert a new document is dominated by the costs of inserting the document into the DHT, and for the other nodes to retrieve the text for that document. If we assume that the average original file size is x, and the size of the text files is on average $x/10$, then the approximate bandwidth overhead per document is $fx + (n/k)(x/10)$ bytes.

We estimate the amount of storage needed by each node as follows. The DHT divides document and table storage among all n nodes in the system: this requires $(d + e)f/n$ GB, where d and e are the amount of storage used for documents and meta-data tables, respectively. Furthermore, each node stores one partition of the inverted index, or i/k GB if i is the total index size.

These bandwidth and storage requirements depend, of course, on the system parameters chosen for OverCite. Some reasonable design choices might be: $n = 100$ (roughly what PlanetLab has obtained through donations), $k = 20$ (so that only a few nodes need to index the full text of each new document), and $f = 2$ (the value DHash uses [6]). With these parameter choices, and the measurements from CiteSeer in Table 1, we find that the OverCite would require 1.84 MB of additional bandwidth per document (above the .735 MB CiteSeer currently uses) and 25 GB of storage per node.

These calculations ignore the cost of DHT routing table and data maintenance traffic. In practice, we expect these costs to be dwarfed by the traffic used to serve documents as we assume nodes are relatively stable.

4.2   Query Resources

Because OverCite partitions the inverted index by document, each query needs to be broadcast in parallel to $k-1$ nodes, one for each of the other index partitions.[1]

---

[1] We assume here that no queries match in the meta-data index; hence, these are worst-case calculations.

Each node caches the meta-data for the documents in its index partition in order to rank search results; this cache need not be up to date. When all k nodes return their top m matches, along with the context of the matches and the value of rank metric, the originating node looks up the meta-data for the top b matches. Figure 1 depicts this process.

The packets containing the queries will be relatively small; however, each response will contain the identifiers of each matching document, the context of each match, and the value of the rank metric. If there are n participating nodes, each DID is 20 bytes, and the context and rank metric value together are 50 bytes, each query consumes about $70mk$ bytes of traffic. Assuming 250,000 searches per day, $k = 20$, and returning $m = 10$ results per query per node, our query design adds 3.5 GB of traffic per day to the network (or 35 MB per node). This is a reasonably small fraction of the traffic currently served by CiteSeer (34.4 GB). This does not include the meta-data lookup traffic for the top b matches, which is much smaller (a reasonable value for b is 10 or 20).

Serving a document contributes the most additional cost in OverCite, since the Web-based front-end must retrieve the document fragments from the DHT before returning it to the user. This will approximately double the amount of traffic from paper downloads, which is currently 21 GB (though this load is now spread among all nodes). However, one can imagine an optimization involving redirecting the user to cached pre-constructed copies of the document on specific DHT nodes, saving this addition bandwidth cost.

OverCite spreads the CPU load of performing each query across multiple nodes, because the cost of an inverted index lookup is linear in the number of documents in the index.

4.3 User Delay

User-perceived delay could be a problem in OverCite, as constructing each Web page requires multiple DHT lookups. However, most lookups are parallelizable, and because we assume a one-hop DHT, the total latency should be low. For example, consider the page generated by a user keyword query. The node initially receiving the query forwards the query, in parallel, to $k-1$ nodes. After receiving responses from all nodes, the node looks up the meta-data for the top matches in parallel. Therefore, we expect that the node can generate the page in response to a search in about twice the average round trip time of the network, plus computation time.

Generating a page about a given document (which includes that document's citations and what documents cite it) will take additional delay for looking up extra meta-data; we expect each of those pages to take an average of three or four round trip times.

5   Features and Potential Impact

Given the additional resources available with OverCite's design, a wider range of features will be possible; in the long run the impact of new capabilities on the way researchers communicate may be the main benefit of a more scalable CiteSeer. This section sketches out a few potential features.

Document Alerts: As the field of computer science grows, it is becoming harder for researchers to keep track of new work relevant to their interests. OverCite could help by providing an *alert* service to e-mail a researcher whenever a paper entered the database that might be of interest. Users could register queries that OverCite would run daily (e.g., alert me for new papers on "distributed hash table" authored by "Druschel"). This service clearly benefits from the OverCite DHT infrastructure as the additional query load due to alerts becomes distributed over many nodes. A recent proposal [11] describes a DHT-based alert system for CiteSeer.

Document Recommendations: OverCite could provide a *recommendation* feature similar to those found in popular Web sites like Amazon. This would require OverCite to track individual users' activities. OverCite could then recommend documents based on either previous downloads, previous queries, or downloads by others with similar interests.

Plagiarism Checking: Plagiarism has only been an occasional problem in major conferences, but with increasing volumes of papers and pressure to publish, this problem will likely become more serious. OverCite could make its database of shingles available to those who wish to check whether one paper's text significantly overlaps any other papers'.

More documents: Most authors do not explicitly submit their newly written papers to CiteSeer. Instead, they rely on CiteSeer to crawl conference Web pages to find new content. CiteSeer could be far more valuable to the community if it could support a larger corpus and, in particular, if it included more preprints and other recently written material. While faster and more frequent crawling might help in this regard, the situation could only be substantially improved if authors took a more active role in adding their material.

As an extreme case, one could imagine that funding agencies and conferences require all publications under a grant and submissions to a conference be entered into OverCite, making them immediately available to the community.[2] Going one step further, one could imagine that program committees annotate submissions in OverCite with comments about the contributions of the paper. Users could then decide based on the comments of the PC which papers to read (using the document-alert feature). This approach would have the additional benefit that users have access to papers that today are rejected from a conference due to limited program time slots.

Potential impact: Radical changes, such as the one above, to the process of dissemination of scientific results are likely to happen only in incremental steps, but are not out of the question. Theoretical physics, for example, uses a preprint collection as its main document repository; insertion into the repository counts as the "publication date" for resolving credit disputes and, more importantly,

---

[2] This would require rethinking anonymous submissions or providing support for anonymous submissions in OverCite.

researchers routinely scan the list of new submissions to find relevant papers. This manual mode works less well for computer science, due in part to the diverse set of sub-disciplines and large number of papers. OverCite, however, could be the enabler of such changes for computer science, because of its scalable capacity and ability to serve many queries.

Acknowledgments

The comments of Jayanthkumar Kannan, Beverly Yang, Sam Madden, Anthony Joseph, the MIT PDOS research group, and the anonymous reviewers greatly improved this work. We also thank C. Lee Giles for his continued support at PSU.

References

1. BAWA, M., MANKU, G. S., AND RAGHAVAN, P. SETS: Search enhanced by topic segmentation. In *Proceedings of the 2003 SIGIR* (July 2003).
2. BRODER, A. Z. On the resemblance and containment of documents. In *Proceedings of the Compression and Complexity of Sequences* (June 1997).
3. BURKARD, T. Herodotus: A peer-to-peer web archival system. Master's thesis, Massachusetts Institute of Technology, May 2002.
4. CHAWATHE, Y., RATNASAMY, S., BRESLAU, L., LANHAM, N., AND SHENKER, S. Making Gnutella-like P2P systems scalable. In *Proc. of SIGCOMM* (August 2003).
5. CHO, J., AND GARCIA-MOLINA, H. Parallel crawlers. In *Proceedings of the 2002 WWW Conference* (May 2002).
6. DABEK, F., KAASHOEK, M. F., LI, J., MORRIS, R., ROBERTSON, J., AND SIT, E. Designing a DHT for low latency and high throughput. In *Proceedings of the 1st NSDI* (March 2004).
7. FAGIN, R., LOTEM, A., AND NAOR, M. Optimal aggregation algorithms for middleware. *Journal of Computer and System Sciences 66* (2003), 614–656.
8. GNAWALI, O. D. A keyword set search system for peer-to-peer networks. Master's thesis, Massachusetts Institute of Technology, June 2002.
9. GUPTA, A., LISKOV, B., AND RODRIGUES, R. Efficient routing for peer-to-peer overlays. In *Proceedings of the 1st NSDI* (Mar. 2004).
10. HUEBSCH, R., HELLERSTEIN, J. M., LANHAM, N., LOO, B. T., SHENKER, S., AND STOICA, I. Querying the Internet with PIER. In *Proceedings of the 19th VLDB* (Sept. 2003).
11. KANNAN, J., YANG, B., SHENKER, S., SHARMA, P., BANERJEE, S., BASU, S., AND LEE, S. J. SmartSeer: Continuous queries over CiteSeer. Tech. Rep. UCB//CSD-05-1371, UC Berkeley, Computer Science Division, Jan. 2005.
12. LAWRENCE, S., GILES, C. L., AND BOLLACKER, K. Digital libraries and autonomous citation indexing. *IEEE Computer 32*, 6 (1999), 67–71. http://www.citeseer.org.
13. LI, J., LOO, B. T., HELLERSTEIN, J. M., KAASHOEK, M. F., KARGER, D., AND MORRIS, R. On the feasibility of peer-to-peer web indexing and search. In *Proceedings of the 2nd IPTPS* (Feb. 2003).
14. LI, J., STRIBLING, J., KAASHOEK, M. F., AND MORRIS, R. Bandwidth-efficient management of DHT routing tables. In *Proceedings of the 2nd NSDI* (May 2005).

15. LITWIN, W., NEIMAT, M.-A., AND SCHNEIDER, D. A. LH* — a scalable, distributed data structure. *ACM Transactions on Database Systems 21*, 4 (1996), 480–525.

16. LOO, B. T., COOPER, O., AND KRISHNAMURTHY, S. Distributed web crawling over DHTs. Tech. Rep. UCB//CSD-04-1332, UC Berkeley, Computer Science Division, Feb. 2004.

17. LOO, B. T., HUEBSCH, R., STOICA, I., AND HELLERSTEIN, J. M. The case for a hybrid P2P search infrastructure. In *Proceedings of the 3rd IPTPS* (Feb. 2004).

18. REYNOLDS, P., AND VAHDAT, A. Efficient peer-to-peer keyword searching. In *Proceedings of the 4th International Middleware Conference* (June 2003).

19. SHI, S., YANG, G., WANG, D., YU, J., QU, S., AND CHEN, M. Making peer-to-peer keyword searching feasible using multi-level partitioning. In *Proceedings of the 3rd IPTPS* (Feb. 2004).

20. SINGH, A., SRIVATSA, M., LIU, L., AND MILLER, T. Apoidea: A decentralized peer-to-peer architecture for crawling the world wide web. In *Proceedings of the SIGIR 2003 Workshop on Distributed Information Retrieval* (Aug. 2003).

21. SUEL, T., MATHUR, C., WU, J.-W., ZHANG, J., DELIS, A., KHARRAZI, M., LONG, X., AND SHANMUGASUNDARAM, K. ODISSEA: A peer-to-peer architecture for scalable web search and information retrieval. In *Proceedings of the International Workshop on the Web and Databases* (June 2003).

22. TANG, C., AND DWARKADAS, S. Hybrid global-local indexing for efficient peer-to-peer information retrieval. In *Proceedings of the 1st NSDI* (Mar. 2004).

23. YANG, B., AND GARCIA-MOLINA, H. Improving search in peer-to-peer networks. In *Proceedings of the 22nd ICDCS* (July 2002).

NetProfiler: Profiling Wide-Area Networks Using Peer Cooperation

Venkata N. Padmanabhan[1], Sriram Ramabhadran[2,*], and Jitendra Padhye[3]

[1] Microsoft Research
padmanab@microsoft.com
[2] University of California at San Diego
sriram@cs.ucsd.edu
[3] Microsoft Research
padhye@microsoft.com

Abstract. Our work is motivated by two observations about the state of networks today. Operators have little visibility into the end users' network experience while end users have little information or recourse when they encounter problems. We propose a system called *NetProfiler*, in which end hosts share network performance information with other hosts over a peer-to-peer network. The aggregated information from multiple hosts allows NetProfiler to *profile* the wide-area network, i.e., monitor end-to-end performance, and detect and diagnose problems from the perspective of *end hosts*. We define a set of attribute hierarchies associated with end hosts and their network connectivity. Information on the network performance and failures experienced by end hosts is then aggregated along these hierarchies, to identify patterns (e.g., shared attributes) that might be indicative of the source of the problem. In some cases, such sharing of information can also enable end hosts to resolve problems by themselves. The results from a 4-week-long Internet experiment indicate the promise of this approach.

1 Introduction

Our work is motivated by two observations about the state of networks today. First, operators have little direct visibility into the end users' network experience. Monitoring of network routers and links, while important, does not translate into direct knowledge of the end-to-end health of the network. This is because any single operator usually controls only a few of the components along an end-to-end path. On the other hand, although end users have direct visibility into *their own* network performance, they have little other information or recourse when they encounter problems. They do not know the cause of the problem or whether it is affecting other users as well.

To address these problems, we propose a system called *NetProfiler*, in which end hosts monitor the network performance and then share the information with other end hosts over a peer-to-peer network. End hosts, or "clients", are

---

* The author was an intern at Microsoft Research during part of this work.

M. Castro and R. van Renesse (Eds.): IPTPS 2005, LNCS 3640, pp. 80–92, 2005.

in the ideal position to do monitoring since they are typically the initiators of end-to-end transactions and have full visibility into the success or failure of the transactions. By examining the correlations, or the lack thereof, across observations made by different clients, NetProfiler can detect network anomalies and localize their likely cause. Besides anomaly detection and diagnosis, this system allows users (and also ISPs) to learn about the network performance experienced by other hosts. The following scenarios illustrate the use of NetProfiler:

– A user who is unable to access a web site can find out whether the problem is specific to his/her host or ISP, or whether it is a server problem. In the latter case, the user's client may be able to automatically discover working replicas of the site.
– A user can benchmark his/her long-term network performance against that of other users in the same city. This information can be used to drive decisions such as upgrading to a higher level of service (e.g., to 768 Kbps DSL from 128 Kbps service) or switching ISPs.
– A consumer ISP such as MSN can monitor the performance seen by its customers in various locations and identify, for instance, that the customers in a certain city are consistently underperforming those elsewhere. This can call for upgrading the service or switching to a different provider of modem banks, backhaul bandwidth, etc. in that city.

We view NetProfiler as an interesting and novel P2P application that leverages peers for network monitoring and diagnosis. Peer participation is critical in NetProfiler, since in the absence of such participation, it would be difficult to learn the end-host perspective from multiple vantage points. This is in contrast to traditional P2P applications such as content distribution, where it is possible to reduce or eliminate dependence on peers by employing a centralized infrastructure. Each end-host is valuable in NetProfiler because of the perspective it provides on the health of the network, and not because of the (minimal) resources such as bandwidth and CPU that it contributes. Clearly, the usefulness and effectiveness of NetProfiler grows with the size of the deployment. In practice, NetProfiler can either be deployed in a coordinated manner by a network operator such as a consumer ISP or the IT department of an enterprise, or can grow organically as an increasing number of users install this new P2P "application".

To put NetProfiler in perspective, the state-of-the-art in end-host-based network diagnosis is an individual user using tools such as ping and traceroute to investigate problems. However, this approach suffers from several drawbacks.

A key limitation of these tools is that they only capture information from the viewpoint of a single end host or network entity. Also, these tools only focus on entities such as routers and links that are on the IP-level path, whereas the actual cause of a problem might be higher-level entities such as proxies and servers. In contrast, NetProfiler considers the entire end-to-end transaction, and combines information from multiple vantage points, which enables better fault diagnosis.

Many of the existing tools also operate on a short time scale, usually on an as-needed basis. NetProfiler monitors, aggregates, and summarizes network performance data on a continuous basis. This allows NetProfiler to detect anomalies in performance based on historical comparisons.

Another important issue is that many of the tools rely on active probing. In contrast, NetProfiler relies on passive observation of existing traffic. Reliance on active probing is problematic due to several reasons. First, the overhead of active probing can be high, especially if hundreds of millions of Internet hosts start using active probing on a routine basis. Second, active probing cannot always disambiguate the cause of failure. For example, an incomplete traceroute could be due to a router or server failure, or simply because of the suppression of ICMP messages by a router or a firewall. Third, the detailed information obtained by client-based active probing (e.g., traceroute) may not pertain to the dominant direction of data transfer (typically server→client).

Thus we believe that it is important and interesting to consider strategies for monitoring and diagnosing network performance that do *not* rely on active probing, and take a broad view of the network by considering the entire end-to-end path rather than just the IP-level path and combining the view from multiple vantage points.

In the remainder of the paper, we discuss the architecture of NetProfiler, some details of its constituent components, open issues and challenges, and related work.

2   NetProfiler Architecture and Algorithms

We now discuss the architecture of NetProfiler and the algorithms used for the acquisition, aggregation, and analysis of network performance data.

2.1   Data Acquisition

Data acquisition is performed by *sensors*, which are software modules residing on end hosts such as users' desktop machines. Although these sensors could perform active measurements, our focus here is primarily on passive observation of existing traffic. The end host would typically have multiple sensors, say one for each protocol or application. Sensors could be defined for the common Internet protocols such as TCP, HTTP, DNS, and RTP/RTCP as well protocols that are likely to be of interest in specific settings such as enterprise networks (e.g., the RPC protocol used by Microsoft Exchange servers and clients). The goal of the sensors is both to characterize the end-to-end communication in terms of success/failure and performance, and also to infer the conditions on the network path.

We have implemented two simple sensors — *TcpScope* and *WebScope* — to analyze TCP and HTTP, respectively. The widespread use of these protocols makes these sensors very useful. We now describe them briefly.

TcpScope: TcpScope is a passive sensor that listens on TCP transfers to and from the end host, and attempts to determine the cause of any performance problems. Our current implementation operates at user level in conjunction with the NetMon or WinDump filter driver on Windows XP. Since the user's machine is typically at the receiving end of TCP connections, it is challenging to estimate metrics such as the connection's RTT, congestion window size, etc. We outline a set of heuristics that are inspired by T-RAT [1] but are simpler since we have access to the client host.

An initial RTT sample is obtained from the SYN-SYNACK exchange. Further RTT samples are obtained by identifying flights of data separated by idle periods during the slow-start phase. The RTT estimate can be used to obtain an estimate of sender's congestion window (cwnd). A rough estimate of the bottleneck bandwidth is obtained by observing the spacing between the pairs of back-to-back packets emitted during slow start. [1] Using estimates of the RTT, cwnd and bottleneck bandwidth, we can determine the likely cause of rate limitation: whether the application itself is not producing enough data or whether an external factor such as a bandwidth bottleneck or packet loss is responsible.

Our initial experiments indicate that the TcpScope heuristics perform well. In ongoing work, we are conducting more extensive experiments in wide-area settings.

WebScope: In certain settings such as enterprise networks, the clients' web connections might traverse a caching proxy. So TcpScope would only be able to observe the dynamics of the network path between the proxy and the client. To provide some visibility into the conditions on the network path beyond the proxy, we have implemented the WebScope sensor. For an end-to-end web transaction, WebScope is able to estimate the contributions of the proxy, the server, and the server–proxy and proxy–client network paths to the overall latency. The main idea is to use a combination of cache-busting and byte-range HTTP requests, to decompose the end-to-end latency.

WebScope produces less detailed information than TcpScope but still offers a rough indication of the performance of the individual components on the client-proxy-server path. WebScope focuses on the first-level proxy between the client and the origin server. It ignores additional intermediate proxies, if any. This is just as well since such proxies are typically not visible to the client and so the client does not have the option of picking between multiple alternatives. Finally, we note that WebScope can operate in a "pseudo passive" mode by manipulating the cache control and byte-range headers on existing HTTP requests.

2.2 Normalization

The data produced by the sensors at each node needs to be "normalized" before it can be meaningfully shared with other nodes. For instance, the throughput observed by a dialup client might be consistently lower that that observed by a LAN client at the same location and yet this does not represent an anomaly. On the other hand, the failure to download a page is information that can be shared regardless of the client's access link speed.

---

[1] We can determine whether two packets were likely sent back-to-back by the sender by examining their IP IDs.

We propose dividing clients into a few different bandwidth classes based on their access link (downlink) speed — dialup, low-end broadband (say under 250 Kbps), high-end broadband (say under 1.5 Mbps), and LAN (10 Mbps and above). Clients could determine their bandwidth class either based on the estimates provided by TcpScope or based on out-of-band information (e.g., user knowledge).

The bandwidth class of a node is included in its set of attributes for the purposes of aggregating certain kinds of information using the procedure discussed in Section 2.3. Information of this kind includes the TCP throughput and possibly also the RTT and the packet loss rate. For TCP throughput, we use the information inferred by TcpScope to filter out measurements that were limited by factors such as the receiver-advertised window or the connection length. Regarding the latter, the throughput corresponding to the largest window (i.e., flight) that experienced no loss is likely to be more meaningful than the throughput of the entire connection.

Certain information such as RTT is strongly influenced by a client's location. So it is meaningful to share this information only with clients at the same location (e.g., same city).

Certain other information can be aggregated across all clients regardless of their location or access link speed. Examples include the success or failure of page download and an indiction of server or proxy load obtained from TcpScope or WebScope.

Finally, certain sites may have multiple replicas, with clients in different parts of the network communicating with different replicas. As such it make sense to report detailed performance information on a per replica basis and also report less detailed information (e.g., just an indication of download success or failure) on a per-site basis. The latter information would enable clients connected to a poorly performing replica to discover that the site is accessible via other replicas.

2.3   Data Aggregation

We now discuss how the performance information gathered at the individual end hosts is shared and aggregated across nodes. Our approach is based on a decentralized peer-to-peer architecture, which spreads the burden of aggregating information across all nodes.

The process of data aggregation and analysis is performed based on a set of client attributes. For both fault isolation and comparative analysis, it is desirable to compare the performance of clients that share certain attributes, as well as those that differ in certain attributes. Attributes may be hierarchical, in which case they define a *logical* hierarchy along which performance data can be aggregated. Examples of hierarchical attributes are

– *Geographical location:* Aggregation based on location is useful for users and network operators to detect performance trends specific to a particular location (e.g. "How are users in the Seattle area performing?"). Location yields a natural aggregation hierarchy, e.g., neighborhood→city→region→country.

- *Topological location:* Aggregation based on topological location is useful for users to make informed choices regarding their service provider (e.g., "Is my local ISP the reason for the poor performance I am seeing?"). It is also useful for network providers to identify performance bottlenecks in their networks. Topological location can also be aggregated along a hierarchy, e.g., subnet→PoP→ISP.

Alternatively, attributes can be non-hierarchical, in which case they are used to filter performance data to better analyze trends specific to that particular attribute. Examples of non-hierarchical attributes include:

- *Destination site:* Filtering based on destination site is useful to provide information on whether other users are able to access a particular website, and if so, what performance they are seeing (e.g. "Are other users also having problems accessing www.cnn.com?"). Although not hierarchical, in the case of replicated sites, destination site can be further refined based on the actual replica being accessed.
- *Bandwidth class:* Filtering based on bandwidth class is useful for users to compare their performance with other users within the same class (e.g. "How are all dialup users faring?") , as well as in other classes ("What performance can I expect if I switch to DSL?").

Aggregation based on attributes such as location is done in a hierarchical manner, with the aggregation tree mirroring the logical hierarchy defined by the attribute space. This is based on the observation that nodes are typically interested in detailed information only from "nearby" peers. They are satisfied with more aggregated information about distant peers. For instance, while a node might be interested in specific information, such as the download performance from a popular web site, pertaining to peers in its neighborhood, it has little use for such detailed information from nodes across the country. Regarding the latter, it is likely to be interested only in an aggregated view of the performance experienced by clients in the remote city or region.

Non-hierarchical attributes such as bandwidth class and destination site are used as filters that qualify performance data as it aggregated up the logical hierarchy described above. For example, each node in the hierarchy may organize the performance reports it receives based on bandwidth class, destination site and perhaps the cross-product. This enables the system to provide more fine-grained performance trends (e.g., "What is the performance seen by dialup clients in Seattle when accessing www.cnn.com?"). Conceptually, this is similar to maintaining different aggregation trees for each combination of attributes; in practice, it is desirable to realize this in a single hierarchy as it limits the number of times an end-host has to report the same performance record. Since the number of bandwidth classes is small, it is feasible to maintain separate hierarchies for each class. However, with destination sites, this is done only for a manageable number of popular sites. For less popular sites, it may be infeasible to maintain per-site trees, so only a single aggregated view of the site is maintained, at the cost of losing the ability to further refine based on other attributes.

Finally, mechanisms are required to map the above logical aggregation hierarchies to a *physical* hierarchy of nodes. To this end, we leverage DHT-based aggregation techniques such as SDIMS [2], which exploits the natural hierarchy yielded by the connectivity structure of the DHT nodes. Aggregation happens in a straightforward manner: nodes maintain information on the performance experienced by clients in their subtree. Periodically, they report aggregated views of this information to their parent. Such a design results in good locality properties, ensures efficiency of the aggregation hierarchy, and minimizes extraneous dependencies (e.g., the aggregator node for a client site lies within the same site).

2.4   Analysis and Diagnosis

We now discuss the kinds of analyses and diagnoses that NetProfiler enables.

Distributed Blame Attribution: Clients that are experiencing poor performance can diagnose the problem using a procedure that we term as *distributed blame attribution*. Conceptually, the idea is for a client to ascribe the poor performance that it is experiencing to the entities involved in the end-to-end transaction. The entities could include the server, proxy, DNS[2], and the network path, where the resolution of the path would depend on the information available (e.g., the full AS-level path or simply the ISP/PoP that the client connects to). The simplest policy is for a client to ascribe the blame equally to all of the entities. But a client could assign blame unequally if it suspects certain entities more, say based on information gleaned from local sensors such as TcpScope and WebScope.

Such blame information is then aggregated across clients. The aggregate blame assigned to an entity is normalized to reflect the fraction of transactions involving the entity that encountered a problem. The entities with the largest blame score are inferred to be the likely trouble spots.

The hierarchical aggregation scheme discussed in Section 2.3 naturally supports this distributed blame attribution scheme. Clients use the performance they experienced to update the performance records of entities at each level of the hierarchy. Finding the suspect entity is then a question of walking up the attribute hierarchy to identify the highest-level entity whose aggregated performance information indicates a problem (based on suitably-picked thresholds). The preference for picking an entity at a higher level reflects the assumption that a single shared cause for the observed performance problems has a greater likelihood than multiple separate causes. For instance, if clients connected to most of the PoPs of Verizon are experiencing problems, then the chances are that there is a general problem with Verizon's network rather than a specific problem at each individual PoP.

---

[2] The DNS latency may not be directly visible to a client if the request is made via a proxy.

Comparative Analysis: A client might benefit from knowledge of its network performance relative to that of other clients, especially those in the same vicinity (e.g., same city). Such knowledge can drive decisions such as whether to upgrade to a higher level of service or switch ISPs. For instance, a user who consistently sees worse performance than others on the same ISP network and in the same neighborhood can demand an investigation by the ISP; in the absence of comparative information, the user wouldn't even know to complain. A user who is considering upgrading from low-end to high-end DSL service could compare notes with existing high-end DSL users in the same locale to see how much improvement an upgrade would actually result in, rather than simply going by the speed advertised by the ISP.

Likewise, a consumer ISP that buys infrastructural services such as modem banks and backhaul bandwidth from third-party providers can monitor the performance experienced by its customers in different location. If it finds, for instance, that its customers in Seattle are consistently underperforming customers elsewhere, it would have reason to suspect the local infrastructure provider(s) in Seattle.

Network Engineering Analysis: A network operator could use detailed information gleaned from clients to make an informed decision on how to re-engineer or upgrade the network. For instance, consider the IT department of a large global enterprise that is tasked with provisioning network connectivity for dozens of corporate sites spread across the globe. There is a plethora of choices in terms of connectivity options (ranging from expensive leased lines to the cheaper VPN over the public Internet alternative), service providers, bandwidth, etc. The goal is typically to balance the twin goals of low cost and good performance. While existing tools and methodologies (based say on monitoring link utilization) are useful, the ultimate test is how well the network serves end-users in their day-to-day activities. NetProfiler provides an end-user perspective on network performance, thereby complementing existing monitoring tools and enabling more informed network engineering decisions. For instance, significant packet loss rate coupled with the knowledge that the egress link utilization is low might point to a problem with chosen service provider and might suggest switching to a leased line alternative. Poor end-to-end performance despite a low packet loss rate could be due to a large RTT, which could again be determined from NetProfiler observations. Remedial measures might include setting up a local proxy cache or server replica.

Network Health Reporting: The information gathered by NetProfiler can be used to generate reports on the health of wide-area networks such as the Internet or large enterprise networks. While auch reports are available today from organizations such as Keynote [3], the advantage of the NetProfiler approach is lower cost, greater coverage, and the ability to operate virtually unchanged in restricted environments such as corporate networks as well as the public Internet.

3   Experimental Results

We present some preliminary experimental observations to provide a flavor of the kinds of problems that the NetProfiler system could address. Our experimental setup consists of a set of a heterogeneous set of clients that repeatedly download content from a diverse set of 70 web sites during a 4-week period (Oct 1-29, 2004). The client set includes 147 PlanetLab nodes, dialup hosts connected to 26 PoPs on the MSN network, and 5 hosts on Microsoft's worldwide corporate network. Our goal was to emulate, within the constraints of the resources at our disposal, a set of clients running NetProfiler and sharing information to diagnose problems. Here are a few interesting observations:

– We observed several failure episodes during which accesses to a web site failed at most or all of the clients. Examples include failure episodes involving www.technion.ac.il and www.hku.hk. The widespread impact across clients in diverse locations suggests a server-side cause for these problems. It would be hard to make such a determination based just on the view from a single client.

– There are significant differences in the failure rate observed by clients that are seemingly "equivalent". Among the MSN dialup nodes, those connected to PoPs with ICG as the upstream provider experienced a much lower failure rate (0.2-0.3%) than those connected to PoPs with other upstream providers such as Qwest and UUNET (1.6-1.9%). This information can help MSN identify underperforming providers and take the necessary action to rectify the problem. Similarly, clients in CMU have a much higher failure rate (1.65%) than those in Berkeley (0.19%). This information can enable users at CMU pursue the matter with their local network administrators.

– Sometimes a group of clients shares a certain network problem that is not affecting other clients. The attribute(s) shared by the group might suggest the cause of the problem. For example, all 5 hosts on the Microsoft corporate network experience a high failure rate (8%) in accessesing www.royal.gov.uk, whereas the failure rate for other clients is negligible. Since the Microsoft clients are located in different countries and connect via different web proxies with distinct WAN connectivity, the problem is likely due to a common proxy configuration across the sites.

– In other instances, the problem is unique to a specific client-server pair. For example, the Microsoft corporate network node in China is never able to access www.nmt.edu whereas other nodes, including the ones at the other Microsoft sites, do not experience a problem. This suggests that the problem is specific to the path between the China node and www.nmt.edu (e.g., site blocking by the local provider). If we had access to information from multiple clients in China, we might be in a position to further disambiguate the possible causes.

4   Discussion

4.1   Deployment Models

We envision two deployment models for NetProfiler: *coordinated* and *organic*. In the coordinated model, NetProfiler is deployed by an organization such as the IT department of a large enterprise, to complement existing tools for network monitoring and diagnosis. The fact that all client hosts are in a single administrative domain simplifies the issues of deployment and security. In the organic model, on the other hand, NetProfiler is installed by end users themselves (e.g., on their home machines) in much the same way as they install other peer-to-peer applications. They might do so to obtain greater visibility into the cause of network connectivity and performance problems that they encounter. This is a more challenging deployment model, since issues of privacy and security as well as bootstrapping the system become more significant. We discuss these challenges next.

4.2   Bootstrapping

To be effective, NetProfiler requires a sufficient number of clients that overlap and differ in attributes to participate, so that meaningful comparisons can be made and conclusions drawn. The coordinated model makes this bootstrapping easy, since the IT department can very quickly deploy NetProfiler on a large number of clients in various locations throughout the enterprise, essentially by fiat.

Bootstrapping is much more challenging in the organic deployment model, where users install NetProfiler by choice. There is a chicken-and-egg problem between having a sufficient number of users to make the system useful and making the system useful enough to attract more users. To help bootstrap the system, we propose relaxing the insistence on passive monitoring by allowing a limited amount of active probing (e.g., web downloads that the client would *not* have performed in normal course). Clients could perform active downloads either autonomously (e.g., like Keynote clients) or in response to requests from peers. Of course, the latter option should be used with caution to avoid becoming a vehicle for attacks or offending users, say by downloading from "undesirable" sites. In any case, once the deployment has reached a certain size, active probing could be turned off.

4.3   Security

The issues of privacy and data integrity pose significant challenges to the deployment and functioning of NetProfiler. These issues are arguably of less concern in a controlled environment such as an enterprise.

Users may not want to divulge their identity, or even their IP address, when reporting performance. To help protect their privacy, we could give clients the option of identifying themselves at a coarse granularity that they are comfortable with (e.g., at the ISP level), but that still enables interesting analyses. Furthermore, anonymous communication techniques (e.g., [4]), that hide whether the sending node actually originated a message or is merely forwarding it, could be used to prevent exposure through direct communication. However, if performance reports were stripped of all client-identifying information, we would only be able to perform very limited analyses and inference (e.g., we might only be able to infer website-wide problems that affect most or all clients).

There is also the related issue of data integrity — an attacker could spoof performance reports and/or corrupt the aggregation procedure. In general, guaranteeing data integrity would require sacrificing privacy (e.g., [5]). However, in view of the likely usage of NetProfiler as an advisory tool, we believe that it would probably be acceptable to have a reasonable assurance of data integrity, even if not iron-clad guarantees. For instance, the problem of spoofing can be alleviated by insisting on a two-way handshake before accepting a performance report. The threat of data corruption can be mitigated by aggregating performance reports along multiple hierarchies and employing some form of majority voting when there is disagreement.

5   Related Work

In this section, we briefly survey existing tools and techniques for network monitoring and diagnosis, and contrast them with NetProfiler.

Several tools have been developed for performing connectivity diagnosis from an end host (e.g., ping, traceroute, pathchar [6], tulip [7]). While these tools are clearly useful, they have some limitations, including dependence on active probing of routers (which may be expensive and also infeasible in many cases), and a focus on just the IP-level path and the view from a single host. In contrast, NetProfiler correlates on *passive* observations of existing end-to-end communication from *multiple* vantage points to diagnose problems.

Network tomography techniques [8] leverage information from multiple IP-level paths to infer network health. However, tomography techniques are based on the analysis of fine-grained packet-level correlations, and therefore have typically involved active probing. Also, the focus is on a server-based, "tree" view of the network whereas NetProfiler focuses on a client-based "mesh" view.

PlanetSeer [9] is a system to locate Internet faults by selectively invoking traceroutes from multiple vantage points. It is a server-based system (unlike NetProfiler), so the direction of traceroutes matches the dominant direction of data flow. PlanetSeer differs from NetProfiler in terms of its dependence on active probing and focus on just the IP-level path.

Tools such as NetFlow [10] and Route Explorer [11] enable network administrators to monitor network elements such as routers. However, these tools do not directly provide information on the end-to-end health of the network.

SPAND [12] is a tool for sharing performance information among end hosts belonging to a single subnet or site. The performance reports are stored in a central database and are used by end hosts for performance prediction and mirror selection. NetProfiler differs from SPAND in several ways, including its focus on fault diagnosis rather than performance prediction and use of a P2P approach that encompasses nodes beyond the local subnet or site.

Several systems have been developed for distributed monitoring, aggregation, and querying on the Internet. Examples include Ganglia [13], Slicestat [14], Iris-Net [15], PIER [16], Sophia [17], SDIMS [2], and Astrolabe [18]. NetProfiler could in principle leverage these systems for data aggregation, albeit with relaxed consistency and timeliness requirements. The primary focus of our work is on leveraging end-host observations to diagnose network problems rather than on developing a new data aggregation system.

The Knowledge Plane proposal [19] shares NetProfiler's goal of enabling users to diagnose network problems. But it is more ambitious in that the knowledge plane is envisaged as encompassing not only the end users' network experience but also network configuration and policy information. In contrast, NetProfiler is designed to be deployable on today's Internet with only the cooperation of (a subset of) end hosts.

Systems such as NETI@home [20] and Keynote [21] also gather end-host-based network performance data. Although it is unclear in what ways this data is further analyzed, NetProfiler's analyses described in Section 2.4 could easily be applied to such data.

Finally, like NetProfiler, STRIDER [22] and PeerPressure [23] also leverage information from peers to do cross-machine troubleshooting of configuration problems, by comparing the configuration settings of a sick machine with that of a healthy machine. NetProfiler is different in that it explicitly deals with information on specific problems (e.g., DNS lookup failures for a particular server) rather than "blackbox" configuration information. Also, given the focus on wide-area network troubleshooting, NetProfiler requires the participation of a larger number of peers in a diverse set of network locations.

6   Conclusion

We have presented NetProfiler, a P2P system to enable monitoring and diagnosis of network problems. Unlike in many previous P2P applications, the participation of peers is fundamental to the operation of NetProfiler. The results from an initial 4-week experiment indicate the promise of the proposed approach. We believe that the capabilities provided by NetProfiler can benefit both end users and network operators, such as consumer ISPs and enterprise IT departments. In ongoing work, we are also exploring using end-host observations to detect large-scale surreptitious communication as might precede a DDoS attack.

Acknowledgements

We thank our colleagues at the Microsoft Research locations worldwide, MSN, and PlanetLab for giving us access to a distributed set of hosts for our experiments. We also thank Sharad Agarwal for his comments on an earlier draft.

References

1. Zhang, Y., Breslau, L., Paxson, V., Shenker, S.: On the Characteristics and Origins of Internet Flow Rates. In: SIGCOMM. (2002)
2. Yalagandula, P., Dahlin, M.: A scalable distributed information management system. In: SIGCOMM. (2004)
3. : Keynote Internet Health Report. (http://www.internethealthreport.com/)
4. Reiter, M.K., Rubin, A.D.: Crowds: anonymity for Web transactions. ACM Transactions on Information and System Security 1 (1998) 66–92
5. Przydatek, B., Song, D., Perrig, A.: Sia: Secure information aggregation in sensor networks (2003)
6. Downey, A.B.: Using pathchar to Estimate Link Characteristics. In: SIGCOMM. (1999)
7. Mahajan, R., Spring, N., Wetherall, D., Anderson, T.: User-level Internet Path Diagnosis. In: SOSP. (2003)
8. Caceres, R., Duffield, N., Horowitz, J., Towsley, D.: Multicast-based inference of network-internal loss characteristics. IEEE Transactions on Information Theory (1999)
9. Zhang, M., Zhang, C., Pai, V., Peterson, L., Wang, R.: PlanetSeer: Internet Path Failure Monitoring and Characterization in Wide-Area Services. In: OSDI. (2004)
10. Feldmann, A., Greenberg, A., Lund, C., Reingold, N., Rexford, J., True, F.: Deriving traffic demands for operational ip networks: Methodology and experience. In: SIGCOMM. (2001)
11. http://www.packetdesign.com/.
12. Seshan, S., Stemm, M., Katz, R.H.: Spand: Shared passive network performance discovery. In: USITS. (1997)
13. Ganglia. http://ganglia.sourceforge.net/.
14. Slicestat. http://berkeley.intel-research.net/bnc/slicestat/.
15. Gibbons, P.B., Karp, B., Ke, Y., Nath, S., Seshan, S.: Irisnet: An architecture for a world-wide sensor web. IEEE Pervasive Computing (2003)
16. Huebsch, R., Hellerstein, J.M., Lanham, N., Loo, B.T., Shenker, S., Stoica, I.: Querying the internet with pier. In: VLDB. (2003)
17. Wawrzoniak, M., Peterson, L., Roscoe, T.: Sophia: An information plane for networked systems. In: HotNets. (2003)
18. van Renesse, R., Birman, K., Vogels, W.: Astrolabe: A robust and scalable technology for distributed system monitoring, management and data mining. ACM Transactions on Computer Systems (2003)
19. Clark, D., Partridge, C., Ramming, J., Wroclawski, J.: A Knowledge Plane for the Internet. SIGCOMM (2003)
20. Simpson, C.R., Riley, G.F.: NETI@home: A Distributed Approach to Collecting End-to-End Network Performance Measurements. PAM (2004)
21. Keynote Systems. http://www.keynote.com.
22. Wang, Y., Verbowski, C., Dunagan, J., Chen, Y., Chun, Y., Wang, H., Zhang, Z.: STRIDER: A Black-box, State-based Approach to Change and Configuration Management and Support. In: Usenix LISA. (2003)
23. Wang, H., Platt, J., Chen, Y., Zhang, R., Wang, Y.: Automatic Misconfiguration Troubleshooting with PeerPressure. In: OSDI. (2004)

A Statistical Theory of Chord Under Churn[*]

Supriya Krishnamurthy[1], Sameh El-Ansary[1], Erik Aurell[2], and Seif Haridi[3]

[1] Swedish Institute of Computer Science, Kista, Sweden
{supriya, sameh}@sics.se
[2] Department of Physics, KTH-Royal Institute of Technology, Sweden
erik.aurell@physics.kth.se
[3] IMIT-Royal Institute of Technology, Kista, Sweden
seif@imit.kth.se

Abstract. Most earlier studies of DHTs under churn have either depended on simulations as the primary investigation tool, or on establishing bounds for DHTs to function. In this paper, we present a complete analytical study of churn using a master-equation-based approach, used traditionally in non-equilibrium statistical mechanics to describe steady-state or transient phenomena. Simulations are used to verify all theoretical predictions. We demonstrate the application of our methodology to the Chord system. For any rate of churn and stabilization rates, and any system size, we accurately predict the fraction of failed or incorrect successor and finger pointers and show how we can use these quantities to predict the performance and consistency of lookups under churn. We also discuss briefly how churn may actually be of different 'types' and the implications this will have for the functioning of DHTs in general.

1 Introduction

Theoretical studies of asymptotic performance bounds of DHTs under churn have been conducted in works like [1,2]. However, within these bounds, performance can vary substantially as a function of different design decisions and configuration parameters. Hence simulation-based studies such as [3,4,5] often provide more realistic insights into the performance of DHTs. Relying on an understanding based on simulations alone is however not satisfactory either, since in this case, the DHT is treated as a black box and is only empirically evaluated, under certain operation conditions. In this paper we present an alternative theoretical approach to analyzing and understanding DHTs, which aims for an accurate prediction of performance, rather than on placing asymptotic performance bounds. Simulations are then used to verify all theoretical predictions.

Our approach is based on constructing and working with master equations, a widely used tool wherever the mathematical theory of stochastic processes is applied to real-world phenomena [6]. We demonstrate the applicability of this approach to one specific DHT: Chord [7]. For Chord, it is natural to define the

---

[*] This work is funded by the Swedish VINNOVA AMRAM and PPC projects, the European IST-FET PEPITO and 6th FP EVERGROW projects.

M. Castro and R. van Renesse (Eds.): IPTPS 2005, LNCS 3640, pp. 93–103, 2005.

state of the system as the state of all its nodes, where the state of an alive node is specified by the states of all its pointers. These pointers (either fingers or successors) are then in one of three states: alive and correct, alive and incorrect or failed. A master equation for this system is simply an equation for the time evolution of the probability that the system is in a particular state. Writing such an equation involves keeping track of all the gain/loss terms which add/detract from this probability, given the details of the dynamics. This approach is applicable to any P2P system (or indeed any system with a discrete set of states).

Our main result is that, for every outgoing pointer of a Chord node, we systematically compute the probability that it is in any one of the three possible states, by computing all the gain and loss terms that arise from the details of the Chord protocol under churn. This probability is different for each of the successor and finger pointers. We then use this information to predict both lookup consistency (number of failed lookups) as well as lookup performance (latency) as a function of the parameters involved. All our results are verified by simulations.

The main novelty of our analysis is that it is carried out entirely from first principles *i.e.* all quantities are predicted solely as a function of the parameters of the problem: the churn rate, the stabilization rate and the number of nodes in the system. It thus differs from earlier related theoretical studies where quantities similar to those we predict, were either assumed to be *given* [8], or *measured* numerically [9].

Closest in spirit to our work is the informal derivation in the original Chord paper [7] of the average number of timeouts encountered by a lookup. This quantity was approximated there by the product of the average number of fingers used in a lookup times the probability that a given finger points to a departed node. Our methodology not only allows us to derive the latter quantity rigorously but also demonstrates how this probability depends on which finger (or successor) is involved. Further we are able to derive an exact relation relating this probability to lookup performance and consistency accurately at any value of the system parameters.

2   Assumptions and Definitions

Basic Notation. In what follows, we assume that the reader is familiar with Chord. However we introduce the notation used below. We use $\mathcal{K}$ to mean the size of the Chord key space and N the number of nodes. Let $\mathcal{M} = \log_2 \mathcal{K}$ be the number of fingers of a node and $\mathcal{S}$ the length of the immediate successor list, usually set to a value $= O(\log(N))$. We refer to nodes by their keys, so a node n implies a node with key $n \in 0 \cdots \mathcal{K} - 1$. We use p to refer to the predecessor, s for referring to the successor list as a whole, and s_i for the ith successor. Data structures of different nodes are distinguished by prefixing them with a node key e.g. $n'.s_1$, etc. Let $fin_i.start$ denote the start of the ith finger (Where for a node n, $\forall i \in 1..\mathcal{M}$, $n.fin_i.start = n + 2^{i-1}$) and $fin_i.node$ denote the actual node pointed to by that finger.

Steady State Assumption. λ_j is the rate of joins per node, λ_f the rate of failures per node and λ_s the rate of stabilizations per node. We carry out our analysis for the general case when the rate of doing successor stabilizations $\alpha\lambda_s$, is not necessarily the same as the rate at which finger stabilizations $(1 - \alpha)\lambda_s$ are performed. In all that follows, we impose the steady state condition $\lambda_j = \lambda_f$. Further it is useful to define $r \equiv \frac{\lambda_s}{\lambda_f}$ which is the relevant ratio on which all the quantities we are interested in will depend, e.g, $r = 50$ means that a join/fail event takes place every half an hour for a stabilization which takes place once every 36 seconds.

Parameters. The parameters of the problem are hence: $\mathcal{K}$, N, α and r. All relevant measurable quantities should be entirely expressible in terms of these parameters.

Chord Simulation. We use our own discrete event simulation environment implemented in Java which can be retrieved from [10]. We assume the familiarity of the reader with Chord, however an exact analysis necessitates the provision of a few details. Successor stabilizations performed by a node n on $n.s_1$ accomplish two main goals: i) Retrieving the predecessor and successor list of of $n.s_1$ and reconciling with n's state. ii) Informing $n.s_1$ that n is alive/newly joined. A finger stabilization picks one finger at random and looks up its start. Lookups do not use the optimization of checking the successor list before using the fingers. However, the successor list is used as a last resort if fingers could not provide progress. Lookups are assumed not to change the state of a node. For joins, a new node u finds its successor v through some initial random contact and performs successor stabilization on that successor. All fingers of u that have v as an acceptable finger node are set to v. The rest of the fingers are computed as best estimates from $v's$ routing table. All failures are ungraceful. We make the simplifying assumption that communication delays due to a limited number of hops is much smaller than the average time interval between joins, failures or stabilization events. However, we do not expect that the results will change much even if this were not satisfied.

Averaging. Since we are collecting statistics like the probability of a particular finger pointer to be wrong, we need to repeat each experiment 100 times before obtaining well-averaged results. The total simulation sequential real time for obtaining the results of this paper was about 1800 hours that was parallelized on a cluster of 14 nodes where we had $N = 1000$, $\mathcal{K} = 2^{20}$, $\mathcal{S} = 6$, $200 \leq r \leq 2000$ and $0.25 \leq \alpha \leq 0.75$.

3   The Analysis

3.1   Distribution of Inter-node Distances

During churn, the inter-node distance (the difference between the keys of two consecutive nodes) is a fluctuating variable. An important quantity used throughout the analysis is the pdf of inter-node distances. We define this quantity below and state a theorem giving its functional form. We then mention three properties of this distribution which are needed in the ensuing analysis. Due to space limitations, we omit the proof of this theorem and the properties here and provide them in [10].

Definition 1. *Let $Int(x)$ be the number of intervals of length x, i.e. the number of pairs of consecutive nodes which are separated by a distance of x keys on the ring.*

Theorem 1. *For a process in which nodes join or leave with equal rates (and the number of nodes in the network is almost constant) independently of each other and uniformly on the ring, The probability $(P(x) \equiv \frac{Int(x)}{N})$ of finding an interval of length x is:*
$$P(x) = \rho^{x-1}(1 - \rho) \text{ where } \rho = \frac{K-N}{K} \text{ and } 1 - \rho = \frac{N}{K}$$

The derivation of the distribution $P(x)$ is independent of any details of the Chord implementation and depends solely on the join and leave process. It is hence applicable to any DHT that deploys a ring.

Property 1. For any two keys u and v, where $v = u + x$, let b_i be the probability that the first node encountered inbetween these two keys is at $u + i$ (where $0 \leq i < x - 1$). Then $b_i \equiv \rho^i(1 - \rho)$. The probability that there is definitely atleast one node between u and v is: $a(x) \equiv 1 - \rho^x$. Hence the conditional probability that the first node is at a distance i *given* that there is atleast one node in the interval is $bc(i, x) \equiv b(i)/a(x)$.

Property 2. The probability that a node and atleast one of its immediate predecessors share the same k^{th} finger is $p_1(k) \equiv \frac{\rho}{1+\rho}(1 - \rho^{2^k-2})$. This is $\sim 1/2$ for $K >> 1$ and $N << K$. Clearly $p_1 = 0$ for $k = 1$. It is straightforward (though tedious) to derive similar expressions for $p_2(k)$ the probability that a node and atleast *two* of its immediate predecessors share the same k^{th} finger, $p_3(k)$ and so on.

Property 3. We can similarly assess the probability that the join protocol (see previous section) results in further replication of the kth pointer. That is, the probability that a newly joined node will choose the kth entry of its successor's finger table as its own k^{th} entry is $p_{join}(k) \sim \rho(1 - \rho^{2^{k-2}-2}) + (1 - \rho)(1 - \rho^{2^{k-2}-2}) - (1 - \rho)\rho(2^{k-2} - 2)\rho^{2^{k-2}-3}$. The function $p_{join}(k) = 0$ for small k and 1 for large k.

3.2   Successor Pointers

In order to get a master-equation description which keeps all the details of the system and is still tractable, we make the ansatz that the state of the system is the product of the states of its nodes, which in turn is the product of the states of all its pointers. As we will see this ansatz works very well. Now we need only consider how many kinds of pointers there are in the system and the states these can be in. Consider first the successor pointers.

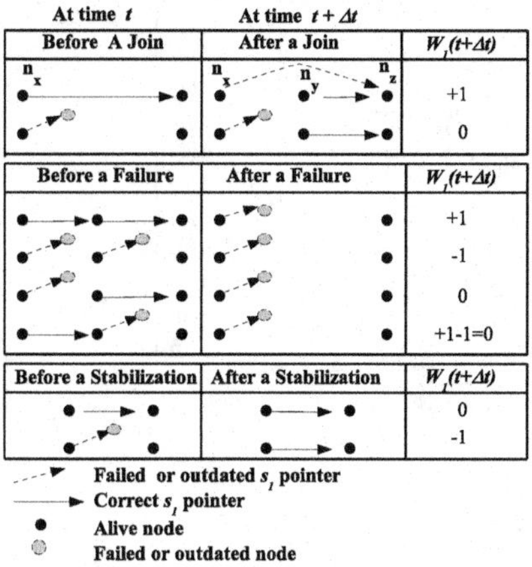

At time t	At time $t + \Delta t$	
Before A Join	**After a Join**	$W_1(t+\Delta t)$
		+1
		0
Before a Failure	**After a Failure**	$W_1(t+\Delta t)$
		+1
		-1
		0
		+1-1=0
Before a Stabilization	**After a Stabilization**	$W_1(t+\Delta t)$
		0
		-1

- - - ▶ Failed or outdated s_1 pointer
────▶ Correct s_1 pointer
● Alive node
◉ Failed or outdated node

Fig. 1. Changes in W_1, the number of wrong (failed or outdated) s_1 pointers, due to joins, failures and stabilizations

Table 1. Gain and loss terms for $W_1(r, \alpha)$: the number of wrong first successors as a function of r and α

Change in $W_1(r,\alpha)$	Rate of Change
$W_1(t+\Delta t) = W_1(t) + 1$	$c_1 = (\lambda_j \Delta t)(1 - w_1)$
$W_1(t+\Delta t) = W_1(t) + 1$	$c_2 = \lambda_f (1 - w_1)^2 \Delta t$
$W_1(t+\Delta t) = W_1(t) - 1$	$c_3 = \lambda_f w_1^2 \Delta t$
$W_1(t+\Delta t) = W_1(t) - 1$	$c_4 = \alpha \lambda_s w_1 \Delta t$
$W_1(t+\Delta t) = W_1(t)$	$1 - (c_1 + c_2 + c_3 + c_4)$

Let $w_k(r, \alpha)$, $d_k(r, \alpha)$ denote the fraction of nodes having a *wrong* k^{th} successor pointer or a *failed* one respectively and $W_k(r, \alpha)$, $D_k(r, \alpha)$ be the respective *numbers*. A *failed* pointer is one which points to a departed node and a *wrong* pointer points either to an incorrect node (alive but not correct) or a dead one. As we will see, both these quantities play a role in predicting lookup consistency and lookup length.

By the protocol for stabilizing successors in Chord, a node periodically contacts its first successor, possibly correcting it and reconciling with its successor list. Therefore, the number of wrong k^{th} successor pointers are not independent quantities but depend on the number of wrong first successor pointers. We consider only s_1 here.

We write an equation for $W_1(r, \alpha)$ by accounting for all the events that can change it in a micro event of time Δt. An illustration of the different cases in which changes in W_1 take place due to joins, failures and stabilizations is provided in figure 1. In some cases W_1 increases/decreases while in others it stays unchanged. For each increase/decrease, table 1 provides the corresponding probability.

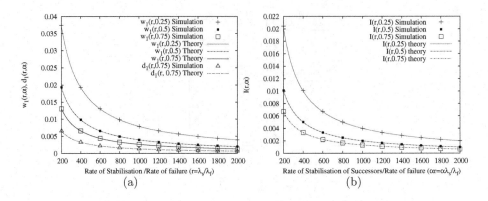

Fig. 2. Theory and Simulation for $w_1(r,\alpha)$, $d_1(r,\alpha)$, $I(r,\alpha)$

By our implementation of the join protocol, a new node n_y, joining between two nodes n_x and n_z, has its s_1 pointer always correct after the join. However the state of $n_x.s_1$ before the join makes a difference. If $n_x.s_1$ was correct (pointing to n_z) before the join, then after the join it will be wrong and therefore W_1 increases by 1. If $n_x.s_1$ was wrong before the join, then it will remain wrong after the join and W_1 is unaffected. Thus, we need to account for the former case only. The probability that $n_x.s_1$ is correct is $1 - w_1$ and from that follows the term c_1.

For failures, we have 4 cases. To illustrate them we use nodes n_x, n_y, n_z and assume that n_y is going to fail. First, if both $n_x.s_1$ and $n_y.s_1$ were correct, then the failure of n_y will make $n_x.s_1$ wrong and hence W_1 increases by 1. Second, if $n_x.s_1$ and $n_y.s_1$ were both wrong, then the failure of n_y will decrease W_1 by one, since one wrong pointer disappears. Third, if $n_x.s_1$ was wrong and $n_y.s_1$ was correct, then W_1 is unaffected. Fourth, if $n_x.s_1$ was correct and $n_y.s_1$ was wrong, then the wrong pointer of n_y disappeared and $n_x.s_1$ became wrong, therefore W_1 is unaffected. For the first case to happen, we need to pick two nodes with correct pointers, the probability of this is $(1 - w_1)^2$. For the second case to happen, we need to pick two nodes with wrong pointers, the probability of this is w_1^2. From these probabilities follow the terms c_2 and c_3.

Finally, a successor stabilization does not affect W_1, unless the stabilizing node had a wrong pointer. The probability of picking such a node is w_1. From this follows the term c_4.

Hence the equation for $W_1(r,\alpha)$ is:

$$\frac{dW_1}{dt} = \lambda_j(1 - w_1) + \lambda_f(1 - w_1)^2 - \lambda_f w_1^2 - \alpha\lambda_s w_1$$

Solving for w_1 in the steady state and putting $\lambda_j = \lambda_f$, we get:

$$w_1(r,\alpha) = \frac{2}{3 + r\alpha} \approx \frac{2}{r\alpha} \tag{1}$$

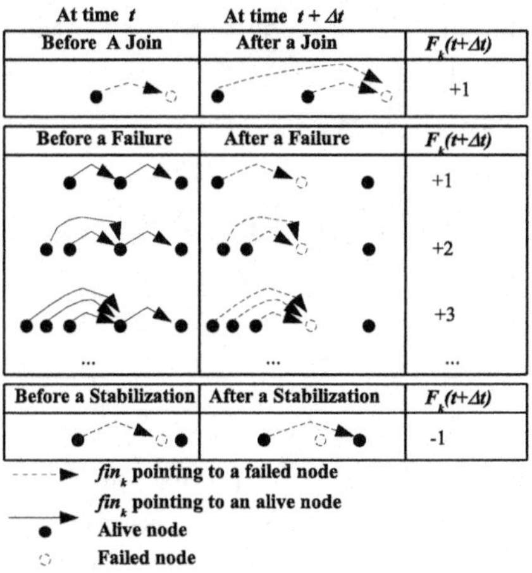

Fig. 3. Changes in F_k, the number of failed fin_k pointers, due to joins, failures and stabilizations

This expression matches well with the simulation results as shown in figure 2. $d_1(r, \alpha)$ is then $\approx \frac{1}{2}w_1(r, \alpha)$ since when $\lambda_j = \lambda_f$, about half the number of wrong pointers are incorrect and about half point to dead nodes. Thus $d_1(r, \alpha) \approx \frac{1}{r\alpha}$ which also matches well the simulations as shown in figure 2. We can also use the above reasoning to iteratively get $w_k(r, \alpha)$ for any k.

Lookup Consistency. By the lookup protocol, a lookup is inconsistent if the immediate predecessor of the sought key has an wrong s_1 pointer. However, we need only consider the case when the s_1 pointer is pointing to an alive (but incorrect) node since our implementation of the protocol always requires the lookup to return an alive node as an answer to the query. The probability that a lookup is inconsistent $I(r, \alpha)$ is hence $w_1(r, \alpha) - d_1(r, \alpha)$. This prediction matches the simulation results very well, as shown in figure 2.

3.3   Failure of Fingers

We now turn to estimating the fraction of finger pointers which point to failed nodes. As we will see this is an important quantity for predicting lookups. Unlike members of the successor list, alive fingers even if outdated, always bring a query closer to the destination and do not affect consistency. Therefore we consider fingers in only two states, alive or dead (failed).

Let $f_k(r, \alpha)$ denote the fraction of nodes having their k^{th} finger pointing to a failed node and $F_k(r, \alpha)$ denote the respective number. For notational simplicity, we write these as simply F_k and f_k. We can predict this function for any k by again estimating the gain and loss terms for this quantity, caused by a join, failure or stabilization event, and keeping only the most relevant terms. These are listed in table 2.

Table 2. Some of the relevant gain and loss terms for F_k, the number of nodes whose kth fingers are pointing to a failed node for $k > 1$

$F_k(t + \Delta t)$	Rate of Change
$= F_k(t) + 1$	$c_1 = (\lambda_j \Delta t) p_{join}(k) f_k$
$= F_k(t) - 1$	$c_2 = (1 - \alpha) \frac{1}{\mathcal{M}} f_k (\lambda_s \Delta t)$
$= F_k(t) + 1$	$c_3 = (1 - f_k)^2 [1 - p_1(k)](\lambda_f \Delta t)$
$= F_k(t) + 2$	$c_4 = (1 - f_k)^2 (p_1(k) - p_2(k))(\lambda_f \Delta t)$
$= F_k(t) + 3$	$c_5 = (1 - f_k)^2 (p_2(k) - p_3(k))(\lambda_f \Delta t)$
$= F_k(t)$	$1 - (c_1 + c_2 + c_3 + c_4 + c_5)$

A join event can play a role here by increasing the number of F_k pointers if the successor of the joinee had a failed k^{th} pointer (occurs with probability f_k) and the joinee replicated this from the successor (occurs with probability $p_{join}(k)$ from property 3).

A stabilization evicts a failed pointer if there was one to begin with. The stabilization rate is divided by $\mathcal{M}$, since a node stabilizes any one finger randomly, every time it decides to stabilize a finger at rate $(1 - \alpha)\lambda_s$.

Given a node n with an alive k^{th} finger (occurs with probability $1 - f_k$), when the node pointed to by that finger fails, the number of failed k^{th} fingers (F_k) increases. The amount of this increase depends on the number of immediate predecessors of n that were pointing to the failed node with their k^{th} finger. That number of predecessors could be 0, 1, 2,.. etc. Using property 2 the respective probabilities of those cases are: $1 - p_1(k)$, $p_1(k) - p_2(k)$, $p_2(k) - p_3(k)$,... etc.

Solving for f_k in the steady state, we get:

$$f_k = \frac{\left[2\tilde{P}_{rep}(k) + 2 - p_{join}(k) + \frac{r(1-\alpha)}{\mathcal{M}}\right]}{2(1 + \tilde{P}_{rep}(k))} - \frac{\sqrt{\left[2\tilde{P}_{rep}(k) + 2 - p_{join}(k) + \frac{r(1-\alpha)}{\mathcal{M}}\right]^2 - 4(1 + \tilde{P}_{rep}(k))^2}}{2(1 + \tilde{P}_{rep}(k))} \tag{2}$$

where $\tilde{P}_{rep}(k) = \Sigma p_i(k)$. In principle its enough to keep even three terms in the sum. The above expressions match very well with the simulation results (figure 4).

3.4 Cost of Finger Stabilizations and Lookups

In this section, we demonstrate how the information about the failed fingers and successors can be used to predict the cost of stabilizations, lookups or in general the cost for reaching any key in the id space. By cost we mean the number of hops needed to reach the destination *including* the number of timeouts encountered en-route. For this analysis, we consider timeouts and hops to add equally to the cost. We can easily generalize this analysis to investigate the case when a timeout costs some factor n times the cost of a hop.

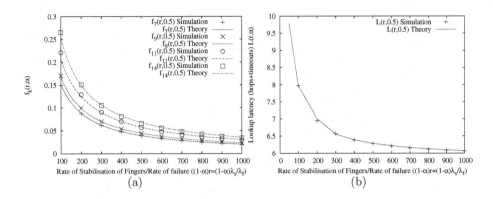

Fig. 4. Theory and Simulation for $f_k(r, \alpha)$, and $L(r, \alpha)$

Define $C_t(r, \alpha)$ (also denoted C_t) to be the expected cost for a given node to reach some target key which is t keys away from it (which means reaching the first successor of this key). For example, C_1 would then be the cost of looking up the adjacent key (1 key away). Since the adjacent key is always stored at the first alive successor, therefore if the first successor is alive (occurs with probability $1 - d_1$), the cost will be 1 hop. If the first successor is dead but the second is alive (occurs with probability $d_1(1 - d_2)$), the cost will be 1 hop + 1 timeout $= 2$ and the *expected* cost is $2 \times d_1(1 - d_2)$ and so forth. Therefore, we have $C_1 = 1 - d_1 + 2 \times d_1(1 - d_2) + 3 \times d_1 d_2(1 - d_3) + \cdots \approx 1 + d_1 = 1 + 1/(\alpha r)$.

For finding the expected cost of reaching a general distance t we need to follow closely the Chord protocol, which would lookup t by first finding the closest preceding finger. For notational simplicity, let us define ξ to be the start of the finger (say the kth) that most closely precedes t. Thus $t = \xi + m$, i.e. there are m keys between the sought target t and the start of the most closely preceding finger. With that, we can write a recursion relation for $C_{\xi+m}$ as follows:

$$C_{\xi+m} = C_\xi \left[1 - a(m)\right]$$
$$+ (1 - f_k) \left[a(m) + \sum_{i=0}^{m-1} b_i C_{m-i}\right]$$
$$+ f_k a(m) \left[1 + \sum_{i=1}^{k-1} h_k(i)\right] \tag{3}$$
$$\sum_{l=0}^{\xi/2^i - 1} bc(l, \xi/2^i)(1 + (i-1) + C_{\xi_i - l + m}) + O(h_k(k))\right]$$

where $\xi_i \equiv \sum_{m=1,i} \xi/2^m$ and $h_k(i)$ is the probability that a node is forced to use its $k - i^{th}$ finger owing to the death of its kth finger. The probabilities a, b, bc have already been introduced in section 3.

The lookup equation though rather complicated at first sight merely accounts for all the possibilities that a Chord lookup will encounter, and deals with them exactly as the protocol dictates. The first term accounts for the eventuality that there is no node intervening between ξ and $\xi + m$ (occurs with probability $1 - a(m)$). In this case, the cost of looking for $\xi + m$ is the same as the cost for looking for ξ. The second term accounts for the situation when a node does intervene inbetween (with probability $a(m)$), and this node is alive (with probability $1 - f_k$). Then the query is passed on to this node (with 1 added to register the increase in the number of hops) and then the cost depends on the distance between this node and t. The third term accounts for the case when the intervening node is dead (with probability f_k). Then the cost increases by 1 (for a timeout) and the query needs to be passed back to the closest preceding finger. We hence compute the probability $h_k(i)$ that it is passed back to the $k - i^{th}$ finger either because the intervening fingers are dead or share the same finger table entry as the kth finger. The cost of the lookup now depends on the remaining distance to the sought key. The expression for $h_k(i)$ is easy to compute using theorem 3.1 and the expression for the f_k's [10].

The cost for general lookups is hence

$$L(r, \alpha) = \frac{\Sigma_{i=1}^{\mathcal{K}-1} C_i(r, \alpha)}{\mathcal{K}}$$

The lookup equation is solved recursively, given the coefficients and C_1. We plot the result in Fig 4. The theoretical result matches the simulation very well.

4   Discussion and Conclusion

We now discuss a broader issue, connected with churn, which arises naturally in the context of our analysis. As we mentioned earlier, all our analysis is performed in the steady state where the rate of joins is the same as the rate of departures. However this rate itself can be chosen in different ways. While we expect the mean behaviour to be the same in all these cases, the fluctuations are very different with consequent implications for the functioning of DHTs. The case where fluctuations play the least role are when the join rate is "per-network" (The *number* of joinees does not depend on the current number of nodes in the network) and the failure rate is "per-node" (the number of failures does depend on the current number of occupied nodes). In this case, the steady state condition is $\lambda_j/N = \lambda_f$ guaranteeing that N can not deviate too much from the steady state value. In the two other cases where the join and failure rate are both per-network or (as in the case considered in this paper) both per-node, there is no such "repair" mechanism, and a large fluctuation can (and will) drive the number of nodes to extinction, causing the DHT to die. In the former case, the time-to-die scales with the number of nodes as $\sim N^3$ while in the latter case it scales as $\sim N^2$ [10]. Which of these 'types' of churn is the most relevant? We imagine that this depends on the application and it is hence probably of importance to study all of them in detail.

To summarize, in this paper, we have presented a detailed theoretical analysis of a DHT-based P2P system, Chord, using a Master-equation formalism. This analysis differs from existing theoretical work done on DHTs in that it aims not at establishing bounds, but on precise determination of the relevant quantities in this dynamically evolving system. From the match of our theory and the simulations, it can be seen that we can predict with an accuracy of greater than 1% in most cases.

Apart from the usefulness of this approach for its own sake, we can also gain some new insights into the system from it. For example, we see that the fraction of dead finger pointers f_k is an increasing function of the length of the finger. Infact for large enough $\mathcal{K}$, all the long fingers will be dead most of the time, making routing very inefficient. This implies that we need to consider a different stabilization scheme for the fingers (such as, perhaps, stabilizing the longer fingers more often than the smaller ones), in order that the DHT continues to function at high churn rates. We also expect that we can use this analysis to understand and analyze other DHTs.

References

1. Liben-Nowell, D., Balakrishnan, H., Karger, D.: Analysis of the evolution of peer-to-peer systems. In: ACM Conf. on Principles of Distributed Computing (PODC), Monterey, CA (2002)
2. Aspnes, J., Diamadi, Z., Shah, G.: Fault-tolerant routing in peer-to-peer systems. In: Proceedings of the twenty-first annual symposium on Principles of distributed computing, ACM Press (2002) 223–232
3. Li, J., Stribling, J., Gil, T.M., Morris, R., Kaashoek, F.: Comparing the performance of distributed hash tables under churn. In: The 3rd International Workshop on Peer-to-Peer Systems (IPTPS'02), San Diego, CA (2004)
4. Rhea, S., Geels, D., Roscoe, T., Kubiatowicz, J.: Handling churn in a DHT. In: Proceedings of the 2004 USENIX Annual Technical Conference(USENIX '04), Boston, Massachusetts, USA (2004)
5. Castro, M., Costa, M., Rowstron, A.: Performance and dependability of structured peer-to-peer overlays. In: Proceedings of the 2004 International Conference on Dependable Systems and Networks (DSN'04), IEEE Computer Society (2004)
6. N.G. van Kampen: Stochastic Processes in Physics and Chemistry. North-Holland Publishing Company (1981) ISBN-0-444-86200-5.
7. Stoica, I., Morris, R., Liben-Nowell, D., Karger, D., Kaashoek, M.F., Dabek, F., Balakrishnan, H.: Chord: A scalable peer-to-peer lookup service for internet applications. IEEE Transactions on Networking **11** (2003)
8. Wang, S., Xuan, D., Zhao, W.: On resilience of structured peer-to-peer systems. In: GLOBECOM 2003 - IEEE Global Telecommunications Conference. (2003) 3851–3856
9. Aberer, K., Datta, A., Hauswirth, M.: Efficient, self-contained handling of identity in peer-to-peer systems. IEEE Transactions on Knowledge and Data Engineering **16** (2004) 858–869
10. El-Ansary, S., Krishnamurthy, S., Aurell, E., Haridi, S.: An analytical study of consistency and performance of DHTs under churn (draft). Technical Report TR-2004-12, Swedish Institute of Computer Science (2004) http://www.sics.se/ sameh/pubs/TR2004_12.

Peering Peer-to-Peer Providers

Hari Balakrishnan[1], Scott Shenker[2], and Michael Walfish[1]

[1] MIT
[2] UC Berkeley and ICSI
`pppp@nms.csail.mit.edu`

Abstract. The early peer-to-peer applications eschewed commercial arrangements and instead established a grass-roots model in which the collection of end-users provided their own distributed computational infrastructure. While this cooperative end-user approach works well in many application settings, it does not provide a sufficiently stable platform for certain peer-to-peer applications (*e.g.*, DHTs as a building block for network services). Assuming such a stable platform isn't freely provided by a benefactor (such as NSF), we must ask whether DHTs could be deployed in a competitive commercial environment. The key issue is whether a multiplicity of DHT services can coordinate to provide a single coherent DHT service, much the way ISPs peer to provide a completely connected Internet. In this paper, we describe various approaches for DHT peering and discuss some of the related performance and incentive issues.

1 Introduction

The peer-to-peer revolution introduced the concept of B.Y.O.I. (Bring Your Own Infrastructure), in that the end-hosts receiving service from peer-to-peer applications (*e.g.*, end-hosts sharing files or participating in application-level multicast) were members of an overlay and performed routing and lookup services for other overlay members. The initial distributed hash table (DHT) proposals arose in this context: the purpose of a DHT was to resolve a large, sparse, and flat namespace for *members* of the DHT.

However, the B.Y.O.I. model is not always appropriate for DHTs. For example, researchers have proposed using DHTs, and other flat name resolution mechanisms, to underpin core network services (see [1,2,3,4,5,6] for a few examples). To be credible, such services cannot depend on the capabilities and caprice of desktop users behind cable modems; rather, these services must run on a set of stable, managed nodes. In addition, as argued in [7,8], running a DHT is a non-trivial task that requires significant expertise and active oversight. As a result, one school of DHT research, led by Open DHT [7,8] (the public DHT service formerly known as OpenHash), is proposing a public DHT *service*, *i.e.*, a managed infrastructure supporting a general-purpose DHT. The approach adopted in Open DHT entails two related changes: moving from several application-specific DHTs to a general-purpose DHT service, and moving from the B.Y.O.I. model to a managed infrastructure.

M. Castro and R. van Renesse (Eds.): IPTPS 2005, LNCS 3640, pp. 104–114, 2005.

While there might be cases when a benevolent entity (such as NSF) would fund a managed DHT service, it would be preferable if one could arise in a competitive commercial environment. For the Internet, a set of competing commercial ISPs coordinate their activity to provide a uniform Internet "dialtone", and the key issue is how ISPs peer with each other. The question we address here is: can a set of DHT service providers (DSPs) similarly coordinate through peering arrangements to give users a unified, globally coherent DHT "dialtone"?

Our focus here is not on whether such an infrastructure *will* emerge—that will depend on market forces which we cannot divine—but rather on whether such an infrastructure *could* emerge. So, for the purposes of this paper, we assume that market demand for DHT service exists (*i.e.*, that people are willing to pay for DHT service directly or for service from DHT-based applications such as the ones cited above), and we investigate, on a technical and economic level, how DSPs can coordinate to meet this demand. We call the peered collection of DSP providers the P^4 (Peering Peer-to-Peer Providers) infrastructure. In the remainder of this paper, we discuss design possibilities for this P^4 infrastructure as well as the challenges that arise.

These challenges fall into two categories. The technical challenge is to define peering relationships that ensure correct operation of the overall DHT service, allowing customers of one DSP to gain access to data stored by customers of another DSP. The economic challenge is to ensure that DSPs have an incentive to peer (rather than function independently), and to faithfully follow the peering rules. We present a simple design that meets both of these challenges. Thus, we posit that it is possible to offer a coherent DHT service in a commercial and competitive environment. For critical network services, DHTs need not endure the vicissitudes of B.Y.O.I. or government funding but can instead be based on hardened and highly capitalized commercial infrastructures.

2   Design Spectrum

We expect that the P^4 infrastructure supports the following high-level usage scenario, depicted in Figure 1. Customers receive "DHT service" much as they receive DNS service today: the DSP informs its customers of the IP address or name of a host—which we call a *DHT proxy*—and this host handles customers' requests of the P^4 infrastructure. To customers, the DHT proxy is opaque; it might contact another DHT proxy or be one hop away from the P^4 infrastructure. Customer requests are either "puts" of key-value pairs or "gets" of keys. After a customer executes a put request on a key-value pair, (k, v), any other customer of any DSP should receive v in response to a get request for k. In this paper, we do not focus on what happens between customers and their DHT proxies.

We now discuss the goals and design possibilities for a P^4 infrastructure that supports the usage scenario above. Throughout, we are concerned with high-level questions about how DSPs peer with each other rather than with the specifics of network protocols to support this peering.

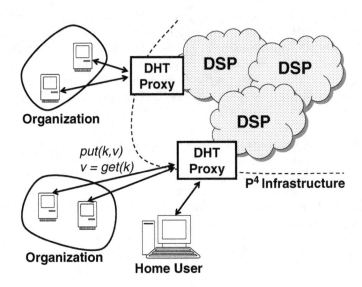

Fig. 1. High-level P^4 scenario. Organizations and home users are customers of a DSP; their interface to the P^4 infrastructure is a DHT proxy supplied by the DSP.

2.1   Goals

We now list a few of the more crucial design goals; these will help us choose from several design options.

Proper incentives, not perfect security. We do not require that P4 ensures, or even monitors, that DSPs execute their responsibilities properly. Instead, we care only that DSPs have an incentive to do so. This incentive arises if a DSP's malfeasance (such as returning incorrect values) causes harm to its own customers (perhaps in addition to harming customers of other DSPs). If so, then the economic incentives caused by customers switching to or from various DSPs will encourage DSPs to perform their tasks properly. We are not concerned that individual customers may receive bad service from individual DSPs; this situation is analogous to the way today's users of IP are vulnerable to their ISPs.

Flat names. We believe that all keys in the P^4 infrastructure should exist in one flat namespace. In particular, one should not be able to look at a key and deduce which DSP was serving the end-host that put the key. The reason for DSP-independent keys is that if the key *did* identify the DSP responsible for a given (k, v) pair, then the owner of the (k, v) pair would not be able to switch its DSP without invalidating its existing keys.

Flexible tradeoffs between writing and reading speeds. While ideally both writes (puts) and reads (gets) would be fast, in distributed systems one usually sacrifices speed in one to achieve it in the other. Since some applications are read-intensive and others write-intensive, we require that the design allow, on a per-key basis, flexible tradeoffs between these two concerns.

2.2   Designs

We now present four general design approaches and test them against our design goals.[1]

All one DHT. The first design we consider is one in which each DSP contributes hosts to a single, global DHT. The advantage of this scenario is that existing DHT mechanisms work without modification. The disadvantage is that it is a classic "tragedy of the commons". Specifically, a particular DSP reaps all the benefit of bringing in additional customers but only receives a small share of the benefit of providing more resources (nodes) to the DHT. The outcome is likely to be a poorly provisioned infrastructure.

Use administrative separation. To avoid the problem of poor incentives that exists in the previous scenario, we can partition the namespace and have the first few bits of the key, k, identify the DSP "responsible" for k, where "responsible" is defined as "storing the authoritative copy of (k, v)". This model is reminiscent of the Skipnet DHT's [9] use of the top bits of the key to identify the organization in which the key originated. The advantages of this scenario are: (1) everyone knows which DSP is responsible for which key, thereby giving DSPs an incentive to be good P^4 citizens and (2) DSPs would have to store only those (k, v) pairs created by their customers; in response to customer requests for other keys, the DSP could use the information in the key to determine which other DSP to contact. The disadvantage of this approach is that it fails to meet the "flat names" requirement.

The next two designs presume that each DSP maintains its own lookup service and exposes that lookup service to the DSP's customers. Each DSP can implement its own lookup mechanism (presumably, but not necessarily, a DHT), and the internal operations of the various DSPs can vary widely. In order for DSPs to correctly answer their customers' get queries for all keys in the P^4 infrastructure, DSPs must exchange updates with each other. The difference between the next two designs is whether these updates occur proactively.

Get-broadcasting, local puts. In this design, when a customer executes a put request for a pair (k, v), the customer's DSP stores (k, v) locally. When a customer requests k, the DSP checks if it has stored k. If not, the DSP *broadcasts* the query for k to the other DSPs to ask them about k. As an optimization, the DSP can do this broadcast in parallel with its own lookup. In §3.4, we discuss a further optimization, namely opportunistic caching of (k, v) pairs originating in other DSPs.

Put-broadcasting, local gets. In this design, DSPs *proactively* exchange updates with each other. After a customer puts a (k, v) pair, its DSP updates the other DSPs with information about k. This update can take two forms: the DSP can either tell the other DSPs about the (k, v) pair, or the DSP can tell the other DSPs about k alone, with the understanding that the other DSPs will fetch v

---

[1] While we can't prove that these are the only design approaches, they do seem to capture the spectrum of approaches taken for similar problems; see §4.

on-demand (from the appropriate DSP) when their own customers execute get requests for k.

These last two peering designs address the shortcomings of the first two. As mentioned above, one of our goals is a flexible tradeoff between put and get speeds. Accordingly, we think the last two designs, which comprise three options—get-broadcasting, put-broadcasting of a key, and put-broadcasting of a key-value pair—can coexist. Our assumption is that the user who executes the put request on key k will make the decision about which propagation regime applies to the pair (k, v). This decision is based on the customer's expectations about put and get frequency as well as the cost charged by DSPs.

The three different options involve splitting the resource consumption between puts and gets differently: get-broadcasting has the least bandwidth-intensive put, but the most bandwidth-intensive get; put-broadcasting of a key-value pair is the opposite (most bandwidth-intensive puts, least bandwidth-intensive gets); and put-broadcasting of a key is intermediate. Presumably the charges imposed by DSPs for the various actions, according to whatever pricing scheme they employ, will reflect these differing burdens.

3   Challenges and Questions

Here, we cover the challenges that result from the last two scenarios of the previous section. We emphasize that there are many DHT-related challenges that pertain to our scenario but are addressed elsewhere. The challenges that result from exposing a general-purpose DHT as a service are articulated and addressed by the Open DHT authors [7,8]. Other challenges, discussed in [4,10], relate to how, in the absence of cues built into flat names, organizations may offer: fate sharing (the hosts of a disconnected organization should be able to gain access to "local" key-value pairs); administrative scoping (key owners should be able to limit a key-value pair to intramural use); and locality (organizations should have fast access for key-value pairs that are frequently requested by its hosts). These solutions are logically between the DHT proxy and the organization.

3.1   Coherence and Correctness

The P^4 infrastructure must offer to customers a coherent and complete view of the namespace while also letting customers choose their keys. These high-level goals induce two requirements. First, as discussed above, key-value pairs put by customers must be visible to customers of other DSPs. To meet this requirement, DSPs propagate puts and gets (§2.2).

The second requirement is that two customers (of the same DSP or of two different ones) must not be able to own the same key or overwrite each other's key-value pairs. To satisfy this requirement, we borrow Open DHT's [7,8] three kinds of put requests (to which correspond three types of get requests).

The first kind is *immutable*: k is a secure, collision-resistant hash of v. The second is *authenticated*: putters supply a public key, and getters request not k

but rather a (k,a) pair; a is a hash of the putter's public key. For both kinds, the same key (meaning k or a (k,a) pair, depending) should never be claimed by two different owners (unless they are storing the same data, in the first case, or they have access to the same private key, in the second case). These facts are independent of whether the DHT infrastructure comprises one or multiple entities. However, Open DHT's approach assumes that the entire DHT infrastructure is trusted. In contrast, P^4 customers need trust only their own DSPs since the DSPs can check the necessary invariants before accepting updates for *immutable* or *authenticated* key-value pairs.

The third type of put is *unauthenticated*; customers can pick the key and value, but such requests are append-only (to prevent customers from overwriting each other's data). Thus, when a DSP receives a key-value pair from a peer (*e.g.*, on a put-broadcast) for a key it already has, the DSP appends the new value to the existing values associated with the key. Observe that under get-broadcasting, *unauthenticated* puts are only *eventually* coherent;[2] For example, if two customers of two different DSPs put (k, v_1) and (k, v_2), then a local get originating in the first DSP will immediately return (k, v_1), not $(k, \{v_1, v_2\})$.

3.2 Incentives

As noted earlier, we do not require that the peering arrangements provide perfect security, preventing any malicious behavior on the part of DSPs. We merely require that the incentive to please customers encourages DSPs to behave well. In what follows, the term *data* refers to key-value pairs, *local* puts or gets are those from a DSP's own customers, and *local* data is data stored from a local put. There are four actions that a DSP executes on behalf of customers:

- Respond to local gets (both by answering directly, or requesting the data from other DSPs)
- Respond to external gets (forwarded from other DSPs) for local data
- Process local puts by both storing locally and optionally forwarding to other DSPs
- Process external puts forwarded by other DSPs

In each case, doing the action correctly adds benefit to the local customers, either by providing them with the correct data or by providing others with the local customer's data. If a DSP fails to execute these operations correctly, then—independent of the payment model among DSPs or between DSPs and customers—the customers will become unhappy (if they detect such behavior, which we assume they eventually will if such cheating is widespread).[3]

---

[2] Under get-broadcasting with TTL-based caching, the other two types of puts are also only eventually coherent, as discussed in §3.4. However, even without caching, the point applies to *unauthenticated* put requests.

[3] A DSP can certainly deny a customer access to a strategic key-value pair; the potential for such abuse appears in many customer/provider relationships (including those discussed in §4).

This discussion of general incentives does not address the question of whether, and how, DSPs would choose to peer. Logically, peering is a pairwise decision in that two DSPs choose to exchange puts and gets. If the two DSPs gain equally, then there will likely be no *settlements* (the common economic term for payments between peers). However, if one of the DSPs benefits substantially more, the DSP benefitting less might demand payment in order to peer.[4] Such settlements would make peering more complicated because they would require detailed monitoring (as explained at the end of this section).

One might think that when a large and small DSP peer, the benefits would be unbalanced. To investigate this hypothesis, consider two DSPs, a and b, who are deciding whether to peer. Assume: (1) that the cost of peering is negligible compared to the other costs of running a DSP[5] and (2) that the profit of a DSP is proportional to the utility its customers derive from its service (the happier the customers are, the more they are willing to pay). Then, the benefit that accrues to a given DSP from peering is proportional to the sum of the benefits that accrue to the DSP's customers from: being able to read data from the other DSP and having their data read by customers of the other DSP.

To calculate these benefits, we use the following definitions:

- b_p: the average benefit a customer derives from having its data read by another customer
- b_g: the average benefit a customer derives from reading a piece of data
- $n_{a \to b}$: number of gets issued by customers of DSP a for data produced by customers of DSP b
- $n_{b \to a}$: number of gets issued by customers of DSP b for data produced by customers of DSP a

The benefit derived by DSP a from peering is proportional to $n_{a \to b} b_g + n_{b \to a} b_p$. Similarly, the benefit derived by DSP b is proportional to $n_{a \to b} b_p + n_{b \to a} b_g$. The difference in benefits is proportional to

$$\Delta = (b_p - b_g)(n_{a \to b} - n_{b \to a}).$$

If the average benefit to a customer from reading data is the same as the average benefit to a customer from having its data read (*i.e.*, if $b_p = b_g$), then both DSPs benefit the same (*i.e.*, $\Delta = 0$), independent of their size. If b_p does not equal b_g, then we must consider the quantity $n_{a \to b} - n_{b \to a}$. We measure the size of DSPs a and b by number of customers and denote these quantities S^a and S^b. Now, assume that the number of gets issued by the customers of a DSP

---

[4] There is a vast economics literature on this two-person *bargaining* problem, where a joint venture benefits two parties unequally. The nature of the solutions doesn't concern us here, except that the literature is unanimous in expecting no payments in the symmetric benefits case.

[5] In practice, this assumption may hold only when the sizes of the two DSPs are the same order of magnitude; a much smaller DSP would incur comparatively more bandwidth cost from peering. However, as discussed in §3.3, we imagine the peering will be done by large players.

is proportional to the DSP's size, with constant of proportionality λ_g (so the number of gets issued by customers of DSP a is $\lambda_g S^a$). Now assume further that the fraction of data items in the P^4 infrastructure owned by a DSP's customers is also proportional to the DSP's size, with proportionality constant λ_d (so the fraction of total data items owned by b's customers is $\lambda_d S^b$). Now assume finally that all gets are targeted randomly in the namespace, so the number of gets destined for a DSP is proportional to the fraction of data items its customers own. Then, $n_{a \to b} = \lambda_g S^a \lambda_d S^b$, which is symmetric in a and b. Thus, if the preceding assumptions hold, DSPs benefit equally, independent of their size.

Clearly these assumptions won't hold in practice exactly. However, if they are a reasonable approximation, DSPs might choose to peer without settlements. If the assumptions aren't even close, and settlements are thus required, then monitoring is necessary (if DSP a locally serves gets for a key-value pair it received on an update from DSP b, then b has no way to know how many gets were thus served, and a has no incentive to be truthful.) The only easily monitored scenario is get-broadcasting with limited caching.

3.3   Scaling

As with ISP peering, put-broadcasting and get-broadcasting do not scale to a large, flat market structure. However, just as in ISP peering, we assume that a forest structure will arise, wherein: a small number of top-level providers peer with each other; it is these top-level providers that do put- and get-broadcasting; and these top-level providers have "children" that are themselves providers (and may offer a different level of customer service). A child has two options. It can either *redirect* customers' put and get requests to a top-level DSP; alternatively, by sending and receiving updates via its parent, it can maintain a local lookup service.

3.4   Latency

We discuss end-to-end latency experienced by customers for put and get requests. For put requests, the DHT proxy supplied by the customer's DSP checks that any required invariants hold (see §3.1 and [8]) and immediately returns an error or success code to the customer. If the key is a put-broadcast key, the DSP will propagate the put request to its peers in the background. Put requests do not suffer from high latency.

For get requests, we separately consider the three propagation regimes: get-broadcast, put-broadcast of the key, and put-broadcast of the key-value pair. For get-broadcast keys, DSPs perform opportunistic, TTL-based caching (with the TTL set by the putter). Thus, the first time a DSP receives a get request for such a key, the lookup may have high latency since the DSP has to contact the other DSPs. Subsequent lookups will be local to the DSP but then this key-value pair may be stale. (To avoid this staleness, the putter can use one of the two put-broadcast types, which presumably require more payment.) For put-broadcast keys, if the key k is broadcast without the value, v, then, as described in §2.2, all of the DSPs will store both k and a pointer to the DSP that actually has v.

The latency situation here is similar to the latency in the get-broadcast regime (in both cases, a get causes a DSP to contact, and wait for, at least one other DSP). Finally, if both the key and value are put-broadcast, all of the DSPs will have copies of (k, v), so latency will not suffer.

Application software acting on behalf of putters can implement an adaptive algorithm that, for each key, decides which propagation regime is optimal, given the costs charged and benefits received.

4   Related Work

The observation that for-profit DSPs could peer to form a federated DHT infrastructure exposing a global namespace was briefly mentioned in [4,2], but no such mechanism was described. This paper fills that void. We now discuss existing federations (arising in different contexts) that present a coherent view of a namespace or of an infrastructure.

Today's competing ISPs federate by exchanging routes with each other to create a global IP dialtone for their customers. The economic incentives in this federation are similar to what we imagine for the P^4 infrastructure, though the technical challenges differ. ISPs can aggregate (while DSPs cannot) the information they exchange with each other, but ISPs must also apply (while DSPs need not) complex policies about what information to expose to peers. Also, no equivalent of get-broadcasting exists with ISPs; route changes are distributed proactively.

The namespace of the Domain Name System (DNS) is hierarchical, and the "providers" of the resolution service are coded directly into the names. These "providers" need not exchange updates, since, on a get request (*i.e.*, a DNS lookup), the end-host knows how to find the responsible provider.

The literature on content internetworking [11,12] describes scenarios in which content distribution networks (CDNs) peer to exchange cached copies of Web objects. Those scenarios and P^4 face similar technical challenges in terms of how entities relate to each other (*e.g.*, when and how to exchange updates) but, within an entity, the solutions differ. CDNs do widespread caching of Web objects that have DNS names, and the hosts comprising a CDN may offer application-specific functions such as serving media files. In contrast, DSPs are optimized for lookup and insertion of small values that have flat names.

While the above federations rest on commercial relationships, other federations rely on a combination of altruism and shared purpose (*i.e.*, the participants are directly interested in each other's data). These non-commercial federations include cooperative Web caches (see citations in [13], esp. [14]), Usenet, and peer-to-peer file sharing networks.

5   Summary

The peer-to-peer revolution, with its B.Y.O.I approach, was a radical departure from the more conventional ways of funding infrastructure. However, commentators on the subject sometimes failed to separate the technical innovations introduced by these peer-to-peer designs—achieving flat name resolution in an unprecedentedly scalable and reliable way—from their economic novelty. In this paper we asked whether one can harness the technical properties of these peer-to-peer designs, specifically DHTs, in a more conventional economic setting.

Our analysis suggests that one can. As we describe, there are peering arrangements that result in a uniform DHT dialtone (for customers) with proper incentives (for DSPs). However, these peering arrangements are a necessary but not sufficient condition for commercially provided DHT service. The market for such DHT service depends on the success of prototypes such as Open DHT [7,8], which in turn will depend on the prevalence and popularity of applications based on a DHT service.

Acknowledgments

We thank Sean Rhea for useful comments. This research was supported by the National Science Foundation under Cooperative Agreement No. ANI-0225660, British Telecom, and an NDSEG Graduate Fellowship.

References

1. Moskowitz, R., Nikander, P.: Host identity protocol architecture (2003) draft-moskowitz-hip-arch-05, IETF draft (Work in Progress).
2. Balakrishnan, H., Lakshminarayanan, K., Ratnasamy, S., Shenker, S., Stoica, I., Walfish, M.: A layered naming architecture for the Internet. In: ACM SIGCOMM. (2004)
3. van Renesse, R., Zhou, L.: P6P: A peer-to-peer approach to Internet infrastructure. In: 3rd Intl. Workshop on Peer-to-Peer Systems (IPTPS). (2004)
4. Walfish, M., Balakrishnan, H., Shenker, S.: Untangling the Web from DNS. In: USENIX Symposium on Networked Systems Design and Implementation (NSDI). (2004)
5. Ramasubramanian, V., Sirer, E.G.: The design and implementation of a next generation name service for the Internet. In: ACM SIGCOMM. (2004)
6. van Steen, M., Ballintijn, G.: Achieving scalability in hierarchical location services. In: 26th International Computer Software and Applications Conference. (2002)
7. Karp, B., Ratnasamy, S., Rhea, S., Shenker, S.: Spurring adoption of DHTs with OpenHash, a public DHT service. In: 3rd Intl. Workshop on Peer-to-Peer Systems (IPTPS). (2004)
8. OpenDHT: (2005) http://opendht.org.
9. Harvey, N.J., Jones, M.B., Saroiu, S., Theimer, M., Wolman, A.: SkipNet: A scalable overlay network with practical locality properties. In: USENIX Symposium on Internet Technologies and Systems (USITS). (2003)
10. Mislove, A., Druschel, P.: Providing administrative control and autonomy in peer-to-peer overlays. In: 3rd Intl. Workshop on Peer-to-Peer Systems (IPTPS). (2004)
11. Day, M., Cain, B., Tomlinson, G., Rzewski, P.: A model for content internetworking (CDI) (2003) RFC 3466.

12. Rzewski, P., Day, M., Gilletti, D.: Content internetworking (CDI) scenarios (2003) RFC 3570.
13. Wolman, A., Voelker, G.M., Sharma, N., Cardwell, N., Karlin, A., Levy, H.M.: On the scale and performance of cooperative Web proxy caching. In: 17th ACM SOSP. (1999)
14. Chankhunthod, A., Danzig, P.B., Neerdaels, C., Schwartz, M.F., Worrell, K.J.: A hierarchical Internet object cache. In: USENIX Technical Conference. (1996)

The Impact of Heterogeneous Bandwidth Constraints on DHT-Based Multicast Protocols

Ashwin R. Bharambe[1], Sanjay G. Rao[2], Venkata N. Padmanabhan[3],
Srinivasan Seshan[1], and Hui Zhang[1]

[1] Carnegie Mellon University, Pittsburgh PA 15213, USA
(ashu+, srini+, hzhang+)@cs.cmu.edu
[2] Purdue University, West Lafayette IN 47907, USA
sanjay@ecn.purdue.edu
[3] Microsoft Research, Redmond WA 98052, USA
padmanab@microsoft.com

Abstract. In this paper, we consider support for bandwidth-demanding applications such as video broadcasting using DHTs. Our investigations focus on the impact of heterogeneity in the outgoing bandwidth capabilities of nodes on Scribe, a representative and relatively mature DHT-based multicast protocol. We expose important issues that arise due to the mismatch between the ID space that underlies the DHT and the outgoing bandwidth constraints on nodes.

1 Introduction

While DHTs were originally developed with applications like peer-to-peer file sharing in mind, there has been considerable interest in recent years in applying DHTs to overlay multicast applications [1,2,3,4,5]. In DHT-based approaches, the focus is on maintaining a structure based on a virtual id space, and enabling scalable and efficient unicast routing based on the node identifiers - the unicast routes are then used to create multicast distribution trees. This approach is in contrast to *performance-centric approaches* such as [6,7,8,9], where the primary consideration while adding links to the overlay topology is application performance.

Two principal reasons have been advocated for a DHT-based approach. First, DHTs provides a generic primitive that can benefit a wide range of applications, among them overlay multicast. Second, the same DHT-based overlay can be used to simultaneously support and maintain a large number of overlay applications and multicast trees. This could help achieve lower overheads as compared to constructing and maintaining several separate overlays. While DHT-based approaches have these potential advantages, a key unknown is application performance. Achieving good performance with DHTs is an active and ongoing area of research.

In this paper, we explore issues in enabling high-bandwidth broadcasting applications using DHTs. Our exploration is guided by design lessons we have learned from our experience deploying an overlay-based broadcasting system [10].

M. Castro and R. van Renesse (Eds.): IPTPS 2005, LNCS 3640, pp. 115–126, 2005.
© Springer-Verlag Berlin Heidelberg 2005

In particular, we focus our investigation by considering the implications of a key issue - heterogeneous *outgoing* bandwidth constraints of nodes in the overlay. Such heterogeneity arises due to the presence of hosts behind various access technologies like cable modem, DSL and Ethernet, as summarized in Figure 1.

We present an initial evaluation of Scribe [3], a representative and relatively mature DHT-based protocol for overlay multicast. Our experiments show that imposing bandwidth constraints on Scribe can result in the creation of distribution trees with high depth, as well as a significant number of *non-DHT links*, i.e. links that are present in the overlay tree but are not part of the underlying DHT. Trees with high depth are undesirable as larger the number of ancestors for a node, higher the frequency of interrupts due to the failure or departure of ancestors, and ultimately poorer the application performance. Non-DHT links are undesirable because they restrict the benefits of the route convergence and loop-free properties of DHT routing, and incur maintenance costs in addition to that of the DHT infrastructure. We find that a key cause for the issues observed is the mismatch between the ID space that underlies the DHT structure and node bandwidth constraints. We discuss potential ways to solve the problem. and conclude that the issues are not straight-forward to address.

Event	Low speed (100 kbps; deg=0)	Medium Speed (1.5 Mbps; deg=2)	High Speed (10 Mbps; deg=10)	Avg. degree
Sigcomm [10]	22%	2%	76%	7.64
Slashdot [10]	74%	4%	22%	2.28
Gnutella [11]	65%	27%	8%	1.34

Fig. 1. Constitution of hosts from various sources. "deg" refers to our model of how many children nodes in each category can support. Sigcomm and Slashdot refer to two different broadcasts with an operationally deployed broadcasting system based on overlay multicast. Gnutella refers to a measurement study of peer characteristics of the Gnutella system.

2   Evaluation Framework

Our evaluation is motivated by video broadcasting applications. Such applications involve data delivery from a single source to a set of receivers. Further, they are non-interactive, and do not place a tight constraint on the end-to-end latency. We assume a constant bit rate (CBR) source stream, and assume only nodes interested in the content at any point in time are members of the distribution tree and contribute bandwidth to the system.

The outgoing bandwidth limit of each host determines its *degree* or *fanout* in the overlay multicast tree, i.e. the maximum number of children that it can forward the stream to. We categorize hosts as being behind: (a) constrained links such as cable and DSL (few hundred Kbps); (b) intermediate speed links such as T1 lines (1.5 Mbps); and (c) high-speed links (10 Mbps or better). Given typical streaming video rates of the order of several hundred kilobits per second [10], we quantize the degrees of the low, medium, and high speed hosts to 0, 2, and 10. The degree 0 nodes are termed *non-contributors*. For higher speed connections, the degree is likely to be bounded by some policy (in view of the shared nature of the links) rather than the actual outgoing bandwidth. Figure 1 summarizes the constitution of hosts seen from measurement studies [11] and real Internet broadcast events [10].

The *Average Degree* of the system is defined as the total degree of all nodes (including the source) divided by the number of receivers (all nodes but the source). In this paper, we focus on regimes with an average degree greater than 1 which indicates that it is feasible to construct a tree.

3   Background

While there have been several DHT-based proposals for multicast in recent years [12,4,5,3], we choose to focus on Scribe. Scribe is one of the more mature proposals among DHT-based approaches with well-defined mechanisms to honor per-node degree constraints. A more recent follow-up work SplitStream [1] builds on top of Scribe and considers data delivery along multiple trees, rather than a single tree to improve the resiliency of data delivery. While we draw on some of the extensions proposed in Splitstream, we only consider single tree data delivery in this paper. We discuss some of the implications of multiple-tree solutions in Section 8.

Scribe is built on top of the Pastry DHT protocol [13], and is targeted at settings which involve support of a large number of multicast groups. Each group may involve only a subset of the nodes in the Pastry system, but members in Pastry not part of a particular multicast group may be recruited to be forwarders in any Scribe tree. In this paper however, our evaluation assumes all participating members in Pastry are also part of the Scribe tree.

Each node in Pastry is assigned a unique 128-bit nodeId which can be thought of as a sequence of digits in base 2^b (b is a Pastry parameter.) A Pastry node in a network of N nodes maintains a routing table containing about $\log_{2^b} N$ rows and 2^b columns. The entries in the rth row of the routing table refer to nodes whose nodeIds share the first r digits with the local node's nodeId. The routing mechanism is a generalization of hypercube routing: each subsequent hop of the route to the destination shares longer *prefixes* with the destination nodeId.

Scribe utilizes Pastry's routing mechanism to construct multicast trees in the following manner: each multicast group corresponds to a special ID called topicId. A multicast tree associated with the group is formed by the union of the Pastry routes from each group member to the topicId. Messages are multicast from the root to the members using reverse path forwarding [14].

A key issue with Scribe is that the number of children of a node A in the Scribe tree can be as high as the *in-degree* of the node in the underlying Pastry infrastructure – that is, the number of nodes in Pastry which use A as the next hop when routing towards the topicId. In general, this may be greater than is

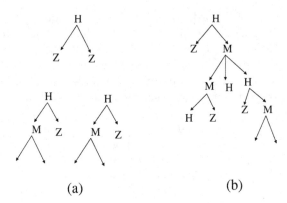

Fig. 2. Issues with heterogeneous degree constraints. H,M, and Z represent nodes of high, medium and zero (non-contributor) degrees respectively; (a) Entire subtrees (bottom) could be rejected when the subtree connected to the source (top) is saturated with non-contributors. (b) Depth xcan be poor with heterogeneous degree constraints.

permitted by the node's bandwidth constraints. In order to tackle this overloading of nodes, the authors of Scribe/SplitStream have proposed two mechanisms:

- *Pushdown:* Whenever an overloaded node A receives a request from a potential child X, it can drop an existing child C, if X is found to be more "desirable" as a child than C. The orphaned node (either C or X) can contact one of the children of A as a potential parent, and this process goes on recursively. Choosing the criteria to determine which child of A (if any) that X should displace is an important issue. We discuss further in Section 5.
- *Anycast:* If all nodes in the system have non-zero degree constraints, pushdown is guaranteed to terminate since leaf nodes will always have capacity. However, in the presence of non-contributor (degree 0) nodes, pushdown could end at a leaf that does not have capacity. This is tackled by an anycast procedure which provides an efficient way to locate a node with free capacity [1].

4   Issues with Heterogeneous Constraints

Our evaluation of Scribe focuses on the following concerns that arise with heterogeneous degree constraints:

- *Rejections:* The tree constructed by a protocol could attain sub-optimal configurations, as for example shown in Figure 2(a). Here, the system as a whole has sufficient bandwidth resources to enable connectivity to all nodes. However, the subtree rooted at the source is saturated with non-contributors, and the bandwidth resources of nodes in the disconnected subtrees remains unutilized. Nodes in the disconnected subtrees are eventually *rejected,* or forced to exit the multicast session.

- *High Depth:* An optimal configuration in terms of depth is one where the nodes that contribute the most (i.e. highest degree) form the highest levels, with lower degree nodes at lower levels. In the absence of mechanisms that explicitly favor construction of such trees, a protocol could produce trees of high depth such as shown in Figure 2(b). We believe that the depth metric is important as it significantly influences application performance. In general, in an overlay multicast application, the performance seen by a node depends on two factors: (i) the frequency of interruptions due to the failure of an ancestor, or due to congestion on an upstream link; and (ii) the time it takes a protocol to recover from the interruptions. The frequency of interruptions a node experiences in turn depends on the number of ancestors the node has, or the depth of the node.

- *Non-DHT Links:*While the two concerns above apply to *performance-centric* protocols as well, DHT-based designs need to deal with additional concerns with regard to preserving the structure of the DHT. In particular, while the pushdown and anycast operations described in Section 3 help Scribe cope with heterogeneous node bandwidth constraints, they may result in the creation of parent-child relationships which correspond to links that are not part of the underlying Pastry overlay. We term such links as *non-DHT* links. We believe these non-DHT links are undesirable because: (i) the route convergence and loop-free properties of DHT routing no longer apply if non-DHT links exist in significant numbers; and (ii) such links require explicit per-tree maintenance which reduces the benefits of DHTs in terms of amortizing overlay maintenance costs over multiple multicast groups (and other applications).

5   Techniques Evaluated

We present two variants of the pushdown algorithm that we evaluated in Scribe. The first policy, *Preempt-ID-Pushdown* is based on the policy implemented in [1], and is not optimized to minimize depth in heterogeneous environments. The second policy, *Preempt-Degree-Pushdown*, is a new policy that we introduced in Scribe to improve depth in heterogeneous environments.

- *Preempt-ID-Pushdown:* When a saturated node A receives a request from a potential child X, X preempts a child C of A if X shares a longer prefix with the topicID than C. Further, the orphaned node (X or C) contacts a child of A and continues the pushdown if the orphaned node shares a prefix match with the child. However, if no child of A shares a prefix with the orphaned node, we continue with the pushdown operation by picking a random child of A.[1] An anycast operation is employed if a leaf node is reached without a parent being found.

---

[1] This is a slight departure from [1], where an anycast operation is employed if no child of A shares a prefix with the orphaned node. We have observed better performance in depth in homogeneous environments with our optimization. The intuition is that pushdown tends to do better at filling up nodes higher in the tree, while anycast tends to choose parents at more random locations in the tree.

– *Preempt-Degree-Pushdown:* Here, node degree is the primary criterion in the pushdown. When a saturated node A receives a request from a potential child X, X preempts the child (say C) of A which has the lowest degree, provided X itself has a higher degree than C. The orphaned node (X or C) picks a random child of A that has a degree equal to or greater than itself and continues the pushdown. An anycast operation is employed if a leaf node is reached without a parent being found.

While *Preempt-Degree-Pushdown* can improve the depth of trees produced by Scribe compared to *Preempt-ID-Pushdown,* it can lead to the creation of a larger number of non-DHT links given that the id is no longer a key criterion in pushdown. Further, *Preempt-Degree-Pushdown* itself cannot create perfectly balanced trees - for example, if node A has a lower degree than node X, there is no mechanism in place for X to displace A. Doing so would require further deviation from the DHT-structure, and the creation of additional non-DHT links. In fact, we believe it is not easy to construct trees with both low depth, as well as a low fraction of non-DHT links. We discuss this further in Section 7.

6   Evaluation Details

We use the original Scribe and Splitstream implementation [15] for our experiments. In the Scribe implementation, Scribe-level links were maintained separately from the underlying Pastry links. Thus, if Pastry changed its routing table (due to its own optimizations), the Scribe level link would appear to be a non-Pastry (i.e. non-DHT) link afterwards. In order to avoid such over-counting, we associate a DHT or non-DHT flag with a Scribe link *only when it is first established.* [2]

Our experiments use a Poisson arrival pattern and a Pareto-distributed stay time for clients. These choices have been motivated by group dynamics charact eristics observed in overlay multicast deployments [10] and Mbone measure-

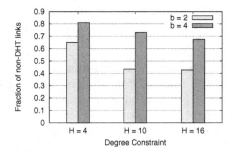

Fig. 3. Fraction of non-DHT links (mean over the session) in homogeneous environments for various values of node degree and b, the base of the node IDs in Pastry

---

[2] It is possible that Pastry route table changes can transform a initial non-DHT Scribe link into a DHT link. However, the probability of this happening is very small.

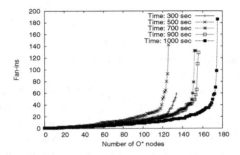

Fig. 4. Distribution of fan-in/in-degree of **0**∗ nodes in Pastry. The Y-Axis is the in-degree of Pastry routing tables. The X-Axis is the number of **0**∗ nodes that have an in-degree less than a particular value. Each curve presents the distribution at different times during the simulation. There exists a sharp skew – indicating a small number of nodes with high in-degree – which persists throughout the simulation.

ments [16]. Our experiments last for a duration of 1000 seconds, and assume a mean arrival rate of 10 joins per second. Further, our experiments assume nodes have a mean stay time of 300 seconds, a minimum stay time of 90 seconds, and a parameter of $\alpha = 1$ in the Pareto distribution. This corresponds to a steady state group size of about 3000 members. Finally, given that our focus is on bandwidth-sensitive and non-interactive applications, we simply consider a uniform-delay network model throughout this paper.

7   Empirical Results

We present the results of experiments with Scribe with both homogeneous and heterogeneous degree constraints.

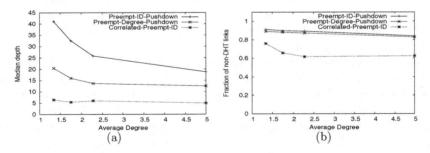

Fig. 5. (a) Depth Vs. Average Degree in heterogeneous settings. We compute mean depth of a node during the session, and compute median across the nodes. The fraction of non-contributors is fixed at 50%. (b) Fraction of non-DHT links Vs. Average Degree in heterogeneous settings. The fraction of non-contributors is fixed at 50%.

Homogeneous Environments

We assume that all nodes have a degree H. Figure 3 plots the fraction of non-DHT links within the Scribe tree as a function of H. There are 3 sets of bars, each set corresponding to a different value of H. Each set consists of bars of 2 shades, corresponding to different values of b, the base of the node IDs in Pastry. Each bar represents the mean of three runs. We find the fraction of non-DHT links is high and over 40% for all configurations we evaluate.

We discuss two factors that contribute to the creation of non-DHT links in Figure 3. Consider a `topicID` of 00...00. Let **0**∗ represent the nodes whose IDs match the topicID in the first digit (that is, the first digit is 0 and the rest of the digits are arbitrary). A join or reconnect request from any node in Scribe should be routed in the first hop to a **0**∗ node, since we would like to match at least the first digit of the `topicID`. So, if there were no pushdown operations, given the reverse-path nature of tree construction in Scribe, all parents in a Scribe tree would be **0**∗ nodes.

A first factor leading to the creation of non-DHT links is that the total bandwidth resources at the **0**∗ nodes may not be sufficient to support all nodes in the tree. Let b be the base of the node IDs in Pastry, and AD be the average degree of the nodes in the system. Then, the **0**∗ nodes represent a fraction $\frac{1}{2^b}$ of the total nodes of the system, and we expect them to only be able to support a fraction $\frac{AD}{2^b}$ of the nodes in the system. Thus, we expect to see $1 - \frac{AD}{2^b}$ links that have non-**0**∗ nodes as parents. Such links are likely to be non-DHT links. This is because: (i) these links must have been created by pushdown operations as described above; and (ii) there are no explicit mechanisms in place to prefer choosing DHT links during a pushdown.

From this discussion, we expect the number of non-DHT links to be equal to $1 - \frac{H}{2^b}$ in a homogeneous environment, where all nodes have a degree H (as the average degree $AD = H$). While this partially explains Figure 3, the fraction of non-DHT links is significantly higher than our estimate. In particular, if $H \geq 2^b$, then we would not expect to see any non-DHT links. However, even when $H = 16$ and $b = 2$ so that $H \gg 2^b$, non-DHT links constitute over 40% of the links in the tree. We believe this is due to a second factor that contributed to the creation of non-DHT links, as we discuss in the next paragraph.

Figure 4 plots the CDF of the fan-ins of the **0**∗s in the system at various times during the simulation. The fan-in of a node is the number of other nodes in the system that have this node as a neighbor in Pastry. We see that there is a significant skew in the fan-ins of the **0**∗s. Due to the skew, Scribe join requests hit the **0**∗s non-uniformly, causing a much larger number of pushdowns, and hence non-DHT links. This also results in poor utilization of the available bandwidth resources at many of the **0**∗ nodes.

We have investigated potential factors that may have led to the skew. For instance, we considered whether it resulted from the uniform delay model used in our simulations. Preliminary experiments indicate that the skew exists even with topologies with non-uniform delays generated using the GeorgiaTech simulator reported in [3]. We believe that the skew arises due to Pastry's join and repair mechanisms in which a new node picks up routing table entries from other nodes in the system. While this reduces join (and repair) times and overheads, it makes nodes that joined earlier far more likely to be picked as neighbors as compared to other nodes. We defer to future work an examination of how fundamental the skew is to the design of Pastry, and whether it can be eliminated using simple heuristics.

Heterogeneous Environments

Our experiments with heterogeneous environments were conducted with 50% of the nodes being non-contributors (degree 0), and for various average degree values. Changing the average degree value results in a different fraction of nodes of medium (degree 2) and higher (degree 10) degree. Figure 5(a) compares the depth of the Scribe multicast tree created with *Preempt-ID-Pushdown* and *Preempt-Degree-Pushdown* in heterogeneous environments. The depth is computed as follows: we compute the mean depth of a node by sampling its depth at different time instances, and then compute the medians across the nodes. The optimal median depth for any of the plotted configurations (not shown in the graph) is about 4. The top 2 curves correspond to *Preempt-ID-Pushdown* and *Preempt-Degree-Pushdown*. *Preempt-ID-Pushdown* performs significantly worse than optimal. This is expected given that there are no mechanisms in place that optimize depth in heterogeneous environments. *Preempt-Degree-Pushdown* performs better than *Preempt-ID-Pushdown* but is still far from optimal, consistent with discussions in Section 5.

Figure 5(b) shows the fraction of non-DHT links from our simulations for *Preempt-Degree-Pushdown,* and *Preempt-ID-Pushdown.* The fraction of non-DHT links is over 80% for a range of average degrees. We believe both factors that we discussed with homogeneous environments – insufficient resources at $0*$ nodes, and the skew in the in-degree of Pastry – have contributed to the creation of non-DHT links. Further, as discussed, even if the skew could be completely eliminated, we would still expect to see $1 - \frac{AD}{2^b}$ non-DHT links due to insufficient resources at $0*$ nodes, where AD is the average degree of the nodes in the system.

A third important factor that could cause non-DHT links in heterogeneous environments is that it may be desirable to use non-$0*$ nodes as parents to minimize the depth of trees. For example, in an environment with nodes of degree H, L, and 0 ($H > L$), the optimal depth tree requires having all nodes of degree H at the highest levels in the tree, and thus as interior nodes. However, only a fraction $\frac{1}{2^b}$ of nodes of degree H are likely to be $0*$ nodes. Thus, optimizing for tree depth in Scribe could potentially result in a larger fraction of non-DHT links due to the need to use non-$0*$ nodes of degree H as interior nodes. Consequently, we would expect *Preempt-Degree-Pushdown* to have a higher fraction of non-DHT links as compared to *Preempt-ID-Pushdown*. However, both policies perform similarly. We believe this is because the other two factors causing non-DHT links dominate in our experiments.

Summary

Our experiments with Scribe indicates trees produced have a high depth, and a large fraction of non-DHT links. There are three factors that cause the creation of non-DHT links with Scribe. First, the bandwidth resources of nodes that share a prefix with the `topicId` may not be sufficient to sustain all nodes in the system. Second, minimizing depth of trees in Scribe requires utilizing higher degree nodes, even though they may not share a prefix with the `topicId`. The third factor is a skew in the in-degree of Pastry. We believe the skew is a result of specific heuristics employed in Pastry, and can potentially be minimized. However, we believe the first two factors are fundamental to the mismatch of node bandwidth constraints and node ids with DHT-based designs. Further, simple analysis shows that the first factor alone could lead to the creation of $1 - \frac{AD}{2^b}$ non-DHT links, where AD is the average degree of the system, and b is the base of the node IDs in Pastry.

8   Feasibility of Potential Solutions

We sketch potential solutions and consider their ability to address the issues raised in the previous section:

–   *ID-Degree Correlation:* A natural question is whether changing the random id assignment of DHTs, and instead employing an assignment where node ids are correlated to node bandwidth constraints can address the issue. To evaluate the potential of such techniques, we consider *Correlated-Preempt-ID* heuristic, where nodes with higher degrees are assigned `nodeIds` which share longer prefixes with the `topicId`. Figure 5(a) shows that this policy indeed is able to achieve depths close to the optimal depth of 4, while Figure 5(b) shows it can significantly lower the fraction of non-DHT links. However, while such a solution could work in scenarios where the DHT is primarily used for a specific multicast group, disturbing the uniform distribution of DHT `nodeIds` can be undesirable, and can adversely affect routing properties of DHTs [17]. Further, DHTs are particularly useful in scenarios where there is a shared infrastructure for a wide variety of applications including multicast sessions. In such scenarios, it is difficult to achieve a correlation between node id and node degree assignments across all trees.

–   *Multiple Trees:* Another question is whether the issues involved can be tackled using the multi-tree data delivery framework used to improve the resiliency of data delivery and for bandwidth management [1,8]. In this framework, 2^b trees are constructed, with the `topicIds` of every tree beginning with a different digit. Each node is an interior node in the one tree where it shares a prefix with the `topicId`, and is a leaf node in the rest. We note that a direct application of the multi-tree approach cannot solve the problem - if nodes belong to multiple degree classes to begin with, then, each of the trees will continue to have nodes of multiple degree classes, and the issues presented in this paper continue to be a concern.

- *Multiple Trees with Virtual Servers:* One potential direction for solving the issues with DHTs is to combine the multi-tree data delivery framework with the concept of virtual servers proposed in [18]. The idea here is that a node can acquire a number of ids proportional to its degree, and then use the multi-tree data delivery framework above. A concern with this approach is that we are not completely concentrating the resources of a higher degree node in one tree, rather, we are distributing it across several trees, thereby giving up on the policy of interior disjointness. The performance implications would need to be carefully evaluated.

9 Summary and Discussion

In this paper, we have considered the impact of heterogeneity in the outgoing bandwidth constraints of nodes on overlay multicast using Scribe. Our results indicate that trees produced by Scribe tend to have a *large depth,* as well as a significant fraction of *non-DHT links.* The key reason for this is the mismatch between the id space that underlies the DHT structure and node bandwidth constraints. We have not found obvious or satisfactory solutions to address the problem, leading us to believe the issues involved are not trivial.

Our work has been motivated by lessons we learned from deploying an overlay-based broadcasting system [10]. Beyond the particular issue of bandwidth heterogeneity considered in this paper, our experience also highlights the importance of considering factors such as heterogeneity in node stabilities, as well as connectivity restrictions due to entities such as NATs and firewalls. While these concerns pertain to both *performance-centric* and *DHT-based* designs, we believe they are more challenging to address in the DHT context given the structure imposed by DHTs. Although there has been significant progress in improving the performance of DHTs, with regard to delay-based metrics such as Relative Delay Penalty (RDP) [6], we believe that it would be important to address the challenges posed by heterogeneity before a compelling case can be made for using DHTs to support bandwidth-demanding broadcasting applications.

Acknowledgments

We thank Anthony Rowstron and Miguel Castro for access to, and for clarifications regarding the Scribe code.

References

1. Castro, M., Druschel, P., Kermarrec, A., Nandi, A., Rowstron, A., Singh, A.: Split-Stream: High-bandwidth Content Distribution in Cooperative Environments. In: Proceedings of SOSP. (2003)
2. Stoica, I., Adkins, D., Zhuang, S., Shenker, S., Surana, S.: Internet Indirection Infrastructure. IEEE/ACM Transactions on Networking (2004)

3. Castro, M., Druschel, P., Kermarrec, A., Rowstron, A.: Scribe: A Large-Scale and Decentralized Application-Level Multicast Infrastructure. In: IEEE Journal on Selected Areas in Communications Vol. 20 No. 8. (2002)

4. Ratnasamy, S., Handley, M., Karp, R., Shenker, S.: Application-level Multicast using Content-Addressable Networks. In: Proceedings of NGC. (2001)

5. Zhuang, S., Zhao, B., Kubiatowicz, J., Joseph, A.: Bayeux: An Architecture for Scalable and Fault-tolerant Wide-area Data Dissemination. In: Proceedings of NOSSDAV. (2001)

6. Chu, Y., Rao, S., Zhang, H.: A Case for End System Multicast. In: Proceedings of ACM Sigmetrics. (2000)

7. Jannotti, J., Gifford, D., Johnson, K.L., Kaashoek, M.F., Jr., J.W.O.: Overcast: Reliable Multicasting with an Overlay Network. In: Proceedings of the Fourth Symposium on Operating System Design and Implementation (OSDI). (2000)

8. Padmanabhan, V., Wang, H., Chou, P.: Resilient Peer-to-peer Streaming. In: Proceedings of IEEE ICNP. (2003)

9. Banerjee, S., Bhattacharjee, B., Kommareddy, C.: Scalable Application Layer Multicast. In: Proceedings of ACM SIGCOMM. (2002)

10. Chu et al.: Early Deployment Experience with an Overlay Based Internet Broadcasting System. In: USENIX Annual Technical Conference. (2004)

11. Saroiu, S., Gummadi, P.K., Gribble, S.D.: A measurement study of peer-to-peer file sharing systems. In: Proceedings of Multimedia Computing and Networking (MMCN). (2002)

12. Liebeherr, J., Nahas, M.: Application-layer Multicast with Delaunay Triangulations. In: IEEE Globecom. (2001)

13. Rowstron, A., Druschel, P.: Pastry: Scalable, distributed object location and routing for large-scale peer-to-peer systems. In: IFIP/ACM International Conference on Distributed Systems Platforms (Middleware). (2001)

14. Deering, S.: Multicast Routing in Internetworks and Extended LANs. In: Proceedings of the ACM SIGCOMM. (1988)

15. Rowstron, A., Castro, M., et al.: SimPastry (Scribe) Implementation, v3.0a (2003)

16. Almeroth, K.C., Ammar, M.H.: Characterization of mbone session dynamics: Developing and applying a measurement tool. Technical Report GIT-CC-95-22, Georgia Institute of Technology (1995)

17. Bharambe, A., Agrawal, M., Seshan, S.: Mercury: Supporting Scalable Multi-Attribute Range Queries. In: Proceedings of ACM SIGCOMM. (2004)

18. Rao, A., Lakshminarayanan, K., Surana, S., Karp, R., Stoica, I.: Load Balancing in Structured P2P Systems. In: Proceedings of the Second International Workshop on Peer-to-Peer Systems (IPTPS). (2003)

Chainsaw: Eliminating Trees from Overlay Multicast

Vinay Pai, Kapil Kumar, Karthik Tamilmani,
Vinay Sambamurthy, and Alexander E. Mohr

Department of Computer Science, Stony Brook University
{vinay, kkumar, tamilman, vsmurthy, amohr}@cs.stonybrook.edu

Abstract. In this paper, we present Chainsaw, a p2p overlay multicast system that completely eliminates trees. Peers are notified of new
packets by their neighbors and must explicitly request a packet from a
neighbor in order to receive it. This way, duplicate data can be eliminated
and a peer can ensure it receives all packets. We show with simulations
that Chainsaw has a short startup time, good resilience to catastrophic
failure and essentially no packet loss. We support this argument with
real-world experiments on Planetlab and compare Chainsaw to Bullet
and Splitstream using MACEDON.

1   Introduction

A common approach taken by peer-to-peer (p2p) multicast networks is to build
a routing tree rooted at the sender. The advantage of a tree-based topology
is that once the tree is built, routing decisions are simple and predictable—a
node receives data from its parent and forwards it to its children. This tends to
minimize both delay and jitter (variation in delay).

However, there are disadvantages to a tree-based approach. Since nodes depend on their parent to deliver data to them, any data loss near the root node
affects every node below it. Moreover, whenever a node other than a leaf node
leaves the system, the tree must be quickly repaired to prevent disruption. Another disadvantage of a tree is that interior nodes are responsible for fanning out
data to all of their children, while the leaf nodes do not upload at all.

Another common feature of p2p multicast systems is that they are *push-based*,
i.e. they forward data based on some routing algorithm without explicit requests
from the recipient. A purely push-based system can't recover from lost transmis-
sions easily. Moreover, if there are multiple senders to a given node, there is a chance
that the node will receive duplicate data, resulting in wasted bandwidth.

In a *pull-based* system, data is sent to nodes only in response to a request
for that packet. As a result, a node can easily recover from packet loss by re-
requesting lost packets. Moreover, there is no need for global routing algorithms,
as nodes only need to be aware of what packets their neighbors have.

We designed Chainsaw, a pull-based system that does not rely on a rigid
network structure. In our experiments we used a randomly constructed graph

M. Castro and R. van Renesse (Eds.): IPTPS 2005, LNCS 3640, pp. 127–140, 2005.
© Springer-Verlag Berlin Heidelberg 2005

with a fixed minimum node degree. Data is divided into finite packets and disseminated using a simple request-response protocol. In our simulations we were able to stream 100kB/sec of data to 10,000 nodes. Our system also withstood the simultaneous failure of half the nodes in the system with 99.6% of the remaining nodes suffering no packet loss at all. Moreover, we observed that new nodes joining the system could start playback within a third of a second without suffering any packet loss. To validate our simulation results, we implemented our protocol in Macedon [1] and ran experiments on PlanetLab [2], and obtained comparable results. We also compared the performance of our system to Bullet [3] and SplitStream [4].

In Section 2 we outline work related to ours. In Section 3 we describe the our system architecture. In Section 4 we present our experimental results. In Section 5 we outline some future work and finally, we conclude.

2   Background

Chu et al. [5] argue that IP is not the correct layer to implement multicast. They proposed *Narada*, a self-organizing application-layer overlay network. Since then many overlay networks [5,6,3,4,7,8] have been proposed, providing different characteristics. We give a brief overview of SplitStream, Bullet and Gossip-style protocols. We also give an overview of BitTorrent, because it is similar in spirit to our system even though it is not a multicast system, but a file-transfer protocol.

2.1   SplitStream

SplitStream [4] is a tree-based streaming system that is built on top of the Scribe [6] overlay network, which in turn is built on top of the Pastry [9] structured routing protocol. In SplitStream, the data is divided into several disjoint sections called *stripes*, and one tree is built per stripe. In order to receive the complete stream, a node must join every tree. To ensure that a node does not have to upload more data than it receives, the trees are built such that every node is an interior node in precisely one tree.

In addition to improving fairness, ensuring that a node is a leaf node in all but one of the trees improves robustness. A node is only responsible for data forwarding on one of the stripes, so if a node suddenly leaves the system, at most one stripe is affected. However, SplitStream does not have any mechanism for recovering from packet loss, and any loss near the root of a tree will affect every node downstream from it.

2.2   Bullet

Bullet [3] is another high-bandwidth data dissemination method. It aims to provide nodes with a steady flow of data at a high rate. A Bullet network consists of a tree with a mesh overlaid on top of it.

The data stream is divided into blocks which are further divided into packets. Nodes transmit a disjoint subset of the packets to each of their children.

An algorithm called RanSub [10] distributes random, orthogonal subsets of nodes every epoch to each node participating in the overlay. Nodes receive a subset of the data from their parents and recover the remaining by locating a set of disjoint peers using these random subsets.

2.3 Gossip-Based Broadcast

Gossip protocols provide a scalable option for large scale information dissemination. Pcast [11] is a two phase protocol in which the exchange of periodic digests takes place independent of the data dissemination. Lpbcast [12] extends pcast in that it requires nodes to have only partial membership information.

2.4 BitTorrent

The BitTorrent [13] file sharing protocol creates an unstructured overlay mesh to distribute a file. Files are divided into discrete *pieces*. Peers that have a complete copy of the file are called *seeds*. Interested peers join this overlay to download pieces of the file. It is pull-based in that peers must request a piece in order to download it. Peers may obtain pieces either directly from the seed or exchange pieces with other peers.

3   System Description

We built a request-response based high-bandwidth data dissemination protocol drawing upon gossip-based protocols and BitTorrent. The source node, called a *seed*, generates a series of new packets with monotonically increasing sequence numbers. If desired, one could easily have multiple seeds scattered throughout the network. In this paper we assume that there is only one seed in the system. We could also support many-to-many multicast applications by replacing the sequence number with a (stream-id, sequence #) tuple. However, for the applications we describe in this paper, a single sender and an integer sequence number suffice.

Every peer connects to a set of nodes that we call its *neighbors*. Peers only maintain state about their neighbors. The main piece of information they maintain is a list of packets that each neighbor has. When a peer receives a packet it sends a NOTIFY message to its neighbors. The seed obviously does not download packets, but it sends out NOTIFY messages whenever it generates new packets.

Every peer maintains a *window of interest*, which is the range of sequence numbers that the peer is interested in acquiring at the current time. It also maintains and informs its neighbors about a *window of availability*, which is the range of packets that it is willing to upload to its neighbors. The window of availability will typically be larger than the window of interest.

For every neighbor, a peer creates a list of *desired packets*, i.e. a list of packets that the peer wants, and is in the neighbor's window of availability. It will then apply some strategy to pick one or more packets from the list and request them via a REQUEST message. Currently, we simply pick packets at random, but more intelligent strategies may yield enhanced improvements (see Section 5.2).

A peer keeps track of what packets it has requested from every neighbor and ensures that it does not request the same packet from multiple neighbors. It also limits the number of outstanding requests with a given neighbor, to ensure that requests are spread out over all neighbors. Nodes keep track of requests from their neighbors and send the corresponding packets as bandwidth allows.

The algorithms that nodes use to manipulate their windows and to decide when to pass data up to the application layer are determined by the specific requirements of the end application. For example, if the application does not require strict ordering, data may be passed up as soon as it is received. On the other hand, if order must be preserved, data would be passed up as soon as a *contiguous* block is available.

For the experiments outlined in this paper, we built our graph by having every node repeatedly connect to a randomly picked node, from the set of known hosts, until it was connected to a specified minimum number of neighbors. Our system does not rely on any specific topology, however we could use other membership protocols like in BitTorrent [13] or Gnutella [14]

For the remainder of this paper, we assume that the application is similar to live streaming. The seed generates new packets at a constant rate that we refer to as the *stream rate*. Nodes maintain a window of interest of a constant size and slide it forward at a rate equal to the stream rate. If a packet has not been received by the time it "falls off" the trailing edge of the window, the node will consider that packet lost and will no longer try to acquire it.

During our initial investigations, we observed that some packets were never requested from the seed until several seconds after they were generated. As a result, those packets wouldn't propagate to all the nodes in time, resulting in packet loss. This is an artifact of picking pieces to request at random and independently from each neighbor, resulting in some pieces not being requested when that neighbor is the seed.

We fixed this problem with an algorithm called *Request Overriding*. The seed maintains a list of packets that have never been uploaded before. If the list is not empty and the seed receives a request for a packet that is not on the list, the seed ignores the sequence number requested, sends the oldest packet on the list instead, and deletes that packet from the list. This algorithm ensures that at least one copy of every packet is uploaded quickly, and the seed will not spend its upload bandwidth on uploading packets that could be obtained from other peers unless it has spare bandwidth available.

In most cases, it is better to have the seed push out new packets quickly, but there are situations when Request Overriding is undesirable. For example, a packet may be very old and in danger of being lost. Therefore, REQUEST packets could have a bit that tells the seed to disable Request Overriding. We have not yet implemented this bit in our simulator or prototype.

4   Experimental Results

We built a discrete-time simulator to evaluate our system and run experiments on large networks. Using it, we were able to simulate 10,000 node networks. We also built a prototype implementation and compared it to Bullet [3] and SplitStream [4].

4.1   No Loss Under Normal Operation

In order to show that our system supports high-bandwidth streaming to a large number of nodes, we simulated a 10,000 node network and attempted to stream 100 kB/sec over it. The seed had an upload capacity of 200 kB/sec, while all other nodes had upload and download capacities of 120 kB/sec and maintained 5 second buffers. The end-to-end round-trip latency between all pairs of nodes was 50 ms.

Figure 1 shows the upload bandwidth of the seed and the average upload and download speeds of the non-seed nodes as a function of time. It took less than three seconds for nodes to reach the target download rate of 100 kB/sec. Once attained, their bandwidth remained steady at that rate through the end of the experiment. On average, the non-seed nodes uploaded at close to 100 kB/sec (well short of their 120 kB/sec capacity), while the seed saturated its upload capacity of 200 kB/sec.

Figure 2 shows another view of the the same experiment. The solid line represents the highest sequence number of contiguous data downloaded by a node,

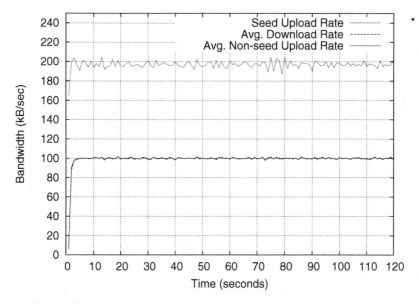

Fig. 1. The seed's upload rate and the average upload and download rate for all other nodes

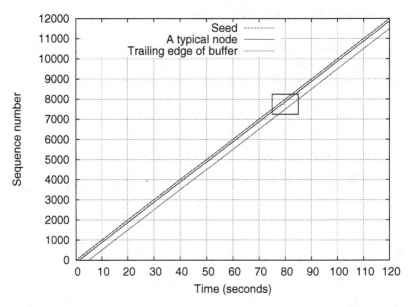

Fig. 2. A plot of the highest sequence number of contiguous data downloaded by a typical node as a function of time. The diagonal line on top (dashed) represents the new pieces generated by the seed, while the bottom line (dotted) represents the trailing edge of the node's buffer.

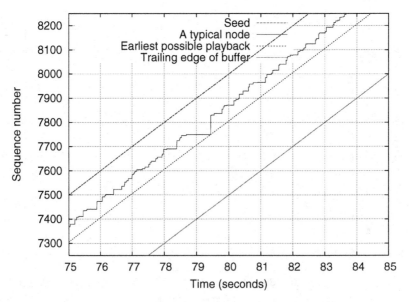

Fig. 3. A zoomed in view of the highlighted portion of Figure 2. The line grazing the stepped solid line represents the minimum buffering delay that avoids packet loss.

as a function of time. The time by which this line lags behind the dashed line representing the seed is the buffering delay for that node. The dotted diagonal line below the progress line represents the trailing edge of the node's buffer. If the progress line were to touch the line representing the trailing edge, that would imply an empty buffer and possible packet loss.

To make it easier to read, we zoom in on a portion of the graph in Figure 3. We also add a third diagonal line that just grazes the node's progress line. The time by which this line lags behind the seed line is the minimum buffering delay required to avoid all packet loss. For this node (which is, in fact, the worst of all nodes) the delay is 1.94 seconds. The remaining nodes had delays between 1.49 and 1.85 seconds.

4.2   Quick Startup Time

When a new node joins the system, it can shorten its playback time by taking advantage of the fact that its neighbors already have several seconds worth of contiguous data in their buffers. Rather than requesting the newest packets generated by the seed, the node can start requesting packets that are several seconds old. It can quickly fill up its buffer with contiguous data by requesting packets sequentially rather than at random.

One of the nodes in the experiment described in Section 4.1 joined the system 50 seconds later than rest. Since other nodes lagged behind the seed by less than 2 seconds, this node started by requesting packets that were 3 seconds old. Figure 4 shows the behavior of this node contrasted with the behavior of an old

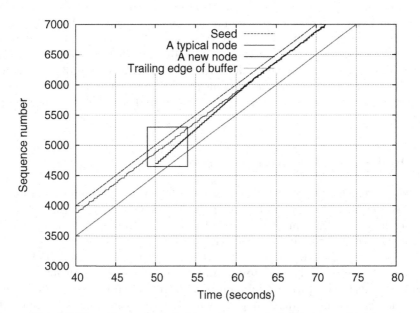

Fig. 4. The bold line shows the behavior of a new node joining at 50 sec contrasted with a node that has been in the system since the start of the experiment

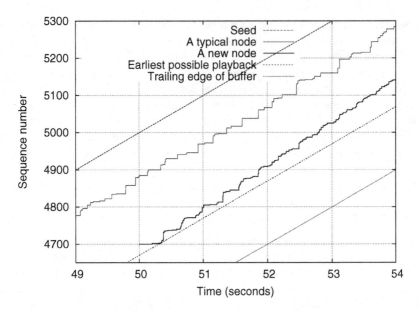

Fig. 5. A zoomed in view highlighting the behavior during the first few seconds of the node joining. The dotted line grazing the bold line shows that the node could have started playback within 330 ms without suffering packet loss.

node. Since the node's download capacity is 20kB/sec higher than the stream rate, it is able to download faster than the stream rate and fill its buffer. In less than 15 seconds, its buffer had filled up to the same level as the older nodes. From this point on, the behavior of the new node was indistinguishable from the remaining nodes.

From the zoomed in view in Figure 5, we observe that the earliest possible playback line for the new node is 3.33 seconds behind the seed, or 330ms behind the point where the node joined. This means the node could have started playback within a third of a second of joining and not have suffered any packet loss.

4.3 Resilience to Catastrophic Failure

We believe that Chainsaw is resilient to node failure because all a node has to do to recover from the failure of its neighbor is to redirect packet requests from that neighbor to a different one. We simulated a catastrophic event by killing off half the non-seed nodes simultaneously.

On average, nodes would be left with half the neighbors they had before the event, but it is likely that some unlucky nodes end up with much fewer. Therefore, we started with a minimum node degree of 40 instead of 30 to minimize the chance of a node ending up with too few neighbors. We used a 10 second buffer instead of a 5 second buffer to prevent momentary disruptions in bandwidth from causing packet loss.

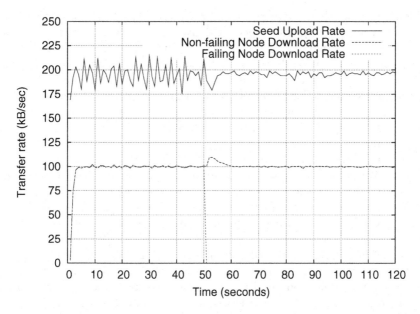

Fig. 6. Observed bandwidth trends when 50% of the nodes are simultaneously failed at 50 seconds

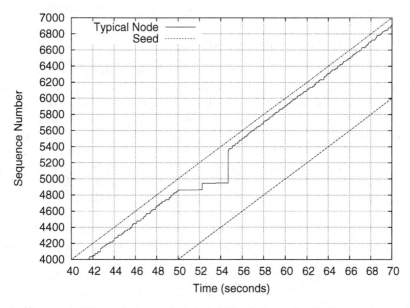

Fig. 7. Progress of a non-failing node when 50% of the nodes in the network simultaneously fail at 50 seconds. All effects of the catastrophic event are eliminated within 5 seconds.

Figure 6 shows the average download rate achieved by the non-failed nodes. Contrary to what one might expect, the average bandwidth briefly *increased* following the node failures! The progress line in Figure 7 helps explain this counter-intuitive behavior. Initially, nodes lagged 1.6 seconds behind the seed. Following the node failures, the lag briefly increased to 5.2 seconds, but then dropped to 0.8 seconds, because with fewer neighbors making demands on their bandwidth, nodes were able to upload and download pieces more quickly than before. The brief spurt in download rate was caused by buffers filling to a higher level than before.

The brief increase in lag was not because of reduced bandwidth, but due to "holes" in the received packets. Some of the failed nodes had received new packets from the seed and not yet uploaded them to any other node. However, since the seed only uploaded duplicate copies of those packets after at least one copy of newer packets had been uploaded, there was a delay in filling in those holes.

Of the 4999 non-seed nodes that did not fail, 4981 nodes (99.6%) suffered no packet loss at all. The remaining 18 nodes had packet loss rates ranging from 0.1% to 17.5% with a mean of 3.74%. These nodes were left with between 9 and 13 neighbors—significantly below the average 20 neighbors. In practice, every node would keep a list of known peers in addition to a neighbor list. When a neighbor disappears, the node picks a neighbor randomly from the known peers list and repeats this process until it has a sufficient number of neighbors. We expect such a mechanism to be robust, even with high rates of churn.

4.4   PlanetLab: Bullet and SplitStream

In order to compare Chainsaw against Bullet [3] and SplitStream [4], we used the Macedon [1] prototyping tool, developed by the authors of Bullet. Macedon allows one to specify the high-level behavior of a system, while letting it take care of the implementation details. The Macedon distribution already includes implementations of Bullet and SplitStream, so we implemented our protocol in their framework to allow a fair comparison between these systems.

We conducted our experiments on the PlanetLab [2] test-bed, using 174 nodes with good connectivity and a large memory capacity. For each of the three protocols, we deployed the application, allowed time for it to build the network and then streamed 600 kbits/sec (75 kB/sec) over it for 360 sec. Half way into the streaming, at the 180 second mark, we killed off half the nodes to simulate catastrophic failure.

Figure 8 shows the average download rate achieved by the non-failing nodes before and after the event. Initially both Chainsaw and Bullet achieved the target bandwidth of 75 kB/sec. However, after the nodes failed, Bullet's bandwidth dropped by 30% to 53 kB/sec and it took 14 seconds to recover, while Chainsaw continued to deliver data at 75 kB/sec with no interruption. SplitStream delivered 65 kB/sec initially, but the bandwidth dropped to 13 kB/sec after the failure event.

In SplitStream, every node is an interior node in one of the trees, so its possible for a node with insufficient upload bandwidth to become a bottleneck.

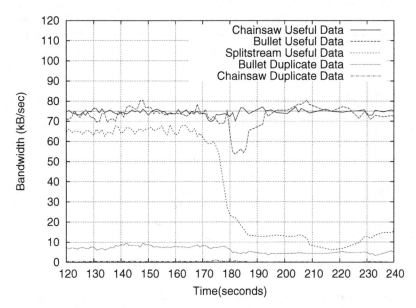

Fig. 8. Useful and duplicate data rates for Chainsaw, Bullet and SplitStream as a function of time from our PlanetLab experiment. 50% of the nodes in the system were killed at the 180 second mark.

When a large number of nodes fail, every tree is is likely to lose a number of interior nodes, resulting in a severe reduction in bandwidth. Macedon is still a work in progress and its authors have not fully implemented SplitStream's recovery mechanisms. Once implemented, we expect SplitStream's bandwidth to return to its original level in a few seconds, once the trees are repaired. Therefore, we ignore SplitStream's packet loss and focus on comparing Chainsaw to Bullet for now.

The packet loss rates for both Chainsaw and Bullet were unaffected by the catastrophic failure. With Chainsaw 73 of the 76 non-failing nodes had no packet loss at all. One of the nodes had an a consistent loss rate of nearly 60% throughout the experiment, whereas two others had brief bursts of packet loss over intervals spanning a few seconds. With Bullet, every node consistently suffered some packet loss rates. The overall packet loss for various nodes varied from 0.88% to 3.64% with a mean of 1.30%.

With Chainsaw, nodes did receive a small number of duplicate packets due to spurious timeouts. However, the duplicate data rate rarely exceeded 1%. With Bullet, on the other hand, nodes consistently received 5-10% duplicate data, resulting in wasted bandwidth.

We think that the improved behavior that Chainsaw exhibits is primarily due to its design assumption that in the common case most of a peer's neighbors will eventually receive most packets. When combined with the direct exchange of "have" information, Chainsaw is able to locate and request packets that it does not yet have within a few RTTs, whereas Bullet's propagation of such information is divided into epochs spanning multiple seconds and is dependent on few assumptions to the RanSub tree remaining relatively intact. As a result Chainsaw has near-zero packet loss, minimal duplicates and low delay.

5   Future Work

In our experiments we have used symmetric links so that aggregate upload bandwidth was sufficient for every node to receive the broadcast at the streaming rate. If large numbers of nodes have upload capacities less than the streaming rate, as might be the case with ADSL or cable modem users, users might experience packet loss. Further work is needed to allocate bandwidth when insufficient capacity exists. Also we have not demonstrated experimentally that Chainsaw performs well under high rates of churn, although we expect that with its pure mesh architecture, churn will not be a significant problem.

5.1   Incentives

So far, we have assumed that nodes are cooperative, in that they willingly satisfy their neighbor's requests. However, studies [15,14] have shown that large fractions of nodes in peer-to-peer networks can be *leeches*, i.e. they try to benefit from the system without contributing. Chainsaw is very similar in design to our unstructured file-transfer system SWIFT [16]. Therefore, we believe that we can adapt SWIFT's pairwise currency system to ensure that nodes that do not contribute are the ones penalized when the total demand for bandwidth exceeds the total supply.

5.2   Packet Picking Strategy

Currently, nodes use a purely random strategy to decide what packets to request from their neighbors. We find that this strategy works well in general, but there are pathological cases where problems occur. For example, a node will give the same importance to a packet that is in danger of being delayed beyond the deadline as one that has just entered its window of interest. As a result it may pick the new packet instead of the old one, resulting in packet loss.

We may be able to eliminate these pathological cases and improve system performance by picking packets to request more intelligently. Possibilities include taking into account the rarity of a packet in the system, the age of the packet, and its importance to the application. Some applications may assign greater importance to some parts of the stream than others. For example, lost metadata packets may be far more difficult to recover from than lost data packets.

6   Conclusion

We built a pull-based peer-to-peer streaming network on top of an unstructured topology. Through simulations, we demonstrated that our system was capable of disseminating data at a high rate to a large number of peers with no packet loss and extremely low duplicate data rates. We also showed that a new node could start downloading and begin play back within a fraction of a second after joining the network, making it highly suitable to applications like on-demand media streaming. Finally, we showed that our system is robust to catastrophic failure. A vast majority of the nodes were able to download data with no packet loss even when half the nodes in the system failed simultaneously.

So far we have only investigated behavior in a *cooperative* environment. However, Chainsaw is very similar in its design to the SWIFT [16] incentive-based file-trading network. Therefore, we believe that we will be able to adapt SWIFT's economic incentive model to streaming, allowing our system to work well in noncooperative environments.

Acknowledgements

We would like to thank Dejan Kostić and Charles Killian for helping us out with MACEDON.

References

1. Rodriguez, A., Killian, C., Bhat, S., Kostić, D., Vahadat, A.: Macedon: Methodology for Automtically Creating, Evaluating, and Designing Overlay Networks. In: NSDI. (2004)
2. Chun, B., Culler, D., Roscoe, T., Bavier, A., Peterson, L., Wawrzoniak, M., Bowman, M.: Planetlab: an overlay testbed for broad-coverage services. SIGCOMM Computer Communication Review (2003)
3. Kostić, D., Rodriguez, A., Albrecht, J., Vahdat, A.: Bullet: high bandwidth data dissemination using an overlay mesh. In: SOSP. (2003)
4. Castro, M., Druschel, P., Kermarrec, A., Nandi, A., Rowstron, A., Singh, A.: Splitstream: High-Bandwidth Multicast in Cooperative Environments. In: SOSP. (2003)
5. Chu, Y., Rao, S.G., Zhang, H.: A case for end system multicast. In: Measurement and Modeling of Computer Systems. (2000)
6. Castro, M., Druschel, P., Kermarrec, A., Rowstron, A.: SCRIBE: A large-scale and decentralized application-level multicast infrastructure. IEEE JSAC (2002)
7. Jannotti, J., Gifford, D.K., Johnson, K.L., Kaashoek, M.F., O'Toole, Jr., J.: Overcast: Reliable multicasting with an overlay network. In: OSDI. (2000)
8. Ratnasamy, S., Handley, M., Karp, R.M., Shenker, S.: Application-level multicast using content-addressable networks. In: Workshop on Networked Group Communication. (2001)
9. Rowstron, A., Druschel, P.: Pastry: Scalable, decentralized object location, and routing for large-scale peer-to-peer systems. In: IFIP/ACM International Conference on Distributed Systems Platforms. (2001)
10. Kostić, D., Rodriguez, A., Albrecht, J., Bhirud, A., Vahdat, A.: Using random subsets to build scalable network services. In: USENIX USITS. (2003)
11. Birman, K.P., Hayden, M., Ozkasap, O., Xiao, Z., Budiu, M., Minsky, Y.: Bimodal multicast. ACM Trans. Comput. Syst. (1999)

12. Eugster, P., Guerraoui, R., Handurukande, S.B., Kouznetsov, P., Kermarrec, A.: Lightweight probabilistic broadcast. ACM Trans. Comput. Syst. (2003)
13. Cohen, B.: BitTorrent (2001) http://www.bitconjurer.org/BitTorrent/.
14. Adar, E., Huberman, B.A.: Free Riding on Gnutella. First Monday 5 (2000)
15. Saroiu, S., Gummadi, P.K., Gribble, S.D.: A measurement study of peer-to-peer file sharing systems. Proceedings of Multimedia Computing and Networking (2002)
16. Tamilmani, K., Pai, V., Mohr, A.E.: SWIFT: A system with incentives for trading. In: Second Workshop on the Economics of Peer-to-Peer Systems. (2004)

FeedTree: Sharing Web Micronews with Peer-to-Peer Event Notification

Daniel Sandler, Alan Mislove, Ansley Post, and Peter Druschel

Department of Computer Science,
Rice University, Houston (TX)
{dsandler, amislove, abpost, druschel}@cs.rice.edu

Abstract. Syndication of micronews, frequently-updated content on the Web, is currently accomplished with RSS feeds and client applications that poll those feeds. However, providers of RSS content have recently become concerned about the escalating bandwidth demand of RSS readers. Current efforts to address this problem by optimizing the polling behavior of clients sacrifice timeliness without fundamentally improving the scalability of the system. In this paper, we argue for a micronews distribution system called FeedTree, which uses a peer-to-peer overlay network to distribute RSS feed data to subscribers promptly and efficiently. Peers in the network share the bandwidth costs, which reduces the load on the provider, and updated content is delivered to clients as soon as it is available.

1 Introduction

In the early days of the Web, static HTML pages predominated; a handful of news-oriented Web sites of broad appeal updated their content once or twice a day. Users were by and large able to get all the news they needed by surfing to each site individually and pressing `Reload`. However, the Web today has experienced an explosion of *micronews:* highly focused chunks of content, appearing frequently and irregularly, scattered across scores of sites. The difference between a news site of 1994 and a weblog of 2004 is its flow: the sheer volume of timely information available from a modern Web site means that an interested user must return not just daily, but a dozen times daily, to get all the latest updates.

This surge of content has spurred the adoption of RSS, which marshals micronews into a common, machine-readable format that can be processed by RSS client programs according to users' interests and preferences. Instead of downloading entire web pages, clients download an RSS "feed" containing a list of recently posted articles. However, RSS specifies a polling-based retrieval architecture, and the scalability of that mechanism is now being tested. There is growing concern in the RSS community over these scalability issues and their impact on bandwidth usage, and providers of popular RSS feeds have begun to abbreviate or eliminate their feeds to reduce the bandwidth stress of polling clients.

M. Castro and R. van Renesse (Eds.): IPTPS 2005, LNCS 3640, pp. 141–151, 2005.

The current RSS distribution architecture, in which all clients periodically poll a central server, has bandwidth requirements that scale linearly with the number of subscribers. We believe that this architecture has little hope of sustaining the phenomenal growth of RSS [1], and that a distributed approach is needed. The properties of peer-to-peer (p2p) overlays are a natural fit for this problem domain: p2p multicast systems scale logarithmically and should support millions of participating nodes. Therefore, we argue that RSS feeds can be distributed in a way that shares costs among all participants. By using p2p event notification to distribute micronews, we can dramatically reduce the load placed on publishers, while at the same time delivering even more timely service to clients than is currently possible. We sketch this system, called FeedTree, and go on to show how it can be deployed incrementally.

The remainder of this paper is organized as follows. Section 2 provides background on RSS and the RSS bandwidth problem. Section 3 discusses related work to improve RSS, and section 4 presents the design of FeedTree. Section 5 describes our prototype FeedTree implementation. Section 6 concludes.

2   Background

2.1   RSS

RSS[1] refers to a family of related XML document formats for encapsulating and summarizing timely Web content. Such documents (and those written in the Atom syndication format [4], a recent entry in the specification fray) are called *feeds*. A Web site makes its updates available to RSS client software (variously termed "readers" and "aggregators") by offering a feed to HTTP clients alongside its conventional HTML content. Because RSS feeds are designed for machines instead of people, client applications can organize, reformat, and present the latest content of a Web site—or many sites at once—for quick perusal by the user. The URL pointing to this feed is advertised on the main Web site.

By asking her RSS reader to *subscribe* to the URL of an RSS feed, a user instructs the application to begin fetching that URL at regular intervals. When it is retrieved, its XML payload is interpreted as a list of RSS *items* by the application. Items may be composed of just a headline, an article summary, or a complete story in HTML; each entry must have a unique ID, and is frequently accompanied by a permanent URL ("permalink") to a Web version of that entry. To the user, each item typically appears in a chronologically-sorted list; in this way, RSS client applications have become, for many users, a new kind of email program, every bit as indispensable as the original. An RSS aggregator is like an inbox for the entire Internet.

---

[1] There is some disagreement [2] over the exact expansion of this acronym. When Netscape first specified version 0.9 of RSS [3], it did so under the name "RDF Site Summary;" the acronym has since been taken to stand for "Rich Site Summary" or "Really Simple Syndication." The subtleties of the many debates over format versions, nomenclature, and ideology are omitted here.

2.2   RSS Bandwidth

Just as major news outlets have begun to discover RSS and to expose their audiences to this burgeoning technology [1,5,6], the RSS technical community is abuzz with weaknesses exposed by its runaway adoption. Chief among these is the so-called "RSS bandwidth problem." Essentially, Web servers which make RSS feeds available tend to observe substantially greater traffic loads as a result, out of proportion to any observable interactive visitor trend. Consequently, some sites have implemented self-defense mechanisms (*e.g.* smaller RSS feed sizes, or enforced limits on access) in an attempt to address the problem [7]. This situation is most likely the effect of many behaviors working in concert:

Polling. For each feed to which a user is subscribed, an RSS application must issue repeated HTTP requests for that feed according to some set schedule. Sites which offer RSS feeds must satisfy one request for every user, many times a day, even if there is no new content.

Superfluity. The RSS data format is essentially static; all entries are returned every time the feed is polled. By convention, feeds are limited to some N most recent entries, but those N entries are emitted for every request, regardless of which of them may be "new" to a client. While this bandwidth problem could be helped by introducing a diff-based polling scheme, all such requests would have to be processed by the RSS provider, which adds more processing load.

Stickiness. Once a user subscribes to an RSS feed, she is likely to retain that subscription for a very long time, so this polling traffic can be counted on for the foreseeable future. If a previously-obscure Web site becomes popular for a day, perhaps by being linked to from popular Web sites, its browsing traffic will spike and then drop off over time. However, if that site offers an RSS feed, users may decide to subscribe; in this case, the drop in direct Web browsing is replaced by a steady, unending load of RSS client fetches. Such a Web site might be popular for a day, but it may have to satisfy a crowd forever [8,9].

Twenty-four-hour traffic. RSS client applications are commonly running on desktop computers at all hours, even when a user is not present; the diurnal pattern of interactive Web browsing does not apply. While the global nature of Web users may generate "rolling" 24-hour traffic, global use of RSS readers generates persistent 24-hour traffic from all over the Earth.

It is easy to see how a website may suffer for publishing RSS feeds. The most popular feed on Bloglines[2] is Slashdot.org, which has about 17,700 subscribers

---

[2] Bloglines (http://bloglines.com), a popular Web-based RSS reading application, offers subscription figures for the feeds it aggregates. We will use these figures (as of late October 2004) as a very crude approximation of reasonable RSS readership. Though Bloglines certainly polls RSS feeds only once for its thousands of subscribers, anecdotal evidence suggests that traditional desktop RSS client usage outweighs Web-based client usage, so we can regard these figures as a lower bound on overall RSS polling load.

as of this writing. If each of those subscribers were using personal aggregation software (desktop clients), Slashdot's headlines-only RSS feed (about 2 kilobytes for a day's worth of entries, and typically polled half-hourly) would be transferred 850,000 times a day, for a total of 1.7 GB of data daily. *The New York Times* recently introduced a suite of RSS feeds for its headlines; the front page alone claims 7,800 subscribers, but the sum of subscribers to all its feeds comes to 24,000. Feeds from the *Times* tend to be around 3 KB, or 3.5 GB of data per day with 30-minute polling. For websites wishing to provide their RSS readers with deeper content, the problem is worse still. Boing Boing, a popular weblog, chooses to publish complete HTML stories in RSS and Atom; 11,500 subscribers might receive 40 KB for each RSS request. To provide this service, Boing Boing must be able to accommodate 22 GB/day of RSS traffic alone. If the BBC News Web site is truly "updated every minute of every day,"[3] its RSS subscribers (18,000 to its various feeds on Bloglines) are unable to take advantage of it: the bandwidth demands of those subscribers polling every minute would be virtually insatiable.

3   Related Work

3.1   Improving the Polling Process

Several proposals have been submitted to ease the pain of RSS on webmasters. Many of these are described in detail in the RSS Feed State HOWTO [10]; examples include avoiding transmission of the feed content if it hasn't changed since the client's last request, `gzip` compression of feed data, and clever ways to shape the timetable by which clients may poll the RSS feed.

Unfortunately, because the schedule of micronews is essentially unpredictable, it is fundamentally impossible for clients to know *when* polling is necessary. Werner Vogels puts it succinctly: Uncontrolled Polling of RSS Resources Does Not Scale [11].

3.2   Outsourcing Aggregation

Several online RSS service providers (essentially, Web-based RSS readers) have proposed alternative solutions [12,13]. In these "outsourced aggregation" scenarios, a centralized service provides a remote procedure interface which end-user applications may be built upon (or refactored to use). Such an application would store all its state—the set of subscribed feeds, the set of "old" and "new" entries—on the central server. It would then poll only this server to receive all updated data. The central RSS aggregation service would take responsibility for polling the authoritative RSS feeds in the wider Internet.

This addresses the bandwidth problem, in a way: A web site owner will certainly service fewer RSS requests as end users start polling the central service

---

[3] As advertised on `http://news.bbc.co.uk`.

instead. The operators of these central services will definitely have bandwidth issues of their own: they will now be at the center of all RSS traffic.

There is a far more insidious danger inherent in this approach, however: a central point of control, failure, and censorship has now been established for all participating users. A central RSS aggregation service may: *(i)* experience unavailability or outright failure, rendering users unable to use their RSS readers, *(ii)* elect to discontinue or change the terms of its service at any time, or *(iii)* silently modify, omit, or augment RSS data without the user's knowledge or consent.

Modification of RSS data by the central aggregator may come in the form of optimized or normalized RSS formatting (a useful feature, since syndication formats found in the wild are frequently incompatible [14]), but might take more dangerous forms as well: it may modify or corrupt the entries in a feed, or it may add advertising or other supplemental yet non-indigenous content to those feeds.

In summary, a third party may not be a *reliable* or *trustworthy* entity, and so it cannot be guaranteed to proxy micronews for client applications. While signed content would allow clients to detect tampering, those clients would have no recourse other than to abandon the central service and retrieve the feed directly from its source. For these reasons, centralized RSS aggregation is most likely not a viable long-term solution.

4   FeedTree

4.1   Group Communication with Overlay Networks

The obvious alternative to polling for data is to distribute that data, as it becomes available, to lists of subscribers. This approach may be adequate for small subscription lists (for example, e-mail lists), but it will not scale to accommodate the growing subscription demands of Web site syndication. Furthermore, while such an approach may reduce the overall bandwidth usage of RSS (by reducing unnecessary fetches), it does nothing to alleviate the per-update stress on network links close to the source.

To address these problems, we look to peer-to-peer overlay networks, which offer a compelling platform for self-organizing subscription systems. Several overlay-based group communication systems, including Scribe [15], offer distributed management of group membership and efficient routing of subscription events to interested parties in the overlay.

We propose FeedTree, an approach to RSS distribution based on peer-to-peer subscription technologies. In FeedTree, timely Web content is distributed to interested parties via Scribe, a subscription-based event notification architecture. Although we chose to base this design on Scribe, there is no reason it could not be deployed on any group communication system that provides similar performance characteristics. In such a system, content may be distributed as soon as it becomes available; interested parties receive these information bursts immediately, without polling the source or stressing network links close to the source.

The use of diverse distribution paths also provides opportunities to recover from any detected corruption or loss of data.

4.2   Scribe

Scribe [15] is a scalable group communication system built on top of a peer-to-peer overlay such as Pastry. Each Scribe group has a 160 bit *groupId* which serves as the address of the group. The nodes subscribed to each group form a multicast tree, consisting of the union of Pastry routes from all group members to the node with nodeId numerically closest to the groupId. Membership management is decentralized and requires less than $\log n$ messages on average, where n is the number of nodes in the overlay.

Scribe has been shown to provide cooperative multicast that is efficient and low overhead [15]. The delay stretch is approximately double that of IP multicast and comparable to other end system multicast systems such as ESM [16] and Overcast [17]. Link stress is also low and less than twice that of IP muliticast. When there are a large number of groups in the system, as is expected in FeedTree, the load is naturally balanced among the participating nodes. Scribe uses a periodic heartbeat mechanism to detect broken edges in the tree; this mechanism is lightweight and is only invoked when there are no messages being published to a group. It has been shown to scale well to both large groups and to a large number of groups. These properties make it a good fit for building large scale event notification systems like FeedTree.

4.3   Architecture

When FeedTree publishing software wishes to deliver an update to subscribers, the following steps are taken (in addition to refreshing a conventional RSS feed URL):

- **A complete RSS document is created** to contain one or more pieces of timely micronews. Each item is assigned a timestamp and a sequence number, to aid clients in the detection of omitted or delayed events.
- The RSS data is then **signed with the publisher's private key.** This is essential to establishing the authenticity of each published item.
- The signed RSS document is **multicast in the overlay** to those peers who have subscribed to a Scribe group whose topic is (a hash of) the feed's **globally unique ID**, trivially defined to be the canonical URL of the advertised RSS feed.
- Peers receiving the message verify its signature, parse the RSS data, and add it to the local RSS application state as if it were a conventional, polled RSS feed. **The user can be notified immediately** of the new entries.

FeedTree-aware client applications should be able to examine conventional RSS feed data to discover if updates to that feed will be published through FeedTree. To do this, FeedTree metadata can be added to the RSS document structure to signal that it is available for subscription in the overlay. In this way, a FeedTree application bootstraps the subscription process with a one-time HTTP request of the conventional feed. All future updates are distributed through incremental RSS items published in FeedTree.

Each RSS feed to be published through FeedTree should advertise a *time-to-live* value, the maximum interval between FeedTree events. (Many RSS feeds already include such a value, to indicate the minimum allowed polling period for clients.) If the publisher observes that no new FeedTree events were generated during this interval, the publisher must generate a heartbeat event. These heartbeats allow subscribers to know conclusively that no published items were lost during the time-to-live period.

It is desirable for all publishers to cryptographically sign their published RSS data, so that clients may be able to trust the Scribe events they receive.[4] The conventional RSS feed should also include the URL and fingerprint of the publisher's certificate, so that clients may retrieve (and cache) the credentials necessary to validate the integrity of signed RSS data.

4.4   Adoption and Deployment

The proliferation of conventional RSS has depended largely on the availability of quality tools to generate RSS data; FeedTree will be no different. Developers have several opportunities to provide support for this system. We break down the deployment scenarios into those that support FeedTree fully, and those that serve as "adapters" to ease transition for legacy RSS systems.

Full FeedTree support

Publishers. Web content management systems (such as weblog publishing packages or traditional workflow-based CMS software) join the overlay by becoming long-lived FeedTree nodes. When new content is posted, the publishing software automatically creates a new FeedTree message and publishes it to the multicast tree.

Readers. RSS-reading applications join the FeedTree peer-to-peer network as well. By doing so, they become part of the global FeedTree service, distributing the network and processing loads of RSS event forwarding. The user interface for an RSS client should remain unchanged; the user subscribes to RSS feeds as she would do ordinarily, and the software takes care of detecting and bootstrapping a FeedTree subscription if it is available. New RSS items are made available to users as soon as the FeedTree events are received by the application.

---

[4] Even though the general benefits of signed content are independent of the FeedTree architecture, we believe our design offers both an excellent opportunity and a compelling need to introduce signed RSS.

Incremental FeedTree support

Publishers. Legacy publishing software that currently emits valid RSS can be adapted to FeedTree with a "republishing" engine running on (or near) the Web server. This tool would poll the legacy RSS feed on an aggressive schedule, sifting out new content and distributing it via FeedTree. Such a republishing tool might even be operated by a third party, in case the owner is slow to deploy FeedTree. This is already a common emergent behavior of the RSS community; several Web sites currently "scrape" the HTML of popular sites and redistribute that content in RSS format. It is up to a user to decide whether or not to trust this third-party proxy feed.

Readers. Until RSS applications support FeedTree natively, users can still contribute to the RSS bandwidth solution by running a local FeedTree proxy. The proxy would listen receive RSS data through FeedTree instead of through conventional means. Existing end-user RSS tools could poll a local FeedTree proxy as often as desired without unnecessary bandwidth usage. Users would then see new FeedTree items sooner than they would under a more conservative polling policy.

4.5   Discussion

Benefits for Participants. The system we propose offers substantial benefits for both producers and consumers of RSS data. The chief incentive for content providers is the lower cost associated with publishing micronews: large Web sites with many readers may offer large volumes of timely content to FeedTree clients without fear of saturating their network links, and a smaller Web site need not fear sudden popularity when publishing a FeedTree feed. FeedTree also offers publishers an opportunity to provide differentiated RSS services, perhaps by publishing simple (low-bandwidth) headlines in a conventional RSS feed, while delivering full HTML stories in FeedTree.

End users will receive even *better* news service with FeedTree than is currently possible. While users currently punish Web sites with increasingly aggressive polling schedules in order to get fresh news, no such schedule will match the timeliness of FeedTree, in which users will see new items within seconds—not minutes or hours. If publishers begin to offer richer micronews through FeedTree, we believe users will be even more likely to use the system. Finally, since RSS readers are generally long-running processes, building FeedTree into the RSS clients will likely result in a stable overlay network for the dissemination of micronews.

Recovery of lost data. Because Scribe offers a best-effort service, failures and node departures within the multicast tree may result in FeedTree clients missing events. In this case, the client will detect a gap in the sequence numbers or an overdue heartbeat. A client may query its parent to recover the missing items; in order to satisfy such a request, each member of the system will keep a small fixed buffer with the last n items in the feed. As a fallback, missing items may be recovered by retrieving the conventional RSS feed by HTTP as in the bootstrapping phase. FeedTree clients may also be offline for periods, during which time they will miss update events. Clients coming online should "catch up" by examining the HTTP-based RSS feed for previously-unseen items during bootstrapping.

A malicious node acting as an interior node in a Scribe tree can suppress events. This attack can be addressed by distributing the responsibility of the Scribe root among several nodes and by routing around non-root interior nodes that fail to forward events. A detailed design of the mechanisms necessary to make FeedTree resilient to these attacks is the subject of ongoing work.

Overhead. The bandwidth demands made on any individual participant in each multicast tree are quite innocuous. For example, an RSS feed generating 4 KB/hour of updates will cause an interior tree node with 16 children to forward less than 20 bytes per second of outbound traffic. Due to the extremely low forwarding overhead, we believe that the motivation for freeloading is very small. In the future, we expect richer content feeds, and consequently, the potential incentive for freeloading may increase. Incentives-compatible mechanisms to ensure fair sharing of bandwidth [18] can be applied if most users subscribe to several feeds, which is a common model of RSS usage. We intend to explore integrating these techniques with FeedTree in future work.

5   Development Status

In order to validate our design for FeedTree, we have developed a software prototype which follows the design outlined in Section 4. The `ftproxy` daemon serves as an intermediary for conventional RSS client software; an HTTP request for a given RSS feed is satisfied by `ftproxy`, which constructs a new ad-hoc RSS document from recent FeedTree messages received for that feed.

When subscribing to a new RSS feed, the proxy first checks to see if that feed is already being published through FeedTree. If the feed is not being published, `ftproxy` will "volunteer" to republish the RSS feed: it begins polling the RSS feed as if it were a conventional RSS reader. New items are published through FeedTree; if a polling interval yields no new items, the proxy publishes a "no news" heartbeat event. This event informs other listening `ftproxy` instances that the feed is already being polled by another volunteer.

In the current implementation, this mechanism is generalized to allow multiple instances of `ftproxy` to poll a single RSS feed cooperatively, providing updates to FeedTree with higher frequency than conventional RSS polling. To "overload" a feed by a factor of N, `ftproxy` will choose to volunteer if it observes fewer than N FeedTree events for that feed during its polling interval. On average, an RSS feed with a minimum polling period of T will have an effective FeedTree refresh period of $\frac{T}{N}$. The polling schedule for volunteers is jittered to help avoid synchronicity.

At the time of this writing, we are running a small FreeTree deployment internally at Rice. We plan to soon expand the distribution to the PlanetLab testbed for further experimentation and validation.

6   Conclusions and Future Work

The current RSS polling mechanism has been said to scale well because "its cost is almost directly proportional to the number of subscribers" [19]. In fact, linear cost is typically an indicator of poor scaling properties, especially when that cost is focused on one member of a distributed system. It is likely that the further growth of RSS adoption will be badly stunted without substantial change to the way micronews is distributed.

The proposed FeedTree subscription system for RSS takes advantage of the properties of peer-to-peer event notification to address the bandwidth problem suffered by Web content providers, while at the same time bringing micronews to end users even more promptly than is currently possible. Self-organizing subscription systems like Scribe offer scalability that cannot be matched by any system designed around resource polling.

Building upon the FeedTree distribution system, we foresee a potential for entirely new services based on RSS which cannot be accomplished today. By using single-writer logs [20] in combination with a distributed storage mechanism such as a DHT [21,22,23], we can record permanently every RSS item published, allowing a distributed archival store of micronews across the Internet. Clients of such a system would easily be able to find out what they "missed" if they had been offline for so long that old RSS items are no longer available in any conventional, static RSS feed. Another area for future work is anonymous RSS feeds involving an anonymizing peer-to-peer routing system, such as AP3 [24]. Finally, we can envision the use of cooperative multicast (such as SplitStream [25]) to distribute large files—such as software, audio, and video—as part of FeedTree feeds.

References

1. Gomes, L.: How the next big thing in technology morphed into a really big thing. The Wall Street Journal (2004)
2. Wikipedia: RSS protocol. (http://en.wikipedia.org/wiki/RSS_(protocol))
3. Netscape Communications Corp.: My Netscape Network. (1999) http://www.purplepages.ie/RSS/netscape/rss0.90.html.
4. IETF Atompub Working Group: (Atom Syndication Format) http://www.atomenabled.org/developers/syndication/.
5. Green, H.: All the news you choose – on one page. BusinessWeek (2004) http://www.businessweek.com/magazine/content/04_43/b3905055_mz011.htm.
6. Kopytoff, V.: One-stop way to read news, blogs online: RSS allows users to get free, automatic feeds. The San Francisco Chronicle (2004) http://www.sfgate.com/cgi-bin/article.cgi?file=/chronicle / archive / 2004 / %10/25/BUG1U9ES301.DTL.

7. Hicks, M.: RSS comes with bandwidth price tag. eWeek (2004) `http://www.eweek.com/article2/0,1759,1648625,00.asp`.

8. Wallace, N.: RSS is sticky traffic. `http://www.synop.com/Weblogs/Nathan/PermaLink.aspx?guid=db37ec96-9271-4e4a-ad8d-6547f27fc1cb`(2004)

9. Scoble, R.: A theory on why RSS traffic is growing out of control. `http://radio.weblogs.com/0001011/2004/09/08.html#a8200` (2004)

10. Morin, R.C.: HowTo RSS Feed State.   `http://www.kbcafe.com/rss/rssfeedstate.html` (2004)

11. Vogels, W.: Once more: Polling does not scale. `http://weblogs.cs.cornell.edu/AllThingsDistributed/archives/000511.html`(2004)

12. Bloglines.com: Bloglines Web Services. (`http://www.bloglines.com/services/`)

13. NewsGator.com: NewsGator Online Service. (`http://www.newsgator.com/ngs/`)

14. Pilgrim, M.:   The myth of RSS compatibility. `http://diveintomark.org/archives/2004/02/04/incompatible-rss` (2004)

15. Castro, M., Druschel, P., Kermarrec, A.M., Rowstron, A.: SCRIBE: A large-scale and decentralized application-level multicast infrastructure. IEEE JSAC **20** (2002)

16. Chu, Y., Rao, S., Zhang, H.: A case for end system multicast. In: ACM Sigmetrics. (2000) 1–12

17. Jannotti, J., Gifford, D., Johnson, K., Kaashoek, M., O'Toole, J.: Overcast: Reliable multicasting with an overlay network. In: OSDI 2000, San Diego, CA (2000)

18. Ngan, T.W.J., Nandi, A., Singh, A., Wallach, D.S., Druschel, P.: On designing incentives-compatible peer-to-peer systems. In: Proc. FuDiCo'04, Bertinoro, Italy (2004)

19. Bell, M.:   RSS for Mac OS X Roundtable. `http://www.drunkenblog.com/drunkenblog-archives/000337.html` (2004)

20. Muthitacharoen, A., Morris, R., Gil, T., Chen, B.: Ivy: A read/write peer-to-peer file system. In: Proc. OSDI'02, Boston, MA (2002)

21. Rowstron, A., Druschel, P.: Storage management and caching in PAST, a large-scale, persistent peer-to-peer storage utility. In: Proc. ACM SOSP'01, Banff, Canada (2001)

22. Kubiatowicz, J., Bindel, D., Chen, Y., Czerwinski, S., Eaton, P., Geels, D., Gummadi, R., Rhea, S., Weatherspoon, H., Weimer, W., Wells, C., Zhao, B.: OceanStore: An architecture for global-scale persistent store. In: Proc. ASPLOS'2000, Cambridge, MA (2000)

23. Dabek, F., Kaashoek, M.F., Karger, D., Morris, R., Stoica, I.: Wide-area cooperative storage with CFS. In: Proc. ACM SOSP'01, Banff, Canada (2001)

24. Mislove, A., Oberoi, G., Post, A., Reis, C., Druschel, P., Wallach, D.S.: AP3: Cooperative, decentralized anonymous communication. In: Proc. SIGOPS-EW, Leuven, Belgium (2004)

25. Castro, M., Druschel, P., Kermarrec, A., Nandi, A., Rowstron, A., Singh, A.: Splitstream: High-bandwidth multicast in cooperative environments. In: Proc. SOSP'03. (2003)

Hybrid Overlay Structure Based on Random Walks

Ruixiong Tian[1,*], Yongqiang Xiong[2], Qian Zhang[2], Bo Li[3],
Ben Y. Zhao[4], and Xing Li[1]

[1] Department of Electronic Engineering, Tsinghua University
[2] Microsoft Research Asia, Beijing China
[3] Department of Computer Science, Hong Kong University of Science and Technology
[4] Department of Computer Science, U.C. Santa Barbara

Abstract. Application-level multicast on structured overlays often suffer several drawbacks: 1) The regularity of the architecture makes it difficult to adapt to topology changes; 2) the uniformity of the protocol generally does not consider node heterogeneity. It would be ideal to combine the scalability of these overlays with the flexibility of an unstructured topology. In this paper, we propose a locality-aware hybrid overlay that combines the scalability and interface of a structured network with the connection flexibility of an unstructured network. Nodes self-organize into structured clusters based on network locality, while connections between clusters are created adaptively through random walks. Simulations show that this structure is efficient in terms of both delay and bandwidth. The network also supports the scalable fast rendezvous interface provided by structured overlays, resulting in fast membership operations.

1 Introduction

Overlay networks are popular as infrastructures for network applications such as streaming multimedia [4], video conferencing and P2P gaming [10]. For these applications, fast membership operations and efficient data delivery are becoming basic usability requirements.

Recent developments of structured [16,13,20] and unstructured [18,9] overlay networks point to a new diagram for overlay research to address these major challenges, i.e., scalability, efficiency and flexibility. Several application-layer multicast systems [14,21] build on these structured overlays by using reverse path forwarding to construct multicast trees.

Structured overlays address the scalability requirements, but their homogeneous design can result in inefficient group communication on heterogeneous networks, by either overloading or under-utilizing resources. This impact is especially visible on bandwidth-demanding multicast services. In contrast, multicast

---

[*] This work is performed while Ruixiong Tian is a visiting student at Microsoft Research Asia.

M. Castro and R. van Renesse (Eds.): IPTPS 2005, LNCS 3640, pp. 152–162, 2005.

nodes on unstructured overlays can choose the number and destinations of their connections, adapting them to network heterogeneity for improved network performance. However, unstructured overlays often require flooding or gossiping to route multicast messages [9], limiting scalability and efficiency.

To combine advantages from both approaches, we propose an application infrastructure called *H*ybrid Overlay Networks (HONet). HONet integrates the regularity of structured overlays with the flexibility of unstructured overlays in a hierarchical structure. For network locality, nodes form clusters, each providing a root node that together form a core network. Local clusters and the core network are separate structured networks. In addition, random connections between members across clusters serve as shortcuts to reduce network delay and bandwidth consumption.

We make these random connections using a random walk algorithm. The number of random connections is chosen according to each node's local service capacity. The neighbors connected to by these links are chosen probabilistically according to the distribution of node service capacities through random walk. This allows these connections to adapt to network heterogeneity.

HONet is an abstract framework and can work with structured overlays such as Chord [16], Pastry [13], Tapestry [20] or De Bruijn networks [11]. In this paper, we use De Bruijn networks as an example, and describe a protocol to construct degree-constrained HONet (called HDBNet). We evaluate the performance of HDBNet through simulation and show that HDBNet is flexible and efficient. The relative delay penalty and cost in HDBNet are roughly $1/5$ and $1/2$ relative to a flat De Bruijn network.

The rest of paper is organized as follows. We describe the problem context and related work in Section 2. Next, we propose the HONet framework in Section 3. Then in Section 4, we present the random walk scheme to construct random connections between clusters. We present simulation results in Section 5, and conclude in Section 6.

2   Related Work

Several approaches have been taken to address routing inefficiency and network heterogeneity in overlay networks. Techniques to exploit topology information to improve routing efficiency in flat structured overlays can be classified into three categories [3]: geographic layout as in Topologically-Aware CAN, proximity routing as in Chord and proximity neighbor selection as in Tapestry and Pastry. However, these optimizations are often limited by the homogeneous design of structured overlays.

Another approach builds auxiliary networks on top of structured overlays, such as Brocade [19] and Expressway [17]. Although these schemes are efficient for message propagation, they are not suitable for bandwidth-demanding multicast services because some nodes with high-degree will be overloaded. HONet routing is similar to Brocade routing with partitioned namespaces plus the addition of randomized inter-cluster links. Canon [7], on the other hand, solves these

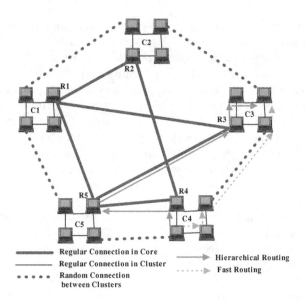

Fig. 1. A HONet composed of clusters ($C1,C2,\dots$). Root nodes ($R1,R2,\dots$) from each cluster form the core network. Messages can route using the hierarchical structure of HONet, or through random connections between members in different clusters (fast routing).

problems by extending the flat structured overlays to a hierarchy. Canon inherits the homogeneous load and functionality offered by a flat design while providing the advantages of a hierarchy. However it can not adapt to nodes' heterogenous service capacities, a problem solved in our scheme by removing the homogeneous flat design.

Hierarchical structure is used in unstructured overlays to address efficiency and scalability issues in systems such as mOverlay [18] and Hierarchical Gossip [9]. Although they achieve good scalability, they often rely on flooding or gossip to multicast messages, resulting in less than ideal efficiency. Random walks are used in [8] to achieve good expansion of unstructured overlays.

3   The HONet Framework

In this section, we describe the general HONet framework, including its structure, construction, and routing mechanisms. Note that HONet is optimized for efficient and fast membership operations, useful for quickly and efficiently joining or switching between multicast groups.

3.1   Overall Structure

As shown in Fig. 1, HONet is organized as a two-level hierarchy. The lower level consists of many clusters, each containing a cluster root node. The cluster roots form the upper level, the core network. The core network and each cluster are constructed as structured overlays with independent ID spaces. Each node is identified by a cluster ID (CID), which is the local cluster root's ID in the core network, and a member ID (MID), which is the node's ID in the local cluster namespace.

Node degree in HONet (*i.e.* the number of neighbors a node knows) includes two components: the regular connections in structured overlays and random connections between clusters. Each node's degree should be constrained by its service capacity and network conditions. If cluster nodes have the capacity to maintain neighbors outside of the regular overlay connections, they can create random connections with members in other clusters. We describe the construction of these random connections in section 4.

We make some general assumptions in our design: (1) The inter-cluster network latencies are larger than intra-cluster latencies, and available bandwidth between clusters is much lower than inside clusters. (2) Nodes' processing capacity and network conditions span a large range. Both assumptions are drawn from the reality of current Internet [15].

In addition to inheriting the scalable routing of structured overlays and the flexibility of unstructured networks, the clustered structure of HONet provides fault-isolation: faults in a cluster will only affect local cluster nodes, with limited impact on other clusters. Each cluster can choose the most stable member to serve as cluster root, resulting in improved global and local stability.

3.2   Node Clustering

HONet is constructed through node clustering. When a node joins the network, it locates a nearby cluster to join. Node clustering provides another way to address topology-awareness in overlays.

Before a node joins, it identifies its coordinates in the network, possibly by using network coordinate systems such as GNP [12] and Vivaldi [5]. In HONet, we implement a simple coordinate system using a set of distances from each node to a group of well-known landmark nodes. The coordinates of cluster roots are stored in a distributed hash table (DHT) on the core network. A new node searches the DHT for cluster roots close by in the coordinate system.

Since most DHTs in structured overlays use a one-dimensional namespace for keys, while coordinates are multidimensional, we need to provide a mapping from the multidimensional coordinate space to the one-dimensional DHT space. The mapping should be: (1) a one-to-one mapping, (2) locality preserving, which means if two points are close in multidimensional space, corresponding mapped numbers are also close. Space filling curves (SFC), such as z-order or Hilbert curves [2,17], have this property. In HONet, we use Hilbert curves to map the coordinates into numbers called locality number (L-number).

With a SFC-based mapping, to find nodes close to a new node coordinate l, the DHT searches the range: $X = \{x : |x - l| < T\}$. This searches for roots with L-numbers within T distance of l, where T is a cluster radius parameter. To find nearby roots, a new node sends out lookup message using l as key. The message routes to nodes responsible for l in the DHT, who search the range X, forwarding the message to close roots in namespace, who then reply to the new node. If the new node cannot locate nearby cluster roots, or if the distance to the closest cluster root is larger than cluster radius T, then this node joins the core network as a new cluster root and announces its L-number and its coordinates in the core network. Otherwise, the node joins the cluster led by the closest cluster root.

Since each node in a DHT maintains a continuous zone of ID space, locality information about close L-numbers (because of SFC's distance-preserving mapping) will be kept in a small set of adjacent nodes. Locating nearby clusters should be fast. Since clusters are significantly smaller than the overall network, joining a local cluster is significantly quicker than joining a flat structured overlay. Finally, a new node can add additional inter-cluster connections according to Section 4.

3.3   Message Routing

If a message is destined for a local cluster node, normal structured overlay routing is used. Otherwise, we can use two approaches, *hierarchical routing* and *fast routing*, both illustrated in Fig. 1. In either case, DHT routing is utilized in the core network and inside local clusters.

Hierarchical Routing. In hierarchical routing, messages are delivered from one cluster to another through the core network. In HONet, the MID for cluster root is fixed and a destination is identified by a (CID, MID) pair. Thus if the destination CID identifies the message as inter-cluster, the message routes to the local root first, then routes through the core network to the destination cluster's root node, and finally to the destination. This is similar to routing in Brocade [19].

Hierarchical routing is important for network construction and maintenance, and is a backup when fast routing fails. Since latencies in the core network are much larger than that inside clusters, we use *fast routing* across random connections to reduce the path delay and bandwidth consumption in the core network.

Fast Routing. Fast routing utilizes the random connections between clusters as inter-cluster routing shortcuts. To implement fast routing, each cluster nodes publishes information about its inter-cluster links in the local cluster DHT. For example, if a node maintains a random connection with neighbor cluster CID C, it stores this information in the local cluster DHT using C as the key. The node storing this information knows all the random connections to destination cluster C, and serves as a reflector to C.

If a source node doesn't know the random connection to the destination cluster, it simply sends the message to the local reflector through overlay routing. The reflector will decide what to do next. If it knows of nodes with random connections to the destination cluster, it forwards the message to one of them, and across the random link to the destination cluster. If the reflector knows of no such random connection, the message routes to the local root and defaults to hierarchical routing. When the message enters another cluster using hierarchical routing, it can check again to see if fast routing is available. Local reflector can tell the source node about the node with the random connection, so that later messages can avoid inefficient triangle routing. Finally, reflectors can also use its knowledge of shortcut links to balance traffic across them.

The difference between hierarchical routing and fast routing is the number of inter-cluster routing hops. Since these latencies are much larger than intra-cluster links, fast routing can significantly reduce end-to-end routing latency and bandwidth consumption between clusters.

4   Random Walks

To construct random connections easily and adaptively, we use a random walk algorithm.

A node's capacity in HONet is measured by a generic fitness metric (denoted by f), which characterizes service capacity and local network conditions. According to the definition of transition probability $p_{i,j}$ in formula (1), the scale of f is not important when determining the quantity of $p_{i,j}$. Thus the fitness metric only needs to be consistent across nodes.

To consider node heterogeneity, a node's fitness metric determines the number of random connections it maintains. Our scheme samples the nodes in HONet according to the node fitness distribution. Since random walks can sample nodes according to some distribution, we propose the following algorithm to construct random connections. Assuming node i with fitness f_i has k_i neighbors, the algorithm is:

1) Node i determines the number of random connections it will create according to f_i.

2) Node i initiates a random walk message with Time-to-Live (ttl) set to s for each random connection. s is the number of skipped steps for the mixing of random walk.

3) If node i has a random walk message with $ttl > 0$, it performs the next step of random walk: select a neighbor j randomly and send the random walk message to node j with probability:

$$p_{i,j} = \frac{1}{k_i} \min\{1, \frac{f_j k_i}{f_i k_j}\} \tag{1}$$

Otherwise the message will stay at node i in next step. $ttl = ttl - 1$.

4) If node i receives a random walk message with $ttl > 0$, goto step 3. Otherwise, it is sampled by the random walk for corresponding random connection.

According to [6], we can see that above algorithm is just a typical Metropolis scheme of Markov Chain Monte Carlo (MCMC) sampling. Since the detailed balance equation

$$f_i p_{i,j} = \min\{\frac{f_i}{k_i}, \frac{f_j}{k_j}\} = f_j p_{j,i} \tag{2}$$

satisfies, if s is large enough, the obtained nodes are samples according to the distribution of fitness. Moreover, since k_i is proportional to f_i in HONet, $p_{i,j} \approx 1/k_i$, the above random walk is similar to the regular random walk in the network. For regular random walk, the mixing time is $O(\log(N)/(1 - \lambda))$, where λ is the second largest eigenvalue of the transition matrix of the regular random walk [8]. Usually λ is much less than 1 and the mixing time is small for general random network if the minimum node degree in the network is large enough. Therefore the s for above random walk is small and each random connection can be created rapidly.

5   Performance Evaluation

We use a De Bruijn graph as the structured overlay network to construct HONet, and call it a Hybrid De Bruijn Network (HDBNet). The performance of HDBNet is evaluated through extensive simulations in this section.

5.1   Simulation Setup

We use GT-ITM to generate transit-stub network topologies for our simulation. We generate 5 topologies each with about 9600 nodes and 57000 edges. We assign different distances to the edges in the topologies (with values from [1]): The distance of intra-stub edges is 1; the distance of the edges between transit node and stub node is a random integer in [5, 15]; and the distance between transit nodes is a random integer in [50, 150]. Nodes in HDBNet are attached to different routers and the size of HDBNet varies from 1000 to 6000. The radix of De Bruijn graph is 2. Five runs are performed on each network topology and the average value reported.

We consider the following metrics:

- Relative Delay Penalty (RDP): the ratio of end-to-end HDBNet routing delay between a pair of nodes over that of a direct IP path. RDP represents the relative cost of routing on the overlay.
- Link cost: the average latency across all connections. The link cost is a convenient, though simplified metric to measure network structure and data delivery performance in different overlays.
- Hop count: the average number of overlay hops in an end-to-end path.

5.2   Evaluation Results of HDBNet

We now compare the performance of HDBNet to a flat De Bruijn overlays. The radix of flat De Bruijn networks is set to 4 to have similar node degrees as HDBNet. Since the cluster radius and random connections are the main factors affecting the performance of HDBNet, we first evaluate the performance with different cluster radii ($R = 20, 30, 40$) when each cluster node has at most 4random connections ($RC = 4$). Then we compare the performance of HDBNet

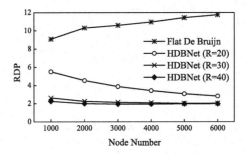

Fig. 2. The average *relative delay penalty (RDP)* between any pair of nodes in flat De Bruijn and HDBNet when $RC=4$

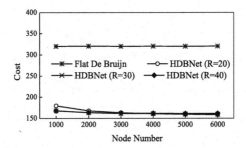

Fig. 3. The *link cost* in flat De Bruijn and HDBNet when $RC=4$

by varying the number of random connections ($RC = 1, 2, 3, 4$) for $R = 30$. These are representative of results run using other radius values. Fast routing is used whenever possible.

Figure 2 shows the comparison of average RDP between any pair of nodes in HDBNet and flat De Bruijn. We can see that the RDP in HDBNet is much smaller than that in flat De Bruijn which does not take the network locality into consideration. For $R = 30$ and $R = 40$, the RDP is very small ($\approx$ 2), roughly 1/5 of the De Bruijn RDP. When the network size is fixed, RDP decreases as cluster radius grows. This is because larger cluster radii imply less clusters, and more clusters are likely to be connected directly via random links.

Figure 3 shows the comparison of link cost in HDBNet and flat De Bruijn. We can see that HDBNet has only half cost compared with flat De Bruijn, which indicates that the HDBNet is much more efficient in terms of end-to-end latency. In fact, most connections in HDBNet are intra-cluster connections, which are much shorter in term of latency than inter-cluster connections. While flat De Bruijn does not take network proximity into account, and many neighbor connections are inter-cluster links.

The comparison of average hop count between any pair of nodes in HDBNet and flat De Bruijn is shown in Fig. 4. Hop count in HDBNet is 2 times or

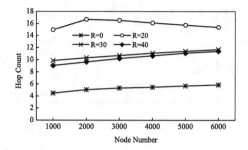

Fig. 4. The *hop count* in flat De Bruijn and HDBNet when *RC=4*

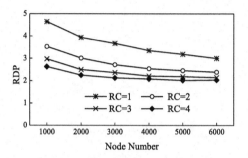

Fig. 5. The average *relative delay penalty (RDP)* in HDBNet when the number of *random connections (RC)* varies and *R=30*

more than in the De Bruijn network. While the inter-cluster hops are reduced in HDBNet, intra-cluster hops increase. Despite this result, the path length still scales as $O(\log N)$.

Figure 5, 6, 7 show the comparison of average RDP, link cost and hop count respectively when $R = 30$, and we vary the maximum number of random connections per node ($RC = 1, 2, 3, 4$). The number of random connections affects performance dramatically. Just a few random connections can improve routing performance dramatically. When more random connections are allowed, messages are more likely to be delivered through random connections. Thus inter-cluster routing will be reduced, resulting in lower RDP. Moreover, fewer inter-cluster hops means less hops in intermediate clusters, resulting in shorter overlay path length. Since the intra-cluster connections are shorter than inter-cluster connections, the link cost increases with allowed random connections.

Our results show that hierarchical structured overlays can perform better than flat structures. These improvements should be applicable to HONets based on other structured overlays. Our proposed mechanisms, node clustering and random connections, offer an orthogonal way to address topology-awareness compared to locality-aware structured overlays such as Tapestry or Pastry. A performance comparison against traditional locality-aware structured overlays is part of our goals for ongoing work.

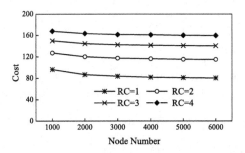

Fig. 6. The *link cost* in HDBNet when the number of *random connections (RC)* varies and *R=30*

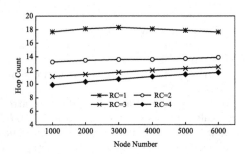

Fig. 7. The *hop count* in HDBNet when the number of *random connections (RC)* varies and *R=30*

6   Conclusions

In this paper, we propose HONet, a locality-aware overlay framework for flexible application-layer multicast that combines the scalability and interface of structured networks and the flexibility of unstructured network. We use random walks to create random connections between clusters of nodes. HONet preserves the key features such as scalability, efficiency, routability and flexibility as in the structured or unstructured overlay networks, and is a desirable platform for flexible group communication.

References

1. The pinger project.
2. ASANO, T., ET AL. Space-filling curves and their use in the design of geometric data structures. *Theoretical Computer Science 181*, 1 (1997), 3–15.
3. CASTRO, M., P.DRUSCHEL, HU, Y., AND ROWSTRON, A. Exploiting network proximity in distributed hash tables. In *International Workshop on Peer-to-Peer Systems* (2002).

4. CHU, Y., RAO, S., SESHAN, S., AND ZHANG, H. Enabling conferencing applications on the internet using an overlay multicast architecture. In *ACM SIGCOMM* (August 2001).

5. DABEK, F., COX, R., KAASHOEK, F., AND MORRIS, R. Vivaldi: a decentralized network coordinate system. In *ACM SIGCOMM* (2004).

6. FILL, A. Reversible markov chains and random walks on graphs.

7. GANESAN, P., GUMMADI, K., AND GARCIA-MOLINA, H. Canon in g major: Designing dhts with hierarchical structure. In *ICDCS* (March 2004).

8. GKANTSIDIS, C., MIHAIL, M., AND SABERI, A. Random walks in peer-to-peer networks. In *IEEE INFOCOM* (March 2004).

9. KERMARREC, A.-M., MASSOULIE, L., AND GANESH, A. J. Probabilistic reliable dissemination in large-scale systems. *IEEE Transactions on Parallel and Distributed systems 14*, 3 (2003), 248–258.

10. KNUTSSON, B., LU, H., XU, W., AND HOPKINS, B. Peer-to-peer support for massively multiplayer games. In *IEEE INFOCOM* (March 2004).

11. LOGUINOV, D., KUMAR, A., RAI, V., AND GANESH, S. Graph-theoretic analysis of structured peer-to-peer systems: Routing distances and fault resilience. In *ACM SIGCOMM* (August 2003).

12. NG, T. S. E., AND ZHANG, H. Towards global network positioning. In *ACM SIGCOMM IMW* (2001).

13. ROWSTRON, A., AND DRUSCHEL, P. Pastry: Scalable, decentralized object location and routing for large-scale peer-to-peer systems. In *ACM Middleware* (Nov. 2001).

14. ROWSTRON, A., KERMARREC, A.-M., CASTRO, M., AND DRUSCHEL, P. Scribe: The design of a large-scale event notification infrastructure. In *NGC* (UCL, London, Nov. 2001).

15. SEN, S., AND WANG, J. Analyzing peer-to-peer traffic across large networks. *IEEE/ACM Trans. on Networking 12*, 2 (2004), 219–232.

16. STOICA, I., MORRIS, R., KARGER, D., KAASHOEK, M. F., AND BALAKRISHNAN, H. Chord: A scalable peer-to-peer lookup service for internet applications. In *ACM SIGCOMM* (August 2001).

17. XU, Z., MATHALINGAM, M., AND KARLSSON, M. Turning heterogeneity into an advantage in overlay routing. In *IEEE INFOCOM* (June 2003).

18. ZHANG, X., ET AL. A construction of locality-aware overlay network: moverlay and its performance. *IEEE JSAC* (Jan. 2004).

19. ZHAO, B. Y., ET AL. Brocade: Landmark routing on overlay networks. In *IPTPS* (2002).

20. ZHAO, B. Y., ET AL. Tapestry: A resilient global-scale overlay for service deployment. *IEEE JSAC 22*, 1 (Jan. 2004), 41–53.

21. ZHUANG, S. Q., ET AL. Bayeux: An architecture for scalable and fault-tolerant wide-area data dissemination. In *NOSSDAV* (2001).

Quickly Routing Searches Without Having to Move Content

Brian F. Cooper

Center for Experimental Research in Computer Systems,
College of Computing, Georgia Institute of Technology
cooperb@cc.gatech.edu

Abstract. A great deal of work has been done to improve peer-to-peer routing by strategically moving or replicating content. However, there are many applications for which a peer-to-peer architecture might be appropriate, but in which content movement is not feasible. We argue that even in such applications, progress can be made in developing techniques that ensure efficient searches. We present several such techniques. First, we show that organizing the network into a square-root topology, where peer degrees are proportional to the square root of the popularity of their content, provides much better performance than power-law networks. Second, we present routing optimizations based on the amount of content stored at peers, and tracking the "best" peers, that can further improve performance. These and other techniques can make searches efficient, even when content movement or replication is not feasible.

1 Introduction

A large number of optimizations have been proposed to improve the performance and effectiveness of peer-to-peer searches. Many of these proposals involve moving or replicating content to achieve high performance. For example, Cohen and Shenker [4] propose replicating files in order to make them easier to find. Super-peer networks [21,14] replicate content metadata from leaf peers to super-peers, where the actual search processing is done. Even distributed hash tables [19,17,18] move data, as content (or pointers to content) are taken from their original peer and moved to a location in the network based on a hash of the object identifier. Other examples of proposals to move or replicate content for efficiency include [20,3,8,7,11,2].

In order for this *content movement* approach to be effective, it must be feasible to move objects around. For example, in the traditional application of multimedia filesharing, it makes sense to move or replicate content: the files and metadata rarely change and are small enough to replicate. However, in many cases content movement may not be feasible. First, the data may be very large, or the index over the data may be very large, and bandwidth and storage requirements for moving content or indexes may be prohibitive. For example, consider a network of digital libraries, each containing multiple gigabytes or terabytes of data. Full text searches can be accomplished efficiently using inverted indexes,

M. Castro and R. van Renesse (Eds.): IPTPS 2005, LNCS 3640, pp. 163–172, 2005.

but such indexes may be as large as the content itself. In this case, replicating either the content or the indexes will certainly tax network links, and may cause problems if storage is limited at peers. Second, if there are many changes in the system, it will be difficult to keep remote indexes and copies up to date. Frequent content changes, or frequent peer membership changes, will require many updates, again taxing bandwidth resources. Third, many content providers are unwilling to export data or index information for intellectual property reasons. For example, an electronic publisher may be willing to process searches and return results, as long as it can record which searches are being processed over its content or attach copyright notices to the content. Such a publisher will oppose replication, and will probably be resistant to exporting indexing information so that other peers end up processing searches of its content. Not every application has these issues, and in many cases content movement makes sense. However, there are many potential applications where such techniques are not feasible.

Can we still use peer-to-peer search techniques to perform information discovery in these applications? We argue that the peer-to-peer approach can still be used and made efficient. In particular, if we do not proactively move content, but instead leave it at its source, we can avoid the cost of shipping replicas or updates altogether. Unfortunately, existing basic peer-to-peer protocols that do not require content movement, such as Gnutella's original flooding approach, are not scalable or efficient. What is needed is a new set of techniques to optimize peer-to-peer searches without content movement.

As evidence for our argument, we present three techniques that can be used to optimize peer-to-peer searches even when content is not moved. Consider a simple protocol of random walk searches over an unstructured network [1,11]. Without content movement, the performance of simple random walks can degrade significantly. Our first optimization is to reorganize the overlay network so that random walks can operate efficiently. We propose the *square-root topology*, where each peer's degree is proportional to the square root of the popularity of its content. Our analysis shows that this topology is optimal for simple random walk searches, and simulations show that other search techniques also perform best on the square-root topology[1]. We also provide an adaptive algorithm for forming the square-root topology without using content movement or global information.

We then present two more optimizations to simple random walks in square-root networks. *Biased document count* and *search memory* work to quickly route searches to peers that have the most content, and thus have the highest probability of storing matching content. These optimizations complement the square-root topology to further improve performance. Simulation results show more than a factor of two performance improvement for our techniques over simple random walk searches in power law networks.

Our optimizations are only a starting point, but they illustrate that high performance can be achieved in networks where replicating or moving con-

---

[1] In fact, the square-root topology is often best even when content movement is used; see [6].

tent is infeasible. There are a few other techniques that also operate without content movement, such as "expanding ring" [11,20] or "directed breadth first search" [20]. However, more work needs to be done. For instance, our results show that the commonly assumed power-law network is not even the best network for walk-based searches, since the square-root topology is optimal. There are potentially a whole host of new techniques that can be developed to search efficiently without using content movement.

In this paper, we first define and analyze the square-root topology (Section 2). Next, we discuss the biased document count and search memory optimizations (Section 3). We present simulation results that show the performance benefit of our techniques (Section 4). We survey related work (Section 5), and then discuss our conclusions (Section 6).

2   The Square-Root Topology

In "unstructured networks," such as that in Gnutella, the topology of the network is built up over time as peers choose neighbors essentially randomly. Without any outside interference, such networks tend toward a power-law distribution, where the number of neighbors of the ith most connected peer is proportional to $1/i^{\alpha}$. Here, α is a constant that determines the skew of the distribution. For such networks, random walk searches have shown to be effective [1,11]. A simple random walk search starts at one peer in the network, and is processed over that peer's content. That peer then forwards the search to a random neighbor, who processes and forwards the query again. In this way, the search "walks" randomly around the network, until it terminates, either because enough results have been found or because a time-to-live (TTL) has been reached [11].

Consider a peer-to-peer network with N peers. Each peer k in the network has degree d_k (that is, d_k is the number of neighbors that k has). The total degree in the network is D, where $D = \sum_{k=1}^{N} d_k$.

We define the square-root topology as a topology where the degree of each peer is proportional to the square root of the popularity of the peer's content. Formally, if we define g_k as the proportion of searches submitted to the system that are satisfied by content at peer k, then the square-root topology has $d_k \propto \sqrt{g_k}$ for all k.

We now show that a square-root topology is optimal for random walk searches. Imagine a user submits a search s that is satisfied by content at a particular peer k. Of course, until the search is processed by the network, we do not know which peer k is. How many hops will the search message take before it arrives at k, satisfying the search? We can model the search process as a Markov chain. Each state in the Markov chain represents a peer, and the transitions between states represent a search being forwarded from a peer to one of its neighbors. For simple random walk searches, the probability of transitioning from peer i to peer j is $1/d_i$ if i and j are neighbors, and 0 otherwise. Under this formulation, Markov chain theory tells us that the expected number of hops for an arbitrary search to reach its goal peer is inversely proportional to the goal peer's degree:

Lemma 1. *If the network is connected (that is, there is a path between every pair of peers) and non-bipartite, then the expected number of hops for search s to reach peer k is D/d_k.*

This result is shown in [13].

To simplify our analysis, we assume a peer forwards a search message to a randomly chosen neighbor, even if that search message has just come from that neighbor or has already visited that neighbor. Lv et al [11] notes that avoiding previously visited peers can improve the efficiency of walks. Simulation results show that the square-root topology is still best; experiments are discussed in Section 4.

If a given search requires D/d_k hops to reach peer k, how many hops can we expect an arbitrary search to take before it finds results? For simplicity, we assume that a search will be satisfied by a single unique peer; this assumption is relaxed in simulation studies in Section 4. We define g_k to be the probability that peer k is the goal peer; $g_k \geq 0$ and $\sum_{k=1}^{N} g_k = 1$. The g_k will vary from peer to peer. The proportion of searches seeking peer k is g_k, and the expected number of hops that will be taken by peers seeking peer k is D/d_k (from Lemma 1), so the expected number of hops per search over all searches (called H) is:

$$H = \sum_{k=1}^{N} g_k \cdot \frac{D}{d_k} \tag{1}$$

How can we minimize the expected number of hops taken by a search message? It turns out that H is minimized when the degree of a peer is proportional to the square root of the popularity of the peer's content. This is the square-root topology.

Theorem 1. *H is minimized when*

$$d_k = \frac{D\sqrt{g_k}}{\sum_{i=1}^{N} \sqrt{g_i}} \tag{2}$$

Proof sketch. We use the method of Lagrange multipliers to minimize equation (1). Our constraint is that $\sum_{k=1}^{N} d_k = D$. Taking the gradient of our constraint, and also of equation (1), and setting them equal to each other gives us a series of N equations of the form $-D \cdot g_k \cdot d_k^{-2} \cdot \hat{\mathbf{u}}_\mathbf{k} = \lambda \hat{\mathbf{u}}_\mathbf{k}$ where λ is the Lagrange multiplier and $\hat{\mathbf{u}}_\mathbf{k}$ is a unit vector. Solving for d_k, and substituting back into the constraint equation (to eliminate λ), gives us the statement of the theorem. The full proof is in [6]. □

Theorem 1 shows that the square-root topology is the optimal topology over a large number of random walk searches. Our analysis shows that D, the total degree in the network, does not impact performance: substituting equation (2) into equation (1) eliminates D. Thus, any value of D that ensures the network is connected is sufficient. Also, the actual topology does not matter, as long as peers have the proper degrees. The result in Lemma 1 is independent of which peers are connected to which other peers.

To construct the square-root topology, each peer k must estimate the popularity of its content (g_k) by dividing Q^k_{match}, the number of queries processed so far that matched the peer's content, by Q^k_{total}, the total number of queries processed by the peer. Since D is unconstrained, we choose $D = d_{max} \cdot \sum_{i=1}^{N} \sqrt{g_i}$, and substituting this equation into equation (2) gives the ideal degree of a peer as $d_k = d_{max} \cdot \sqrt{Q^k_{match}/Q^k_{total}}$. The d_{max} value is a constant we choose and fix as part of the peer-to-peer protocol. Each peer continually tracks its queries and calculates its ideal d_k, and then adds or drops connections to achieve its ideal degree (rounding d_k as necessary). In order to keep the network connected, we also choose a constant d_{min}, which is the minimum number of connections a peer can have.

3   Optimizations to Random Walks

The square-root topology is optimal for simple random walk searches. But are simple random walk searches the best search strategy for the square-root topology? Previous work [11,4,1] has shown that content movement can improve simple random walks significantly. However, we can still optimize random walks for cases where content movement is not feasible. In this section, we describe two optimizations that work together to improve search efficiency for random walks in square-root networks. Both optimizations introduce determinism into the routing process, so to avoid routing loops between the same sets of nodes, statekeeping must be used [11]. With statekeeping, nodes remember where they have forwarded searches and avoid forwarding them to the same neighbors over and over again.

3.1   Biased Document Count

With the *biased document count* technique, peers forward searches to the neighbors that have the most documents. Then, searches are quickly processed over a large amount of content, increasing the probability of finding matches. This technique is similar to biasing random walks toward high degree peers [1], which quickly routes searches to peers that know many other peers (and consequently know about a large amount of content). When it is too expensive for peers to track their neighbors' content, we can do the next best thing: forward queries to peers that have the most content themselves.

3.2   Search Memory

Search memory tracks the "best" peers the search has seen so far, and forwards the search directly to those best peers. Consider for example the network fragment shown in Figure 1. Imagine that a search is at peer p_1. This peer has two neighbors, p_2 (with 1,000 documents) and p_3 (with 500 documents). Using the biased document count technique, peer p_1 would forward the query to p_2. Peer

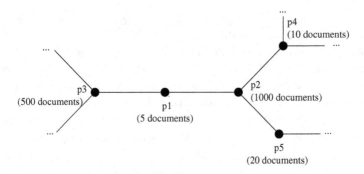

Fig. 1. Search memory example

p_2 has neighbors p_4 (with 10 documents), p_5 (with 20 documents) and p_1 (with 5 documents). Under the biased document count strategy alone, the search would next be forwarded to p_5. However, if the search message tracks that it has seen, but was not forwarded to, peer p_3 with 500 documents, peer p_2 can determine that p_3 is a better choice than any of its neighbors. Peer p_2 would then send the message to p_3 using UDP or a temporary TCP connection.

Searches are likely to encounter many possible peers along their path, and remembering document counts for all of them will significantly increase the size of the search message. For example, consider a system where peers are identified by their 32 bit IP address and 16 bit port number, and a 16 bit document count is "remembered" for each peer. In our simulations of search memory in a 20,000 peer network, the average search message had to remember 7,460 peers and counts, adding 58 KB on average to the search message size. Since peer-to-peer searches otherwise require a few hundred bytes at most, adding 58 KB per message will prohibitively increase the bandwidth used by search messages.

We can approximate search memory at much lower cost by remembering only the best n peers. For example, if a search message remembers 10 peers, this adds only 80 bytes to the message. Our experimental results (reported in the next section) show that even this limited search memory can result in performance improvement.

With the search memory optimization, search messages are not strictly routed according to the overlay topology. However, the overlay is still important as a mechanism for discovering peers; a search message learns about new peers because they are the neighbors of the current peer. Thus, the square-root topology is still a good network organization, because it ensures the probability that a search message learns about a new peer is in proportion to the popularity of the content at the peer.

4   Experimental Results

In this section we present simulation results to confirm our analysis for scenarios where queries may match content at multiple peers. We use simulation because we wish to examine the performance of large networks (i.e., tens of thousands of peers) and it is difficult to deploy that many live peers for research purposes on the Internet.

Our primary metric is to count the total number of messages sent under each search method. We used a message-level peer-to-peer simulator that we have developed to model networks with 20,000 peers storing a total of 631,320 documents. A total of 100,000 searches were submitted to random peers in the system, and each query sought to find 10 results. Because the square-root topology is based on the popularity of documents stored at different peers, it is important to accurately model document and peer popularity; we use a content model based on traces of real documents, peers and queries [5].

First, we conducted an experiment to examine the performance of random walk searches in the square root topology. We generated two square-root topologies: one constructed *a priori* with global knowledge, and another constructed adaptively using only local information at peers (with $d_{max} = 160$, $d_{min} = 3$ and $d_k = 4$ when a peer first joins the network). We compared these topologies to low-skew ($\alpha = 0.58$) and high-skew ($\alpha = 0.74$) power-law networks, both generated using the PLOD algorithm [15].

Figure 2 shows the number of messages per search, calculated as a running average every 1,000 queries. As the figure shows, the adaptive square-root topology quickly converges to the ideal *a priori* square root topology (after about 8,000 queries). The square-root topology is significantly better than the power-law topologies, requiring 26 percent fewer messages than the low-skew network, and 45 percent fewer messages than the high-skew network.

Other results (not shown) indicate that the square-root topology is in fact better than a power-law topology for several other types of peer-to-peer routing techniques, and when statekeeping [11] is used. In fact, the square-root topol-

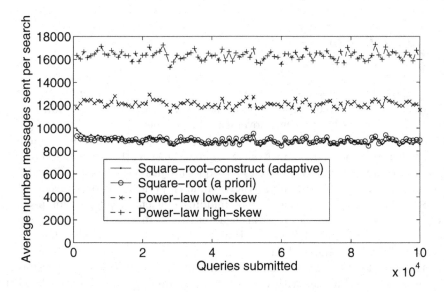

Fig. 2. The square-root topology versus power-law topologies

Table 1. Results for optimizations

Routing	Topology	Msgs per search
Random walk	Power-law (high skew)	16340
Random walk	Power-law (low skew)	12110
Random walk	**Square-root**	8850
Doc count	**Square-root**	7780
Doc count + memory	**Square-root**	7030

ogy is often best even when content movement is allowed. Detailed results are reported in [6].

Next, we conducted an experiment to measure the effect of the biased document count and search memory optimizations for searches in the square-root topology. Table 1 shows the results averaged over 100,000 queries. As the table shows, using the biased document count and limited memory optimizations provided good performance, with 21 percent fewer messages than random walks in the square-root topology. Even though we used limited memory, we achieved high performance; for comparison, unlimited search memory only reduced the message cost by a further 3 percent in our experiments. The combination of all three of our techniques (square-root topology, biased document count and limited memory) results in 42 percent fewer messages than random walks in the low skew power-law topology, and 57 percent fewer messages than random walks in the high-skew power-law topology. Clearly, it is possible to achieve high performance even without content movement.

Other optimizations may be possible to further improve performance, and examining such optimizations is worthy of further study.

5   Related Work

A variety of techniques for efficient peer-to-peer searches have been proposed. Many investigators have proposed ways to move or replicate content, or replicate indexes over content, in order to improve performance [11,4,20,8,3,2,7,19,17,18,21,14,4]. For applications where content movement is too expensive or resisted by peers, other techniques must be developed. There have been several proposed techniques that do not use content movement, such as expanding ring [11] or directed breadth first search [20]. We argue that these techniques are just a starting point, and that there is unexplored potential for further significant performance enhancements.

Some investigators have looked at building efficient topologies for peer-to-peer searches. For example, Pandurangan et al [16] discuss building low diameter networks for efficient flooding. However, random walk searches have been shown to be more scalable than flooding [11]. Lv et al [12] presented a dynamic algorithm for load balancing when random walks are used. It may be possible to combine these techniques with our square-root topology in order to take both popularity and peer capacity into account.

Several investigators have examined peer-to-peer systems analytically, including models for peer behavior [9], download traffic [10], and so on. To our knowledge, there have been no published analytical results on the optimal topology for random walk searches.

6   Conclusions

We have argued that new techniques must be developed to deal with networks where it is infeasible to move or replicate content. Although many of the most effective techniques developed so far utilize content movement, we believe that progress can be made on efficient searching while leaving content at its original peer. We have presented three techniques as support for our assertion, and as a starting point for further investigation. First, we have shown that for simple random walk searches, the optimal topology is a square-root topology, not a power-law network. This topology can be constructed using purely local information at peers. Second, biasing searches towards peers with a large amount of content further improves performance. Third, adding search memory allows messages to be quickly routed to the best peers. These techniques show the viability of further research into routing in unstructured networks, even when we cannot move or replicate content.

References

1. L. Adamic, R. Lukose, A. Puniyani, and B. Huberman. Search in power-law networks. *Phys. Rev. E*, 64:46135–46143, 2001.
2. M. Bawa, R. J. Bayardo Jr., S. Rajagopalan, and E. Shekita. Make it fresh, make it quick — searching a network of personal webservers. In *Proc. WWW*, 2003.
3. Y. Chawathe, S. Ratnasamy, L. Breslau, N. Lanham, and S. Shenker. Making Gnutella-like P2P systems scalable. In *Proc. SIGCOMM*, 2003.
4. E. Cohen and S. Shenker. Replication strategies in unstructured peer-to-peer networks. In *Proc. SIGCOMM*, 2002.
5. B. F. Cooper. A content model for evaluating peer-to-peer searching techniques. In *Proc. ACM/IFIP/USENIX Middleware Conference*, 2004.
6. B. F. Cooper. An optimal overlay topology for routing peer-to-peer searches. Technical report, available at http://www.cc.gatech.edu/~cooperb/-pubs/squareroot.pdf, April 2005.
7. B.F. Cooper and H. Garcia-Molina. Studying search networks with SIL. In *Proc. IPTPS*, 2003.
8. A. Crespo and H. Garcia-Molina. Routing indices for peer-to-peer systems. In *Proc. ICDCS*, 2002.
9. Z. Ge, D.R. Figueiredo, S. Jaiswal, J. Kurose, and D. Towsley. Modeling peer-peer file sharing systems. In *Proc. INFOCOM*, 2003.
10. K.P. Gummadi, R.J. Dunn, S. Saroiu, S.D. Gribble, H.M. Levy, and J. Zahorjan. Measurement, modeling and analysis of a peer-to-peer file-sharing workload. In *Proc. SOSP*, 2003.
11. Q. Lv, P. Cao, E. Cohen, K. Li, and S. Shenker. Search and replication in unstructured peer-to-peer networks. In *Proc. Int'l Conf. on Supercomputing (ICS)*, 2002.

12. Q. Lv, S. Ratnasamy, and S. Shenker. Can heterogeneity make Gnutella scalable? In *Proc. IPTPS*, 2002.

13. R. Motwani and P. Raghavan. *Randomized Algorithms*. Cambridge University Press, New York, NY, 1995.

14. W. Nejdl, M. Wolpers, W. Siberski, C. Schmitz, M. Schlosser, I. Brunkhorst, and A. Loser. Super-peer-based routing and clustering strategies for RDF-based peer-to-peer networks. In *Proc. WWW*, 2003.

15. C. Palmer and J. Steffan. Generating network topologies that obey power laws. In *Proc. GLOBECOM*, 2000.

16. G. Pandurangan, P. Raghavan, and E. Upfal. Building low-diameter P2P networks. In *Proc. IEEE FOCS*, 2001.

17. S. Ratnasamy, P. Francis, M. Handley, R. Karp, and S. Shenker. A scalable content-addressable network. In *Proc. SIGCOMM*, Aug. 2001.

18. A. Rowstron and P. Druschel. Pastry: Scalable, decentralized object location and routing for large-scale peer-to-peer systems. In *Proc. IFIP/ACM International Conference on Distributed Systems Platforms*, 2001.

19. I. Stoica, R. Morris, D. Karger, M. F. Kaashoek, and H. Balakrishnan. Chord: A scalable peer-to-peer lookup service for internet applications. In *Proc. SIGCOMM*, Aug. 2001.

20. B. Yang and H. Garcia-Molina. Efficient search in peer-to-peer networks. In *Proc. ICDCS*, 2002.

21. B. Yang and H. Garcia-Molina. Designing a super-peer network. In *Proc. ICDE*, 2003.

Practical Locality-Awareness for Large Scale Information Sharing*

Ittai Abraham[1], Ankur Badola[2], Danny Bickson[1], Dahlia Malkhi[3], Sharad Maloo[2], and Saar Ron[1]

[1] The Hebrew University of Jerusalem, Jerusalem, Israel
{ittaia, daniel51, ender}@cs.huji.ac.il
[2] IIT Bombay, India
{badola, maloo}@cse.iitb.ac.in
[3] Microsoft Research Silicon Valley and The Hebrew University of Jerusalem, Israel
dalia@microsoft.com

Abstract. Tulip is an overlay for routing, searching and publish-lookup information sharing. It offers a unique combination of the advantages of both structured and unstructured overlays, that does not co-exist in any previous solution. Tulip features locality awareness (stretch 2) and fault tolerance (nodes can route around failures). It supports under the same roof exact keyed-lookup, nearest copy location, and global information search. Tulip has been deployed and its locality and fault tolerance properties verified over a real wide-area network.

1 Introduction

Driven by the need to bridge the gap between practically deployable P2P systems, which should be easy and robust, and academic designs which have nice scalability properties, we present the Tulip overlay. The Tulip information sharing overlay obtains a combination of features not previously met simultaneously in any system. In a nutshell, these can be characterized as follows:

Locality-awareness: The algorithms for searching and retrieving information are designed to provably contain every load as locally as possible. Formally, this is expressed using the standard network-theoretical measure *stretch*, which bounds the ratio between routes taken in the algorithm and optimal routes. Formally, the Tulip overlay guarantees stretch-2 routing.

Flexibility and Simplicity: All protocols have firm, formal basis, but intentionally accommodate fuzzy deployment which applies optimizations that deviate from the theory, in order to cope with high churn and scalability.

Diverse tools: Tulip addresses under the same roof exact-match keyed lookup, nearest object location, and global data search.

Experimentation: In addition to formal proofs of locality and fault tolerance we analyze Tulip's performance with real measurements on a real planetary-scale

---

* Work supported in part by EC *Evergrow*.

M. Castro and R. van Renesse (Eds.): IPTPS 2005, LNCS 3640, pp. 173–181, 2005.

deployment. Tulip is deployed and tested over PlanetLab. Its locality awareness and fault tolerance properties are evaluated in a WAN setting. Furthermore, experience gained from practical deployment is fed back in Tulip to the formal design.

Tulip adopts the successful space-to-communication tradeoff introduced by Kelips [4], which allows nodes to maintain links to many, but not to all other nodes, and achieve highly efficient information dissemination paths. In Tulip, each node maintains roughly $2\sqrt{n}\log n$ links, where n is the number of nodes. Routes take 2 hops. Search or event data can be disseminated to $O(\sqrt{n})$ nodes, and retrieved from $O(\sqrt{n})$ nodes.

We believe this tradeoff is the right one for P2P overlays. In terms of space, even a large system of several millions of nodes requires storing only several thousands node addresses, which is not a significant burden. That said, this does not lead us to attempt at maintaining global information as in [3]. Indeed, we maintain sufficient slack to tolerate a large degree of stale and/or missing information. As a result of this design choice, Tulip exhibits extremely good fault tolerance (see Section 4). Furthermore, this slack also enables *static resilience*, which means that even as the system undergoes repair it can continue routing data efficiently. Some previous DHTs like Kademlia [5] and Babmboo [6] appear to cope well with churn with a lower node degree and more rigid structure. However, we believe that having $O(\sqrt{n})$ links with a semi-structured two hop network may give a very high level of resiliency.

Tulip enhances the Kelips approach in a number of important ways, detailed henceforth. The first feature in Tulip is **locality awareness**. Building self maintaining overlay networks for information sharing in a manner that exhibits locality-awareness is crucial for the viability of large internets.

Tulip guarantees that the costs of finding and retrieving information are proportional to the actual distances of the interacting parties. Building on the formal foundations laid by Abraham et al. in [1], Tulip provides provable stretch 2 round-trip routing between all sources and destinations [1]. Tulip extends the formal algorithm in [1] with methods that accommodate changes in the network. These include background communication mechanisms that bring links up to date with provably sub-linear costs.

The second feature of Tulip is its **flexibility and simplicity**. Structured p2p overlays often appear difficult to deploy in practical, Internet-size networks. In particular, they are sensitive to changes and require substantial repair under churn. They lack flexibility in that they require very accurate links in order to operate correctly. And faced with high dynamism, they may break quite easily.

By maintaining $O(\sqrt{n}\log n)$ links at each node and a simple two hop design, Tulip has sufficient redundancy to maintain a good level of service even when some links are broken, missing or misplaced. A multi-hop algorithm similar to Kelips [4] allows routing around failed or missing links with $O(1)$ communication

---

[1] The standard definition of stretch, as in [1], looks at source-destination routing but in a DHT it is natural to examine round-trip routing since the source requires a reply from the target.

costs. Furthermore, the repair procedures can be done in the background, while heuristics keep Tulip's service quality even while it is under repair.

The third feature of our system is its support of **diverse tools** for information sharing. This goal stems from our vision of a convergence of technologies empowering network leaf-nodes. These technologies include overlay networks supporting Grid and p2p file sharing, web caching, and large scale content delivery services. Though these are different services, the overlays that support them are converging toward a common set of protocols. The Tulip routing overlay can be utilized as an overlay for keyed lookup, for finding nearest copies of, replicated objects, for event notification and for global searching.

We have built a **real deployment** of the Tulip overlay and have conducted experimentation on wide area networks (WANs). All of our protocols are deployed and tested extensively over the PlanetLab WAN test-bed. In particular, Tulip's locality behavior, its stretch factor, distance measurements and fault tolerance are all ascertained over a real-life, planetary-wide network. To the best of our knowledge, our stretch performance data are the first to be measured over a real WAN, not via synthetic simulation. We also assess Tulip's behavior under intentional and unintentional churn.

2   Formal Foundations

The Tulip system builds on the locality-aware compact routing algorithm of Abraham et al. in [1]. It uses $O(\sqrt{n}\log n)$ space per node, where n is the number of nodes in the system. It provides a 2-hop routing strategy whose cost over optimal routing (the *stretch*) is at most 2. Continuous background gossip mechanism with a reasonable overhead is used to maintain and update the system and guarantee quick convergence after changes in the system.

Let $d(s,t)$ denote the communication cost between nodes s and t. It is natural to assume that $d()$ forms a metric space. However, to be precise, our lookup stretch result requires only that $d()$ is symmetric, or that it upholds the triangle inequality. In addition, the analysis of message complexity of the join algorithm and the protocol for finding nearest copies of data assume growth bounded densities, defined as follows. A growth-bound limits the number of nodes in a ball of radius $2r$ by a constant multiple of the number of nodes within radius r.

Vicinity balls. For every node $u \in V$, let the vicinity of u be the set of $\sqrt{n}\log n$ closest nodes to u according to $d()$, breaking ties by lexicographical order of node names.

Coloring. Our construction uses a partition of nodes into $\sqrt{n}$ color-sets, with the following two properties:

(i) Every color-set has at most $2\sqrt{n}$ nodes.
(ii) Every node has in its vicinity at least one node from every other color-set.

Each node belongs to one of the color groups determined by using a consistent hashing function to map node's identifier (IP address and port number) to one of the $\sqrt{n}$ values. This mapping is done by taking the first $\log \sqrt{n}$ bits of the hash value. We denote by $c(u)$ node u's color. The use of cryptographic hash function such as SHA-1 ensures that the expected number of nodes in each group is around $\sqrt{n}$, and is under $\sqrt{n} \log n$ with high probability.

Routing information. Each node u maintains information classified under:

• *Vicinity list*: From each of the other color groups in the system, node u maintains information about the closest $\log n$ nodes of a particular color.

• *Color list*: A list containing information about all nodes belonging to the same color as u, i.e, to the color-set $c(u)$.

Each entry also carries an additional field of network distance. Each of the lists is sorted based on the relative distance value from the node.

Keyed Lookup. The lookup tool supports exact-match keyed lookup and routing for objects or nodes whose names are known precisely. It guarantees locating any target with lookup stretch of at most 2, and with up to 2 lookup hops.

An object is stored on the node whose identifier is the longest prefix of the object's hash value. Objects are also mapped to colors by taking the first $\log \sqrt{n}$ bits of their hash. Given a source node s that is looking for an object o with color $c(o)$ that is stored in node t:

• *First hop*: Node s routes to the node w in s's vicinity list that has the same color as the object $c(w) = c(o)$, and whose identifier is closest to the object's hash. If this node contains the object then the lookup has stretch 1.

• *Second hop*: Otherwise, using w's color list, s routes to node t (this is possible since $c(o) = c(w) = c(t)$). In this case we have $d(s, w) \leq d(s, t)$ and from symmetry the cost of the path $s \rightsquigarrow w \rightsquigarrow s \rightsquigarrow t \rightsquigarrow s$ is at most *twice* the cost of the path $s \rightsquigarrow t \rightsquigarrow s$ (see Figure 1).

Note that, the above scheme is *iterative*, and achieves stretch 2 without requiring triangle inequality. A *recursive* version would give stretch 2 but require triangle inequality, without requiring symmetry.

Finding nearest copy. This mechanism allows objects to be stored on any node the designer wants. Moreover, several copies of the same object may exist on different nodes. Assuming latencies form a metric space, we guarantee to retrieve the copy closest to the initiator of the searching node, with lookup stretch of at most 4, and with up to 2 hops.

Let node x store a replica of object o. A pointer of the form $\langle o \rightarrow x \rangle$ is stored in the following nodes:

• *Vicinity pointers:* All nodes u such that x is in u's vicinity list store a pointer $\langle o \rightarrow x \rangle$. Under the growth bound assumption, only $O(\sqrt{n})$ nodes will store such a pointer.

• *Color pointers:* All nodes u such that $c(u) = c(o)$ store a pointer $\langle o \rightarrow u(o) \rangle$ where $u(o)$ is the name of the node closest to u that stores a replica of o.

Lookup uses the pointers to shortcut directly to a replica. If the source does not have a direct pointer to the desired object it routes to the node w in its vicinity such that $c(w) = c(o)$. In such a case, node w will have a pointer to the closest replica from w.

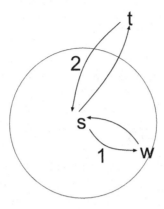

Fig. 1. Example of a 2 hop, stretch 2 round-trip path from source s to destination t and back

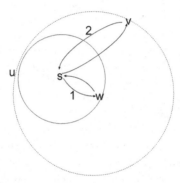

Fig. 2. Example of 2 hop, stretch 4, nearest copy search from s to v and back

• *Analysis.* Given source s searching for object o, let u be the closest node to s storing a replica of o, let w be the node in the vicinity of s such that $c(w) = c(o)$ let v be the closest node to w storing a replica of o. Then $d(w,v) \le d(w,u)$ and by triangle inequality $d(s,v) \le d(s,w) + d(w,v) \le 3d(s,u)$, summing up and using symmetry $d(s,w)+d(w,s)+d(s,v)+d(v,s) \le d(s,u)+d(s,u)+3d(s,u)+3d(s,u)$, hence the ratio between the cost of lookup and the cost of directly accessing the closest replica (stretch) is at most 4 (see Figure 2).

Global information search. This tool builds a *locality aware quorum system.* Information can be published to a global shared memory and later users can perform arbitrary search queries on all the published information. The search mechanism is locality aware, it requires communication only with nodes in the vicinity of the query.

Publishing an object o is done by storing information about o on all the nodes whose color is the closest to o's hash value. Each node may either store the full o content, or summary data used for searching o, along with a pointer to the actual stored location. This creates roughly $\sqrt{n}$ replicas of the information.

Global searching is done in a locality aware manner. An initiator sends a query only to the nodes that are in its vicinity list. The computation of a query is maintained locally since each search involves only the $\sqrt{n}$ closest nodes. This is the first read/write quorum system whose read operations are locality aware.

3   Maintaining Locality Under Churn

Considerable effort is invested in Tulip's deployment in order to deal with the dynamics of scalable and wide spread networks. This includes protocols for node joining and deletion, and a background refresh mechanism that maintains locality under churn. Surprisingly, under reasonable assumptions, all of these mechanisms have sub-linear complexity. Our deployment also entails multi-hop query routing to cope with churn simultaneously with ongoing repair. The evaluation of this heuristical protocol is done experimentally.

Joining: A joining node requires one existing contact node in the system. The mechanism for obtaining a contact node can be a web site or a distributed directory such as DNS. Our approach for handling joins is for the joiner to first acquire a somewhat rough initial vicinity. Then, through normal background refresh mechanism (detailed below), the joiner gathers more accurate information about its vicinity and its color list.

More specifically, a joiner u first queries its contact point for the list of nodes in its vicinity. From this list, u selects a random node x. It then finds a node w from x's color list that is closest to u. Under reasonable growth bounded density assumptions w's vicinity has a sizable overlap with the u's vicinity. Node u adopts w's vicinity as its own initial vicinity, and informs its vicinity about its own arrival.

The communication complexity of the approximate closest-node finding and the establishment of an initial vicinity is $O(1)$ and $O(\sqrt{n}\log n)$ computational complexity.

Deletion: A departing or a failed node gradually automatically disappears from the routing tables of all other nodes, once they fail to communicate with it. Naturally, the departure of a node also means the loss of the data it holds. Clearly, any robust information system must replicate the critical information it stores. We leave out of the discussion in this short paper such issues.

Refresh mechanisms: Existing view and contact information is refreshed periodically within and across color groups. During each cycle, a node re-evaluates the distance of some nodes in its two lists (vicinity and color), and refreshes entries in them. Formally, these mechanisms maintain the following property: An individual node that misses information or has incorrect information (e.g., this is the case of a new joiner) learns information that significantly improves its vicinity and color list with $O(1)$ communication overhead and $O(\sqrt{n}\log n)$ computation overhead.

All our methods have sub linear communication complexity of $O(1)$ and $O(\sqrt{n}\log n)$ computational complexity. The three methods used in each cycle for refresh are as follows:

• *Vicinity list merging:* Node u chooses a random node x in its vicinity list and requests for x's vicinity list, while sending its own vicinity list to that random node (a combined push and pull flat model gossip). Both nodes merge the two vicinities, while keeping the list sorted according to distance and maintaining (if possible) at least one member from each existing color in the list. Intuitively, due to the expected overlap between the vicinities of close nodes, this step provides for quick propagation of knowledge about changes within the vicinity. This mechanism is quick and efficient in practice. However, formally it cannot guarantee by itself that nodes obtain all relevant vicinity information.

• *Same color merging:* Node u contacts a random node x from its color list and and requests for x's color list, while sending its own color list to that random node. Again, both nodes merge the two color lists.

• *Failed nodes detection:* When a failed node is detected (a node that had failed to respond to an outgoing communication), that node is immediately removed from all active nodes' lists. That node is then inserted into a failed nodes list, which also holds information about the failure detection time (a node's "death certificate"). This list is being propagated in two methods:

1. *Passive fault tolerance mechanism:* a node which is refreshing its color or vicinity list also sends its failed nodes list with its request and receives the other node's failed nodes list with the response. Both nodes then merge both lists, and remove all new found failed nodes from all their active nodes lists.

2. *Active fault tolerance mechanism:* a node that sends a routing info request to a node x also pushes its failed nodes list as a part of the request. Before processing the request, the receiving node merges its own failed nodes list with the received list, and removes the new found failed nodes from all active nodes lists. This somewhat prevents x from sending a next hop route data which includes a newly detected failed node.

A node is removed from the failed nodes list only after a period of time which is greater then the estimated gossip propagation time in the network.

Multi-Hop Query Routing: The scale and wide spreading of the systems we envision implies that the information held at nodes' routing lists at any snapshot in time may contain inaccessible nodes, failed links, and inaccurate distances. Although eventually the refresh mechanisms repair such errors, the system must continue routing data meanwhile. To this end, we adopt similar, heuristic strategies as in Kelips [4] to accommodate changes, while enhancing them with locality consideration, and in addition, evaluating them with real wide-area experimentation (in the next section).

Given a source node s that is looking for an object that is stored in node t, the two heuristics employed are as follows:

- If s cannot contact any node with color $c(t)$ from its vicinity list, then it contacts a random node x in the vicinity list and forwards the query for x to handle.
- If during a lookup, an interim node w with the target's color $c(t) = c(w)$ does not have t in its color list, then w responds with sending the details of a node v from its vicinity list, drawn randomly with preference to closer nodes.

4   Experimental Results

The Tulip client is implemented in C++ and the overlay is fully operational. Tulip is deployed in 220 nodes over the PlanetLab wide-area testbed [2] as of October 2004.

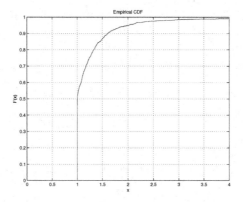

Fig. 3. Cumulative density of lookup stretch

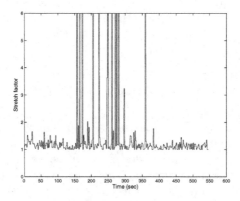

Fig. 4. Average stretch over time while randomly killing half the nodes at time 150

Figure 3 depicts the actual routing stretch experienced in our deployed system. The graph plots the cumulative density function of the stretch factor of one thousand experiments. In each experiment, one pair of nodes is picked at random and the routing stretch factor between them is measured. The measured stretch factor is the ratio between lookup duration and the direct access duration: The lookup duration is the time a lookup takes to establish connections, reach the destination node storing the object via the Tulip overlay, and return to the source. The direct access duration is the time it takes to form a direct (source to destination) TCP connection and to get a reply back to the source.

The graph shows that about 60 percent of the routes has stretch 1, and therefore experience nearly optimal delay. Over 90 percent of the routes incur stretch lower than 2, and stretch 3 is achieved in nearly 98 percent of the routes. These results are comparable, and to some extent better, than the simulation stretch results provided for Pastry [7] and Bamboo [6].

The graph also demonstrates that due to dynamic nature of the network and due to fuzziness, stretch 4 is exceeded in about one percent of the cases. The graph is cut at stretch 4, and thus excludes a very small number of extremely costly routes; these do occur, unfortunately, in the real world deployment, due to failures and drastic changes in the network conditions.

Figure 4 depicts fault tolerance tests results on the PlanetLab testbed. We have used 200 Tulip nodes on different computers. Lookup requests were induced into the system at a rate of 2 per second. The graph depicts average stretch of every 4 lookup requests (reflecting two seconds each). At time 150 we randomly killed half the nodes in the system. The results show that after time 300 the systems has almost completely regained its locality properties.

References

1. I. Abraham, C. Gavoille, D. Malkhi, N. Nisan, and M. Thorup. Compact name-independent routing with minimum stretch. The Sixteenth ACM Symposium on Parallelism in Algorithms and Architectures (SPAA 04).
2. Brent Chun, David Culler, Timothy Roscoe, Andy Bavier, Larry Peterson, Mike Wawrzoniak, and Mic Bowman. Planetlab: an overlay testbed for broad-coverage services. *SIGCOMM Comput. Commun. Rev.*, 33(3):3–12, 2003.
3. A. Gupta, B. Liskov, and R. Rodrigues. One hop lookups for peer-to-peer overlays. In *Ninth Workshop on Hot Topics in Operating Systems (HotOS-IX)*, pages 7–12, Lihue, Hawaii, May 2003.
4. I. Gupta, K. Birman, P. Linga, A. Demers, and R. van Renesse. Kelips: Building an efficient and stable P2P DHT through increased memory and background overhead. In *Proceedings of the 2nd International Workshop on Peer-to-Peer Systems (IPTPS '03)*, 2003.
5. P. Maymounkov and D. Mazieres. Kademlia: A peer-to-peer information system based on the xor metric. In *Proceedings of IPTPS02*, March 2002.
6. S. Rhea, D. Geels, T. Roscoe, and J. Kubiatowicz. Handling churn in a dht. Technical Report Technical Report UCB//CSD-03-1299, The University of California, Berkeley, December 2003.
7. A. Rowstron and P. Druschel. Pastry: Scalable, distributed object location and routing for large-scale peer-to-peer systems. In *IFIP/ACM International Conference on Distributed Systems Platforms (Middleware)*, pages 329–350, 2001.

An Empirical Study of Free-Riding Behavior in the Maze P2P File-Sharing System

Mao Yang [1,*], Zheng Zhang[2], Xiaoming Li[1], and Yafei Dai[1]

[1] School of Electronics Engineering and Computer Science,
Beijing University, 100871 Beijing, China
{ym, lxm, dyf}@net.pku.edu.cn
[2] Microsoft Research Asia, Beijing, China
{zzhang}@microsoft.com

Abstract. Maze[1] is a P2P file-sharing system with an active and large user base. It is developed, deployed and operated by an academic research team. As such, it offers ample opportunities to conduct experiments to under-stand user behavior. Embedded in Maze is a set of incentive policies designed to encourage sharing and contribution. This paper presents an in-depth analysis of the effectiveness of the incentive policies and how users react to them. We found that in general the policies have been effective. But they also encourage the more selfish users to cheat by whitewashing their ac-counts as a variation of Sybil attack. We examine multiple factors that may contribute to the free-riding behavior. Our conclusions are that upload speed, NAT and amount of shared files are not the problems, and selfish behavior is demonstrated more by shorter online time. Since free-riders are also avid consumers of popular files, we suggest a two-pronged approach to reduce free-riding further: mechanisms to direct queries to sources that would otherwise be free-riders, and policies to encourage users make their resources more available.

1 Introduction

Maze[1] is a peer-to-peer file-sharing application that is developed and deployed by an academic research team. Maze is similar in structure to Napster, with a centralized, cluster-based search engine, but is additionally outfitted with a social network of peers. This hybrid architecture offers keyword-based search, simple locality-based download optimizations, and also reduces dependency on the central cluster. Maze has a set of evolving incentive policies which, complemented by direct user feedbacks via forum, discourage free-loading, a problem plaguing many similar networks. More details of the Maze architecture are available in [2][3].

Maze is in its 4th major software release, and is currently deployed across a large number of hosts inside China's internal network. As of October 2004, Maze includes a user population of about 410K users and supports searches on more than 150 million files totaling over 200TB of data. At any given time, there are over 10K users online simultaneously, and over 200K transfers occurring per day.

---

[*] Work done as intern in MSR-Asia.
[1] This work is partially supported by NSFC grant 90412010 (China).

M. Castro and R. van Renesse (Eds.): IPTPS 2005, LNCS 3640, pp. 182 – 192, 2005.
© Springer-Verlag Berlin Heidelberg 2005

Maze provides an excellent platform to observe many important activities inside the network and some of our measurement results have been reported in [2]. In this paper, we focus on the reputation and incentive aspects of the Maze architecture. We found that, in general, the incentive policies are effective to encourage contribution. However, one consequence is that free-riders start cheating by account whitewashing. The fact that the free-riders are avid consumers of popular con-tents should have made them the sources of contributors. However, the slow updating of the Maze central indexing makes it harder to direct queries to these users. Looking at the free-riding behavior further, we found that one of the more direct measurements of the selfish degree is the online session time: free-riding users usually stay only one-third as long as the server-like users. Although 40% of users are behind firewall, NAT is generally not the source to blame, nor is the upload speed. However, high upload speed and not being hindered by firewall are advantageous for motivated users to contribute.

The roadmap of the paper is as follows. Section-2 gives a quick overview of the Maze architecture. Section-3 describes the data collected . Section-4 is the main body of this paper, where we take a closer look at the incentive policies and the free-riding behavior in Maze. Secition-5 contains related work and we conclude in Section-6.

2   Maze Architecture Overview

Maze grew out of the need to address the downloading problem of the FTP part of a Web search project called T-net[4]. As the service became popular, the limited number of FTP servers has led to degrading performance. The first step of Maze is to allow parallel downloading from peer users. Each peer will authenticate itself to the Maze central server, send periodical heartbeats, and upload the index of the files that it has in its local Maze directory. This allows full-text queries to be conducted over the set of the online peers. A download request fans out to multiple sources to for different chunks of the file, with simple locality hint that gives priority to peers that share more prefix of the initiator's IP address. Maze has an evolving set of incentive policies designed to discourage free-loadings. The policies award or deduct points according to user behaviors. At the end of each transaction, the peers involved report to the central server which adjusts their points accordingly.

Recognizing that we eventually need to reduce the dependencies upon the central server, Maze in addition let each peer to have several peer lists. The first is the "friend-list," which is bootstrapped from the central server with a list of other peers when the user first registered, and can be modified later on. Frequently, the user adds those who have satisfied her queries before. Thus, the friend-lists collectively form a social network that evolves continuously. The second is the "neighborhood-list," which is given by the central server upon a peer logon, contains a set of online peers sharing the B-class address. Finally, Maze gives a small list called "good peer-list" of peers who currently have high reputation scores as an incentive to reward good sharing behaviors. Users on this list can be thought as a "celebrities" in the entire user population. A peer can recursively browse the contents of the Maze directories of any level of these lists, and directly initiate downloading when they find interesting contents. These lists form the bases over which we plan to add P2P search capabilities. As we will show shortly, these lists comprise a surprisingly large source of finding interesting files.

A NAT client can download from a non-NAT client, or another NAT client behind the same firewall. However, we have not implemented relay mechanism and currently a NAT user can not download from another NAT user behind a different firewall.

Maze also has an associated online forum. This is where many discussions among the users take place, and is also the venue that Maze developers gather feedbacks. Our experience has proven that this forum is invaluable.

3   Data Collected

The Maze5.04 release we issued on September 26th has a component to report their download behavior includes the source or sink of the transfer, file type, file size, file signature (MD5) and the transfer bit rate. The central servers also log the following information per client: online time, IP address and network information (such as NAT or non-NAT), the files shared, the change of the user's reputation point, and finally the register information. Table 1 gives the summary of the logs. Unless otherwise stated, results are analyzed using logs from 9/28 to 10/28. We use mysql to process these logs.

Notice that that the number of transfers is almost 3 times more than the number of queries. This suggests that at most one-third of download follows a query to the central server. What that means is that more than two-third of transfers occur as a result of browsing the three peer lists. Thus, it is evident that the Maze social links have been effective.

Table 1. Summary of log information (9/28~10/28)

Log duration	30 days
# of active users	130,205
# of NAT users	51,613
# of transfer files	6,831,019
Total transfer size	97,276GB
Average transfer file size	14,240KB
Average transfer speed	327,841 bps
# of unique transfer files	1,588,409
# of querying	2,282,625

4   Reputation and Incentive Mechanism

In this section, we will start with a description of the Maze incentive policies, and then look at its overall impact overtime. Next, we will focus on the free-riders, followed by a more detailed analysis of possible courses of free-riding.

4.1   The Maze Incentive Policies

In Maze, we use an incentive system where users are rewarded points for uploading, and expend points for successful downloads. Recall that Maze has an active forum.

This point system was discussed in the forum and agreed-upon before implemented. The rules are:

1. New users are initialized with 4096 points.
2. Uploads: +1.5 points per MB uploaded
3. Downloads:
   - -1.0/MB downloaded within 100MB
   - -0.7/MB per additional MB between 100MB and 400MB
   - -0.4/MB between 400MB and 800MB
   - -0.1/MB per additional MB over 800MB
4. Download requests are ordered by T = requestTime − 3logP, where P is a user's point total.
5. Users with P < 512 have a download bandwidth of 200Kb/s.

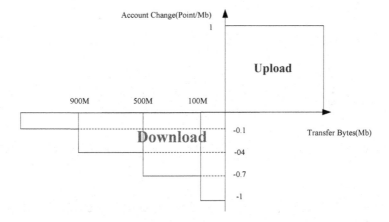

Fig. 1. The account system

Maze uses service differentiation as the way of rewarding/punishing good/bad behavior. It was designed to give downloading preference to users with high scores. These users add to their request time a negative offset whose magnitude grows logarithmically with their score. In contrast, a bandwidth quota is applied to downloads of users with lower scores (<512). Although the quota seems to be high, it is consistent with our observation that a large number of users have access to high-bandwidth links. Finally, while we encouraged uploads and deducted points for downloads, we recognized that the majority of bytes exchanged on Maze were large multimedia files, and made the download point adjustment graduated to weigh less heavily on extremely large files. For instance, the user will spend all the start points if she downloads 4k 1MB size files, or 133 400MB size files, or about 9 800MB size files.

Our policies award at least 50% more points for uploading than downloading. This is based on our belief that the contributing users should earn more rights to download. For instance, when a user has uploaded 267MB files, he will earn enough points to download 628MB files. Therefore, those who contribute contents shall see their points increase quickly. On the other hand, if a user downloads more than uploads, his score will decrease over time, and will eventually drop to so low as he may decide to leave the system altogether. Since the number of downloads and uploads are equal, the total points of the entire Maze population will grow. For the time being, we do not believe this is an issue.

For convenience of discussion, we will define the server-like and client-like users for those users whose points are above and below their initial point (4096), respectively. As of 10/28, the ratio between these two classes of users is 4.4:1. We found that client-like users are responsible for 51% downloads but only 7.5% uploads. These statistics suggest the existence of free-loading. Fig. 2 depicts the CDF curves of number of upload and download activities against user reputation scores. Our reputation metrics has reflected the user behavior in general.

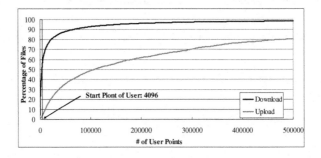

Fig. 2. CDF distribution of uploads and downloads against user reputation scores up to 500000

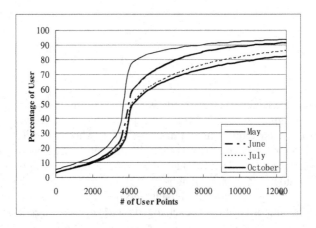

Fig. 3. CDF distribution of user points up to 12000 for the month of May, June, July and October

One of the top score users that we interviewed share out many popular course materials, which are video files of various formats and are large enough to earn points quickly. The motivation for a Maze user to earn extremely high score is primarily to gain social status in the community, rather than earning points to download. There seems to exist a self-enforcing cycle that propels the riches get richer.

A set of good incentive policies should have the net effect of moving users towards more sharing behaviors. Since its very first release, Maze has the incentive policies in place. However, before 5/20 of 2004 (the release date of Maze3.02), the policies are quite different. For each MB of transfer, a download will deduct one point, whereas an upload will add one point. Furthermore, the scores are not used in anyway as to enforce the QoS measures that this new set of policies do. The new policies were extensively discussed in the Maze online forum, and officially launched in May. Over the period of several months, we are able to gather the scores and observe the effects.

The impact of the policies is best understood with the upload and the download logs, which are only available after the Maze5.04 release of 9/26. The complete information that we have are the reputation scores, which are kept on the Maze central server. Fig. 3 shows the changes of the reputation CDFs from May till October. There are around 20~30% of users who stay at their starting points (4096); these are the registered but inactive users. These set of curves are difficult to analyze because, as we mentioned earlier, the total point of the system continue to increase and thus the "center of the gravity" shall move towards right unless there are absolutely no activities. However, we do believe that the policies are effective to some extent. For instance, the proportion of client-like users decreases from 76.4 % in May, to 56.2% in June, to 48.1% in July and finally to 46.8% in October. Also, if the policies were ineffective to change user behavior, the client-like users shall see their point totals drop quite rapidly. This does not happen. In the future, we will collect more statistics to study this aspect.

4.2 The Free-Riders

For simplicity of discussion, we will call the client-like users the free-riders. When a free-rider sees her point drops, she has several choices. For instance, she may start to aggressively promote himself. Indeed, we have found that once a request for content was posed on the forum, it is soon followed by many invitations – typically from those with low points – to advise the availability of the content. There are several things a user can do to cheat the system. One route he might pursue, for instance, is simply to leave the system and re-enter with a different Maze user ID. These are the whitewashers. Whitewashers can be detected, but we currently do not ban them. If a user has several Maze accounts, he can mount the more elaborate Sybil's attack [5] by downloading among these accounts to earn credits for each one of them. We know for a fact that these behaviors exist, and are investigating how much fraction they account for.

Fig. 4 plots the breakdown of user population according to how many different user IDs they own from the time that they first registered. The last bracket includes whitewashers with 8 or more. We are surprised to find that a tiny fraction of whitewashers went so far as to own up to 23 different user IDs, although the majority of the Maze user have only one user ID (75%). We have verified that those who have owned multiple IDs typically spend their points completely before registering a new ID.

One would expect that there is a strong correlation between owning multiple IDs and free-riding behaviors. Our result shows that this is indeed the case. The percentage of free-riders increases steadily with number of user IDs. Within the category of one user ID, there are only 22% free-riders, whereas for those that owns 8 IDs or more, this percentage increases to 77%.

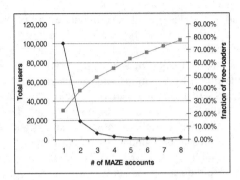

Fig. 4. The distribution of user over number of accounts they have owned and the proportion of free-riders

4.3 Understanding the Source of Free-Riding

The only way that the free-riders can survive the Maze system without cheating is through contribution. Since the free-riders account for the majority of download activities, they will quickly own many of the popular items as well. For the period of 9/28~10/28, we found that the top 10% popular files account for more than 98.8% of total transfer traffic, and over half of which were downloads from the client-like users. Therefore, they can easily make back their deficits provided that 1) the Maze system can quickly direct queries to them and 2) their contents are available.

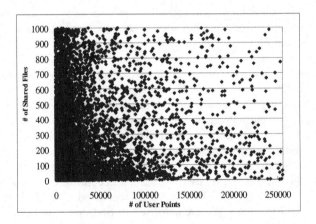

Fig. 5. Number of shared files versus points

The first factor is hindered by one of the artifacts that challenges the scalability of Maze recently. Because the Maze central server has limited power, as more and more contents become available, we have to slow down the indexing process. On October 8th, 4 out of the 10 Maze central index servers were decommissioned because of bad hard disks. This exacerbates the situation even further. Currently, new content of a peer does not make into the index until a few days later. Complemented with friend/neighborhood-lists and the high-reputation users that Maze recommends, this has not made searching for popular items too difficult. It is difficult to quantify how this affects the low-point peers to earn back their scores until we perform detailed simulation to see how many free-riders can become download targets if the index is always up to date. However, we believe that this is indeed a factor. We are replacing the bad indexing servers. Still, a more complete solution is to implement the P2P searching in the future releases. Since popular contents spread out quickly, P2P search will allow more download sources to be discovered at a timely fashion.

Even if a user downloaded a popular object, he may choose to move the file out of his Maze partition. The study in [6] shows that 70% of Gnutella users do have any files to share. This is clearly not the case in Maze. Fig. 5 shows the distribution of total files shared out versus users' reputation score. In fact, the average number of shared files of client-like users is 491, versus 281 of the server-like users. It is logical to infer that these users also contain a good portion of interesting files.

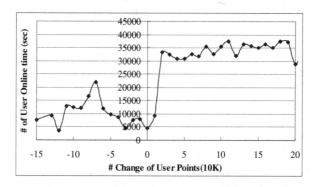

Fig. 6. Online session time versus point changes. Each point is the average of a 10K point change segment

Besides the fact that the slow updating of the central index delays queries to be sent to these potential sources, there are many other reasons. For instance, the user may choose to turn off the Maze server or shut down the machine, either due to resource constraints or selfish behavior. Fig. 6 depicts the correlation of the user session time and users reputation of 65K randomly picked users. Overall, users with positive point changes have longer session time, on average 2.89 times more than those with negative point changes (218 minutes versus 75 minutes). The figure also shows that there are users who have earned high points and then stopped contributing and only perform downloading.

Even when queries have been directed to a Maze user, there are other factors that could make her earn points less aggressively. A Maze client employs parallel downloading from all sources that the index server advices. A source with higher upload bandwidth (and machine power as well) will account for higher proportion of the file being downloaded, and hence is advantageous to earn more points. Fig. 7 draws the scatter graph of the effective upload speed versus the change of reputation points. The effective upload speed is the average upload speed weighted over the transfer size.

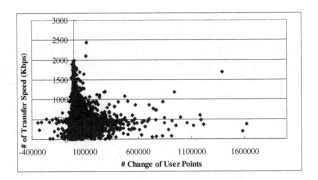

Fig. 7. Upload speed versus point change

The users with negative point changes and those with positive point changes up to 30K have similar upload speed around 310kbps. However, those with changes above 30K have upload speed more than 400kbps. Thus, upload speed makes a difference for those users want to earn high points, but is not a significant factor for the free-riders.

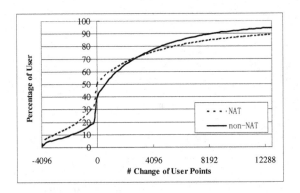

Fig. 8. CDF of point changes for NAT and non-NAT users

There is also the problem of NAT. We have found that 40% of Maze users are behind firewall. Thus, 16% of upload can not happen because the source and the sink are behind different firewalls. This does not in general make the NAT problem an issue, since there are still 84% of chances that a NAT user can upload to a non-NAT user and therefore earn points. In fact, when we look at the point change distribution of the NAT versus non-NAT users (Fig. 8), we found that there are more low score NAT users than low score non-NAT users. It is true, however, that the non-NAT users are easier to earn higher points, 91% of the top500 users are non-NAT users. In other words, although there is significant number of NAT users, firewall traversal is an important but not deciding factor in the free-riding behavior. Notice the sharp drop of both curves at the -4096 point, these correspond to users that have spent all their initial quota and either leave the system or enter again by re-registration.

In summary, the selfish behavior has been demonstrated more by reducing online session time than other factors. In particular, neither the upload speed nor being behind the firewall can be legitimate excuses. On the other hand, high upload speed and/or not being hindered by the NAT issue are necessary for motivated users to contribute.

5 Related Work

There are many works on incentive policies. Due to space constraint, we can not include all of them. Many of the works [9][10] focus on modeling, for which the empirical data we obtained would be useful. In terms of measurement studies, [6] was the first study that pointed out the degree of free-riding in Gnutella. Our data confirms the effect but shows that free-riding is not as pronounced in Maze. Our incentive policies could be one of the reasons.

John Douceur [5] proved that if distinct identities for remote entities are not established either by an explicit certification authority or by an implicit one, these systems are susceptible to Sybil attacks. We believe that incentive policies will not remove these attacks. Quite the contrary, it might actually encourage that, as proven by the whitewashing behavior in Maze, simply because this is an easier way out for the selfish users. The centralized registration in Maze makes it possible to counter these attacks.

Several measurement studies have characterized the properties of peer-to-peer file-sharing systems [7][8]. Some of our other experiment results match what these studies have found. However, this paper focuses on free-riding and the contributing factors.

6 Conclusion and Future Work

This preliminary study on the free-riding behavior in the Maze system has yielded a few interesting insights. First of all, the incentive policies have been effective in general, but they are circumvented by free-riders using account white-washing. We have examined several factors that could contribute to the free-riding behavior.

We are reasonably confident to reduce the free-riding behaviors further. Since popular contents dominate the sharing activities, we should be able to devise mechanisms and policies to spread the load more easily. As we discussed earlier, this entails two different aspects: direct queries to sources that would otherwise become free-riders, and to ensure that contents are available when queries do arrive. The first is the responsibility of the query and search mechanism, and we can accomplish it by installing P2P searching mechanism and/or increasing the frequency of updating the central index. The second is simply human nature, and the only way to influence that is through more savvy incentive policies (e.g. encourage people to increase their online session durations).

References

1. http://maze.pku.edu.cn.
2. Mao Yang, Ben Y. Zhao, Yafei Dai and Zheng Zhang. "Deployment of a large scale peer-to-peer social network", Proceedings of the 1st Workshop on Real, Large Distributed Systems

3. Hua Chen, Mao Yang, et al. "Maze: a Social Peer-to-peer Network". The International Conference on e-Commerce Technology for Dynamic e-Business (CEC-EAST'04). Beijing, China. September, 2004.
4. http://e.pku.edu.cn.
5. John Douceur. "The Sybil Attack". In Proceedings of the 1st International Workshop on Peer-to-Peer Systems, pages 251–260, Boston, MA, USA, March 2002.
6. E. Adar and B. Huberman. "Free Riding on Gnutella". October, 2000.
7. S. Saroiu, P. K. Gummadi, and S. D. Gribble. "A measurement study of peer-to-peer file sharing systems". In Proceedings of Multimedia Computing and Networking (MMCN) 2002.
8. Krishna P. Gummadi, Richard J. Dunn and et al. "Measurement, Modeling, and Analysis of a Peer-to-Peer File-Sharing Workload". Proceedings of the 19th ACM Symposium on Operating Systems Principles (SOSP-19), Bolton Landing, NY.
9. http://p2pecon.berkeley.edu.
10. C. Buragohain, D. Agrawal, and S. Suri. "A game theoretic framework for incentives in p2p systems". In Proc. 3rd Intl. Conf. on Peer-to-Peer Computing, 2003.

Clustering in P2P Exchanges and Consequences on Performances

Stevens Le Blond[1,2], Jean-Loup Guillaume[1], and Matthieu Latapy[1]

[1] LIAFA – CNRS – Université Paris 7, 2 place Jussieu, 75005 Paris, France
{guillaume, latapy}@liafa.jussieu.fr
[2] Faculty of Sciences – Vrije Universiteit, De Boelelaan 1081A,
1081 HV, Amsterdam, The Netherland
slblond@few.vu.nl

Abstract. We propose here an analysis of a rich dataset which gives an exhaustive and dynamic view of the exchanges processed in a running eDonkey system. We focus on correlation in term of data exchanged by peers having provided or queried at least one data in common. We introduce a method to capture these correlations (namely the data clustering), and study it in detail. We then use it to propose a very simple and efficient way to group data into clusters and show the impact of this underlying structure on search in typical P2P systems. Finally, we use these results to evaluate the relevance and limitations of a model proposed in a previous publication. We indicate some realistic values for the parameters of this model, and discuss some possible improvements.

1 Preliminaries

P2P networks such as KaZaA, eDonkey or Gnutella and more recently BitTorrent [15] are nowadays the most bandwidth consuming applications on the Internet, ahead of Web traffic [7,11]. Their analysis and optimisation therefore appears as a key issue for computer science research. However, the fully distributed nature of most of these protocols makes it difficult to obtain relevant information on their actual behavior, and little is known on it [2,8,9]. The fact that these behaviors have some crucial consequences on the performance of the underlying protocol (both in terms of answer speed and in term of used bandwidth) makes it a challenge of prime interest to collect and analyze such data. The observed properties may then be used for the design of efficient protocols.

1.1 Context

In the last few years, both active and passive measurements have been used to gather information on peers behaviors in running P2P networks. These studies gave evidence for a variety of properties which appear as fundamental characteristics of such systems. Among them, let us notice the high ratio of free-riders

M. Castro and R. van Renesse (Eds.): IPTPS 2005, LNCS 3640, pp. 193–204, 2005.
© Springer-Verlag Berlin Heidelberg 2005

[1,3], the heterogeneous distribution (often approximated by a power law) of the number of queries by peer [7,12], and recently the presence of semantic clustering in file sharing networks [3,13].

This last property captures the fact that the data exchanged by peers may overlap significantly: if two peers are interested in a given data, then they probably are in some other data. By connecting directly such peers, it is possible to take benefit from this semantic clustering to improve search algorithms and scalability of the system.

In [3], the authors propose a protocol based on this idea, which reaches very high performances. It however relies on a static classification which can hardly be maintained up to date.

Another approach using the same underlying idea is to add a link in a P2P overlay between peers exchanging files [13,14]. This has the advantage of being very simple and permits significant improvement of the search process.

In [3,6] the authors use traces of a running eDonkey network, obtained by crawling caches of a large number of peers. They study some statistical properties like replication patterns, various distributions, and clustering based on file types and geography. They then use these data to simulate protocols and to evaluate their performances in real-world cases. The use of actual P2P traces where previous works used models (whose relevance is hard to evaluate) is an important step. However, the large number of free-riders, as well as other measurements problems, makes it difficult to evaluate the relevance of the data. Moreover, such measurements miss the dynamic aspects of the exchanges and the fact that fragment of files are made available by peers *during* the download of the files.

1.2   Framework and Contribution

Our work lies in this context and proposes a new step in the direction opened by previous works. We collected some traces using a modified eDonkey server [10], which made it possible to grab accurate information on *all* the exchanges processed by a large number of peers through this server during a significant portion of time. The server handled up to 50 000 users simultaneously and we collected 24 hour traces. The size of a typical trace at various times is given in Figure 1. See [2,4,5], for details on the measurement procedure, on the protocol and on the basic properties of our traces.

	6h	12h	18h	24h
peers	26187	29667	43106	47245
data	187731	244721	323226	383163
links in $\mathcal{Q}$	811042	1081915	1571859	1804330
links in $\mathcal{D}$	12238038	20364268	31522713	38399705

Fig. 1. Time-evolution of the basic statistics for $\mathcal{Q}$ and $\mathcal{D}$

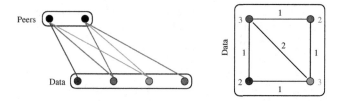

Fig. 2. A query graph (left) and the associated (weighted) data graph (right)

A natural way to encode the gathered data is to define a bipartite graph $\mathcal{Q} = (P, D, E)$, called *query graph*, as follows (see Figure 2, left):

- P is the set of peers in the network, D is the set of data,
- $E \subseteq P \times D$ is a set of undirected edges, where $\{p, d\} \in E$ if and only if the peer p is *active* for the data d, which means that p was interested for the data d or was a provider of d.

Notice that this graph evolves during time, and we will indeed consider it at various dates.

In order to analyze our data, we will also consider the (weighted) *data graph* $\mathcal{D} = (D, E, w)$ obtained from the query graph $\mathcal{Q}$ as follows (see Figure 2, right):

- D is the set of data,
- $E \subseteq D \times D$ is a set of undirected edges, where $\{d_1, d_2\} \in E$ if and only if there exists a peer active for both d_1 and d_2 in $\mathcal{Q}$,
- w is a weight function over the nodes and the edges such that $w(d)$ is the number of data having been exchanged by peers active for d in $\mathcal{Q}$ and $w(d_1, d_2)$ is the number of data exchanged by peers in both d_1 and d_2 in $\mathcal{Q}$.

The sizes of query graphs and data graphs obtained from a typical trace at various times are given in Figure 1. We use these graphs, which have properties representative of what we observed of this kind of graphs, throughout this paper.

In the following, we use these graphs and tools from the recent field of complex network analysis to deepen the study of the dynamic traces. We focus in particular on the *data clustering*, which captures how much the exchanges processed by two sets of peers are similar. In other words, it is a measure of how much peers active for at least one common data will exchange the same other data. We then show that these properties have significant impact on the efficiency of searches in the network, and therefore may be used in the design of efficient P2P protocols. Finally, we will use this analysis to study the relevance of a previously proposed model.

2   Data Clustering Analysis

Our aim now is to analyze similarities between data in terms of exchanges processed by peers active for them. In particular, given two data u and v exchanged by a given peer p we are interested in the number of other common data exchanged by peers actives for u or v. This can be measured using the following parameter over the edges in $\mathcal{D}$:

$$c(u, v) = \frac{w(u, v)}{w(u) + w(v) - w(u, v)}$$

Indeed, the two data u and v induce an edge $\{u, v\}$ in D, the weight $w(u, v)$ is nothing but the number of common data exchanged by peers active for u or v, and the expression $w(u) + w(v) - w(u, v)$ gives the total number of data exchanged by peers active for u or v. Finally, $c(u, v)$ therefore measures how much these exchanges overlap. Notice that its value is between 0 and 1.

The value of $c(u, v)$ may however be strongly biased if one of the two nodes has a high weight and the other a low one: the value would then be very low. For example, if a data with an high popularity[1] is connected to an unpopular one, then the clustering will probably be low, even if the few data exchanged by the lowest population are completely included in the large set of data exchanged by the highest one.

In order to capture these cases, we will also consider the following statistical parameter:

$$\bar{c}(u, v) = \frac{w(u, v)}{\min(w(u), w(v))}$$

which is still in $[0; 1]$ but is always larger than $c(u, v)$ and does not have this drawback. For instance, in the case described above the obtained value is 1.

We will call $c(u, v)$ the *clustering* of $\{u, v\}$ and $\bar{c}(u, v)$ its *min-clustering*. In summary, the clustering captures the overlap between data exchanged by two sets of peers with no consideration of the heterogeneity between the number of data exchanged, whereas min-clustering takes into account and captures eparticularly well the fact that a small set of exchanged data can actually be a subset of a another much larger one.

Figure 3 and 4 show the time-evolution of the distributions[2] of $c(u, v)$ and $\bar{c}(u, v)$, respectively. First notice that the general shape of these distributions is very stable along time, which indicates that the observations we will derive are not biased by the timescale or date considered.

Now let us observe (Figure 3) that around 60% of the edges always have a clustering lower than 0.2. This may indicate that the overlap of exchanges is not as high as expected. However, this may be a consequence of the fact that both the peer activity and the data popularity are very heterogeneous: there are very active peers while most of them are not, and there are very popular data while most are not. This induces in $\mathcal{D}$ many links between data of very different popularity and a low clustering.

---

[1] The popularity of a data is the number of peers active for that data.

[2] The distribution of a parameter x is, for each possible value of x, the ratio between the number of instances of this value and the total number of instances. Here we will directly plot the number of instances of each value, which makes it possible to visualize traces of various sizes (*i.e.* at various dates) in a same plot.

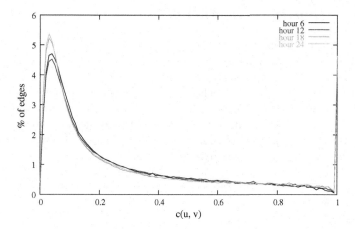

Fig. 3. Time evolution of the $c(u, v)$ distribution

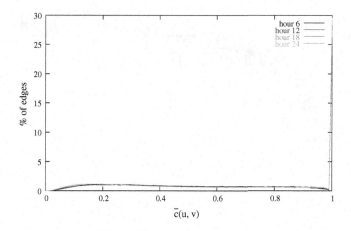

Fig. 4. Time evolution of the $\bar{c}(u, v)$ distribution

This can be corrected using the distribution of min-clustering (Figure 4): only 15% of the edges have a min-clustering lower than 0.2 while for nearly 60% higher or equal to 0.5. This indicates that the overlap is indeed high; for instance, 30% of the overlaps between all exchanges actually are a complete inclusion.

Such results may indicate the presence of a hierarchy among exchanges: while few popular data form the core of $\mathcal{D}$, a large number of less popular ones have their exchanges mostly included into the ones of the core. If this structure indeed exists, it may be used to dynamicaly build a multicast tree from a P2P overlay. We will discuss the presence of such a hierarchy and its implications later in this contribution.

3   Consequences on Searching

Following several previous works (e.g. [3,6,13,14]), one may wonder if the properties highlighted in previous section may be used to improve search in P2P systems. To answer this question, we will process the following experiment. We suppose that each peer has a knowledge of the peers active for the same data as itself. Then, when a peer p sends a query for a data d, it first looks at the other peers already active for a data p is active for. If one of them provides d, then it sends it directly to p. In this case, the clustering has been used and the data was found using only one hop search.

The time-evolution of this hit ratio is plotted in Figure 5. Despite it is quite low in the first few minutes (due to the server bootstrap), the ratio quickly converges to a value close to 50%.

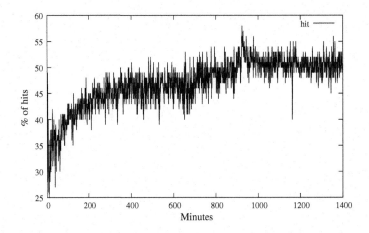

Fig. 5. Time evolution of the hit % using the one hop protocol

To deepen our understanding of what happens, let us consider Figure 6, in which we plotted the percentage of all the peers, the percentage of all the queries, and the replication of each data[3] corresponding to the percentage of hits using a one hop search.

The first thing to notice is that nearly 25% of the peers do not find *any* data using the proposed approach. This is quite surprising, since we observed in Figure 5 that 50% of *all* the queries are routed with success using the same approach. This can be understood by observing that this 'null hit' population generated only 7% of the queries and so only slighly influenced the high hit rate previously observed. Additionally, the queried data appear to be very rare at the time they were asked. This low volume of queries together with the low replication explain the null hit rate; these peers are not active for enough data nor enough replicated ones to find them using the one hop search.

---

[3] The *replication* of a data is the percentage of all the peers active for a given data.

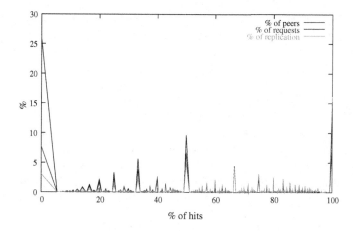

Fig. 6. Correlation between the % of peers, the associated % of queries they generated, the % of replication of the queried data and the % of hits they obtained after 24h using the one hop protocol

On the other hand, more than 10% of the peers have a *perfect* success rate. One could think that such a result would imply a prohibitive amount of queries; Figure 6 indicates that it is not the case: the percentage of queries is close to the number of peers who processed them. Notice however that data found this way appear to be highly replicated (the population being active for these data at the time they were asked represents 15% of the peers active for other queried data) which explains the high success rate. Finally, notice that the average peer's success rate increases from 40% to nearly 60% if the 'null hit' population is removed from the calculus.

4   Modeling Peer and Data Clusters

In [14] the authors propose a model to represent the semantic structure of P2P file sharing networks and use it to improve searching. They assume the existence of semantic types labelled by $n \in \{1, \ldots, N\}$ with N denoting the number of such types. They assume that each data and each peer in the system has exactly one type. A data of type n is called a n-data, and a peer of type n is called a n-peer. They denote respectively by d_n and u_n the number of n-data and the number of n-peer (u for *user*).

They denote by $p_n(m)$ the probability that a query sent by a n-user is for a m-data.

Clearly, a classification of peers and users captures clustering if, for all n and m, either $p_n(m)$ is close to 0 (n-peers almost never seek m-data) or it is quite large (n-peers often seek m-data). If it is either 0 or 1 then the clustering is perfect: n-peers only seek m-data for that value of m such that $p_n(m) = 1$.

This formalism is useful in helping to consider the hierarchical organisation induced by clustering, for the purpose of simulations for instance. We will see here that the statistical properties observed in previous section may be used to compute clusters of data, which make it possible to validate the model describe above. Moreover, we will give some information on parameters which may be used with the model to make its use realistic.

4.1 Cluster Computation

Notice that computation of relevant clusters in general is a challenging task, computationaly extensive and untractable in practice on large graphs such as the one we consider. We can however propose a simple procedure based on the statistical properties of $\mathcal{D}$ observed in previous section: for two given integers $1 < \perp < \top < |\mathcal{D}|$,

- sort edges by increasing values of their clustering
- for each edge taken in this order:
  - if its removal does not induce a connected component with less than $\perp$ vertices then remove it
  - if the size of the largest connected component if lower than $\top$ then terminate

We define the data clusters as the connected components finally obtained. The integers $\perp$ and $\top$ are respectively the minimal and the maximal sizes of these clusters.

The idea behind this cluster definition is that edges between data of different clusters should have a low clustering, indicating that the clusters put together data with similar sets of exchanges.

In our case, we observed that $\top = 1000$ and $\perp = 10$ give good results, and that changing their values does not change significantly the results. We will illustrate this in the following by using $\top = 1000$ and $\perp \in \{10, 30, 60, 90\}$. Notice that these values ensure both that the clusters will not be too small (they contain at least $\perp$ data) and not too large (their size is bounded by $\top$).

4.2 Cluster Properties

Figure 7 shows that the size distribution of clusters, *i.e.* the distribution of d_n, is well fitted by a power law (for all considered $\perp$). Notice however that the average clusters sizes are highly influenced by $\perp$, for instance, for $\perp \in \{10, 30, 60, 90\}$, the average clusters sizes are 30, 60, 100 and 150 respectively. There is indeed a natural correlation between $\perp$ and the average size of clusters since, despite some contain up to $1\,000$ data, most clusters are small, with size close to $\perp$. This indicates that, when using the model proposed in [14], one may suppose a power law distribution for d_n.

Let us now associate to each data cluster all the peers active for a data in the cluster. The number of peers associated this way is the *popularity* of the cluster. One may expect that these popularities will vary much, and that large clusters will be very popular, possibly concerning almost all the peers in the system.

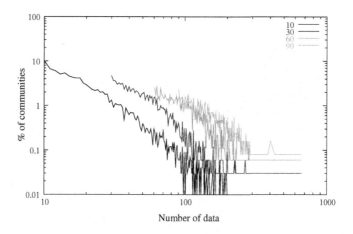

Fig. 7. Distribution of the number of data per cluster for $\bot \in \{10, 30, 60, 90\}$

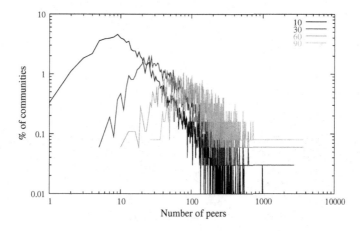

Fig. 8. Distribution of the number of peers per cluster for $\bot \in \{10, 30, 60, 90\}$

Figure 8 shows that this is not the case: very few clusters have a low popularity, and none has a huge popularity, the maximum being lower than $4,000$ peers (to be compared to the total number of peers in the system, around $50,000$).

These statistics show that the clusters we defined, despite their simplicity, do capture non-trivial information concerning the peers. This might indicate that data clusters also define peer clusters, as assumed in [14].

In order to check this, we plot in Figure 9 the correlations between the number of data peers are active for, and the average number of clusters this population queried in. This plot displays almost linear correlations until peers reach a degree 100 in $\mathcal{D}$, but the correlation seems to be inverted after this limit: the most active peers queried data in very few clusters.

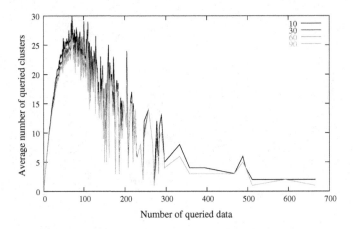

Fig. 9. Correlation between the number of data queried and the average number of queried cluster for $\perp \in \{10, 30, 60, 90\}$

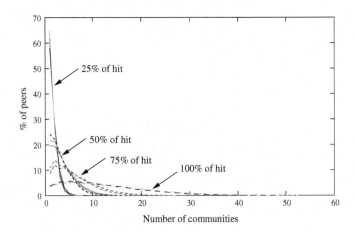

Fig. 10. Number of clusters which has to be queried to get $p_n(m) = 25\%$, 50%, 75% and 100% for $\perp \in \{10, 30, 60, 90\}$

Several important observations can be done here. First, most of the peers do not ask for data in a constant number of clusters but rather in a number of clusters which depends on the number of queries they processed. In other words, peers do not ask for data in only one well identified cluster, in contradiction with what is assumed in [14].

This could make us conclude that, either the model should be improved to take this diversity into account, or a more subtle definition of clusters is necessary. Indeed, there are many ways in which data can be put into clusters, and the very simple one we proposed capture some features, but not all, of data/peers relations.

Notice that the previous plots do not capture the fact that a peer generally asks for many data in the same cluster (they only show that they ask for data in many clusters). This is exactly what $p_n(m)$, the ratio of m-data asked for by n-peers, represents.

For each peer, we therefore have taken different values of $p_n(m)$ and see how many clusters have to be queried by this peer to reach each of these values. We obtained this way the distributions of $p_n(m)$ plotted in Figure 10.

It appears that approximately 60% of the peers can find 25% of the data they look for in only *one* cluster. This percentage of peers goes over 95% when we consider up to 3 clusters. Using the same procedure, we can see that asking only 5 clusters permits to 80% of the peers to find 50% of the data they look for. Likewise, considering still 5 clusters permits to more than 50% of the peers to find 75% of the data they look for.

Finally, this analysis shows that our simple cluster definition is enough to argue that the model proposed in [14] is relevant concerning the data and may be used with power law distributions of the size of clusters. It however shows that, despite non-trivial correlations are captured, either the cluster definition or the model fails in capturing a strict equivalence between a peer and a cluster. It rather indicates that most of the peers ask their data from a *small* set clusters, and not only one.

5   Conclusion

In this contribution, we proposed simple statistical parameters to capture the correlations between the set of peers active for a given data. We used these parameters first to confirm the previously noticed fact that semantic clustering can be used to improve search algorithms. Second, we used them to define a very simple and efficient way to compute data clusters. We have shown that these clusters succeed in capturing similarities between data.

We used these clusters to discuss the validity of a model of data clustering proposed in [14]. We obtained information on realistic parameters which should be used with this model. We also shown that the clusters we define can not be used directly with this simple model, which indicates that either a more subtle cluster definition should be considered, or that the model should be extended. We pointed out some direction for this.

Notice that we focused here on *data*, but the same kind of approach may be fruitful with peers. A combination of the clusters we defined on data and clusters defined in a similar way on peers would probably bring significant improvement. More subtle cluster computations would also probably help, but we must keep in mind the huge size of the trace, which forbids intricate methods.

Finally, let us insist on the fact that the analysis of large real-world traces like the one we presented here is only at its beginning, and that much remains to understand from it. The lack of relevant statistical parameters (concerning for example the dynamics of the trace), and of efficient algorithms to deal with such traces are among the main bottleneck to this, but studies like the one we presented here show that simple methods can already bring much information.

References

1. E. Adar and B. Huberman. Free riding on gnutella, 2000.
2. Stevens Le Blond, Matthieu Latapy, and Jean-Loup Guillaume. Statistical analysis of a p2p query graph based on degrees and their time evolution. IWDC'04, 2004.
3. F. Le Fessant, S. Handurukande, A.-M. Kermarrec, and L. Massoulié. Clustering in peer-to-peer file sharing workloads. 3rd International Workshop on Peer-to-Peer Systems (IPTPS), September 2004.
4. Jean-Loup Guillaume and Stevens Le Blond. P2p exchange network: Measurement and analysis. 2004.
5. Jean-Loup Guillaume and Stevens Le Blond. Statistical properties of exchanges in p2p systems. Technical report, PDPTA'04, 2004.
6. S. Handurukande, A.-M. Kermarrec, F. Le Fessant, and L. Massoulié. Exploiting semantic clustering in the edonkey p2p network. 11th ACM SIGOPS European Workshop (SIGOPS), September 2004.
7. Nathaniel Leibowitz, Aviv Bergman, Roy Ben-Shaul, and Aviv Shavit. Are file swapping networks cacheable? characterizing p2p traffic. 7th International Workshop on Web Content Caching and Distribution (WCW), August 2002.
8. Nathaniel Leibowitz, Matei Ripeanu, and Adam Wierzbicki. Deconstructing the kazaa network. The Third IEEE Workshop on Internet Applications, June 2003.
9. Jian Liang, Rakesh Kumar, and Keith Ross. Understanding kazza, 2004.
10. Lugdunum. lugdunum2k.free.fr/.
11. S. Saroiu, K. Gummadi, R. Dunn, S. Gribble, and H. Levy. An analysis of internet content delivery systems, 2002.
12. Subhabrata Sen and Jia Wang. Analyzing peer-to-peer traffic across large networks. Internet Measurement Workshop 2002, November 2002.
13. K. Sripanidkulchai, B. Maggs, and H. Zhang. Efficient content location using interest-based locality in peer-to-peer systems. Internet Measurement Workshop 2002, November 2002.
14. S. Voulgaris, A.-M. Kermarrec, L. Massoulie, and M. van Steen. Exploiting semantic proximity in peer-to-peer content searching. 10th IEEE Int'l Workshop on Future Trends in Distributed Computing Systems (FTDCS), May 2004.
15. rfc-gnutella.sourceforge.net/developer/testing/index.html
www.bittorrent,   www.kazaa.com,   www.edonkey2000.com.

The Bittorrent P2P File-Sharing System: Measurements and Analysis

Johan Pouwelse, Paweł Garbacki, Dick Epema, and Henk Sips

Delft University of Technology, Delft, The Netherlands
j.a.pouwelse@ewi.tudelft.nl
Department of Computer Science, Parallel and Distributed systems group

Abstract. Of the many P2P file-sharing prototypes in existence, Bit-Torrent is one of the few that has managed to attract millions of users. BitTorrent relies on other (global) components for file search, employs a moderator system to ensure the integrity of file data, and uses a bartering technique for downloading in order to prevent users from freeriding. In this paper we present a measurement study of BitTorrent in which we focus on four issues, viz. availability, integrity, flashcrowd handling, and download performance. The purpose of this paper is to aid in the understanding of a real P2P system that apparently has the right mechanisms to attract a large user community, to provide measurement data that may be useful in modeling P2P systems, and to identify design issues in such systems.

1 Introduction

Even though many P2P file-sharing systems have been proposed and implemented, only very few have stood the test of intensive daily use by a very large user community. The BitTorrent file-sharing system is one of these systems. Measurements on Internet backbones indicate that BitTorrent has evolved into one of the most popular networks [8]. In fact, BitTorrent traffic made up 53 % of all P2P traffic in June 2004 [12]. As BitTorrent is only a file-download protocol, it relies on other (global) components, such as web sites, for finding files. The most popular web site for this purpose at the time we performed our measurements was suprnova.org.

There are different aspects that are important for the acceptance of a P2P system by a large user community. First, such a system should have a high availability. Secondly, users should (almost) always receive a good version of the content (no fake files) [10]. Thirdly, the system should be able to deal with flashcrowds. Finally, users should obtain a relatively high download speed.

In this paper we present a detailed measurement study of the combination of BitTorrent and Suprnova. This measurements study addresses all four aforementioned aspects. Our measurement data consist of detailed traces gathered over a period of 8 months (Jun'03 to Mar'04) of more than two thousand global components. In addition, for one of the most popular files we followed all 90,155 downloading peers from the injection of the file until its disappearance (several

M. Castro and R. van Renesse (Eds.): IPTPS 2005, LNCS 3640, pp. 205–216, 2005.

months). In a period of two weeks we measured the bandwidth of 54,845 peers downloading over a hundred newly injected files. This makes our measurement effort one of the largest ever conducted.

The contributions of this paper are the following: first, we add to the understanding of the operation of a P2P file-sharing system that apparently by its user-friendliness, the quality of the content it delivers, and its performance, has the right mechanisms to attract millions of users. Second, the results of this paper can aid in the (mathematical) modeling of P2P systems. For instance, in the fluid model in [13], it is assumed that the arrival process and the abort and departure processes of downloaders are Poisson, something that is in obvious contradiction with our measurements. One of our main conclusions is that within P2P systems a tension exists between availability, which is improved when there are no global components, and data integrity, which benefits from centralization.

2   The BitTorrent File-Sharing System

BitTorrent [5] in itself is only a file-downloading protocol. In BitTorrent, files are split up into chunks (on the order of a thousand per file), and the *downloaders* of a file *barter* for chunks of it by uploading and downloading them in a tit-for-tat-like manner to prevent parasitic behavior. Each peer is responsible for maximizing its own download rate by contacting suitable peers, and peers with high upload rates will with high probability also be able to download with high speeds. When a peer has finished downloading a file, it may become a *seed* by staying online for a while and sharing the file for free, i.e., without bartering.

Table 1. Popular BitTorrent web sites (Oct 2004)

Site name	Available files	File transfers
Suprnova.org	46,766	2,267,463
Youceff.com	47,137	1,145,889
Piratebay.org	39,294	749,133
Lokitorrent.com	30,957	816,435

To find a file in BitTorrent, users access web sites which act as global directories of available files. In Table 1, we show for the most popular of these web sites the number of different files and the number of active file transfers at a certain time. In december 2004, the top two of these web sites went offline. In this paper we assume Suprnova as the directory web site.

The Suprnova web site uses a *mirroring system* to balance user requests across its mirror sites. The web pages on Suprnova show for each available file the name and size, the current numbers of downloaders and seeds, and the name of the person who uploaded the file. To start the download of a file, a user clicks on a link pointing to .`torrent` meta-data file. These meta-data files are not stored on Suprnova or its mirrors, but are distributed among a number of .`torrent` file servers. In turn, each .`torrent` file points to a *tracker*, which keeps a global registry of all the downloaders and seeds of the corresponding file. The tracker responds to a user's request with a list of some of the peers having (part of) the requested file, with whom the user can establish direct connections to barter for chunks of the file. One tracker can supervise the simultaneous downloads of multiple files.

New content is injected into BitTorrent by uploading a `.torrent` file to the Suprnova web site and creating a seed with the first copy of the file. In order to reduce the pollution level, new content is first manually inspected by *moderators*, who weed out fake content, content with low perceptual quality, and content with incorrect naming. A normal user who injects content is called a *moderated submitter*. To lower the burden on the moderators, a user who frequently injects correct content is promoted to the rank of *unmoderated submitter*, and is allowed to directly add content. Unmoderated submitters can request a promotion to moderator status to existing moderators.

Together, BitTorrent and Suprnova form a unique infrastructure that uses mirroring of the web servers with its directory structure, meta-data distribution for load balancing, a bartering technique for fair resource sharing, and a P2P moderation system to filter fake files.

3   Experimental Setup

In this section, we will discuss some details of our measurement software and the collected data. Our measurement software consists of two parts with three scripts each. The first part is used for monitoring the global BitTorrent/Suprnova components, and consists of the *Mirror script* which measures the availability and response time of the Suprnova mirrors, the *HTML script* which gathers and parses the HTML pages of the Suprnova mirrors and downloads all new `.torrent` files, and the *Tracker script* which parses the `.torrent` files for new trackers and checks the status of all trackers.

The second part of our software is used for monitoring actual peers. To follow thousands of peers at one minute time resolution we used 100 nodes of our Distributed ASCI Supercomputer (DAS, `cs.vu.nl/das2`). The *Hunt script* selects a file to follow and initiates a measurement of all the peers downloading this particular file, the *Getpeer script* contacts the tracker for a given file and gathers the IP addresses of peers downloading the file, and the *Peerping script* contacts numerous peers in parallel and (ab)uses the BitTorrent protocol to measure their download progress and uptime. The Hunt script monitors once per minute every active Suprnova mirror for the release of new files. Once a file is selected for measurement, the Getpeer and Peerping scripts are also activated at the same time resolution. In this way we are able to obtain the IP addresses of the peers that inject new content and we can get a good estimate of the average download speed of individual peers.

In doing our measurements, we experienced three problems. First, our measurements were hindered by the wide-spread usage of firewalls [11]. When a peer is behind a firewall, our Getpeer script can obtain its IP number, but the Peerping script cannot send any message to it. Therefore, our results for download speed are only valid for non-firewalled peers. The second problem was our inability to obtain all peer IP numbers from a tracker directly. The BitTorrent protocol specifies that a tracker returns only a limited number (with a default of 20) of randomly selected peer IP numbers. We define the *peer coverage* as the fraction of all peers that we actually discovered. In all our measurements we obtained a peer coverage of over 95 %. Our final measurement problem was caused by modifications made to the BitTorrent system itself. Which created minor gaps in our traces.

4   Measurement Results

In this section, we first show the number of users downloading or seeding on BitTorrent/Suprnova. Then we present detailed performance measurements of the availability, the integrity, the flashcrowd effect, and the download performance of the system.

4.1   Overall System Activity

The number of users over time on BitTorrent/Suprnova gives a good indication of both the general performance and the dynamics of the system. We show the popularity of BitTorrent/Suprnova in terms of the number of downloads over time and its dependence on technical failures in the system.

Figure 1 shows the total number of downloads, and the number of downloads of three types of content (games, movies, and music) in progress in BitTorrent around Christmas 2003. We have selected this month for presentation because it shows

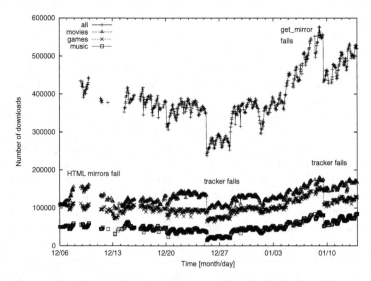

Fig. 1. The number of users downloading or seeding on BitTorrent/Suprnova for one month (Dec'03-Jan'04)

a large variance in the number of downloads due to several BitTorrent/Suprnova failures. The lowest and highest number of downloads in Figure 1 are 237,500 (on Christmas day) and 576,500 (on January 9). Our HTML script requests every hour all pages from one of the active Suprnova mirrors. The consecutive data points have been connected with a line when there was no overall systems failure.

There are two things to be noted in Figure 1. The first is the daily cycle; the minimum and maximum (at around 23:00 GMT) number of downloads occur at roughly the same time each day, which is similar to the results found in [14]. The second is the large variation due to failures of either the mirroring system across the Suprnova mirrors, of the mirrors themselves, of the .torrent servers, or of the trackers. For example, on December 8 and 10, gaps occurred due to failures of the mirroring system and of 6 out of 8 Suprnova mirrors, and on Christmas day, a large tracker went off-line for 98 hours. The failure of this single tracker alone reduced the number of available movies from 1675 to 1017, and resulted in a sharp reduction in the number of downloads. From January 5 to 10, the mirroring system was also off-line a few times, causing suprnova.org to be unusable and the Suprnova mirrors not being updated, which is visible in the figure as a few gaps in the "all" line. The figure suggests that users are not discouraged by such failures.

We conclude that the number of active users in the system is strongly influenced by the availability of the global components in BitTorrent/Suprnova.

4.2 Availability

In this section we present measurements of the availability of both the global Suprnova components and the BitTorrent peers.

The BitTorrent/Suprnova architecture is vulnerable because of potential failures of the four types of *global components*. The main suprnova.org server sometimes switched IP number and was down several times. The various mirrors rarely survive longer than a few days due to the high demands of over 1,200,000 daily visitors (Oct 2004), and sometimes, fewer than five mirrors were up. Occasionally, no .torrent file servers were available, blocking all new downloads. In general, trackers are a frequent target for denial-of-service attacks and are costly to operate due to GBytes of daily bandwidth consumption.

Figure 2 shows the results of our availability measurements of 234 Suprnova mirrors, 95 .torrent file servers, and 1,941 BitTorrent trackers (Suprnova.org itself is not shown). In the figure we plot the average uptime in days for these global components ranked according to decreasing uptime. Only half of the Suprnova mirrors had an average uptime of over 2.1 days, which is a good indication of their (un)availability. In addition, only 39 mirrors had a continuous uptime period longer than two weeks. We can conclude that reliable webhosting of Suprnova pages is a problem. As shown in the figure, the .torrent file servers are even less reliable. A few trackers show a high degree of availability, with one tracker even showing a continuous uptime period of over 100 days. Half of the trackers had an average uptime of 1.5 day or more, and the 100 top ranking trackers had an average uptime of more than 15.7 days.

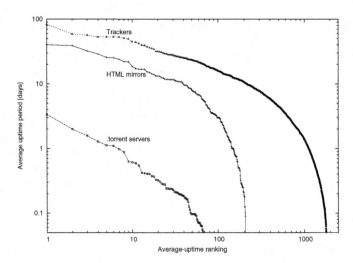

Fig. 2. The uptime ranking of three types of BitTorrent/Suprnova global components

In Figure 1 we have shown that unavailability has a significant influence on popularity. Combined with the high frequency of such failures as apparent from Figure 2, we conclude that there is an obvious need to decentralize the global components. However, all the features that make BitTorrent/Suprnova exceptional (easy single-click-download web interface, low level of pollution, and high download performance) are heavily dependent on these global components.

The availability of *individual peers* over a long time period has never been studied, despite its importance. We measured peer availability for over three months, which is significantly longer than reported in [2], [4], and [14].

On December 10, 2003 the popular PC game "Beyond Good and Evil" from Ubisoft was injected into BitTorrent/Suprnova and on March 11, 2004 it died. We followed this content and obtained 90,155 peer IP numbers using our Getpeer script. Of these IP numbers, only 53,883 were not behind firewalls and could be traced by our Peerping script. We measured the uptime of all non-firewalled peers with a one minute resolution.

Figure 3 shows the results of our uptime measurements. Here we plot the peer uptime in hours *after* they have finished downloading with the peers ranked according to decreasing uptime. The longest uptime is 83.5 days. Note that this log-log plot shows an almost straight line between peer 10 and peer 5,000. The sharp drop after 5,000 indicates that the majority of users disconnect from the system within a few hours after the download has been finished. This sharp drop has important implications because the actual download time of this game spans several days. Figure 3 shows that seeds with a high availability are rare. Only 9,219 out of 53,883 peers (17 %) have an uptime longer than one hour after they finished downloading. For 10 hours this number has decreased to only 1,649 peers (3.1 %), and for 100 hours to a mere 183 peers (0.34 %).

Our two availability figures depict crucial information for architectural improvements. To increase the availability of the whole system, the functionality

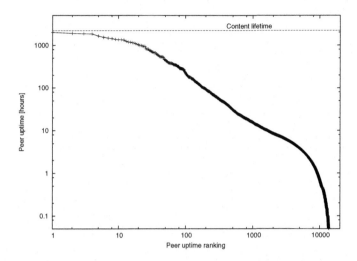

Fig. 3. The uptime distribution of the 53,833 peers downloading "Beyond Good and Evil"

of the global components would have to be distributed, possibly across the ordinary peers. However, as peers with a high uptime are currently very rare, then peers should be given incentives to lengthen their uptimes.

4.3   Integrity

This section analyses the integrity in BitTorrent/Suprnova of both the content itself and of the associated meta-data, which is a notorious problem in P2P systems.

In order to test the integrity of meta-data, we donated to Suprnova an account for hosting a mirror. By installing spyware in the HTML code, we have registered each `.torrent` download and could have easily corrupt the meta-data. We conclude that using donated resources for hosting meta-data entails substantial integrity and privacy risks.

As to the integrity of the content, P2P message boards and other sources strongly indicate that BitTorrent/Suprnova is virtually pollution free. However, a direct measurement of fake or corrupted files is difficult; manually checking the content of many files is not really a viable option. Instead, we actively tried to pollute the system. We created several accounts on different computers from which we tried to insert files that were obviously fake. We failed; the moderators filtered out our fake files.

The system of moderators seems to be very effective in removing fake and corrupted files. The following measurements show that only a few of such volunteers are needed. Figure 4 shows the numbers of files that have been injected by the 20 moderators, the 71 unmoderated submitters, and the 7,933 moderated submitters that were active between June 2003 and March 2004. The ten most active moderated submitters injected 5,191 files, versus 1,693 for the unmoderated submitters and 274 for the moderators. We are surprised that a

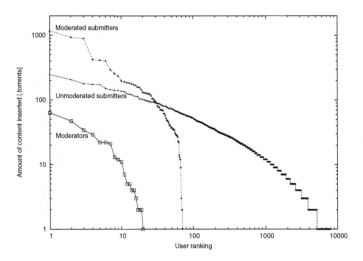

Fig. 4. The activity of the different content submitters on Suprnova to prevent pollution

mere 20 moderators were able to effectively manage the numerous daily content injections with such a simple system. Unfortunately, this system of moderation relies on global components and is extremely difficult to distribute.

4.4   Flashcrowds

We now focus on the system's reaction to the sudden popularity of a single (new) file. This phenomenon is also called the *flashcrowd* effect. Figure 5 shows the number of downloads for a single file as a function of time (the Lord of the Rings III movie with size 1.87 GByte). We have selected this file because it uses a tracker (Future-Zone.TV) which provides access to detailed statistics, which we collected every five minutes with our Tracker script. The top line shows the sum of the number of downloads in progress and the number of seeds according to this tracker, while the bottom line only shows the number of seeds. During the first five days, no peer finished downloading the file and the injector of the file was continuously online. This long time period provides a clear opportunity to identify copyright violators. The statistics from Suprnova were fetched by our HTML script every hour, and are in agreement with the total tracker results to such an extent that the lines overlap almost completely. Only on December 23, 2003 there was a problem with the tracker for a few minutes, which is not visible in the Suprnova data. The results from the Peerping script show a significantly lower number of downloads, which is due to the firewall problem (40 % of the peers were firewalled). The gaps in the Peerping results were due to disk quota problems on the DAS, which ran our measurement software. From the measurements we conclude that the global BitTorrent/Suprnova components are capable of efficiently handling very large flashcrowds. Also, because of the strong sudden increase in the number of downloaders, it is clear that the arrival process is not Poisson.

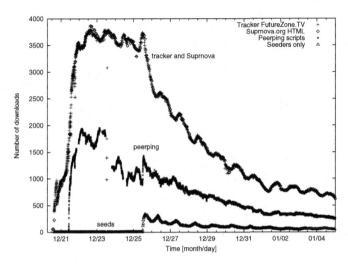

Fig. 5. Flashcrowd effect of "Lord of the Rings III"

4.5   Download Performance

In this section, we examine the efficiency (download speed) and the effectiveness (number of available files) of downloading.

Figure 6 presents the results of a two-week experiment in which the average download bandwidth of 54,845 peers was measured. To obtain these measurements, our Hunt script followed the first 108 files that where added to Suprnova on March 10, 2004. The figure also shows the Cumulative Distribution Function (CDF) of the fraction of peers with a certain download speed. It turns out that 90% of the peers had a download speed below 520 kbps; the average download

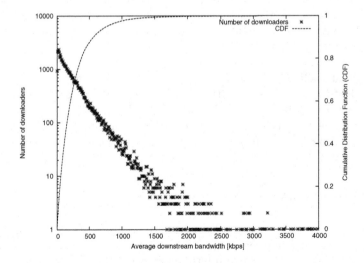

Fig. 6. The average download speed of peers

speed of 240 kbps allowed peers to fetch even large files in one day. An important observation is the exponential relation between the average download speed and the number of downloads at that speed.

In BitTorrent the availability of content is unpredictable. When the popularity drops and the last peer/seed with certain content goes offline, the content dies. Figure 7 shows the content lifetime of all large files (at least 500 MByte) on

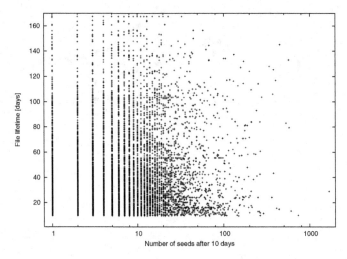

Fig. 7. The content lifetime versus the number of seeds after 10 days for over 14,000 files

BitTorrent/Suprnova we have followed. Each file is represented as a data point with on the horizontal axis the number of seeds for the file 10 days after its injection time, and on the vertical axis its content lifetime. Important observations are that the number of seeds after 10 days is not an accurate predictor for the content lifetime, and that files with only a single seed can still have a relatively long content lifetime.

BitTorrent itself does not have incentives to seed, but there are Suprnova-like websites that do so. For instance, the software from `Yabtuc.org` consists of such a website with an integrated tracker which registers seeding behaviour. When users do not upload sufficiently, their access is temporarily denied. However, this system is even more centralized then Suprnova due to the integration of website and tracker at a single location.

5   Related Work

Previous work on BitTorrent has focused on measurements [5,12,8,7], theoretical analysis [13], and improvements [16]. In [7], the log of a Bittorrent tracker is analysed; it shows for a single file the flashcrowd effect and download speed. In [13] a fluid model is used to determine the average download time of a single file. This remarkable model assumes Poisson arrival and departure processes for downloaders and seeds, equal upload and download bandwidths for all peers, and no flashcrowd effect. However, their assumption of Poisson processes is contradicted by the results of this paper, indicating the strong need for proper workload characterization to validate P2P models.

Improvements to BitTorrent-like software are presented in [16]. Their system effectively decentralizes the tracker. However, due to the complete lack of integrity measures it will be trivial to corrupt this system.

For other P2P systems than BitTorrent, several measurement studies of P2P networks have addressed the issues of availability [2,4,6], integrity [10], flashcrowds [5,9], and download performance [1,15,14,3,4]. Most of the availability studies only span a few days [2] or weeks [4], making it difficult to draw conclusions on long-term peer behavior. The only long-term study is a 200-day trace of the Kazaa traffic on the University of Washington backbone [6], but the well-connected users with free Internet access in this environment are not average P2P users. Integrity of P2P systems has received little attention from academia. A unique study found that for popular songs on Kazaa, up to 70 % of the different versions are polluted or simply fake [10]. The Kazaa moderation system based on voting is therefore completely ineffective. In one of the first studies (August 2000) related to download performance [1], over 35,000 Gnutella peers where followed for one day. Nearly 70 % of the peers did not contribute *any* bandwidth. In [15] it is found that less than 10 % of the IP numbers fill about 99 % of all P2P bandwidth. In [14], SProbe (`sprobe.cs.washington.edu`) was used to measure the bandwidth of 223,000 Gnutella peers in May 2001. It turned out that roughly 8 % of the Gnutella peers downloaded files at speeds lower than 64 kbps.

Content lifetime is still a poorly understood and unexplored research area. Only one paper has investigated when content appeared on a P2P network, but not when it disappeared [3].

6 Discussion and Conclusions

In this paper we have presented a detailed measurement study and an analysis of the BitTorrent/Suprnova P2P system. We believe that this study is a contribution to the ongoing effort to gain insight into the behavior of widely used P2P systems. In order to share our findings we have published all raw data files (anonymized), measurement software, and documentation on `peer-2-peer.org`.

One of the big advantages of BitTorrent/Suprnova is the high level of integrity of both the content and the meta-data due to the working of its global components. We have shown that only 20 moderators combined with numerous other volunteers solve the fake-file problem on BitTorrent/Suprnova. However, this comes at a price: system availability is hampered by the global nature of these components. Decentralization would provide an obvious solution, but makes the meta-data more vulnerable. Also, a decentralized scheme such as in Kazaa has no availability problems but lacks integrity, since Kazaa is plagued with many fake files. Clearly, decentralization is an unsolved issue that needs further research.

Another future design challenge for P2P file sharing is creating incentives to seed. For example, peers that seed files should be given preference to barter for other files.

References

1. E. Adar and B. A. Huberman. Free riding on gnutella. Technical report, Xerox PARC, August 2000.
2. R. Bhagwan, S. Savage, and G. M. Voelker. Understanding availability. In *International Workshop on Peer to Peer Systems*, Berkeley, CA, USA, February 2003.
3. S. Byers, L. Cranor, E. Cronin, D. Kormann, and P. McDaniel. Analysis of security vulnerabilities in the movie production and distribution process. In *The 2003 ACM Workshop on DRM*, Washington, DC, USA, Oct 2003.
4. J. Chu, K. Labonte, and B. Levine. Availability and locality measurements of peer-to-peer file systems. In *ITCom: Scalability and Traffic Control in IP Networks*, Boston, MA, USA, July 2002.
5. B. Cohen. Incentives build robustness in bittorrent. In *Workshop on Economics of Peer-to-Peer Systems*, Berkeley, USA, May 2003. http://bittorrent.com/.
6. K. Gummadi, R. Dunn, S. Saroiu, S. Gribble, H. Levy, and J. Zahorjan. Measurement, modeling, and analysis of a peer-to-peer file-sharing workload. In *19-th ACM Symposium on Operating Systems Principles*, Bolton Landing, NY, USA, October 2003.
7. M. Izal, G. Urvoy-Keller, E. Biersack, P. Felber, A. Al Hamra, and L. Garces-Erice. Dissecting bittorrent: Five months in a torrent's lifetime. In *Passive and Active Measurements*, Antibes Juan-les-Pins, France, April 2004.
8. T. Karagiannis, A. Broido, N. Brownlee, kc claffy, and M. Faloutsos. Is p2p dying or just hiding? In *Globecom*, Dallas, TX, USA, November 2004.
9. N. Leibowitz, M. Ripeanu, and A. Wierzbicki. Deconstructing the kazaa network. In *3rd IEEE Workshop on Internet Applications (WIAPP'03)*, San Jose, CA, USA, June 2003.
10. J. Liang, R. Kumar, Y. Xi, and K. Ross. Pollution in p2p file sharing systems. In *IEEE Infocom*, Miami, FL, USA, March 2005.
11. T. Oh-ishi, K. Sakai, T. Iwata, and A. Kurokawa. The deployment of cache servers in p2p networks for improved performance in content-delivery. In *Third International Conference on Peer-to-Peer Computing (P2P'03)*, Linkoping, Sweden, September 2003.
12. A. Parker. The true picture of peer-to-peer filesharing, 2004. http://www.cachelogic.com/.
13. D. Qiu and R. Srikant. Modeling and performance analysis of bit torrent-like peer-to-peer networks. In *ACM SIGCOMM*, Portland, OR, USA, August 2004.
14. S. Saroiu, P. K. Gummadi, and S. D. Gribble. A measurement study of peer-to-peer file sharing systems. In *Multimedia Computing and Networking (MMCN'02)*, San Jose, CA, USA, January 2002.
15. S. Sen and J. Wang. Analyzing peer-to-peer traffic across large networks. *IEEE/ACM Transactions on Networking*, 12(2):219–232, 2004.
16. R. Sherwood, R. Braud, and B. Bhattacharjee. Slurpie: A cooperative bulk data transfer protocol. In *IEEE Infocom*, Honk Kong, China, March 2004.

Dynamic Load Balancing in Distributed Hash Tables [*]

Marcin Bienkowski[1], Miroslaw Korzeniowski[1],
and Friedhelm Meyer auf der Heide[2]

[1] International Graduate School of Dynamic Intelligent Systems,
Computer Science Department, University of Paderborn,
D-33102 Paderborn, Germany
{young, rudy}@upb.de
[2] Heinz Nixdorf Institute and Computer Science Department,
University of Paderborn, D-33102 Paderborn, Germany
fmadh@upb.de

Abstract. In Peer-to-Peer networks based on consistent hashing and ring topology, each server is responsible for an interval chosen (pseudo-) randomly on a unit circle. The topology of the network, the communication load, and the amount of data a server stores depend heavily on the length of its interval.

Additionally, the nodes are allowed to join the network or to leave it at any time. Such operations can destroy the balance of the network, even if all the intervals had equal lengths in the beginning.

This paper deals with the task of keeping such a system balanced, so that the lengths of intervals assigned to the nodes differ at most by a constant factor. We propose a simple fully distributed scheme, which works in a constant number of rounds and achieves optimal balance with high probability. Each round takes time at most $\mathcal{O}(\mathcal{D} + \log n)$, where $\mathcal{D}$ is the diameter of a specific network (e.g. $\Theta(\log n)$ for Chord [15] and $\Theta\left(\frac{\log n}{\log \log n}\right)$ for the continous-discrete approach proposed by Naor and Wieder [12,11]).

The scheme is a continuous process which does not have to be informed about the possible imbalance or the current size of the network to start working. The total number of migrations is within a constant factor from the number of migrations generated by the optimal centralized algorithm starting with the same initial network state.

1 Introduction

Peer-to-Peer networks are an efficient tool for storage and location of data since there is no central server which could become a bottleneck and the data is evenly distributed among the participants.

[*] Partially supported by DFG-Sonderforschungsbereich 376 "Massive Parallelität: Algorithmen, Entwurfsmethoden, Anwendungen" and by the Future and Emerging Technologies programme of EU under EU Contract 001907 DELIS "Dynamically Evolving, Large Scale Information Systems".

M. Castro and R. van Renesse (Eds.): IPTPS 2005, LNCS 3640, pp. 217–225, 2005.

The Peer-to-Peer networks which we are considering are based on consistent hashing [6] with ring topology like Chord [15], Tapestry [5], Pastry [14], and a topology inspired by de Bruijn graph [12,11]. The exact structure of the topology is not relevant. It is, however, important that each server has direct links to its successor and predecessor on the ring and that there is a routine that lets any server contact the server responsible for any given point in the network in time $\mathcal{D}$.

A crucial parameter of a network defined in this way is its *smoothness* which is the ratio of the length of the longest interval to the length of the shortest interval. The smoothness is a parameter, which informs about three aspects of load balance.

- Storage load of a server: The longer its interval is, the more data has to be stored in the server. On the other hand, if there are n servers and $\Omega(n \cdot \log n)$ items distributed (pseudo-) randomly on the ring, then, with high probability, the items are distributed evenly among the servers provided that the *smoothness* is constant.
- Degree of a node: A longer interval has a higher probability of being contacted by many short intervals which increases its in-degree.
- Congestion and dilation: Having constant smoothness is necessary to get small such routing parameters for example in [12,11] .

Even if we choose the points for the nodes fully randomly, the smoothness is as high as $\Omega(n \cdot \log n)$ with high probability[1] , whereas we would like it to be constant (n denotes the current number of nodes).

1.1   Our Results

We present a fully distributed algorithm which makes the smoothness constant using $\Theta(\mathcal{D} + \log n)$ direct communication steps per node. The algorithm can start with any distribution of nodes on the ring. It does not need to know $\mathcal{D}$ or n. A knowledge of an upper bound of $\log n$ suffices.

1.2   Related Work

Load balancing has been a crucial issue in the field of Peer-to-Peer networks since the design of the first network topologies like Chord [15]. It was proposed that each real server works as $\log n$ virtual servers, thus greatly decreasing the probability that some server will get a large part of the ring. Some extensions of this method were proposed in [13] and [4], where more schemes based on virtual servers were introduced and experimentally evaluated. Unfortunately, such an approach increases the degree of each server by a factor of $\log n$, because each server has to keep all the links of all its virtual servers.

The paradigm of many random choices [10] was used by Byers *et al* [3] and by Naor and Wieder [12,11]. When a server joins, it contacts $\log n$ random places in the network and chooses to cut the longest of all the found intervals. This yields constant *smoothness* with high probability.

---

[1] With high probability (w.h.p.) means with probability at least $1 - \mathcal{O}\left(\frac{1}{n^l}\right)$ for arbitrary constant l.

A similar approach was proposed in [1]. It extensively uses the structure of the hypercube to decrease the number of random choices to one and the communication to only one node and its neighbors. It also achieves constant *smoothness* with high probability.

The approaches above have a certain drawback. They both assume that servers join the network sequentially. What is more important, they do not provide analysis for the problem of balancing the intervals afresh when servers leave the network.

One of the most recent approaches due to Karger and Ruhl is presented in [7,8]. The authors propose a scheme, in which each node chooses $\Theta(\log n)$ places in the network and takes responsibility for only one of them. This can change if some nodes leave or join, but each node migrates only among the $\Theta(\log n)$ places it chose and after each operation $\Theta(\log \log n)$ nodes have to migrate on expectation. The advantage of our algorithm is that the number of migrations is always within a constant factor from optimal centralized algorithm. Both their and our algorithms use only tiny messages for checking the network state, and in both approaches the number of messages in half-life[2] can be bounded by $\Theta(\log n)$ per server. Their scheme is claimed to be resistant to attacks thanks to the fact that each node can only join in logarithmically bounded number of places on the ring. However, in [2] it is stated that such a scheme cannot be secure and that more sophisticated algorithms are needed to provide provable security. The reasoning for this is that with IPv6 the adversary has access to thousands of IP numbers and she can join the system with the ones falling into an interval that she has chosen. She does not have to join the system with each possible IP to check if this IP is useful, because the hash functions are public and she can compute them offline.

Manku [9] presented a scheme based on a virtual binary tree that achieves constant *smoothness* with low communication cost for servers joining or leaving the network. It is also shown that the *smoothness* can be diminished to as low as $(1 + \epsilon)$ with communication cost per operation increased to $\mathcal{O}(1/\epsilon)$. All the servers form a binary tree, where some of them (called *active*) are responsible for perfect balancing of subtrees rooted at them. Our scheme treats all servers evenly and is substantially simpler.

2   The Algorithm

In this paper we do not aim at optimizing the constants used, but rather at the simplicity of the algorithm and its analysis. For the next two subsections we fix a situation with some number n of servers in the system, and let $l(I_i)$ be the length of the interval I_i corresponding to server i. For the simplicity of the analysis we assume a static situation, i.e. no nodes try to join or leave the network during the rebalancing.

---

[2] Half-life of the network is the time it takes for half of the servers in the system to arrive or depart.

2.1   Estimating the Current Number of Servers

The goal of this subsection is to provide a scheme which, for every server i, returns an estimate n_i of the total number of nodes, so that each n_i is within a constant factor of n, with high probability.

Our approach is based on [2] where Awerbuch and Scheideler give an algorithm which yields a constant approximation of n in every node assuming that the nodes are distributed *uniformly at random* in the interval $[0, 1]$.

We define the following infinite and continuous process. Each node keeps a connection to one random position on the ring. This position is called a marker. The marker of a node is fixed only for $\mathcal{D}$ rounds during which the node is looking for a new random location for the marker.

The process of constantly changing the positions of markers is needed for the following reason. We show that for a fixed random configuration of markers our algorithm works properly with high probability. However, since the process runs forever, and nodes are allowed to leave and join (and thus change the positions of their markers), a bad configuration may (and will) appear at some point in time. We assure that the probability of failure in time step t is independent of the probability of failure in time step $t + \mathcal{D}$, and this enables the process to recover even if a bad event occurs.

Each node v estimates the size of the network as follows. It sets initially $l := l_v$ which is the length of its interval and $m := m_v$ which is the number of markers its interval stores. As long as $m < \log \frac{1}{l}$, the next not yet contacted successor is contacted, and both l and m are increased by its length and the number of markers, respectively.

Finally, l is decreased so that $m = \log \frac{1}{l}$. This can be done locally using only the information from the last server on our path.

The following Lemma from [2] states how large l is when the algorithm stops.

Lemma 1. *With high probability, $\alpha \cdot \frac{\log n}{n} \leq l \leq \beta \cdot \frac{\log n}{n}$ for constants α and β.*

In the following corollary we slightly reformulate this lemma in order to get an approximation of the number of servers n from an approximation of $\frac{\log n}{n}$.

Corollary 1. *Let l be the length of an interval found by the algorithm. Let n_i be the solution of $\log x - \log \log x = \log(1/l)$. Then with high probability $\frac{n}{\beta^2} \leq n_i \leq \frac{n}{\alpha^2}$.*

In the rest of the paper we assume that each server has computed n_i. Additionally, there are global constants l and u such that we may assume $l \cdot n_i \leq n \leq u \cdot n_i$, for eeach i.

2.2   The Load Balancing Algorithm

We call the intervals of length at most $\frac{4}{l \cdot n_i}$ *short* and intervals of length at least $\frac{12 \cdot u}{l^2 \cdot n_i}$ *long*. Intervals of length between $\frac{4}{l \cdot n_i}$ and $\frac{12 \cdot u}{l^2 \cdot n_i}$ are called *middle*. Notice that *short* intervals are defined so that each *middle* or *long* interval has length at least $\frac{4}{n}$. On the other hand, *long* intervals are defined so that by halving a *long* interval we never obtain a *short* interval.

The algorithm will minimize the length of the longest interval, but we also have to take care that no interval is too short. Therefore, before we begin the routine, we force all the intervals with lengths smaller than $\frac{1}{2 \cdot l \cdot n_i}$ to leave the network. By doing this, we assure that the length of the shortest interval in the network will be bounded from below by $\frac{1}{2 \cdot n}$. We have to explain why this does not destroy the structure of the network.

First of all, it is possible that we remove a huge fraction of the nodes. It is even possible that a very long interval appears, even though the network was balanced before. This is not a problem, since the algorithm will rebalance the system. Besides, if this algorithm is used also for new nodes at the moment of joining, this initialization will never be needed. We do not completely remove the nodes with too short intervals from the network. The number of nodes n and thus also the number of markers is unaffected, and the removed nodes will later act as though they were simple *short* intervals. Each of these nodes can contact the network through its marker.

Our algorithm works in rounds. In each round we find a linear number of *short* intervals which can leave the network without introducing any new *long* intervals and then we use them to divide the existing *long* intervals.

The routine works differently for different nodes, depending on the initial server's interval's length. The *middle* intervals and the *short* intervals which decided to stay help only by forwarding the contacts that come to them. The pseudocodes for all types of intervals are depicted in Figure 1.

---

short
    state := staying
    if (predecessor is *short*)
       with probability $\frac{1}{2}$ change state to leaving
    if (state = leaving **and** predecessor.state = staying)
    {
       p := random(0..1)
       P := the node responsible for p
       contact consecutively the node P and its $6 \cdot \log(u \cdot n_i)$ successors on the ring
       if (a node R accepts)
          leave and rejoin in the middle of the interval of R
    }
    At any time, if any node contacts, reject.

middle
    At any time, if any node contacts, reject.

long
    wait for contacts
    if any node contacts, accept

Fig. 1. The algorithm with respect to lengths of intervals (one round)

Theorem 1. *The algorithm has the following properties, all holding with high probability:*

1. *In each round each node incurs a communication cost of at most $O(D + \log n)$.*
2. *The total number of migrated nodes is within a constant factor from the number of migrations generated by the optimal centralized algorithm with the same initial network state.*
3. *Each node is migrated at most once.*
4. *$O(1)$ rounds are sufficient to achieve constant smoothness.*

Proof. The first statement of the theorem follows easily from the algorithm due to the fact that each *short* node sends a message to a random destination which takes time D and then consecutively contacts the successors of the found node. This incurs additional communication cost of at most $r \cdot (\log n + \log u)$. Additionaly in each round each node changes the position of its marker and this operation also incurs communication cost D.

The second one is guaranteed by the property that if a node tries to leave the network and join it somewhere else, it is certain that its predecessor is *short* and is not going to change its location. This assures that the predecessor will take over the job of our interval and it will not become *long*. Therefore, no *long* interval is ever created. Both our and the optimal centralized algorithm have to cut each *long* interval into *middle* intervals. Let M and S be the upper thresholds for the lengths of a *middle* and *short* interval, respectively, and $l(I)$ be the length of an arbitrary *long* interval. The optimal algorithm needs at least $\lceil l(I)/M \rceil$ cuts, wheras ours always cuts an interval in the middle and performs at most $2^{\lceil \log(l(I)/S) \rceil}$ cuts, which can be at most constant times larger because M/S is constant.

The statement that each server is migrated at most once follows from the reasoning below. A server is migrated only if its interval is *short*. Due to the gap between the upper threshold for *short* interval and the lower threshold for *long* interval, after being migrated the server never takes responsibility for a *short* interval, so it will not be migrated again.

In order to prove the last statement of the theorem, we show the following two lemmas. The first one shows how many *short* intervals are willing to help during a constant number of rounds. The second one states how many helpful intervals are needed so that the algorithm succeeds in balancing the system.

Lemma 2. *For any constant $a \geq 0$, there exists a constant c, such that in c rounds at least $a \cdot n$ nodes are ready to migrate, w.h.p.*

Proof. As stated before, the length of each *middle* or *long* interval is at least $\frac{4}{n}$ and thus at most $\frac{1}{4} \cdot n$ intervals are *middle* or *long*. Therefore, we have at least $\frac{3}{4} \cdot n$ nodes responsible for *short* intervals.

We number all the nodes in order of their position in the ring with numbers $0, \dots, n-1$. For simplicity we assume that n is even, and divide the set of all nodes into $n/2$ pairs $P_i = (2i, 2i+1)$, where $i = 0, \dots, \frac{n}{2} - 1$. Then there are at least $\frac{1}{2} \cdot n - \frac{1}{4} \cdot n = \frac{1}{4} \cdot n$ pairs P_i, which contain indexes of two *short* intervals. Since the first element of a pair is assigned state `staying` with probability at least $1/2$ and the second element state `leaving` with probability $1/2$, the probability that the second element is eager to migrate is at least $1/4$. For two different pairs P_i and P_j migrations of their second elements are independent. We stress here that this reasoning only only bounds the number of nodes able to migrate from below. For example, we do not consider first elements of pairs which also may migrate in some cases. Nevertheless, we are able to show that the number of migrating elements is large enough. Notice also that even if in one round many of the nodes migrate, it is still guaranteed that in each of the next rounds there will still exist at least $\frac{3}{4} \cdot n$ *short* intervals.

The above process stochastically dominates a Bernoulli process with $c \cdot n/4$ trials and single trial success probability $p = 1/4$. Let X be a random variable denoting the number of successes in the Bernoulli process. Then $E[X] = c \cdot n/16$ and we can use Chernoff bound to show that $X \geq a \cdot n$ with high probability if we only choose c large enough with respect to a.   □

In the following lemma we deal with cutting one *long* interval into *middle* intervals.

Lemma 3. *There exists a constant b such that for any long interval I, after $b \cdot n$ contacts are generated overall, the interval I will be cut into middle intervals, w.h.p.*

Proof. For the further analysis we will need that $l(I) \leq \frac{\log n}{n}$, therefore we first consider the case where $l(I) > \frac{\log n}{n}$. We would like to estimate the number of contacts that have to be generated in order to cut I into intervals of length at most $\frac{\log n}{n}$. We depict the process of cutting I on a binary tree. Let I be the root of this tree and its children the two intervals into which I is cut after it receives the first contact. The tree is built further in the same way and achieves its lowest level when its nodes have length s such that $\frac{1}{2} \cdot \frac{\log n}{n} \leq s \leq \frac{\log n}{n}$. The tree has height at most $\log n$. If a leaf gets $\log n$ contacts, it can use them to cover the whole path from itself to the root. Such covering is a witness that this interval will be separated from others. Thus, if each of the leaves gets $\log n$ contacts, interval I will be cut into intervals of length at most $\frac{\log n}{n}$.

Let b_1 be a sufficiently large constant and consider first $b_1 \cdot n$ contacts. We will bound the probability that one of the leaves gets at most $\log n$ of these contacts. Let X be a random variable depicting how many contacts fall into a leaf J. The probability that a contact hits a leaf is equal to the length of this leaf and the expected number of contacts that hit a leaf is $E[X] \geq b_1 \cdot \log n$. Chernoff bound guarantees that, if b_1 is large enough, the number of contacts is at least $\log n$, w.h.p.

There are at most n leaves in this tree, so each of them gets sufficiently many contacts with high probability. In the further phase we assume that all the intervals existing in the network are of length at most $\frac{\log n}{n}$.

Let J be any of such intervals. Consider the maximal possible set K of predecessors of J, such that their total length is at most $2 \cdot \frac{\log n}{n}$. Maximality assures that $l(K) \geq \frac{\log n}{n}$. The upper bound on the length assures that even if the intervals belonging to K and J are cut ("are cut" in this context means "have been cut", "are being cut" and/or "will be cut") into smallest possible pieces (of length $\frac{2}{n}$), their number does not exceed $6 \cdot \log n$. Therefore, if a contact hits some of them and is not needed by any of them, then it is forwarded to J and can reach its furthest end. We consider only the contacts that hit K. Some of them will be used by K and the rest will be forwarded to J.

Let b_2 be a constant and Y be a random variable denoting the number of contacts that fall into K in a process in which $b_2 \cdot n$ contacts are generated in the network. We want to show that, with high probability, Y is large enough, i.e. $Y \geq 2 \cdot n \cdot (l(J) + l(K))$. The expected value of Y can be estimated as $E[Y] = b_2 \cdot n \cdot l(K) \geq b_2 \cdot \log n$. Again, Chernoff bound guarantees that $Y \geq 6 \cdot \log n$, with high probability, if b_2 is large enough. This is sufficient to cut both K and J into *middle* intervals.

Now taking $b = b_1 + b_2$, finishes the proof of Lemma 3.   □

Combining Lemmas 2 and 3 and setting $a = b$, finishes the proof of Theorem 1.   □

3   Conclusion and Future Work

We have presented a distributed randomized scheme that continously rebalances the lengths of intervals of a Distributed Hash Table based on a ring topology. We proved that the scheme succeeds with high probability and that its cost measured in the terms of migrated nodes is comparable to the best possible.

Our scheme still has some deficiencies. The constants which emerge from the analysis are huge. We are convinced that these constants are much smaller than their bounds implied by the analysis. In the experimental evaluation one can play with at least a few parameters to see which configuration yields the best behavior in practice. The first parameter is how well we approximate the number of servers n present in the network. Another one is how many times a help-offer is forwarded before it is discarded. And the last one is the possibility to redefine the lengths of *short*, *middle* and *long* intervals. In the future we plan to redesign the scheme so that we can approach the *smoothness* of $1 + \epsilon$ with additional cost of $1/\epsilon$ per operation, as it is done in [9].

Another drawback at the moment is that the analysis demands that the algorithm is synchronized. This can probably be avoided with more careful analysis in the part where nodes with *short* intervals decide to stay or help. On the one hand, if a node tries to help, it blocks its predecessor for $\Theta(\log n)$ rounds. On the other, only one decision is needed per $\Theta(\log n)$ steps.

Another issue omitted here is counting of nodes. Due to the space limitations we have decided to use the scheme proposed by Awerbuch and Scheideler in [2]. We developed another algorithm which is more compatible to our load balancing scheme. It inserts $\Delta \geq \log n$ markers per node and instead of evening the lengths of intervals it evens their weights defined as the number of markers contained in an interval. We can prove that such scheme also rebalances the whole system in constant number of rounds, w.h.p.

As mentioned in the introduction our scheme can be proven to use $\Theta(\log n)$ messages in a half-life, provided that the half-life is known. Our proof, however, is based on the assumption that join (or leave) operations are distributed evenly in a half-life and not generated in an adversarial fashion (for example if nothing happens for a long time and then many new nodes join at once). We are working on bounding the communication cost using techniques from online analysis.

References

1. M. Adler, E. Halperin, R. Karp, and V. Vazirani. A stochastic process on the hypercube with applications to peer-to-peer networks. In *Proc. of the 35th ACM Symp. on Theory of Computing (STOC)*, pages 575–584, June 2003.
2. B. Awerbuch and C. Scheideler. Group spreading: A protocol for provably secure distributed name service. In *Proc. of the 31st Int. Colloquium on Automata, Languages, and Programming (ICALP)*, pages 183–195, July 2004.
3. J. Byers, J. Considine, and M. Mitzenmacher. Simple load balancing for distributed hash tables. In *2nd International Workshop on Peer-to-Peer Systems (IPTPS)*, pages 80–87, Feb. 2003.
4. B. Godfrey, K. Lakshminarayanan, S. Surana, R. Karp, and I. Stoica. Load balancing in dynamic structured P2P systems. In *23rd Conference of the IEEE Communications Society (INFOCOM)*, Mar. 2004.
5. K. Hildrum, J. D. Kubiatowicz, S. Rao, and B. Y. Zhao. Distributed object location in a dynamic network. In *Proc. of the 14th ACM Symp. on Parallel Algorithms and Architectures (SPAA)*, pages 41–52, Aug. 2002.
6. D. R. Karger, E. Lehman, T. Leighton, M. Levine, D. Lewin, and R. Panigrahy. Consistent hashing and random trees: Distributed caching protocols for relieving hot spots on the world wide web. In *Proc. of the 29th ACM Symp. on Theory of Computing (STOC)*, pages 654–663, May 1997.
7. D. R. Karger and M. Ruhl. Simple efficient load balancing algorithms for peer-to-peer systems. In *3rd International Workshop on Peer-to-Peer Systems (IPTPS)*, 2004.
8. D. R. Karger and M. Ruhl. Simple efficient load balancing algorithms for peer-to-peer systems. In *Proc. of the 16th ACM Symp. on Parallelism in Algorithms and Architectures (SPAA)*, pages 36–43, June 2004.
9. G. S. Manku. Balanced binary trees for id management and load balance in distributed hash tables. In *Proc. of the 23rd annual ACM symposium on Principles of Distributed Computing (PODC)*, pages 197–205, 2004.
10. M. Mitzenmacher, A. W. Richa, and R. Sitaraman. The power of two random choices: A survey of techniques and results. In *Handbook of Randomized Computing. P. Pardalos, S.Rajasekaran, J.Rolim, and Eds. Kluwer*, 2000.
11. M. Naor and U. Wieder. Novel architectures for P2P applications: the continuous-discrete approach. In *Proc. of the 15th ACM Symp. on Parallel Algorithms and Architectures (SPAA)*, pages 50–59, June 2003.
12. M. Naor and U. Wieder. A simple fault tolerant distributed hash table. In *2nd International Workshop on Peer-to-Peer Systems (IPTPS)*, Feb. 2003.
13. A. Rao, K. Lakshminarayanan, S. Surana, R. Karp, and I. Stoica. Load balancing in structured P2P systems. In *2nd International Workshop on Peer-to-Peer Systems (IPTPS)*, Feb. 2003.
14. A. Rowstron and P. Druschel. Pastry: Scalable, decentralized object location, and routing for large-scale peer-to-peer systems. *Lecture Notes in Computer Science*, 2218:329–350, 2001.
15. I. Stoica, R. Morris, D. R. Karger, M. F. Kaashoek, and H. Balakrishnan. Chord: A scalable peer-to-peer lookup service for internet applications. In *Proc. of the ACM SIGCOMM*, pages 149–160, 2001.

High Availability in DHTs: Erasure Coding vs. Replication

Rodrigo Rodrigues[1] and Barbara Liskov[2]

[1] INESC-ID / Instituto Superior Técnico, Lisbon, Portugal
[2] MIT Computer Science and Artificial Intelligence Laboratory,
Cambridge MA, USA

Abstract. High availability in peer-to-peer DHTs requires data redundancy. This paper compares two popular redundancy schemes: replication and erasure coding. Unlike previous comparisons, we take the characteristics of the nodes that comprise the overlay into account, and conclude that in some cases the benefits from coding are limited, and may not be worth its disadvantages.

1   Introduction

Peer-to-peer distributed hash tables (DHTs) propose a logically centralized, physically distributed, hash table abstraction that can be shared simultaneously by many applications [1,2,3,4]. Ensuring that data objects in the DHT have high availability levels when the nodes that are storing them are not themselves 100% available requires some form of data redundancy. Peer-to-peer DHTs have proposed two different redundancy schemes: replication [2,3] and erasure coding [1,4]. This paper aims to provide a comprehensive discussion about the advantages of each scheme.

While previous comparisons exist [4,5,6] they mostly argue that erasure coding is the clear victor, due to huge storage savings for the same availability levels (or conversely, huge availability gains for the same storage levels). Our conclusion is somewhat different: we argue that while gains from coding exist, they are highly dependent on the characteristics of the nodes that comprise the overlay. In fact, the benefits of coding are so limited in some cases that they can easily be outweighed by some disadvantages and the extra complexity of erasure codes.

We begin this paper by performing an analytic comparison of replication and coding that clearly delineates the relative gains from using coding vs. replication as a function of the server availability and the desired DHT object availability (Section 2). We present a model [7] that allows us to understand server availability (Section 3). Then we use measured values from three different traces to find out exact values for the parameters of the model (Section 4). This allows us to draw more precise conclusions about the advantages of using coding or replication (Section 5).

M. Castro and R. van Renesse (Eds.): IPTPS 2005, LNCS 3640, pp. 226–239, 2005.
© Springer-Verlag Berlin Heidelberg 2005

2   Coding vs. Replication – Redundancy Levels

This section summarizes the two redundancy schemes and presents an analytic comparison that highlights the main advantage of coding: the savings in terms of the required redundancy. Section 5 outlines other positive and negative aspects of the two schemes.

2.1   Replication

Replication is the simplest redundancy scheme; here k identical copies of each data object are kept at each instant by system members.

The value of k must be set appropriately depending on the desired per object unavailability target, ϵ (i.e., $1 - \epsilon$ has some "number of nines"), and on the average node availability, a. Assuming that node availability is independent and identically distributed (I.I.D.), and assuming we only need one out of the k replicas of the data to be available in order to retrieve it (this would be the case if the data is immutable and therefore a single available copy is sufficient to retrieve the correct object), we compute the following values for ϵ.

$$\begin{aligned}
\epsilon &= P(\text{object } o \text{ is unavailable}) \\
&= P(\text{all } k \text{ replicas of } o \text{ are unavailable}) \\
&= P(\text{one replica is unavailable})^k \\
&= (1 - a)^k
\end{aligned}$$

which upon solving for k yields

$$k = \frac{\log \epsilon}{\log(1 - a)} \tag{1}$$

2.2   Erasure Coding

With an erasure-coded redundancy scheme, each object is divided into m fragments and recoded into n fragments which are stored separately, where $n > m$. The key property of erasure codes is that the original object can be reconstructed from any m fragments (where the combined size for the m fragments is approximately equal to the original object size). This means that the effective redundancy factor is $k_c = \frac{n}{m}$.

We now exhibit the equivalent of Equation (1) for the case of erasure coding. (This is a summary of a complete derivation that can be found in [8].) Object availability is given by the probability that at least m out of $k_c \cdot m$ fragments are available:

$$1 - \epsilon = \sum_{i=m}^{k_c m} \binom{k_c m}{i} a^i (1 - a)^{k_c m - i}.$$

Using algebraic simplifications and the normal approximation to the binomial distribution (see [8]), we get the following formula for the erasure coding redundancy factor:

$$k_c = \left(\frac{\sigma_\epsilon \sqrt{\frac{a(1-a)}{m}} + \sqrt{\frac{\sigma_\epsilon^2 a(1-a)}{m} + 4a}}{2a} \right)^2 \qquad (2)$$

where σ_ϵ is the number of standard deviations in a normal distribution for the required level of availability. E.g., $\sigma_\epsilon = 3.7$ corresponds to four nines of availability.

Note that we considered the use of deterministic coding schemes with a constant rate of encoding (e.g., Reed-Solomon [9] or IDA [10]). Our analysis does not extend to rateless codes [11], since it is not consensual how to use such codes in a storage environment like a DHT.

2.3 Comparing the Redundancy

The previous discussion highlights the main reason for using coding: the increased redundancy allows the same level of availability to be achieved with much smaller additional storage.

The exact gains are depicted in Figure 1. This plots the ratio between the required replication and the required erasure coding expansion factor (i.e., the ratio between equations 1 and 2) for different server availability levels (assuming server availability is I.I.D.) and for three different per-object availability targets: 3, 4, and 5 nines of availability. In this figure we set the number of fragments needed to reconstruct an object to be 7 (i.e., we set $m = 7$ in Equation 2). This is the value used by Chord [4]. Increasing m would lead to more redundancy savings, but at the cost of exacerbating the disadvantages of coding we detail in Section 5.

The conclusion is that erasure coding is going to matter more if you store the data in unreliable servers (lower server availability levels) or if you target better guarantees from the system (higher number of nines in object availability). The redundancy gains from using coding range from 1 to 3-fold.

The remainder of our discussion assumes a per-object availability target of 4 nines. Targeting higher levels of availability seems exaggerated since other aspects of the system will not keep up with such high availability levels. For instance, a measurement study of MIT's client access link found that a host at MIT was able to reach the rest of the Internet 99.9% of the time [12]. The same study pointed out that the MIT access link was more reliable than two other links (a DSL line and a 100 Mbits/s link from Cogent).

Since the overall end-to-end availability will be given by the product

$$end\text{-}to\text{-}end\ avail. = client\ access\ link\ avail. \cdot DHT\ object\ avail.$$

and considering that the client access link only has 3 nines of availability, then making a distinction between, for instance, 5 and 6 nines of of DHT object

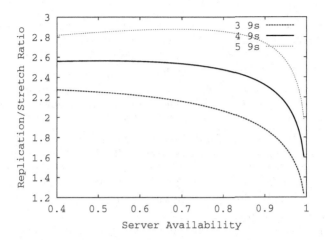

Fig. 1. Ratio between required replication and required expansion factors as a function of the server availability and for three different per-object availability levels. We used $m = 7$ in equation 2, since this is the value used in the Chord implementation [4].

availability is irrelevant since the end-to-end object availability is dominated by the uplink quality (or other factors we are not considering), and the extra DHT availability is in the noise.

A question we may ask is why are redundancy savings important? Obviously, they lead to lower disk usage. Also they may improve the speed of writes, since a smaller amount of data has to be uploaded from the writer to the servers, and therefore, if client upload bandwidth limits the write speed, then coding will lead to faster writes.

But more important than these two aspects is the savings in the bandwidth required to restore redundancy levels in the presence of a changing membership. This importance is due to the fact that bandwidth, and not spare storage, is most likely the limiting factor for the scalability of peer-to-peer storage systems [7].

3   Basic Model

This section presents a simple model that allows us to (1) quantify the bandwidth cost for maintaining data redundancy in the presence of membership changes (as a function of the required redundancy), and (2) understand the concept of server availability in a peer-to-peer DHT so we can measure it. The core of the model, described in Sections 3.1 and 3.2, was presented in a previous publication [7], so we will only summarize it.

3.1   Assumptions

Our model assumes a large, dynamic collection of nodes that cooperatively store data. The data set is partitioned and each subset is assigned to different nodes using a well-known data placement mapping (i.e., a function from the current membership to the set of replicas of each block). This is what happens, for instance, in consistent hashing [13], used by storage systems such as CFS [4].

We make a number of simplifying assumptions. The main simplification comes from the fact that we will only focus on an average-case analysis. When considering the worse-case values for certain parameters, like the rate at which nodes leave the system, the model underestimates the required bandwidth.

We assume a fixed redundancy factor and identical per-node space contributions. A previous system [5] dropped these two assumptions and used a variable redundancy factor where many copies are created initially, and, as flaky nodes leave the system, the redundancy levels will drop. This leads to a biased system where the stable nodes donate most of the storage, therefore drastically reducing bandwidth costs. This affects some of our conclusions, and, as future work, we would like to understand how our analysis would change in this new design.

We assume a constant rate of joining and leaving and we assume that join and leave events are independent. We also assume a constant steady-state number of nodes.

3.2   Data Maintenance Model

We consider a set of N identical hosts that cooperatively provide guaranteed storage over the network. Nodes are added to the set at rate α and leave at rate λ, but the average system size is constant, i.e. $\alpha = \lambda$. On average, a node stays a member for $T = N/\lambda$ (this is a queuing theory result known as Little's Law [14]).

Our data model is that the system reliably stores a total of D bytes of unique data stored with a redundancy factor k, for a total of $S = kD$ bytes of contributed storage. k is either the replication factor or the expansion due to coding and must be set (depending on a desired availability target and on the node availability of the specific deployment) according to equations 1 and 2.

Each node *joining* the system must download all the data that it must serve later, however that subset of data might be mapped to it. The average size of this transfer is S/N, since we assume identical per-node storage contributions. Join events happen every $\frac{1}{\alpha} = \frac{1}{\lambda}$ time units on average. So the aggregate bandwidth to deal with nodes joining the overlay is $\frac{\lambda S}{N}$, or S/T.

When a node *leaves* the overlay, all the data it housed must be copied over to new nodes; otherwise redundancy would be lost. Thus, each leave event also leads to the transfer of S/N bytes of data. Leaves therefore also require an aggregate bandwidth of $\frac{\lambda S}{N}$, or S/T.

In some cases the cost of leaving the system can be avoided: for instance, if the level of redundancy for a given block is sufficiently high, a new node can both join and leave without requiring data movement.

We will ignore this optimization and therefore the total bandwidth usage for data maintenance is $\frac{2S}{T} = \frac{2kD}{T}$, or a per node average of:

$$B/N = 2\frac{kD/N}{T}, \quad \text{or} \quad BW/node = 2\frac{space/node}{lifetime} \tag{3}$$

3.3   Restoring Redundancy with Coding

When coding is used, creating new fragments to cope with nodes holding other fragments leaving the system is not a trivial task. The problem is that to create a new fragment we must have access to the entire data object. We envision two alternative approaches. The more expensive alternative would be to download enough fragments to reconstruct the object and then create a new fragment. This is costly since, for each fragment that is lost and needs to be reinstated, some system node needs to download $m - 1$ fragments (assuming it has another fragment already) and upload the new fragment. Thus the amount of data that needs to be transferred is m times higher than the amount of redundancy lost.

The alternative is to maintain a full copy of the object at one of the nodes, along with the fragments at the remaining nodes that share the responsibility for the object. In practice, this corresponds to increasing the redundancy factors for erasure coding by one unit.

Note that the analysis above is still correct when we mix fragments with complete copies, namely the fact that the amount of data that needs to be moved when nodes leave is equal to the amount of data the departing node stored. This is correct because to restore a fragment, the node that keeps a complete copy can create the new fragment and push it to the new owner, and to restore a complete copy the node that will become responsible for that copy can download m fragments with the combined size approximately equal to the size of the object.

In the remainder of the paper we will assume that a system using coding keeps the additional complete copy for each object stored in the system.

3.4   Distinguishing Downtime vs. Departure

In the model we presented, we refer to *joins* and *leaves* as joining the system for the first time or leaving forever, and data movement is triggered only by these events.

In other words, we try to make a simple distinction between session times and membership lifetimes (as other authors have noted [8,15]). This distinction is illustrated in Figure 2: A session time corresponds to the duration of an interval when a node is reachable, whereas a membership lifetime is the time from when the node enters the system for the first time until it leaves the system permanently.

This distinction is important since it avoids triggering data movement to restore redundancy due to a temporary disconnection. The side effect of doing

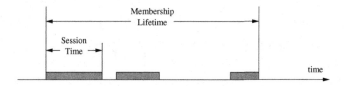

Fig. 2. Distinction between sessions and lifetimes

this is that nodes will be unavailable for some part of their membership lifetime. We define *node availability*, *a*, as the fraction of the time a member of the system is reachable, or in other words, the sum of the node's session times divided by the node's membership lifetime.

3.5   Detecting Permanent Departures

The problem with this simple model for distinguishing between sessions and membership lifetimes is that it requires future knowledge: applications have no means to distinguish a temporary departure from a permanent leave at the time of a node's disconnection. To address this problem we introduce a new concept, a *membership timeout*, τ, that measures how long the system delays its response to failures. In other words, the process of making new hosts responsible for a host's data does not begin until that host has been out of contact for longer than time τ, as illustrated in Figure 3.

There are two main consequences of increasing the membership timeout: First, a higher τ means that member lifetimes are longer since transient failures are not considered leaves (and as a consequence the total member count will also increase). Second, the average host availability, a, will decrease if we wait longer before we evict a node from the system.

Translating this into our previous model, T and N will now become $T(\tau)$ and $N(\tau)$, and a will now become $a(\tau)$, which implies that k will become $k(a(\tau), \epsilon)$ (set accordingly to the equations above). Note that a decreases with τ, whereas T, N, and k increase with τ. By our definition of availability, $N(\tau)$ can be deduced as $N(0)/a(\tau)$.

Another consequence is that some joins are not going to trigger data movement, as they will now be re-joins and the node will retain the data it needs to serve after re-joining the system. According to the measurements we will present later, this has a minor impact on data movement when we set long membership timeouts (i.e., if τ is large enough then there will hardly exist any re-joins) so we will ignore this issue.

Equation 3 can therefore be rewritten as

$$B/N(\tau) = 2\frac{k(a(\tau), \epsilon)D/N(\tau)}{T(\tau)} \qquad (4)$$

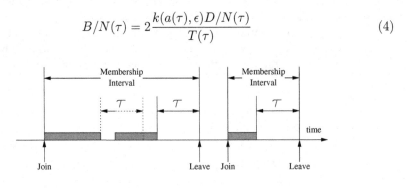

Fig. 3. Membership timeout, τ

Note that $B/N(\tau)$ is the average bandwidth used by system members. At any point in time some of these members are not running the application (the unavailable nodes) and these do not contribute to bandwidth usage. Thus we may also want to compute the average bandwidth used by nodes while they are available (i.e., running the application). To do this we replace the left hand side of Equation 4 with $a(\tau)B/N(0)$ and compute $B/N(0)$ instead.

4   Measured Dynamics and Availability

In this section we present results from measurements of how the membership dynamics and the node availability change as a function of the membership timeout (τ), and derive the corresponding redundancy requirements and maintenance bandwidth (for both replication and coding).

We use numbers from three different traces that correspond to distinct likely deployments of a peer-to-peer storage system:

- Peer-to-peer (volunteer-based) – We used the data collected by Bhagwan et al. on their study of the Overnet file sharing system [8]. This tracked the reachability of 2,400 peers (gathered using a crawl of the system membership) during 7 days by looking up their node IDs every 20 minutes.
- Corporate Desktop PCs – We used the data collected by Bolosky et al. [16] on their study of the availability of 51,663 desktop PCs at Microsoft Corporation over the course of 35 days by pinging a fixed set of machines every hour.
- Server Infrastructure – This data was collected by Stribling [17] and reflects the results of pinging every pair among 186 hosts of the Planet Lab testbed every 15 minutes. We used the data collected over the course of 70

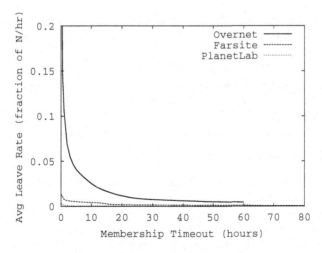

Fig. 4. Membership dynamics as a function of the membership timeout (τ)

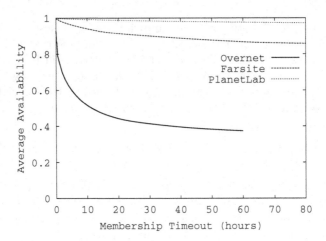

Fig. 5. Average node availability as a function of the membership timeout (τ)

days between October and December 2003. Here we considered a host to be reachable if at least half of the nodes in the trace could ping it.

Our graphs only show the average case behavior of the system.

Figure 4 shows how increasing the membership timeout τ decreases the dynamics of the system. In this case, the dynamics are expressed as the average fraction of system nodes that leave the system during an hour (in the y axis). Note that by leave we are now referring to having left for over τ units of time (i.e., we are referring to membership dynamics, not session dynamics).

As expected, the system membership becomes less dynamic as the membership timeout increases, since some of the session terminations will no longer be considered as membership leaves, namely if the node returns to the system before τ units of time.

As mentioned, the second main effect of increasing τ is that the node availability in the system will decrease. This effect is shown in Figure 5.

Node availability is, as one would expect, extremely high for PlanetLab (above 97% on average), slightly lower for Farsite (but still above 85% on average), and low for the peer-to-peer trace (lower than 50% when τ is greater than 11 hours).

Note that we did not plot how N varies with τ but this can be easily deduced from the fact that $N(\tau) = N(0)/a(\tau)$.

4.1   Needed Redundancy and Bandwidth

Finally, we measure the bandwidth gains of using erasure coding vs. replication in the three deployments.

First, we compute the needed redundancy for the two redundancy schemes as a function of the membership timeout (τ). To do this we used the availability values of Figure 5 in Equations (1) and (2), and plotted the corresponding redundancy factors, assuming a target average per-object availability of four nines.

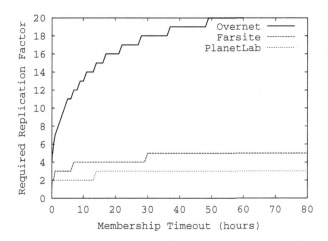

Fig. 6. Required replication factor for four nines of per-object availability, as a function of the membership timeout (τ)

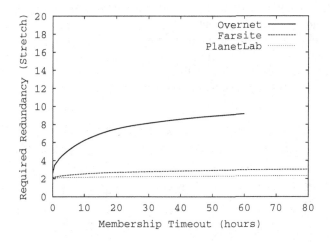

Fig. 7. Required coding redundancy factor for four nines of per-object availability, as a function of the membership timeout (τ) as determined by Equation 2, and considering the extra copy required to restore lost fragments

The results for replication are shown in Figure 6. This shows that Overnet requires the most redundancy, as expected, reaching a replication factor of 20. In the other two deployments replication factors are much lower, on the order of a few units. Note that the replication values in this figure are rounded off to the next integer, since we cannot have a fraction of copies.

Figure 7 shows the redundancy requirements (i.e., the expansion factor) for the availability values of Figure 5 (using Equation 2 with $m = 7$ and four nines of target availability). The redundancy values shown in Figure 7 include the extra copy of the object required to create new fragments as nodes leave the system (as we explained in Section 3.3).

As shown in Figure 7, Overnet still requires more redundancy than the other two deployments, but for Overnet coding leads to the most substantial storage savings (for a fixed amount of unique data stored in the system) since it can reduce the redundancy factors by more than half.

Finally, we compare the bandwidth usage of the two schemes. For this we use the basic equation for the cost of redundancy maintenance (Equation 3) and apply for membership lifetimes the values implied by the leave rates from Figure 4 (recall the average membership lifetime is the inverse of the average join or leave rate). We will also assume a fixed number of servers (10, 000), and a fixed amount of *unique* data stored in the system (10 TB). We used the replication factors from Figure 6, and for coding the redundancy factors from Figure 7.

Figure 8 shows the average bandwidth used for the three different traces and for different values of τ. An interesting effect can be observed in the Farsite trace, where the bandwidth has two "steps" (around $\tau = 14$ and $\tau = 64$ hours). These correspond to the people who turn off their machines at night, and during the weekends, respectively. Setting τ to be greater than each of these downtime periods will prevent this downtime from generating a membership change and the corresponding data movement.

Figure 9 shows the equivalent of Figure 8 for the case when coding is used instead of replication. The average bandwidth values are now lower due to the smaller redundancy used with coding, especially in the Overnet deployment where we achieve the most substantial redundancy savings.

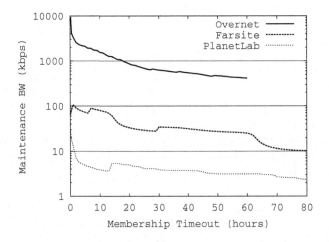

Fig. 8. Maintenance bandwidth – Replication. Average bandwidth required for redundancy maintenance as a function of the membership timeout (τ). This assumes that 10, 000 nodes are cooperatively storing $10TB$ of *unique* data, and replication is used for data redundancy.

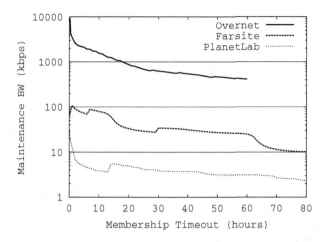

Fig. 9. Maintenance bandwidth – Erasure coding. Average bandwidth required for redundancy maintenance as a function of the membership timeout (τ). This assumes that $10,000$ nodes are cooperatively storing $10TB$ of *unique* data, and coding is used for data redundancy.

5   Discussion and Conclusion

Several conclusions can be drawn from Figures 8 and 9.

For the Overnet trace, coding is a win since server availability is low (we are on the left hand side of Figure 1) but unfortunately the maintenance bandwidth for a scalable and highly available storage system with Overnet-like membership dynamics can be unsustainable for home users [7] (around 100 kbps on average for a modest per-node contribution of a few gigabytes). Therefore, cooperative storage systems should target more stable environments like Farsite or PlanetLab.

For the PlanetLab trace, coding is not a win, since server availability is extremely high (corresponding to the right hand side of Figure 1).

So the most interesting deployment for using erasure codes is Farsite, where intermediate server availability of 80–90% already presents visible redundancy savings.

However, the redundancy savings from using coding instead of full replication come at a price.

The main point against the use of coding is that it introduces complexity in the system. Not only there is complexity associated with the encoding and decoding of the blocks, but the entire system design becomes more complex (e.g., the task of redundancy maintenance becomes more complicated as explained in Section 3).

As a general principle, we believe that complexity in system design should be avoided unless proven strictly necessary. Therefore system designers should question if the added complexity is worth the benefits that may be limited depending on the deployment.

Another point against the use of erasure codes is the download latency in a environment like the Internet where the inter-node latency is very heterogeneous. When using replication, the data object can be downloaded from the replica that is closest to the client, whereas with coding the download latency is bounded by the distance to the mth closest replica. This problem was illustrated with simulation results in a previous paper [4].

The task of downloading only a particular subset of the object (a sub-block) is also complicated by coding, where the entire object must be reconstructed. With full replicas sub-blocks can be downloaded trivially.

A similar observation is that erasure coding is not adequate for a system design where operations are done at the server side, like keyword searching.

A final point is that in our analysis we considered only immutable data. This assumption is particularly important for our distinction between session times and membership lifetimes, because we are assuming that when an unreachable node rejoins the system, its state is still valid. This would not be true if it contained mutable state that had been modified in the meantime. The impact of mutability on the redundancy choices is unclear, since we have to consider how a node determines whether its state is accurate, and what it does if it isn't. A study of redundancy techniques in the presence of mutability is an area for future work.

Acknowledgements

We thank Jeremy Stribling, the Farsite team at MSR, and the Total Recall team at UCSD for supplying the data collected in their studies. We thank Mike Walfish, Emil Sit, and the anonymous reviewers for their helpful comments. Special thanks to Steven Richman that helped process the Overnet trace, and to Chuck Blake that was part of the genesis of this series of papers and wrote some of the scripts that were reused here.

This research is supported by DARPA under contract F30602-98-1-0237 and by the NSF under Cooperative Agreement ANI-0225660. Rodrigo Rodrigues was supported by a fellowship from the Calouste Gulbenkian Foundation, and was previously supported by a Praxis XXI fellowship.

References

1. Kubiatowicz, J., Bindel, D., Chen, Y., Czerwinski, S., Eaton, P., Geels, D., Gummadi, R., Rhea, S., Weatherspoon, H., Weimer, W., Wells, C., Zhao, B.: OceanStore: An architecture for global-scale persistent storage. In: ASPLOS-IX: Proceedings of the ninth international conference on Architectural support for programming languages and operating systems. (2000) 190–201
2. Ratnasamy, S., Francis, P., Handley, M., Karp, R., Shenker, S.: A scalable content-addressable network. In: SIGCOMM '01: Proceedings of the 2001 conference on Applications, technologies, architectures, and protocols for computer communications, San Diego, California, United States (2001) 161–172

3. Rowstron, A., Druschel, P.: Storage management and caching in PAST, a large-scale, persistent peer-to-peer storage utility. In: Proceedings of the 18th ACM Symposium on Operating System Principles, Banff, Canada (2001)
4. Dabek, F., Li, J., Sit, E., Robertson, J., Kaashoek, F., Morris, R.: Designing a DHT for low latency and high throughput. In: Proceedings of the First ACM/Usenix Symposium on Networked Systems Design and Implementation (NSDI), San Francisco, California (2004)
5. Bhagwan, R., Tati, K., Cheng, Y.C., Savage, S., Voelker, G. In: Proceedings of the First ACM/Usenix Symposium on Networked Systems Design and Implementation (NSDI), San Francisco, California, United States (2004)
6. Weatherspoon, H., Kubiatowicz, J.D.: Erasure coding vs. replication: A quantitative comparison. In: Proc. 1st International Workshop on Peer-to-Peer Systems (IPTPS'02), Cambridge, Massachusetts, United States (2002)
7. Blake, C., Rodrigues, R.: High availability, scalable storage, dynamic peer networks: Pick two. In: Proceedings of The Ninth Workshop on Hot Topics in Operating Systems (HotOS-IX), Lihue, Hawaii, United States (2003)
8. Bhagwan, R., Savage, S., Voelker, G.: Understanding availability. In: Proceedings of the 2nd International Workshop on Peer-to-Peer Systems (IPTPS'03), Berkeley, California (2003)
9. Reed, S., Solomon, G.: Polynomial codes over certain finite fields. J. SIAM **8** (1960) 300–304
10. Rabin, M.: Efficient dispersal of information for security, load balancing, and fault tolerance. J. ACM **36** (1989)
11. Luby, M.: LT codes. In: Proceedings of the 43rd Symposium on Foundations of Computer Science (FOCS 2002), Vancouver, Canada (2002)
12. Andersen, D.: Improving End-to-End Availability Using Overlay Networks. PhD thesis, MIT (2005)
13. Karger, D., Lehman, E., Leighton, T., Levine, M., Lewin, D., Panigrahy, R.: Consistent hashing and random trees: Distributed caching protocols for relieving hot spots on the World Wide Web. In: Proc. 29th Symposium on Theory of Computing, El Paso, Texas (1997) 654–663
14. Bertsekas, D., Gallager, R.: Data Networks. Prentice Hall (1987)
15. Rhea, S., Geels, D., Roscoe, T., Kubiatowicz, J.: Handling churn in a DHT. In: Proceedings of the USENIX Annual Technical Conference. (2004)
16. Bolosky, W.J., Douceur, J.R., Ely, D., Theimer, M.: Feasibility of a serverless distributed file system deployed on an existing set of desktop PCs. In: Proceedings of the international conference on measurement and modeling of computer systems (SIGMETRICS). (2000) 34–43
17. Stribling, J.: Planetlab - all pairs pings. http://pdos.lcs.mit.edu/~strib/pl_app (2005)

Conservation vs. Consensus in Peer-to-Peer Preservation Systems

Prashanth P. Bungale, Geoffrey Goodell, and Mema Roussopoulos

Harvard University, Cambridge, MA 02138, USA
{prash, goodell, mema}@eecs.harvard.edu

Abstract. The problem of digital preservation is widely acknowledged, but the underlying assumptions implicit to the design of systems that address this problem have not been analyzed explicitly. We identify two basic approaches to address the problem of digital preservation using peer-to-peer systems: *conservation* and *consensus*. We highlight the design tradeoffs involved in using the two general approaches, and we provide a framework for analyzing the characteristics of peer-to-peer preservation systems in general. In addition, we propose a novel conservation-based protocol for achieving preservation and we analyze its effectiveness with respect to our framework.

1 Introduction

Recently, a number of peer-to-peer approaches have been proposed to address the problem of *preservation* (e.g., [4,7,11,2,3,6]). In their attempt to preserve some data so that it is available in the future, these systems face a number of challenges including dealing with natural degradation in storage media, catastrophic events or human errors, attacks by adversaries attemtping to change the data preserved, as well as providing incentives to other peers to help in the preservation task. These systems differ in their approaches and the systems' designers characterize their approaches in different ways: archiving, backup, digital preservation. But these peer-to-peer systems share a basic premise: that each peer is interested in preserving one or more *archival units* (AUs) and uses the aid and resources of other peers to achieve its goal.

In this paper we provide a framework for analyzing the characteristics and highlighting the design tradeoffs of peer-to-peer preservation approaches. Suppose that our preservation system involves each AU of interest being replicated on a subset of the peer population. Consider a particular archival unit being replicated on a subset consisting of n peers, denoted $(p_1, p_2, ..., p_n)$. We use $p_i(t)$ to denote the copy of the archival unit held by peer p_i at time t. To simplify the scenario somewhat, presume that all peers enter the system at time t_0. We assert that there are two basic approaches to providing preservation:

- CONSENSUS. The goal is for all peers in the system to come to a uniform agreement over time; that is to say that as $t \rightarrow \infty$, we have that $\forall i, j :$ $p_i(t) = p_j(t)$. In essence, each peer always believes that the version of the

M. Castro and R. van Renesse (Eds.): IPTPS 2005, LNCS 3640, pp. 240–251, 2005.

AU it has may be questionable and is willing to use the aggregate opinion of the community to influence its own copy, even if that sometimes involves replacing the current copy with a new one.

- CONSERVATION. The goal is for each peer to retain indefinitely the exact copy of the AU that it holds initially; that is to say that as $t \to \infty$, we have that $\forall i, t : p_i(t) = p_i(t_0)$. In essence, each peer believes that the version of the AU it starts with is the "right" version, and it always attempts to preserve this copy, even if other peers disagree. When it suffers a damage to its AU, it seeks the help of other peers to recover this right version.

There is a fundamental trade-off between these two approaches. If a peer happens to have a wrong version, conserving the data as it is is detrimental to preservation, whereas consensus helps preserve the right version if the other peers happen to supply the right version as the consensus version. On the other hand, if a peer happens to have the right version, conserving the data as it is helps preserve the right version, whereas consensus can potentially cause it to get infected with a wrong version (if the other peers happen to supply a wrong version to it as the consensus version).

2   Framework for Design Considerations

The design choice between conservation and consensus is not straightforward, but involves balancing and prioritizing various conflicting goals and choosing the best suited approach. To aid this process, we discuss below a list of considerations for designing a peer-to-peer preservation system. There may be other useful considerations, but we've found this list to be particularly useful.

Trust in the source of the AU. If the original source of the AU is perfectly trusted to supply the right version of the AU always, consistently, to all the subscriber peers (i.e., peers that will hold replicas of this AU), conservation might be a better preservation strategy. On the other hand, if the source supplies the right version to some subscriber peers and a wrong version to some others, consensus could help, as long as the subscribers with the right version outnumber those with a wrong version and are thus able to convince those with the wrong version to replace their archived documents.

Trust in the means of procuring the AU. If peers in the system use an unreliable means of obtaining the AUs to be archived, then it is likely that only a fraction of the peers will obtain the correct copy at the outset. This circumstance may provide an argument in favor of a consensus-based approach, since conservation alone will lead to preservation of invalid copies.

Frequency of storage faults. If storage degradation is frequent because of the environment or particular storage medium chosen, then, it could prove difficult to achieve consensus on an AU. This is because if a substantial portion of peers are in damaged state at any point of time, then a deadlock situation could arise. The peers need to get a consensus copy to recover from their damage, and on the other hand, the peers need to first recover from their damage in order to achieve good consensus. Thus, the consensus approach may not be well-suited for systems with high frequencies of storage faults. On the other hand, a conservation approach might avoid this problem because all it requires to recover from a damage is any one peer being able to respond with the AU being conserved.

Frequency of human error. If system operators are likely to commit errors, for instance, while loading an AU to be preserved or while manually recovering the AU from a damage occurrence, conservation could be detrimental because the system may end up preserving an incorrect AU, whereas consensus could help recover the right AU from other peers.

Resource relavance to participants. Relevance [10] is the likelihood that a "unit of service" within a problem (in our case, an archival unit) is interesting to many participants. When resource relevance is high, both consensus and conservation could benefit from the relevance and would be equally suitable. However, when the resource relevance is low, because cooperation would require artificial or exrinsic incentives to make the peer-to-peer solution viable, conservation would be better suited as it would require less frequent interactions (specifically, only during recovery from damage) and smaller number of peers participating as compared to consensus.

Presence of adversaries. Preservation systems may be subject to various attacks from adversaries. We focus on two kinds of attacks that exploit peer interactions in the system: *stealth-modification attack* and *nuisance attack*. In a stealth-modification attack, the adversary's goal is to modify the data being preserved by a victim peer, but without being detected. In a nuisance attack, the adversary's goal is to create nuisance for a victim peer, for instance by raising intrusion detection alarms that may require human operator intervention. The design of a preservation system that takes these attacks into account would involve the following two considerations:

- *Tolerance for stealth-modification*: Is it acceptable to the users of the preservation system for some peers being successfully attacked by a stealth modification adversary, and possibly recovering eventually? i.e., Is it tolerable for some of the peers to have an incorrect AU sometimes? If the answer is 'yes', then both conservation and consensus may be equally suitable approaches. But, if the system has very low tolerance for stealth-modification attacks, conservation may be appropriate as it is less influenced by (and thus, less susceptible to) other peers. Consider the case in which there is substantial likelihood that adversaries may have subverted peers, or if there is fear that adversarial peers form a large percentage of the overall peer population. In this circumstance, consensus is a dangerous strategy because it may cause all of the well-behaved peers that have the right version to receive an invalid version, and thus conservation may be appropriate. However, there is also a downside to using conservation in that once the adversary is somehow able to carry out a stealth-modification attack successfully, the victim peer, by definition, believes that its copy is the right one and is thus prevented from being able to recover, even after the adversary has stopped actively attacking it.

- **Tolerance for nuisances**: Can the users tolerate frequent nuisances? The frequency of possible nuisance attacks is limited by the frequency of invoking peer participation. Thus, if there is low tolerance to nuisance attacks, then a conservation approach may be preferable because each peer relies on other peers only when it suffers a damage.

3   LOCKSS - An Example of the Consensus Approach

In this section, we consider LOCKSS, an example of a preservation system following the consensus approach, and discuss its design with respect to our framework.

The LOCKSS system [7,9] preserves online academic journals using a peer-to-peer auditing mechanism. The system provides a preservation tool for libraries, whose budgets for preservation are typically quite small [1]. Each (library) peer crawls the websites of publishers who have agreed to have their content preserved and downloads copies of published material (e.g. academic journals) to which the library in question has subscribed. The cached information is then used to satisfy requests from the library's users when the publisher's website is unavailable.

Web crawling is an unreliable process, making it difficult for peers to determine without manual inspection of the crawled material whether complete and correct replicas of the AUs of interest have been downloaded. Peers therefore need some automated way to determine if their copy is correct. LOCKSS uses consensus for this purpose. Peers perform sampled-auditing of their local copies to ensure that it agrees with the consensus of peers.

The LOCKSS design is based on the following characteristics and/or assumptions in our design framework:

Trust in the source of the AU and trust in the means of procuring the AU: low, as long as only a relatively small portion of the overall peer population initially acquires an incorrect AU either from the source or through the procurement means.

Frequency of storage faults: extremely low (assumed to be once in 200 machine years on an average); *Frequency of human error*: can be high; *Resource relevance to participants*: high (as libraries often subscribe to the same AU's from the publishers).

Presence of adversaries: at most one-third to 40% of the peer population could be adversarial; the adversary is assumed to have unlimited computation power and unlimited identities. Tolerance for stealth-modification and for nuisances: *medium*.

Looking at these characteristics and assumptions, and considering the suitability of the approaches described in our design framework, we can clearly see why the system designers have chosen the consensus approach. We descibe below the design of the consensus protocol of LOCKSS, and discuss the factors relevant to our framework on the way.

Each peer maintains two lists: a *friends list* and a *reference list*. The reference list is a list of peers that the peer in question has recently discovered in the process of participating in the LOCKSS system. The friends list is a list of peers (*friends*) that the peer knows externally and with whom it has an out-of-band relationship before entering the system. When a peer joins the system, his reference lists starts out containing the peers on his friends list.

Periodically, at a rate faster than the rate of natural bit degradation, a peer (the *poller* conducts an *opinion poll* on an AU. The peer takes a random sample of peers as a *quorum* from its reference list and invites the chosen peers as *voters* into a poll. The voters vote on the AU by sending hashes of their individual copies of the AU to the peer initiating the poll. The poller compares the votes it receives with its local copy. If an overwhelming majority of the hashes received agrees with the poller's hash, then the poller concludes that its copy is good, (i.e., it agrees with the consensus) and it resets a refresh timer to determine the next time to check this AU. If an overwhelming majority of hashes disagree, then the peer fetches a *repair* by obtaining a copy of the AU from one of the disagreeing peers and re-evaluating the votes it received. That is, the peer alters its copy of the AU so that it agrees with the consensus. If there is neither landslide agreement nor landslide disagreement, then the poll is deemed *inconclusive* and the poller raises an alarm.

Because natural storage degradation is assumed to be a relatively infrequent occurrence, it is unlikely that many peers will simultaneously be experiencing degradation. If an inconclusive poll results, it is an indication that an attack might be in progress. LOCKSS uses alarms as a way of performing intrusion detection, so that when an attack is suspected, humans are called upon to examine, heal, and restart the system. This requirement of humans being expected to examine, heal, and restart the system every time an alarm is raised, which could happen on every poll in the theoretically worst case, is the reason why the system cannot tolerate frequent nuisance attacks. Therefore, the designers aim for nuisance attacks being only infrequently possible.

At the conclusion of a poll, the poller updates its reference list as follows. First, it removes those peers that voted in the poll so that the next poll is based on a different sample of peers. Second, the poller replenishes its reference list by adding *nominated peers* and peers from the friends list. Nominated peers, or *nominees*, are peers that are introduced by the voters when the voters are first invited to participate in the poll. Nominees are used solely for discovery purposes so that the poller can replenish its reference list. Nominees vote on the AU, but their votes are not considered in determining the outcome of the poll. Instead, their votes are used to implement admission control into the reference list. Nominees whose votes agree with the poll outcome are added to the reference list.

The bias of friends to nominees added is called *churn*. The contents of the reference list determine the outcome of future polls. Adding more friends to the reference list than nominees makes the poller vulnerable to targeted attacks aimed at its friends. Adding more nominees than friends to the reference list increases the potential for Sybil attacks [5].

Using a combination of defense techniques such as rate-limitation, effort-balancing, reference list refreshes and churn, among others, the LOCKSS protocol achieves strong, but imperfect, defense against a stealth-modification adversary. Experimental results show that the probability that, at any point in time, the user at a peer would access a bad AU was increased by just 3.5%. However, it was also observed that around one-third of the loyal (i.e., non-adversarial) peers end up being attacked by a stealth-modification adversary who starts with an initial subversion of 40% of the overall peer poulation. Although the LOCKSS authors have reported that successful nuisance attacks have been observed to be seldom, they have not looked into what exactly happens when an alarm is raised at a peer (i.e., to what extent the adversary is rooted out), and so we cannot analyze the real impact of nuisance attacks at this time.

4   Sierra - An Example of the Conservation Approach

The key notion of the conservation approach is that each peer, being fully confident that the version of the AU it stores is the right version, attempts to conserve its own version. To do so, the peer ignores what the version may look like at other peers, except when it suffers a "bit-rot", i.e., a storage failure or some other event that results in its AU being damaged, at which point it looks to other peers for recovery.

Given just the conservation notion, one might consider a simple solution for implementing conservation such as storing the AU, along with a signed hash of the AU remotely on other peers, and relying on this information while recovering from a bit-rot. This solution may be perfectly acceptable in peer-to-peer backup applications. However, in a LOCKSS-like application that would want to exploit the high resource relevance existing in the system (to reduce unnecessary storage overhead) and avoid long-term secrets (which may be unreasonable for long-term preservation on the order of decades), this simple solution may not be suitable.

We propose Sierra as a conservation-based alternative to the LOCKSS protocol. Sierra shares some features with LOCKSS in that it exploits resource relevance and does not depend on long-term secrets. It also borrows some techniques from LOCKSS such as calling opinion polls using a sample of the peer population. However, Sierra's primary goal departs fundamentally from that of LOCKSS. While Sierra makes use of opinion polls (which have a consensus flavor), it does not blindly rely on the results of the polls. We thus refer to Sierra as using a *tamed-consensus* approach towards achieving the conservation goal.

Following are the characteristics and/or assumptions we use that are relevant to our design framework:

Trust in the source of the AU and trust in the means of procuring the AU: high; *Frequency of storage faults*: low; *Frequency of human error*: low; *Resource relevance to participants*: high.

Presence of adversaries: up to 60% of the peer population could be adversarial; the adversary is assumed to have unlimited computation power and unlimited identities; Tolerance for stealth-modification: *zero-tolerance*; Tolerance for nuisances: *low*.

Since we prioritize allowing higher presence of adversaries, and yet having zero-tolerance for stealth-modification attacks and low tolerance for nuisance attacks, we are forced to make the stronger assumption of high trust in the source and procurement means for the AU.

Since a conservation-based system assumes complete confidence in the local AU, a bit-rot occurrence is the only *"time-of-need"* when a peer might have to rely on the other peers to recover its AU. During the remaining time, the peer would be *"self-sufficient"* in terms of preserving the AU. Alongside each stored AU, a peer stores a hash of that AU and periodically checks the AU against the hash to determine if it is self-sufficient or in its time of need.

In addition, we introduce a host of defense techniques to help a peer *conserve* its AU. Peers call polls periodically as in LOCKSS. If the stored AU and hash match, then the poller ignores the result of the poll. However, the poller updates its reference list as in the LOCKSS protocol with the following change. Any voters whose votes disagree with the poller's AU are removed from the reference list and also *blacklisted* from providing votes to this poller in the future.

If the AU and local hash do not match when the poller calls its next poll, it enters a "time-of-need" state and remains in this state for the next n polls, where n is a system-defined parameter. During (and only during) a time-of-need poll, the poller checks to see if any of the peers that are in the minority agree with each other. If a *minority threshold* number of peers agree with each other, the poller raises an alarm to notify its local operators. Otherwise, the poller repairs using the version of the AU stored by the majority. A minority alarm indicates that either the majority or the minority is potentially adversarial. When this alarm is raised, the operator is expected to examine and choose the right one among the different contending versions of the AU and then, the peers who supplied the incorrect versions will be blacklisted. Note that the larger n is, the more likely a stealth-modification attack will be detected because the higher the chance that the poller will find, in a subsequent poll, a minority threshold number of peers that agree with each other.

In Sierra, voters only vote if they are in the self-sufficient state (i.e., their stored AU and hash match) and decline the poll invitation otherwise.

4.1   Analysis

The Sierra protocol uses the basic underlying features of the LOCKSS protocol for calling polls and managing the peer-to-peer network, and thus to analyze its effects theoretically, we start by examining existing theoretical properties of LOCKSS. Due to lack of space, we omit the details of the LOCKSS analysis [8] here.

Attaining a presence in a victim peer's reference list is the only means through the protocol by which an adversary can launch a stealth-modification or a nui-

symbol	default description
C	0.1 churn rate (ratio)
M_0	1000 initial number of malign peers
Q	100 quorum # of voters needed per poll
P	10000 total population
T	600 reference list size
Int	3 months mean inter-poll interval

Fig. 1. Parameters for Sierra analysis

sance attack. We call the strength of adversarial presence, i.e., the proportion of reference list peers that are adversarial, the adversary's *foothold*. The only way for an adversary to attain higher foothold in a peer's reference list is to *lurk*, i.e., to *act* loyal (or non-malign) by voting using the correct version of the AU and nominating its minions for entrance into the poller's reference list.

Consider an adversary in LOCKSS that lurks. We can model the expected number of malign (i.e., adversarial) peers, M_{rt}, in a loyal peer's reference list at time t, given a uniform distribution of adversaries throughout the population, as a function of time and a set of system parameters (See Figure 1) [8]:

$$M_{r(t+1)} = -\frac{X}{T^2}M_{rt}^2 + \left(1 - \frac{Q + 2X}{T}\right)M_{rt} + \frac{CTM_0}{P} \qquad (1)$$

where X, the expected number of nominees in steady-state equilibrium, is given by:

$$X = Q + T\left(\frac{1 - C^2}{1 + C} - 1\right) \qquad (2)$$

However, because Sierra introduces blacklisting as a means by which a peer may eradicate those who vote with invalid copies from its reference list, the recurrence equation for Sierra is somewhat different. The only opportunity for an adversary to have its set of malign peers $(p_{m1}, ..., p_{mk})$ vote with an invalid copy and still increase its expected foothold in the reference lists of some target peer p_t occurs when p_t suffers a bit-rot and enters its time-of-need state.

Suppose that μ is the threshold for raising an alarm in the event of minority agreement. Given that a stealth-modification adversary seeks to win a poll and avoid detection, the malign peers must vote with the invalid copy of the AU only if there exist at least $Q - \mu$ malign peers in a given poll called by p_t, and further if the poll happens to be a time-of-need poll. Otherwise, if the adversary attacks with its bad copy, it ends up losing all of its hard-earned foothold due to blacklisting. Therefore, the optimal strategy for the stealth-modification adversary in the case where there are less than $Q - \mu$ malign peers in a poll is to lurk, so that it can try to increase its foothold further. Thus, the recurrence equation does not change for the stealth-modification adversary if we assume an optimal adversary strategy (and therefore no blacklisting).

If an adversary wants to simply create a nuisance that raises an alarm, then at least μ malign peers must vote with a non-majority copy of the AU. Since the act of creating a nuisance does not benefit from having more than μ peers vote with the invalid copy, it is in the best interest of the adversary to have only μ peers, $(p_{m1}, ..., p_{m\mu})$ perform this task. The adversary would now lose some foothold due to blacklisting whenever it creates a nuisance, and therefore, the recurrence equation changes. Next, we introduce three other variables: F, the mean time between failures (in terms of number of polls) for the particular storage system, d, the likelihood that an adversary will choose to create a nuisance when it can, and K, the likelihood that an adversary will create a nuisance even when a peer is *not* in time-of-need. K represents the extent to which the adversary has knowledge of when a bit-rot occurs for a particular loyal peer. If the adversary has perfect knowledge (through some covert channel or out-of-band means), then $K = 0$, but we believe that in most realistic cases, K would be closer to 1. Whenever the adversary tries to create a nuisance for a given peer p_t by supplying μ malicious votes, p_t will evict μ adversarial peers from its reference list. Thus, our new recurrence is represented by the following equations:

$$M'_{r(t+1)} = -\frac{X}{T^2}M_{rt}^2 + (1 - \frac{Q + 2X}{T})M_{rt} + \frac{CTM_0}{P} \tag{3}$$

$$M_{rt} = M'_{rt} - \frac{d\mu(1 + K(F - 1))}{F} \tag{4}$$

Since we are interested in powerful adversaries, we assume for the rest of our analysis that an adversary somehow has perfect knowledge about peers suffering bit-rots and will attack or create a nuisance only when a peer is in time-of-need.

Effectiveness against Stealth Modification Attacks. We first consider the question of what conditions can actually lead to an adversary being able to carry out a stealth-modification attack successfully (i.e., without being detected). An attack is possible only if:

- The adversary has somehow achieved very high (close to 100%) foothold in the victim's reference list – because it would otherwise be detected through the minority threshold alarm within the n polls called during the time-of-need.
- More importantly, the adversary is able to sustain that foothold for a sufficient number of consecutive polls – specifically, during the n time-of-need polls.
- The adversary is able to somehow magically attack exactly when a damage has just occurred at the victim, i.e., should have perfect knowledge of the victim's damage occurrences.

We now use the mathematical model discussed earlier to show that the adversary is not able to carry out stealth-modification attacks successfully. Recall that the the optimal adversary strategy for stealth-modification is lurking continuously until it attains enough foothold. We find that the adversary is unable to lurk and attain footholds high enough (i.e., enough to ensure at least $Q - \mu$ poll invitations) to be able to carry out successful attacks. Figure 2 shows the result of using equations 3 and 4 with $d = 0$ to obtain the equilibrium foothold value (which is the maximum expected number of malicious peers on the reference list of a given loyal peer) for different initial subversion values. As we can see from this graph, even for initial subversions as high as 60%, the equilibrium foothold never reaches 80%, which is the foothold required to ensure at least $Q - \mu$ poll invitations.

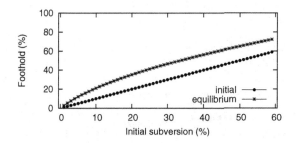

Fig. 2. EQUILIBRIUM FOOTHOLD ACHIEVED WITH VARYING INITIAL SUBVERSION. *Presuming MTBF $F = 10$ years, nuisance probability $d = 0$, and minority threshold $\mu = 20$.*

Note that we have assumed that the adversary has perfect knowledge of the victim's damage occurrences. If the adversary has no out-of-band means to acquire this knowledge, it is close to impossible for the adversary to be able to lurk for the entire period that the victim peer is healthy (to avoid being blacklisted) and then attack exactly when it suffers a damage.

Effectiveness against Nuisance Attacks. First, we note that in Sierra, the maximum frequency at which an adversary can create nuisance is limited to once every bit-rot occurrence instead of once every poll as in LOCKSS. Next, we observe that creating a nuisance comes with an associated penalty: peers voting with an invalid copy are blacklisted by the operator upon being notified by the alarm, and they cannot return to the reference list. We want to show that the penalty associated by blacklisting creates some disincentive for nuisance attacks. For the following analysis, we consider adversaries having an initial subversion of 10% of the peer population. First, this subversion ratio is enough for the adversary to be able to carry out nuisance attacks. Second, while an adversary with a higher subversion ratio could very well carry out nuisance attacks, it does not lose much foothold because it can quickly make up for the loss it suffers (due to blacklisting) by nominating its minions.

Figure 3 shows what happens when we vary the probability in which an adversary creates a nuisance. Observe that even if an adversary has complete

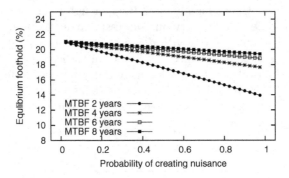

Fig. 3. VARYING NUISANCE PROBABILITY. *Presuming 10% initial subversion and minority threshold $\mu = 20$.*

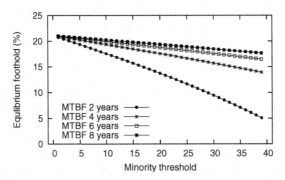

Fig. 4. VARYING MINORITY THRESHOLD. *Presuming 10% initial subversion and nuisance probability $d = 1$. Note that the x-axis shows the minority threshold as an absolute number of peers and the quorum is 100.*

knowledge of when a given peer's AU is damaged, it may still have substantial incentive not to create a nuisance too frequently, particularly if the MTBF is sufficiently short that the adversary does not have time to restore its representation on the peer's reference list between successive failures.

Finally, Figure 4 shows the effect of varying the minority threshold. We see that with lower minority thresholds, the adversary incurs lesser penalty and therefore, the adversary has less of an incentive not to create a nuisance. On the other hand, we know intuitively that increasing the threshold, while contributing to a better defense against nuisance attacks, leads to more opportunities for stealth modification attacks.

5   Conclusions

Preservation is not a straighforward problem. Peer-to-peer systems aimed at providing a preservation solution face a number of conflicting design considerations that force designers to make difficult choices. We have presented a framework for considering the tradeoffs involved in designing such a system. We have also discussed two example systems with respect to this framework, LOCKSS and Sierra, that embody the two basic approaches to preservation: consensus and conservation, respectively. We observe that LOCKSS allows assumptions of distrustful source and procurement means for the AU, while achieving moderately strong defense against stealth-modification and nuisance attacks. On the other hand, Sierra achieves much stronger defense against both attacks, but at the expense of making assumptions of high trust in the source and procurement means for the AU.

Acknowledgments

We would like to thank the following people for their very helpful feedback and suggestions: Mary Baker, T. J. Giuli, Rachel Greenstadt, Petros Maniatis, Radhika Nagpal, Bryan Parno, Vicky Reich, and David S. H. Rosenthal.

References

1. ARL – Association of Research Libraries. ARL Statistics 2000-01. http://www.arl.org/stats/arlstat/01pub/intro.html, 2001.
2. T. Burkard. Herodotus: A Peer-to-Peer Web Archival System, Master's thesis, MIT, Jun 2002.
3. B. F. Cooper and H. Garcia-Molina. Peer-to-peer data preservation through storage auctions. *IEEE Transactions on Parallel and Distributed Systems, to appear.*
4. Landon P. Cox and Brian D. Noble. Samsara: Honor Among Thieves in Peer-to-Peer Storage. In *Proceedings of the Nineteenth ACM Symposium on Operating Systems Principles*, pages 120–132, Bolton Landing, NY, USA, October 2003.
5. J. Douceur. The Sybil Attack. In *1st Intl. Workshop on Peer-to-Peer Systems*, 2002.
6. HiveCache, Inc. Distributed disk-based backups. Available at http://www.hivecache.com/.
7. P. Maniatis, M. Roussopoulos, TJ Giuli, D. S. H. Rosenthal, M. Baker, and Y. Muliadi. Preserving Peer Replicas By Rate-Limited Sampled Voting. In *SOSP*, 2003.
8. B. Parno and M. Roussopoulos. Predicting Adversary Infiltration in the LOCKSS System. Technical Report TR-28-04, Harvard University, October 2004.
9. D. S. H. Rosenthal, M. Roussopoulos, P. Maniatis, and M. Baker. Economic Measures to Resist Attacks on a Peer-to-Peer Network. In *Workshop on Economics of Peer-to-Peer Systems*, Berkeley, CA, USA, June 2003.
10. M. Roussopoulos, TJ Giuli, M. Baker, P. Maniatis, D. S. H. Rosenthal, and J. Mogul. 2 P2P or Not 2 P2P? In *IPTPS*, 2004.
11. D. Wallach. A Survey of Peer-to-Peer Security Issues. In *Intl. Symp. on Software Security*, 2002.

Locality Prediction for Oblivious Clients

Kevin P. Shanahan and Michael J. Freedman

New York University
www.coralcdn.org

Abstract. To improve performance, large-scale Internet systems require clients to access nearby servers. While centralized systems can leverage static topology maps for rough network distances, fully-decentralized systems have turned to active probing and network coordinate algorithms to scalably predict inter-host latencies. Internet applications seeking immediate adoption, however, must inter-operate with unmodified clients running existing protocols such as HTTP and DNS.

This paper explores a variety of active probing algorithms for locality prediction. Upon receiving an external client request, peers within a decentralized system are able to quickly estimate nearby servers, using a minimum of probes from multiple vantages. We find that, while network coordinates may play an important role in scalably choosing effective vantage points, they are not directly useful for predicting a client's nearest servers.

1 Introduction

Many replicated Internet systems can improve performance by servicing clients at nearby hosts. The performance of a distributed web mirror, for example, is highly dependent on the network distance between client and server. Commercial content distribution networks (CDNs) like Akamai [1] build large maps of the Internet topology and use this information to redirect clients to nearby hosts. These hosts are carefully deployed at specific access sites or behind bottleneck links. This technique for locality prediction, however, requires centralized mapping, aggregation, extensive network knowledge, and often ISP-specific heuristics. But by using existing protocols like HTTP and DNS, these systems can achieve immediate and wide-spread use.

More recent distributed systems use self-organizing techniques to reduce the infrastructure's administrative and operational overhead, while still providing service to unmodified clients. Such peer-to-peer systems include static and dynamic CDNs [5,6], distributed hash storage services [7], and new Internet naming systems [13,14]. Such decentralized systems, however, cannot easily produce aggregated static topology maps nor specify host deployments [4].

Active probing provides a simple alternative to static topology mapping that can be easily realized in a decentralized system. In its simplest form, when an unmodified client contacts any system peer, this ingress peer probes the client and directs other so-called *landmarks* to do the same. By collecting these round-trip-time (RTT) measurements, the ingress concludes which corresponding peer is closest to the client in terms of network distance, requiring no *a priori* knowledge of

M. Castro and R. van Renesse (Eds.): IPTPS 2005, LNCS 3640, pp. 252–263, 2005.

a client's location. Coupled with some application-level mechanism such as DNS redirection, this approach can be leveraged to service clients from nearby hosts.

Recent network coordinate systems [8,10,12,9,2,3] offer new methodologies for active probing. These systems allow peers to estimate inter-host latency without topological maps or explicit all-pairs measurements, by assigning synthetic coordinates to each peer. The distance between peers in the coordinate space accurately predicts their RTT. Thus, for example, by combining active probing with network coordinates, a peer can map its client onto the system's underlying coordinate space. Then, it can use these coordinates to estimate the client's location and redirect it accordingly, potentially to a *destination* other than from among the landmarks.

This paper explores various methodologies for locality prediction using active probing. We concentrate our analysis on four main properties: (1) the method used for *landmark selection*, (2) the *number of landmarks* selected, (3) the method used for *destination determination*, and (4) the *number of redirection iterations* performed by a client.

We present and analyze several algorithms for landmark selection, destination determination, and methods of iterative redirection. We find that network coordinates *enable* landmark-selection algorithms that yield better client redirection, but are not as useful in *directly* finding a client's nearby hosts via coordinate distance estimation.

2   Design

In an abstract model, we consider a network comprised of a core decentralized system and external clients. Internal system peers communicate with one another, sharing liveness information and measuring internal round-trip-times, potentially as part of a network coordinate system.

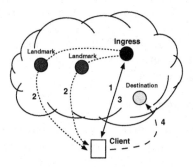

Fig. 1. *Redirection architecture.* When an oblivious client c contacts any system peer (step 1), this ingress peer directs other known landmark peers to probe the client to determine RTT (step 2). The ingress accumulates these measurements and selects some destination peer that is closest to c. It returns this peer (step 3), which the client can subsequently contact for application-level operation (step 4). The destination may or may not be restricted to the set of landmarks (latter condition shown).

We assume that an external client has some method of contacting a random system peer, via DNS for example.[1] As shown in Figure 1, upon receiving a request, this *ingress* peer selects some subset of system peers to act as *landmarks* for probing the client. All landmark peers probe the client after receiving a corresponding request from the ingress. Landmarks respond to the ingress with all measured RTTs to the client.

2.1   Network Coordinates

In network coordinate systems, peers derive synthetic coordinates based on measurements to a limited subset of other peers, either using a fixed set of public landmarks [8,10,12] or in a fully-decentralized fashion [9,2,3]. Given another peer's coordinates, a peer can accurately predict its RTT without physical measurement.

In our decentralized model, hosts within the core peer-to-peer infrastructure can easily maintain and disseminate network coordinates as a by-product of other communication: (1) A peer includes its coordinates in all application-level messages it sends. (2) Whenever communication is two-way, the sender learns the RTT to the recipient using packet timestamps.(1)).

For concreteness, we use the decentralized Vivaldi algorithm [3] for our network coordinate system. Vivaldi coordinates are represented by a (x, y, h, e) tuple, corresponding to a two-dimensional Euclidean coordinate space (x, y), with an additional height scalar h and an error term e. Conceptually, the Euclidean coordinates model the peer's location in the high-speed Internet backbone, the height models the additional access link latency at the Internet's edge, and the error term captures the host's confidence in its coordinates. The distance $D_{a,b} = \|C_a - C_b\|$ between two peers' coordinates C_a, C_b approximates their RTT; it is calculated by taking the Euclidean distance of their (x, y) coordinates and adding the height vectors. A peer updates its own coordinates whenever communicating with other peers, taking the others' error estimates into account.

External *unmodified* clients cannot themselves engage in the network coordinate algorithms. However, an ingress can estimate a client's coordinates, if desired, by collecting the landmarks' RTT measurements and coordinates. Then, it can synthesize client coordinates by running the centralized Vivaldi algorithm repeatedly on these measurements.[2]

2.2   Design Considerations

The landmark selection and redirection mechanisms we explore rely on two assumptions. First, all internal peers can select a *random* subset of other peers

---

[1] For example, if the system is named with a particular domain and every peer runs a DNS server authoritative for the name, clients initially contact one of 13 or so peers listed with a registrar. Nameserver caching from prior requests can increase the client's view to the entire system.

[2] The Vivaldi algorithm is analogous to a mass spring network, which does not converge immediately, but rather has a period of oscillation before resting at the (locally) lowest energy-level configuration.

from the network. Second, peers can obtain a subset of those peers closest to some distance d from a particular peer.

The second assumption requires some practical consideration. Without using network coordinates, each peer must maintain complete $O(n^2)$ network state, and each peer must continually probe all others to generate these RTTs. Network coordinates, however, allow peers to predict all pair-wise latencies with only n state. In fact, each peer need only continually probe a small number of other peers, independent of n. To learn all n coordinates, a peer can then perform some gossiping protocol in an unstructured overlay. Alternatively, new distributed data structures may be designed to support closest-point queries (like a dynamic Voronoi diagram) using significantly less communication. We leave this as an open problem.

Based on having n^2 RTT estimates via n network coordinates, our results serve as an upper-bound for the performance benefit of more complex redirection algorithms over mere random selection. If less state is available at an ingress, this performance gap shrinks. System designers should therefore weigh this benefit in locality prediction against its usage and maintenance cost.

System designers must consider other practical issues when performing active probing. To handle packet losses or excessive queuing delays, an ingress peer may choose to use $k + \alpha$ landmarks to ensure k timely results. Second, clients may be behind firewalls or NATs, where UDP probes, TCP requests to high ports, or ICMP packets have varied success. If client requests use connection-based protocols, RTTs can be measured directly during connection establishment. Or, fast traceroute-like scans can at least report timing information to the client's firewall. Still, the system should seek to use a minimal number of probes whenever possible, as additional probing increases network traffic, response time, and the probability of abuse complaints.

2.3 Selecting Landmarks

We consider three different metrics for choosing k landmarks with which to probe the client.

Random. k peers are selected uniformly at random from the system, fresh for each query.

Well-distributed. This approach attempts to select landmarks that have good coverage throughout the network—*e.g.*, spread across North America, Europe, and Asia—without requiring static configuration. Thus, our algorithm works by selecting random subsets of k peers, then choosing the subset that minimizes the following:

$$|mean(\mathcal{D}_n) - mean(\mathcal{D}_k)|^2 + var(\mathcal{D}_k)$$

where $\mathcal{D}_k$ is the set of all pair-wise distances for the k peers in the subset (resp. n peers in the network).

Intuitively, minimizing the difference in mean distance between peers in the subset and those in the network ensures that landmarks are not all clustered together. Minimizing variance ensures that peers are approximately equidistant from one another. Taken together, these properties attempt to spread landmarks evenly throughout the network. Experimental analysis (not included) showed that minimizing only one property yielded strictly worse performance than that obtained using this given metric.

While this well-distributed metric is computationally more expensive, an ingress peer need not perform this selection process online nor upon each client request. For example, it may only reselect the set of well-distributed landmarks once every five minutes.

Sphere.   In our third metric, the ingress attempts to choose landmarks that are likely to be closer to the client. Specifically, an ingress selects landmarks whose distances from the ingress are closest to the distance between ingress and client. This implies, of course, that the ingress must first calculate the RTT r to the client before choosing $k-1$ other such landmarks. We select $k-1$ non-ingress landmarks in order to fairly compare this metric with the former two, based on the total number of vantage points probing the client (k).

Intuitively, if one is working in a three-dimensional coordinate space, the resulting set of $k-1$ landmarks and the client are located on the surface of a sphere with radius r, centered about the ingress peer. Thus, any particular landmark on this sphere is $\leq 2r$ from the client, provided the triangle inequality holds. While Vivaldi uses instead a 2-D space with a height vector, (x, y, h), we use this nomenclature for illustrative clarity.

Note that neither the sphere nor the well-distributed metrics strictly require network coordinates: The distance calculations used when selecting landmarks could be based on measured RTTs instead of coordinate distances, although this practice would significantly limit the system's scalability.

2.4   Selecting Destinations

We consider two different metrics for determining the destination peer to which the client is redirected.

Direct RTT measurements.   Given the k RTTs between landmarks and the client, based on direct network probes, the ingress peer chooses the landmark with the smallest measured RTT.

Estimated coordinate distance.   After collecting the k RTT measurements from landmarks, as well as the landmarks' latest coordinates, the ingress peer synthesizes the client's coordinates C_c per Section 2.1. Then, given the coordinates of all other system peers, the ingress chooses the peer d that is closest to the client in the coordinate space, i.e., minimizes $D_{c,d} = \|C_c - C_d\|$. Note that, unlike the direct measurement approach, this destination is not restricted to the set of landmarks.

2.5   Iterating Redirection

Finally, we consider whether repetitions of the redirection mechanism will improve the system's predictive accuracy, where each step of the algorithm attempts to find a destination closer to the client.[3] Thus, the destination from iteration $i - 1$ is contacted by the client as an ingress peer for iteration i. Although such iteration does not make sense for random landmark selection, we can consider iteration for the latter selection metrics.

For the *well-distributed* landmark metric, we attempt to decrease the mean distance between peers by half during each iteration, using $var(D_k) + |2^{-i} \cdot mean(D_n) - mean(D_k)|^2$ for the ith iteration. The ingress peer *must* include itself among the landmark set for $i > 0$, given that the algorithm should select some set of well-distributed peers that are closer to the client at each iteration.

For the *sphere* metric, each iteration proceeds as expected. Intuitively, the ingress from iteration i selects landmarks from a sphere with radius $r_i \leq r_{i-1}$. To ensure forward progress, landmarks should not be reused between iterations. As the ingress of iteration i can use its measured RTT to the client from $i-1$ whenever possible, it selects k other landmarks for $i > 0$, not $k-1$ as described for $i = 0$ above.

3   Evaluation

This section evaluates the proposed selection metrics for choosing both landmarks and destinations, as well as the effect of the number of landmarks and of iterations.

3.1   Methodology and Terminology

We performed wide-area experiments on the PlanetLab testbed [11] and then simulated client-system interactions. On 105 randomly-chosen PlanetLab hosts (as of November 2004), we ran peers that implemented the Vivaldi network coordinate algorithm [3], where each peer regularly probed 32 others. These peers functioned as landmarks to allow the collection of RTT measurements accompanied by their sources' network coordinates. Peers sent ICMP echo messages as probes; we used the response's kernel timestamp to minimize the effect of scheduling latency.

A non-PlanetLab server directed *all* peers to probe each client once, with a 25 ms delay between each probe request to reduce congestion at the specified client. These clients were restricted to the same set of PlanetLab peers, although peers did not simultaneously play the roll of client and landmark. Each peer was simulated as a client three times. We collected the resulting ~30,000 RTT measurements for subsequent analysis.

Figure 2 briefly characterizes the predictive error of our Vivaldi implementation, defined by the difference between predicted distance in network coordinate space and the measured RTT for any two peers a, b: $|D_{a,b} - RTT_{a,b}|$. This is plotted alongside the cumulative distribution function (CDF) of all measured pair-wise RTTs. Additionally, we plot the error of the client coordinates synthesized by the ingress using only 3 landmarks, against all peers as before. Thus, we

---

[3] An iterative redirection mechanism is readily feasible even for unmodified clients. For example, custom DNS servers can synthesize artificially-hierarchical hostnames, as in [5], causing DNS resolvers to resolve the names recursively.

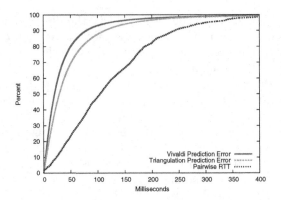

Fig. 2. Coordinate predictive error vs. network RTTs

find that client coordinates can achieve relatively good accuracy, even though these coordinates are "fitted" against only a few points. Using 32 landmarks yielded client results indistinguishable from that of internal peers.

For our analysis, we consider how effectively a mechanism can predict the system's *optimal* destination o. Given that our experiments calculate RTTs between a client c and all system peers, we call the peer with minimum RTT optimal. We say that the metric's *predictive error* is the absolute RTT difference between the client with the predicted destination d and with the optimal peer: $|RTT_{c,d} - RTT_{c,o}|$.[4]

3.2   Results

We now evaluate the specified metrics and parameters for active probing. For predictive sphere selection, a random peer was selected as an ingress peer for each client test. For random landmark selection, a random subset was selected for each client test. For the distributed metric, 10,000 subsets were considered, chosen uniformly at random with replacement.[5] The subset that minimized the well-distributed metric (per Section 2.3) was used for the duration of the experiment. The following figures are the combined results from 10 such evaluations on all clients. As a baseline, each graph includes the error CDF of using one randomly-selected destination.

Landmark selection metrics.   Figure 3 compares the efficacy of the three landmark selection metrics for decreasing predictive error. All three CDFs shown use three landmarks and the direct RTT measurement approach for selecting a destination. An error of 0 ms corresponds to predicting the optimal destination.

---

[4] We note that an alternate metric to consider is the relative RTT difference, or stretch, which normalizes the absolute difference by the optimal RTT. We do not include such analysis in this paper, however, due to our interest in the system's absolute performance: An increase from 2ms to 5ms, while having high stretch, is irrelevant in practice.

[5] Testing all $\binom{n}{k}$ possible subsets was computationally infeasible.

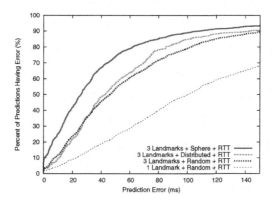

Fig. 3. Comparison of landmark selection metrics

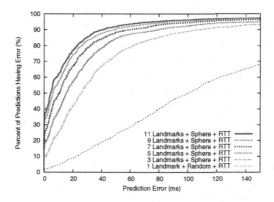

Fig. 4. The effect of the multiple landmarks

The sphere metric makes the most accurate predictions, with a median error of 25.9 ms and optimal selection of 6.8%. The distributed metric has a median error of 42.8 ms and optimal selection of 2.1%. Randomly selected landmarks have a median error of 45.9 ms and optimal selection of 2.3%.

Number of landmarks. Figure 4 shows the effect of multiple landmarks on predictive error. Increasing the number of landmarks improves the accuracy of destination selection, with decreasing returns as the set size increases. Thus, even a moderate number of landmarks greatly improves performance: Using 3 landmarks results in a destination with median predictive error that is 4x better than that of random selection (*i.e.*, 1 landmark).

Destination selection metrics. Figure 5 compares the two methods for selecting destinations, that of direct RTT measurement versus using network coordinates to estimate a client's location and predict a nearby peer. Somewhat surprisingly, we find that the coordinate prediction approach yields strictly worse performance. These results are shared across all landmark selection metrics and all evaluated landmark set sizes (up to 11).

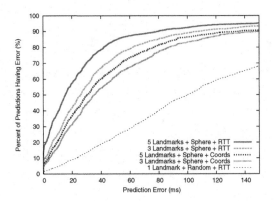

Fig. 5. Comparison of destination selection metrics

A (strong) form of the destination selection problem is the following: generate a sorted list of peers with increasing distance from the client. The RTT metric samples from this list in some (possibly biased) manner. The coordinate metric uses the same set of peers, but sorts on coordinate distance. Therefore, any inaccuracy in the coordinate system—which is inherent whenever mapping the Internet onto a lower-dimensional space—is reflected in the differences between the orderings of these two lists and hence in their first elements. This intuition is reflected by the data: the median error in destination prediction when using coordinates is 35.5 ms, while the median error in the coordinates' accuracy themselves (Figure 2) is 29.4 ms. Lower-error coordinate systems can potentially improve the accuracy of destination selection based on network coordinates.

Number of iterations.   Next, we examine the effect of iteratively repeating the redirection mechanism. Each iteration uses a set of k landmarks not included in previous iterations. We find that iteration improves accuracy, but again with diminishing results. The results are similar across all evaluated selection metrics (noting that random selection cannot be expressed as an iteration problem).

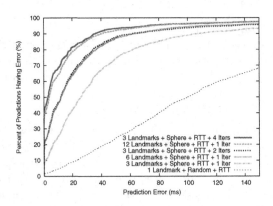

Fig. 6. Redirection iteration vs. landmark number

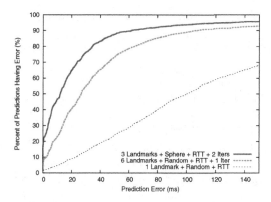

Fig. 7. Simple random vs. iterative distance metrics

One must consider whether these benefits are simply caused by increasing the total number of landmarks, instead of any additional "forward progress" made during each iteration step. Figure 6 compares the predictive error of k landmarks against i iterations of j landmarks each, where $i \cdot j = k$, again using the sphere and RTT metrics. We find that iterations do have some additional benefit beyond merely increasing the number of landmarks, although it is quite small. Thus, system designers must weigh whether the gain from iteration (in returning a closer destination) outweighs its cost (in added latency during the redirection protocol) for their particular application domain.

Repeated probing. Additionally, one might consider the effect of taking multiple probes versus using only a single probe per landmark, given that any transient network congestion can cause queuing delays and affect RTT measurements. However, we found no real difference in predictive errors between the two cases.

Minimizing complexity. In summary, Figure 7 shows the benefit of using the more complex locality prediction mechanisms explored in this paper. We compare the simple random approach to our "best" solution, which couples iteration with the sphere landmark metric. We see that 6 random landmarks achieve a median predictive error of 26.7 ms and a 90th percentile of 105.4 ms. Using two iterations of three sphere-chosen landmarks, we decrease the median error to 12.0 ms (a 2.2x improvement) and the 90th percentile to 61.5 ms (1.7x better). Certainly, both are better than random selection, with its median of 101.1 ms and 90th percentile of 230.5 ms. Thus, while the advantage of the more complex redirection mechanism is significant, we also conclude that the simplest approach can in fact achieve reasonable results.

4   Conclusions

To improve performance, large-scale Internet systems require clients to access nearby servers. Unfortunately, the techniques usually associated with generating static topology maps—centralized mapping, trustworthy aggregated results, extensive network knowledge, ISP-specific heuristics, infrastructure deployment, etc.—are not readily available to fully-decentralized systems. Thus, such systems have turned to active probing and network coordinate algorithms to scalably predict inter-host latencies.

This paper explores various methodologies for locality prediction using active probing, showing that a distributed system can achieve high accuracy with minimal probing. We concentrate on four properties. (1) We conclude that, when selecting landmarks, a peer should choose ones that are more likely to be close to the client (the so-called sphere metric). If such selection is not feasible, well-distributed landmarks perform better than randomly-selected peers, but only when using smaller numbers of landmarks. (2) Increasing the number of landmarks improves the system's predictive accuracy, although with diminishing returns. (3) Iteratively redirecting clients provides minimal improvements over that obtained only from increasing the number of landmarks. (4) Choosing a client's destination based on coordinate distances yields strictly worse accuracy than simply using the landmark with smallest RTT. Thus, network coordinates enable certain landmark-selection algorithms—like the sphere metric—to scale to large systems, but are not as directly useful for determining a client's nearest hosts.

Acknowledgments. Special thanks to Russ Cox, Frank Dabek, Jinyang Li, David Mazières, and members of the NYU Systems Group for helpful discussions. This research was conducted as part of the IRIS project (http://project-iris.net/), supported by the NSF under Cooperative Agreement No. ANI-0225660. Michael Freedman is supported by an NDSEG Fellowship.

References

1. Akamai Technologies. http://www.akamai.com/, 2004.
2. M. Costa, M. Castro, A. Rowstron, and P. Key. PIC: Practical Internet coordinates for distance estimation. In *Conference on Distributed Systems*, Tokyo, Japan, March 2004.
3. F. Dabek, R. Cox, F. Kaashoek, and R. Morris. Vivaldi: A decentralized network coordinate system. In *ACM SIGCOMM*, Portland, OR, August 2004.
4. P. Francis, S. Jamin, C. Jin, Y. Jin, D. Raz, Y. Shavitt, and L. Zhang. IDMaps: A global Internet host distance estimation service. *IEEE/ACM Trans. on Networking*, Oct 2001.
5. M. J. Freedman, E. Freudenthal, and D. Mazières. Democratizing content publication with Coral. In *USENIX/ACM NSDI*, San Francisco, CA, March 2004.
6. R. Grimm, A. Kravetz, G. Lichtman, N. Michalakis, S. Raza, A. Elliston, and J. Miller. OpenEdge: A unified architecture for edge-side content creation, transformation, and caching. Technical report, NYU, February 2005.
7. B. Karp, S. Ratnasamy, S. Rhea, and S. Shenker. Spurring adoption of DHTs with OpenHash, a public DHT service. In *3rd Intl. Workshop on Peer-to-Peer Systems*, San Diego, CA, February 2004.
8. E. Ng and H. Zhang. Predicting Internet network distance with coordinates-based approaches. In *IEEE INFOCOM*, New York, NY, June 2002.

9. E. Ng and H. Zhang. A network positioning system for the Internet. In *USENIX Conference*, Boston, MA, March 2004.
10. M. Pias, J. Crowcroft, S. Wilbur, S. Bhatti, and T. Harris. Lighthouses for scalable distributed location. In *2nd Intl. Workshop on Peer-to-Peer Systems*, February 2003.
11. PlanetLab. http://www.planet-lab.org/, 2004.
12. L. Tang and M. Crovella. Virtual landmarks for the Internet. In *Internet Measurement Conference*, Miami Beach, FL, October 2003.
13. M. Walfish, H. Balakrishnan, and S. Shenker. Untangling the Web from DNS. In *USENIX/ACM NSDI*, San Francisco, CA, March 2004.
14. M. Walfish, J. Stribling, M. Krohn, H. Balakrishnan, R. Morris, and S. Shenker. Middleboxes no longer considered harmful. In *USENIX OSDI*, San Francisco, CA, December 2004.

Impact of Neighbor Selection on Performance and Resilience of Structured P2P Networks

Byung-Gon Chun[1], Ben Y. Zhao[2], and John D. Kubiatowicz[1]

[1] Computer Science Division, U.C. Berkeley
{bgchun, kubitron}@cs.berkeley.edu
[2] Department of Computer Science, U.C. Santa Barbara
ravenben@cs.ucsb.edu

Abstract. Recent work has shown that intelligent neighbor selection during construction can significantly enhance the performance of peer-to-peer overlay networks. While its impact on performance has been recognized, few have examined the impact of neighbor selection on network resilience. In this paper, we study the impact with a generalized cost model for overlay construction that takes into consideration different types of heterogeneity, such as node capacity and network proximity. Our simulation results show that the resulting performance improvement comes at the cost of static resilience against targeted attacks and adding random redundancy can improve the resilience significantly.

1 Introduction

Recent research has shown structured peer-to-peer overlay networks to provide scalable and resilient abstractions to large-scale applications [20, 12, 15, 9, 11]. They support routing to endpoints or nodes inside a network requiring only logarithmic routing state at each node. Nodes in structured peer-to-peer networks choose their neighbors based on optimization metrics. A recent study by Gummadi et al. [7] shows that neighbor selection based on network proximity significantly improves overall performance.

However, such neighbor selection can lead to an unbalanced overlay structure. Figure 1 shows a snapshot of the number of incoming edges (in-degree) and outgoing edges (out-degree) of nodes in a Bamboo [11] overlay running on PlanetLab [5]. Because the overlay uses proximity neighbor selection, some nodes in the system are more popular (have higher in-degree) than others. The impact of such a skewed degree distribution on the static resilience of networks has yet to be quantified. The focus of our study is to look at the impact of different neighbor selections on static resilience and performance of networks.

To better model neighbor selection across these networks, we first present a generalized cost model. While the heterogeneity of Internet hosts in bandwidth, inter-node latency and availability are well measured [13], most current protocols only consider network proximity in neighbor selection. Thus we use different neighbor selection models based on network proximity and node capacity. We study the impact they have on lookup latency and static resilience by incorporating the neighbor selection algorithms into ring and tree geometries, and show that the performance improvement from exploiting network proximity or node capacity comes at a price of increased vulnerability

M. Castro and R. van Renesse (Eds.): IPTPS 2005, LNCS 3640, pp. 264–274, 2005.

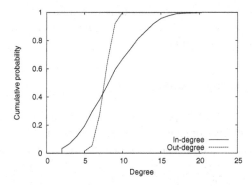

Fig. 1. Cumulative distribution of node degrees of a 205-node Bamboo overlay running on PlanetLab. In-degree and out-degree represent the number of incoming edges and the number of outgoing edges of each overlay node. The graph does not include default links (*i.e.*, leafset) used for failure tolerance. This is a snapshot taken on August 26, 2004.

against targeted attacks. Finally, we show that adding random redundancy can significantly improve static resilience against targeted attacks.

The paper is organized as follows. We discuss related work in Section 2 and describe details of the neighbor selection model in Section 3. We then measure the impact of different cost functions on both resilience and performance in Section 4 and conclude in Section 5.

2 Related Work

The closest work to ours was done by Gummadi et al. [7]. The authors quantified the impact of *routing geometry* on performance and static resilience. In contrast, we focus on the impact of *neighbor selection* on these factors. Albert et al. [1] show a clear correlation between the scale-free nature of networks and resilience to attacks and failures. Chun et al. [6] show the tradeoff between performance and network resilience of selfishly constructed unstructured overlays.

Castro et al. studied a defense mechanism against Eclipse attacks where attackers fake proximity to increase the fraction of bad routing entries in structured peer-to-peer networks using proximity neighbor selection [2]. They proposed to use two routing tables — proximity-based one and constrained one. Singh et al. proposed to bound the degree of overlay nodes in one proximity-based routing table to defend against Eclipse attacks [14]. In our work, attackers affect network connectivity by taking down nodes with high degree.

Several research efforts propose optimizing overlay construction of structured overlays using the network proximity metric [3, 10, 16, 18, 20], but generally ignore other factors such as CPU load, storage and bandwidth capacity. Brocade [19] proposes the use of supernodes for more efficient routing, but requires static selection of supernodes.

Other work [8] proposes the use of multiple "virtual servers" for load balancing among nodes of varying resource capacity, but does not consider network proximity for routing performance. Gia [4] performs continuous topology adaptation on an unstructured overlay such that nodes participate with network degree matching their resource capacity, without considering network proximity.

3   Structured Overlay Construction

In the construction of structured peer-to-peer networks, each node chooses neighbors that meet logical identifier constraints (e.g., prefix matching or identifier range), and builds directional links to them. These constraints are flexible such that a number of nodes are possible neighbors for each routing table entry. Intelligent selection of neighbors from the set of possible neighbor nodes significantly impacts the overlay's performance, resilience, and load balancing properties.

The neighbor selection problem can be reduced to a generalized cost minimization problem. We present here a generalized cost model that captures general node and link characteristics during neighbor selection. Ideally, optimizing neighbor selection for node i means minimizing the sum of the cost from i to all other nodes. The cost from i to j consists of two factors: cost incurred by intermediate overlay nodes (node cost: c_n) and cost incurred by overlay network links (edge cost: c_e). Let N be the network size. The cost of node i (C_i) is:

$$C_i = \sum_{j=1}^{N} t(i,j) c_p(i,j) \text{ where}$$
$$c_p(i,j) = \sum_{n \in V(i,j)} c_n(n) + \sum_{e \in P(i,j)} c_e(e) \tag{1}$$

where $t(i,j)$ is the traffic from i to j, $c_p(i,j)$ is the cost of the path from i to j, $P(i,j)$ is the path (a set of edges) from i to j, $V(i,j)$ is the set of intermediate overlay nodes in the path $P(i,j)$ (it does not include i and j), e is an edge in the path $P(i,j)$, n is a node in $V(i,j)$, $c_n(n)$ is the cost of node n, and $c_e(e)$ is the cost of edge e. If $t(i,j)$=0, there is no incentive for the node to optimize the path from i to j. In this model, c_n captures the heterogeneity in node capacity, which is a function of bandwidth, computation power, disk access time, and so on. c_e captures network proximity.

For structured networks such as Chord, Pastry, and Tapestry, the cost function can be rearranged as follows:

$$C_i = \sum_{b=1}^{N_b} \sum_{j \in R_b} t(i,j) c_p(i,j,n_b) \text{ where}$$
$$c_p(i,j,n_b) = [c_n(n_b) + c_e(i,n_b)] + [\sum_{n \in V(n_b,j)} c_n(n) + \sum_{e \in P(n_b,j)} c_e(e)] \tag{2}$$
$$= [c_n(n_b) + c_e(i,n_b)] + c_p(n_b,j)$$

where b is the neighbor index, n_b is the neighbor indexed by b, N_b is the number of neighbors, R_b is the set of destinations routed through the neighbor n_b, $c_n(i)$ is the node cost value of i, $c_e(k,l)$ is the edge cost between two nodes k and l, and $c_e(e)$ is the edge cost of e. $c_p(i,j,n_b)$ is the cost of the path from i to j with n_b as a first hop; we see that this includes terms from the first hop $[c_n(n_b) + c_e(i,n_b)]$ and terms from the remainder of the path $c_p(n_b,j)$.

Depending on the optimization goal, we can choose different metrics for c_n and c_e, including latency, throughput, reliability, availability, monetary cost, or any combination thereof. For example, choosing high capacity nodes as neighbors can decrease lookup latency and increase the overall lookup processing capacity of the system. On

Table 1. Cost functions studied. $c_n(i)$ represents the processing delay in node i. This is a decreasing function of capacity of node i. $c_e(i, n_b)$ represents the direct overlay link delay between node i and node n_b.

Model	Cost (C_i)
Random	None
Dist	$\sum_{b=1}^{N_b} c_e(i, n_b)$
Cap	$\sum_{b=1}^{N_b} c_n(n_b)$
CapDist	$\sum_{b=1}^{N_b} \{ c_n(n_b) + c_e(i, n_b) \}$

the other hand, using availability as a metric creates a more stable network or using monetary cost can create a network that is more economically incentivized.

Note that our idealized cost function assumes full knowledge of the network components, and is therefore not feasible in practice. Since most peer-to-peer protocols focus on optimizing neighbor tables locally, we will focus on the application of our cost function to the cost of the first overlay hop. In this work we focus on neighbor selections that consider the first hop and optimize latency under uniform traffic ($t(i, j) = 1, \forall i, j$).

Table 1 shows the four neighbor selection cost functions. *Random* chooses neighbors randomly. *Dist* chooses neighbors physically closest in the network to adapt to the underlying network topology. Currently, Bamboo, Pastry, and Tapestry use this mechanism. *Cap* chooses neighbors that have the smallest processing delay. *CapDist* chooses neighbors that gives the smallest combined latency, which is the sum of the node processing delay and the overlay link delay.

4   Simulation Results

In this section, we first present simulation results that quantify the performance benefits of using intelligent neighbor selection algorithms. We then examine the impact such algorithms have on the static resilience of the resulting overlay to randomized failures and targeted attacks.

4.1   Simulation Setup

We simulate the Tapestry [20] and Chord [15] protocols as representatives of their respective geometries (tree and ring). When each node optimizes its cost function, it performs random sampling to select neighbors and choose the best one among the samples. In our experiments, we use 32 samples for each routing level in Tapestry or each finger in Chord.

We use practical greedy routing algorithms for both Tapestry and Chord. For Tapestry, each node forwards messages to the first live neighbor matching one more prefix digit. The lookup fails if all primary and backup links in the routing entry fail. For our Chord experiments, each node forwards messages to the live neighbor that is closest to the destination in the identifier space. The lookup fails if all neighbors before the destination in the namespace fail. Note that the measured network resilience depends on the routing algorithms we use.

Our simulations use 5100 node transit-stub network topologies generated using the
GT-ITM library [17]. We construct Chord and Tapestry overlays of 4096 nodes by placing overlay nodes to random physical locations. We gather results with 9 different configurations for GT-ITM, generate 3 transit-stub topologies each, and choose 3 overlay
node placements on each topology.

4.2   Performance

We begin by quantifying the effects of neighbor selection algorithms on performance.
We look at two different distributions of node processing delay: uniform and bimodal.
Because Tapestry and Chord results are similar in both cases, we will only show
Tapestry results.

We start by assigning node processing delay from a coarse-grained uniform distribution. We choose one of 10 values uniformly from the range $(0, \alpha]$, where α is the

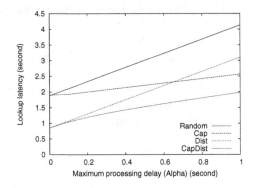

Fig. 2. Average lookup latency for uniform processing delay distribution. When processing delay
variation is low, neighbor selections that exploit network proximity (*Dist* and *CapDist*) have low
latency. However, when processing delay variation is high, neighbor selections that exploit node
capacity (*Cap* and *CapDist*) have low latency.

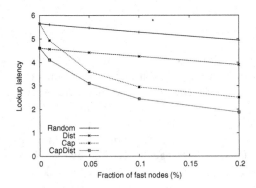

Fig. 3. Average lookup latency for bimodal processing delay distribution. As the fraction of fast
nodes increases, neighbor selections using node capacity can have better lookup latency than
those that do not use node capacity.

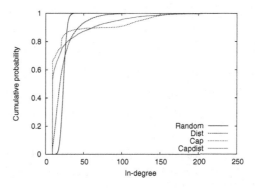

Fig. 4. CDF of the number of incoming edges for uniform processing delay distribution. *Random* shows an even in-degree distribution, but the others have very skewed distributions.

maximum processing delay. Figure 2 shows average lookup latency over all node pairs in Tapestry. By exploiting network proximity and heterogeneous capacity, *CapDist* achieves the best lookup performance. When processing delay variation is high (α=1s), *CapDist* performs 30% better than *Dist* and 48% better than *Random*. When no variation exists (*i.e.*, α=0s), *Dist* and *CapDist* exploit network proximity to outperform *Random* and *Cap*.

We now look at a bimodal model for processing capacity, where nodes are either fast or slow. Fast nodes process 100 lookup messages per second while slow nodes process 1 message per second. Figure 3 shows that as we vary the fraction of fast nodes from 0% to 20%, neighbor selection using capacity (*Cap* and *CapDist*) favors routes through fast nodes and achieves better performance. For instances where the variation in processing capacity is extremely high, we expect that capacity utilization at fast nodes will be limited by the routing constraints of the protocol, and the deployment of virtual nodes is necessary to fully exploit the excess processing capacity.

Using latency optimization creates uneven distributions of nodes' incoming node degrees. Nodes near the center of the network (*i.e.*, transit domains) and nodes with high capacity are preferred, and minimize path latency by utilizing low latency links or low processing delay. Figure 4 shows the cumulative distribution function (CDF) of nodes' in-degrees in Tapestry networks with different neighbor selection algorithms. Unlike *Random*, results from cost-optimized overlays show slow transitions and long tails. We also observe that the CDF of nodes in transit domains is more skewed and has longer tails than that of nodes in stub domains.

4.3 Static Resilience

Previous work by Albert et al. showed an inherent tradeoff for unstructured networks between resilience against random node failures and resilience against targeted attacks [1]. In this section, we explore the impact that neighbor selection algorithms have on static resilience.

We measure resilience as the proportion of all pairs of *live* endpoints that can still route to each other via the overlay after an external event, either randomized node fail-

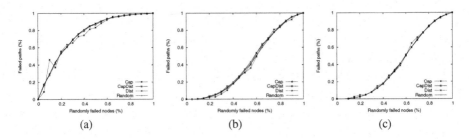

Fig. 5. Tapestry under random node failures. (a) Tapestry varying neighbor selection on one primary link (e.g., *Dist*: primary link chosen to optimize the *Dist* cost function), (b) Tapestry varying neighbor selection on one primary link and two backup links (e.g., *Dist*: all three links chosen to optimize the *Dist* cost function), (c) Tapestry varying neighbor selection on one primary link and choosing two backup links randomly (e.g., *Dist*: primary link chosen to optimize the *Dist* cost function and two backup links chosen randomly).

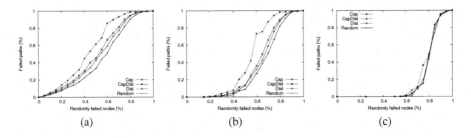

Fig. 6. Chord under random node failures. Chord varying finger selection on finger table having (a) one sequential neighbor, (b) four sequential neighbors, and (c) 12 sequential neighbors.

ures or targeted attacks. We assume attacks focus on removing nodes with the highest in-degree in order to maximize damage to overall network reachability. For these experiments, we assume nodes have a uniform processing delay distribution with $\alpha = 0.5$s.

For Tapestry, we examine resilience of the base protocol, the base protocol plus additional backup links (all chosen using a number of neighbor selection algorithms), and the base protocol plus backup links chosen at random. We maintain backup links for each routing level, so adding two backup links triples the number of neighbors. For Chord, we examine the base protocol (i.e., protocol with one sequential neighbor) and the base protocol plus multiple sequential neighbors. Sequential neighbors are successors in the identifier space. They can make progress to route to all destinations.

Random Node Failures. We first examine the impact of randomized node failures. In general, we would expect that using selection algorithms that prefer high capacity nodes results in more hierarchy in the network, where many weaker nodes are connected by highly interconnected high capacity nodes. In such cases, we expect that randomized failures will disconnect weaker nodes from the network, but have a relatively low impact on overall connectivity.

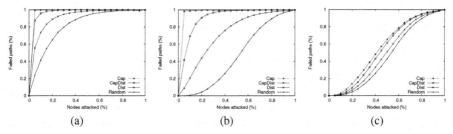

Fig. 7. Tapestry under attack. (a) Tapestry varying neighbor selection on one primary link (e.g., $Dist$: primary link chosen to optimize the $Dist$ cost function), (b) Tapestry varying neighbor selection on one primary link and two backup links (e.g., $Dist$: all three links chosen to optimize the $Dist$ cost function), (c) Tapestry varying neighbor selection on one primary link and choosing two backup links randomly (e.g., $Dist$: primary link chosen to optimize the $Dist$ cost function and two backup links chosen randomly).

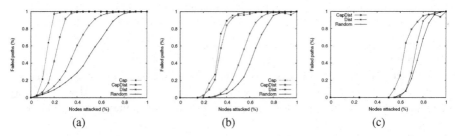

Fig. 8. Chord under attack. Chord varying finger selection on finger table having (a) one sequential neighbor, (b) four sequential neighbors, and (c) 12 sequential neighbors. For (c), we do not present *Cap*. We cannot find an order to launch targeted attacks, since *Cap* creates networks where many nodes have the same node degree.

Figures 5 and 6 show the failure tolerance of Tapestry and Chord, respectively. Surprisingly, we see the failure tolerance is a little affected by neighbor selections. The tighter outgoing link constraints of structured peer to peer networks allow less variation in the resulting topology than unstructured networks. Every node has at least $O(logN)$ outgoing links, and randomized naming also smoothens out distribution of outgoing links. Since each lookup takes $O(logN)$ hops regardless of neighbor selection cost functions, the probability of meeting randomly failed nodes in a lookup will be similar.

Adding backup links in Tapestry and sequential neighbors in Chord dramatically improves failure tolerance (Figures 5(b), 5(c), 6(b), and 6(c)). Note that in Tapestry, failure behavior changes from extremely brittle (concave downward with increasing node failure) to smoothly varying (an S-shaped curve with increasing node failure) with the addition of path diversity.

Targeted Node Attacks. While structured peer to peer overlays define a minimum number of outgoing links per node, a node's number of incoming links is unrestricted. This means that neighbor selection algorithms considering capacity or network proximity will skew the network such that powerful or central nodes have significantly higher in-degrees than weaker or boundary nodes. This means that structured peer to peer overlays that consider capacity or network proximity in neighbor selection can be vulnerable to attacks.

As shown in Figures 7(a) and 8(a), attacking nodes with high in-degree affects network connectivity severely. *Random* shows the best attack tolerance among neighbor selections. *CapDist* has worse attack tolerance than *Dist*, although it has the best performance among neighbor selections we examine. In Tapestry, when 30% of nodes are attacked, 0.4% of pairs of live nodes can communicate in the networks created with *CapDist*, but 20.4% of pairs of live nodes can still communicate in the networks created with *Random*. In Chord, when 50% of nodes are attacked, 0.2% of pairs of live nodes can communicate in the networks created with *CapDist*, but 51.8% of pairs of live nodes can still communicate in the networks created with *Random*.

This result demonstrates a fundamental tradeoff between performance and attack resilience in structured overlay construction. The performance gain from neighbor selection algorithms increases the variability of in-degrees among nodes. Nodes with high capacity or nodes near the center of the network end up with high in-degrees and have a disproportionately large impact on network connectivity when they are attacked.

Adding Redundancy. From Figures 5(a) and 7(a) we observe that the resilience of *Random* under random failures is the same as that under targeted attacks. This result shows that randomness can shield against attacks targeting biases. If we can bring the randomness back into the system, we may improve the resilience against targeted attacks.

Paying the additional cost of maintaining extra links improves static resilience against targeted attacks. Figures 7(c) and 8(c) show that adding backup links or sequential neighbors can increase attack tolerance significantly. When 30% of nodes are attacked in Tapestry with one primary link optimizing *CapDist* and two random backup links, 76% of pairs of live nodes can communicate. When 50% of nodes are attacked in Chord with 12 sequential neighbors, all nodes can still communicate. Randomly choosing backup links in Tapestry and sequential neighbors in Chord avoids routing hotspots that are vulnerable to targeted attacks. In Tapestry for example, cost-optimized backup links are less effective at improving attack tolerance than random backup links (Figure 7(b)). Using sequential neighbors gains good attack resilience with the overhead of high lookup latency under attacks.

5   Conclusion

Previous research argued for the consideration of network or physical characteristics of nodes in overlay construction. In this paper, we take a quantitative approach to examining the benefits and costs of considering such criteria in overlay construction.

We present a generalized model for neighbor selection that incorporates metrics for network proximity and available resources (capacity), and show that while considering these factors can lead to significant gains in routing performance, these benefits come with their associated costs. We find that the choice of neighbor selection algorithm drives a tradeoff between performance and resilience to attacks.

Optimized structured overlays have unbalanced structures. These overlays do not bound the number of incoming links per node. Thus central nodes in a network or nodes with more resources will have much higher in-degree than others. Should high degree nodes be attacked, the impact on network connectivity is severe. On the other hand, the minimum out-degree means even for overlays that optimize towards proximity or available resources, most nodes achieve enough resilience against randomized failures. Finally, we show that adding random redundancy can improve the resilience significantly.

As future work, we intent to investigate the resilience of different geometries under different neighbor selection algorithms. We also plan to investigate the impact of these neighbor selection algorithms on dynamic resilience, such as when maintenance algorithms repair failures over time.

References

1. ALBERT, R., JEONG, H., AND BARABASI, A.-L. Error and attack tolerance of complex networks. *Nature 406* (July 2000), 378–381.
2. CASTRO, M., DRUSCHEL, P., GANESH, A., AND ROWSTRON, A. Secure routing for structured peer-to-peer overlay networks. In *Proc. of USENIX OSDI* (December 2002).
3. CASTRO, M., DRUSCHEL, P., HU, Y. C., AND ROWSTRON, A. Exploiting network proximity in peer-to-peer overlay networks, technical report msr-tr-2002-82, 2002.
4. CHAWATHE, Y., RATNASAMY, S., BRESLAU, L., LANHAM, N., AND SHENKER, S. Making gnutella-like p2p systems scalable. In *Proc. of ACM SIGCOMM* (2003).
5. CHUN, B., CULLER, D., ROSCOE, T., BAVIER, A., PETERSON, L., WAWRZONIAK, M., AND BOWMAN, M. Planetlab: An overlay testbed for broad-coverage services. In *ACM Computer Communication Review* (July 2003).
6. CHUN, B.-G., FONSECA, R., STOICA, I., AND KUBIATOWICZ, J. Characterizing selfishly constructed overlay routing networks. In *Proceedings of IEEE INFOCOM* (2004).
7. GUMMADI, K. P., GUMMADI, R., GRIBBLE, S. D., RATNASAMY, S., SHENKER, S., AND STOICA, I. The impact of dht routing geometry on resilience and proximity. In *Proc. of ACM SIGCOMM* (2003).
8. RAO, A., LAKSHMINARAYANAN, K., SURANA, S., KARP, R., AND STOICA, I. Load balancing in structured p2p systems. In *Proc. of IPTPS* (2003).
9. RATNASAMY, S., FRANCIS, P., HANDLEY, M., KARP, R., AND SHENKER, S. A scalable content-addressable network. In *Proc. of SIGCOMM* (August 2001), ACM.
10. RATNASAMY, S., HANDLEY, M., KARP, R., AND SHENKER, S. Topologically-aware overlay construction and server selection. In *Proc. of IEEE INFOCOM* (2002).
11. RHEA, S., GEELS, D., ROSCOE, T., AND KUBIATOWICZ, J. Handling churn in a dht. In *Proc. of the USENIX Annual Technical Conference* (June 2004).
12. ROWSTRON, A., AND DRUSCHEL, P. Pastry: Scalable, distributed object location and routing for large-scale peer-to-peer systems. In *Proc. of Middleware* (Nov 2001), ACM.
13. SAROIU, S., GUMMADI, P. K., AND GRIBBLE, S. D. A measurement study of peer-to-peer file sharing systems. In *Proc. of MMCN* (2002).
14. SINGH, A., CASTRO, M., DRUSCHEL, P., AND ROWSTRON, A. Defending against eclipse attacks on overlay networks. In *Proc. of the ACM SIGOPS European Workshop* (September 2004).
15. STOICA, I., MORRIS, R., KARGER, D., KAASHOEK, M. F., AND BALAKRISHNAN, H. Chord: A scalable peer-to-peer lookup service for internet applications. In *Proc. of SIGCOMM* (August 2001), ACM.

16. WALDVOGEL, M., AND RINALDI, R. Efficient topology-aware overlay network. In *Proc. of HotNets* (2002).
17. ZEGURA, E. W., CALVERT, K. L., AND BHATTACHARJEE, S. How to model an internetwork. In *Proc. of IEEE INFOCOM* (1996).
18. ZHANG, H., GOEL, A., AND GOVINDAN, R. Incrementally improving lookup latency in distributed hash table systems. In *Proc. of ACM SIGMETRICS* (2003).
19. ZHAO, B. Y., DUAN, Y., HUANG, L., JOSEPH, A., AND KUBIATOWICZ, J. Brocade: Landmark routing on overlay networks. In *Proc. of IPTPS* (2002).
20. ZHAO, B. Y., HUANG, L., RHEA, S. C., STRIBLING, J., JOSEPH, A. D., AND KUBIATOWICZ, J. D. Tapestry: A global-scale overlay for rapid service deployment. *IEEE J-SAC* 22, 1 (January 2004), 41–53.

Evaluating DHT-Based Service Placement for Stream-Based Overlays

Peter Pietzuch, Jeffrey Shneidman, Jonathan Ledlie,
Matt Welsh, Margo Seltzer, and Mema Roussopoulos

Harvard University, Cambridge MA 02138, USA
hourglass@eecs.harvard.edu

Abstract. *Stream-based overlay networks* (SBONs) are one approach
to implementing large-scale stream processing systems. A fundamental
consideration in an SBON is that of *service placement*, which determines
the physical location of in-network processing services or operators, in
such a way that network resources are used efficiently. Service placement
consists of two components: *node discovery*, which selects a candidate set
of nodes on which services might be placed, and *node selection*, which
chooses the particular node to host a service. By viewing the placement
problem as the composition of these two processes we can trade-off quality and efficiency between them.

We evaluate the appropriateness of using DHT routing paths for service placement in an SBON, when aiming to minimize network usage. For
this, we consider two DHT-based algorithms for node discovery, which
use either the *union* or *intersection* of DHT routing paths in the SBON,
and compare their performance to other techniques. We show that current DHT-based schemes are actually rather poor node discovery algorithms, when minimizing network utilization. An efficient DHT may
not traverse enough hops to obtain a sufficiently large candidate set for
placement. The union of DHT routes may result in a low-quality set of
discovered nodes that requires an expensive node selection algorithm. Finally, the intersection of DHT routes relies on route convergence, which
prevents the placement of services with a large fan-in.

1 Introduction

A marriage between the database and networking communities has produced a
series of interesting systems for continous queries, large-scale stream processing,
and application-level multicast. These systems are examples of a generic class of
stream-based overlay networks (SBONs). SBON applications include real-time
processing of financial data (Aurora [1], Borealis [2]), Internet health monitoring (PIER [3]) and querying geographically diverse sensor networks (IrisNet [4]).

SBONs pose two important challenges. First, a suitable choice of services,
such as database operators, multicast points, or stream processors, must be
provided by the system to satisfy user requirements. Second, these services must
be deployed efficiently in the network according to user queries. Thus far, most

M. Castro and R. van Renesse (Eds.): IPTPS 2005, LNCS 3640, pp. 275–286, 2005.
© Springer-Verlag Berlin Heidelberg 2005

existing research into SBONs has focused on the former question, with much less emphasis on efficient service placement. However, network-aware service placement becomes a crucial factor that determines the scalability and impact of an SBON when deployed in a shared network. Therefore, a service placement algorithm should be scalable and adaptive, and perform well based on several cost metrics, such as network utilization and application latency.

Service placement is actually composed of two mechanisms: *node discovery* and *node selection*. Discovery is the process of identifying a set of nodes capable of hosting a service; we call this set of nodes the *candidate set*. Selection is the act of selecting a particular member of the candidate set to actually host the service. Traditionally, these two mechanisms have been intertwined, but by viewing them as separable processes, it is possible to gain greater insight into the performance of existing systems and develop new approaches to placing services.

In this paper, we investigate how well-suited current DHTs are to the task of node discovery with respect to efficient network utilization. We evaluate two DHT-based placement algorithms in comparison to non-DHT-based approaches, such as a globally optimal placement algorithm and a scheme based on spring relaxation [5]. Our analysis highlights the tight relationship between discovery and placement. A bad discovery mechanism can sometimes yield a good placement, but at the cost of an expensive selection mechanism. For the topologies we have considered, DHT-based schemes produce candidate sets that are marginally distinguishable from a random sampling. In particular, the union of DHT paths from producers to consumers creates a large collection of nodes and selecting the best one does yield a good placement, but we would have done equally well by selecting nodes at random. When considering the intersection of routing paths, services with a large fan-in are always placed at consumer nodes.

We conclude that current DHTs are not well-suited to this particular challenge of optimizing network utilization. We suggest that one should turn toward alternate solutions, such as the relaxation-based approach analyzed here, or a new generation of DHTs that are designed to address the needs of SBONs.

The outline of paper is as follows. Section 2 summarizes SBONs and describes the service placement problem. Section 3 introduces several node discovery and selection schemes that are then evaluated in Section 4. In Section 5 we review related work and Section 6 concludes.

2   Stream-Based Overlay Networks

An SBON is an overlay network that streams data from one or more producers to one or more consumers, possibly via one or more operator services that perform in-network processing. In an SBON, *circuits* interconnect multiple *services*. A circuit is a tree that specifies the identities and relationships between services in a data stream and corresponds to a query. Services that are part of a circuit are connected with *circuit links*.

We model a circuit as a logical query statement that is then *realized* on physical nodes. Some logical elements are constrained when the query is first stated.

For example, the destination and data sources are specific physical nodes. We call these elements *consumer* and *producer* services, respectively, and consider them *pinned* because their logical-to-physical mapping is fixed. Other services, *e.g.*, a *join* operator, might be placed at any appropriate node in the network. We call these unassigned logical services *unpinned*. Logically, a join operator resides between two or more producers and one or more consumers, but its physical mapping is unassigned, *i.e.*, it is initially *unplaced*.

2.1 Placement Problem

Determining a placement for unpinned services is the fundamental placement problem in an SBON. Some placements are better than others: each placement has a *cost* and the quality of a placement is revealed by a *cost function*. Therefore, a solution to the placement problem calculates a valid placement for all unplaced services that minimizes the total incurred cost in the SBON.

Cost functions in an SBON can be categorized into two classes. Minimizing *application-specific* costs, such as circuit delay and jitter, addresses the application's desire for quality of service in the SBON. *Global* cost functions, such as network utilization and resource contention, attempt to capture the impact of a placement decision on other participants of the SBON.

In this paper, we concentrate on the global cost of utilizing the network when streaming data through the SBON, which is important in cooperative network environment, such as PlanetLab. One way to capture overall network utilization is the *bandwidth-latency* (BW-Lat) product, which is the sum of the *data rates* consumed by circuit links multiplied by their communication *latencies* calculated over all circuit links. The BW-Lat product captures network utilization as the amount of in-transit data in the network at a particular point in time.

The rationale behind this cost function is that the less data is put into the network by a placed circuit, the more network capacity is available to other circuits or applications. The BW-Lat cost function makes the assumption that high latency network links are more costly to use than low latency ones. Often high latency indicates network congestion or long geographical distance that means higher network operating costs. In both cases, the utilization of such links should be reduced. By factoring in the used bandwidth of a circuit link into the BW-Lat metric, the cost is proportional to the amount of network traffic used by a circuit. In other words, overall network utilization can be reduced more when good placement decisions are chosen for circuits with a high data rate.

3   Placement Algorithms

Many service placement algorithms can be viewed as consisting of two steps: *node discovery* and *node selection*. *Node discovery* identifies a subset of all nodes in the SBON as a possible candidate set for service placement, and *node selection* chooses a suitable node for the actual placement. An optimal node selection would consider all nodes in the SBON, but requiring global knowledge is clearly not feasible for a scalable system. Even in a moderately-sized network, such as

PlanetLab, up-to-date node characteristics for 500 nodes cannot be gathered in a resource efficient manner. Therefore, most placement algorithms use the results of a node discovery scheme as the input for node selection to cope with the complexity of the placement problem. Other placement algorithms, such as the Relaxation placement scheme described below, reverse the ordering of the two steps or coalesce them into one.

3.1   Node Discovery

The goal of *node discovery* is to generate a list of physical nodes on which an unpinned service can be placed. This list is known as the *candidate set*. The quality of the candidate set, in terms of the placement cost, is an important consideration: if no nodes with a low placement cost are part of the candidate set, a good placement cannot be found even with an optimal node selection algorithm. The size of the candidate set and the distribution of placement costs for the included nodes determines the flexibility that the node selection algorithm has when the best choice from the set cannot support the placement due to resource limitations. In this section, we describe several possible candidate sets.

All. Setting the candidate set to be the entire overlay network gives the node selection algorithm the most flexibility to make a good placement. However, it is infeasible to maintain global knowledge about all nodes in a large-scale distributed system and process a large set of candidate nodes efficiently.

Consumer. This algorithm returns the node hosting the consumer service as the placement location, which models a centralized data warehouse system. While it trivially solves the placement problem, it makes no attempt to optimize the placement decision.

Producer. Since data producers are pinned services in the circuit, one can select these nodes as the candidate set. Using known producer nodes solves the discovery problem, but can result in a small, badly-chosen candidate set.

Random. A candidate set of k random nodes can be discovered through some mechanism. However, the average quality of this set may be worse than that of any other scheme that favors nodes with lower placement costs.

DHT Routing Path. A natural way to build a candidate set is to route a message between pinned services through an overlay network, such as a DHT. In a DHT setting, a message will traverse $\lceil \log_b(N) \rceil$ hops in the worst case, where N is the number of nodes in the DHT and b is the numeric base used for hash keys during routing. There are two obvious ways to generate a candidate set when a circuit contains a consumer and multiple producers:

   1. **DHT Union** takes the total set of overlay nodes in the paths from producers to the consumer as the candidate set. The service is then placed at one of these nodes.

   2. **DHT Intersection** takes the intersection of overlay nodes in the routing path from producers to the consumer. The service is then placed at one of these ordered nodes, such as the node closest to the producers.

The goal of this paper is to explore the performance of these two DHT routing schemes in comparison with the other schemes and to determine their applicability for service placement in an SBON.

3.2 Node Selection

For each unplaced service in a circuit, the *node selection* algorithm must place the service on some node in the candidate set. In this paper, we consider three general selection algorithms. Other selection schemes are possible, but will produce placements no better than optimal selection. Of course, no selection algorithm is necessary when the candidate set contains only a single node.

Random. selects a node out of the candidate set with uniform probability. This is a trivial scheme to implement, and may do well with a well-chosen candidate set. However, it does not attempt to optimize the placement decision.

Optimal. chooses the best node from the candidate set with respect to some metric, such as network utilization or application latency. In this paper, we consider the BW-Lat product from Section 2.1. If the candidate set is well-chosen or large, optimal may find a globally-optimal placement. However, an efficient implementation of optimal selection is hard. An exhaustive search over all possibilities may result in a large amount of network probing and computational overhead for non-trivial circuits.

Relaxation. [5] places services using a spring-relaxation model in an artificial coordinate space [6], in which distance corresponds to latency between physical nodes in the SBON. The placement coordinate is then mapped back to physical network space to perform the actual service placement. Prior work has shown that relaxation placement performs well compared to other algorithms and supports scalable and dynamic cross-circuit optimization decision [5]. However, relaxation requires additional overhead in calculating the latency space in a distributed fashion and maintaining a mapping back to physical space.

4 Evaluation

In this section we present our evaluation of DHT-based service placement compared to other, non-DHT-based placement schemes. The goal is to determine the performance of the DHTUnion and DHTIntersection algorithms when applied to different topologies and DHT parameters. Our evaluation focuses on the efficiency of network utilization, as captured by the BW-Lat product. Throughout this section, we refer to a placement algorithm by its discovery and selection schemes, *e.g.*, *All/Random*. The Optimal selection scheme uses the BW-Lat product as its metric.

4.1 Experimental Set-Up

To evaluate the placement efficiency for a large number of circuits, we implemented a discrete-event simulator that operates either on the PlanetLab [7] topology with 186 nodes generated from all-pairs-ping measurements [8], or an artificial 600-node transit-stub topology created by the GATech topology generator [9]. After placing 1000 circuits each consisting of 4 pinned producers, 1 unpinned service, and 1 pinned consumer, the simulator calculates the placement cost per circuit for each of the placement algorithms. The four producers in the circuits produce streams with a data rate of 2 kb/s each, which are then aggregated into a single 1 kb/s stream by the unpinned service.

Two separate DHT implementations were used for the DHT-based placement schemes. We leverage a recent DHT implementation by crawling the *Open-Hash* [10] routing tables running on PlanetLab, which uses the *Bamboo* [11] routing algorithm. OpenHash has a DHT key base of 2 and a leaf set size of 8. We performed latency measurement with *Scriptroute* [12] to fill in the missing Bamboo nodes in the all-pair pings data. We also implemented our own Pastry-like DHT, called *Pan*, which allowed us to vary the key base. A comparison of Pan and Bamboo routing with key base 2 shows that the average routing hop count of Pan is within 2 % of Bamboo's value. Both DHTs used are proximity-aware because otherwise the DHT routing paths would be essentially random. Pan follows Pastry's approach to achieve proximity awareness by preferring DHT nodes for its routing tables that are close in terms of latency.

4.2   Network Utilization

The experiment in Figure 1 depicts the efficiency of network utilization in terms of the amount of data in the network for five different, non-DHT placement schemes. Each curve shows the BW-Lat distribution as a CDF after placing 1000 circuits. As expected, *All/Opt* performs best and *All/Random* worst. *All/-Relaxation* is close to optimal, and outperforms the random selection of a producer (*Producer/Random*) and consumer placement (*Consumer/—*). We will use these placement schemes as baselines for comparison to DHT-based placement. All our experimental results for DHT-based service placement are summarized in Table 1. The data is listed as the ratio of the 80th percentile of the BW-Lat product compared to the 80th percentile of *All/Opt* after placing 1000 circuits

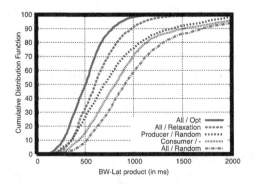

Fig. 1. Non-DHT: CDF of the BW-Lat product on the PlanetLab topology

Table 1. 80th percentile of the BW-Lat product as a ratio of the 80th percentile of *All/Opt* after placing 1000 circuits for two topologies with DHT bases 2 and 64

Node		Topology			
Discovery	Selection	PlanetLab		Transit-Stub	
		b=2	b=64	b=2	b=64
All	Optimal	1.00		1.00	
All	Relax.	1.24		1.09	
RandomSet(6)	Optimal	1.26		1.36	
Producer	Random	1.60		1.43	
Consumer	—	1.70		1.63	
All	Random	1.96		1.84	
DHTUnion	Optimal	1.13	1.13	1.14	1.18
DHTUnion-NoProd	Optimal	1.17	1.31	1.16	1.31
DHTUnion	Random	1.60	1.63	1.56	1.52
DHTIntersec.	—	1.68	1.67	1.63	1.63
DHTIntersec.-Split	—	1.61	1.55	1.59	1.54
DHTIntersec.-Data	—	2.82	1.96	3.31	2.25

using various placement schemes. In the next two sections, we discuss the results for two DHT-based node discovery schemes, *DHTUnion* and *DHTIntersection*, using several topologies and DHT parameters.

DHTUnion. The DHTUnion scheme for node selection uses the DHT routing paths from the producers to the consumer in a circuit to obtain a set of candidate nodes for service placement. The size and the quality of the set with respect to the placement cost function, will depend on the network topology and the specifics of the particular DHT, such as its network awareness, key base and leaf set size. Most DHTs are optimized for efficient key retrieval, which means that the number of routing hops is kept low by choosing a large key base. However, this reduces the size of the candidate set for node selection when using a DHT, potentially missing good placement nodes from the set. In terms of quality, the choice of the routing path by the DHT will determine the suitability of the candidate set for service placement.

PlanetLab Topology. In Figure 2, we plot the distribution of the BW-Lat product for three variations of the DHTUnion scheme on the PlanetLab topology using the Bamboo DHT. For such a small topology, many nodes are included in the candidate set because the Bamboo deployment on PlanetLab has a large average routing path length of 3.18 hops due to its binary key base. Therefore, the figure shows that *DHTUnion/Opt* placement performs well compared to *All/Opt*: the candidate set covers a significant fraction of all nodes and therefore is likely to include at least one good placement node. However, this good placement node must be found through an expensive exhaustive search.

The DHT contributes little to placement efficiency, which is supported by the fact that *RandomSet(6)/Opt* (1.26) performs similarly to *DHTUnion/Opt* (1.13). RandomSet uses a node size of six because this is close to the average number of nodes in the DHTUnion candidate set. A random choice of six nodes out of 186 is likely to include a good placement candidate. This is especially the case for the PlanetLab network, which mainly interlinks well-provisioned educational institutions. In general, performing optimal node selection on large candidate sets is not desirable because of the probing and computational overheads when placing complex circuits with multiple unpinned services. The *DHTUnion/Random* algorithm (1.60) has a similar cost as *Producer/Random* (1.60) and *Consumer/—* (1.70) because of the probability that either the producer or consumer nodes are chosen randomly.

We study the effect of a more efficient DHT deployment on PlanetLab by simulating a DHT with a larger key base of 64. For this DHT, the average routing path length drops to 1.6 hops. Table 1 shows that the performance of DHTUnion/Opt is still good (1.13) when compared to *All/Opt*. Although the DHT routing paths are shorter due to the larger key base, the candidate set now becomes dominated by the 5 nodes hosting either pinned producers or consumers. We verify this claim with the DHTUnion-NoProd scheme: when the producer nodes are removed from the candidate set in *DHTUnion-NoProd/Opt* placement, the placement cost increases to 1.31. This means that the in-network DHT routing path is not long enough to contribute a good placement node.

Transit-Stub Topology. The problem of a small, low-quality candidate set, as returned by DHTUnion, is even more pronounced in larger topologies. In Figure 2, we consider an efficient DHT deployment with a key base of 64 deployed on a 600-node transit-stub topology. The average DHT path length here is 1.89 hops. In this topology, *DHTUnion/Opt* (1.18) performs worse than *All/Relaxation* (1.09). Removing the producer nodes (*DHTUnion-NoProd/Opt*) reduces the efficiency to 1.31, resulting in only a small gain when compared to *RandomSet(6)/Opt* (1.36).

An obvious way to enlarge the candidate set is to consider the round-trip DHT routing path. However, increasing the size of candidate set without picking good nodes does not lead to efficient service placement in a large topology. The

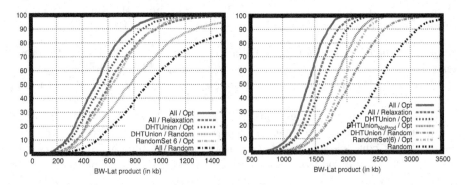

Fig. 2. DHTUnion: CDF of the BW-Lat product with Bamboo (base=2) on the Planet-Lab topology (left) and CDF of the BW-Lat product with Pan (base=64) on 600-node transit-stub topology (right)

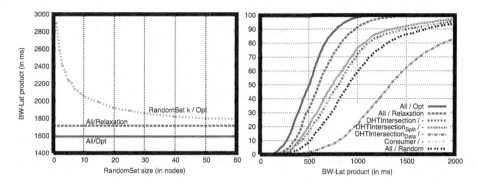

Fig. 3. RandomSet/Opt: BW-Lat product with Pan (base=64) on 600-node transit-stub topology (left). DHT-Intersection: CDF of the BW-Lat product with Bamboo (base=2) on the PlanetLab topology (right).

experiment in Figure 3 with the same 600-node transit-stub topology investigates the minimum size of a randomly chosen candidate set (RandomSet(k)) that is necessary to perform a good node selection with an exhaustive search (Opt). Even when the candidate set includes 10 % of all nodes, it does not achieve the performance of *All/Relaxation* placement. Note that RandomSet performs worse on the transit-stub topology than before because this network is not as homogeneous as PlanetLab.

DHTIntersection. The DHTIntersection discovery scheme considers the nodes in the intersection of all DHT routing paths between the producers and the consumer as the candidate set. It relies on the route convergence property of DHT routing [13], which states that routing paths to the same destination are likely to converge. A service is then placed on the farthest node along the path that is shared by all other routing paths. In this case, node discovery is equivalent to selection, so the selection scheme is represented by —.

In Figure 3, we evaluate three types of DHTIntersection. The overlapping curves of *DHTIntersection/—* and *Consumer/—* reveal that DHTIntersection performs only marginally better than consumer selection. In most cases the intersection of the four routing paths from the producers to the consumer contains only the node hosting the consumer. This means that DHTIntersection is not a good scheme for unpinned services with a large fan-in. Since the candidate set returned by DHTIntersection contains a single node in most cases, varying the node selection scheme is unnecessary.

The DHTIntersection-Split scheme recognizes this lack of convergence of multiple routes by assuming that an unpinned service can be *split* into sub-services. These sub-services can then be placed independently. A sub-service is created at the intersection between any two routing paths from producers to consumer. This is similar to the setup of multicast trees in DHT-based systems, such as Scribe [13], where a multicast node is created at the node joining the path from a new subscriber to the root of the multicast tree. The graph shows that splitting services improves the fraction of cases, in which services are placed in-network. However, it does not reach the performance of *All/Relaxation*, which optimizes for the BW-Lat product. Moreover, it is not applicable if services cannot be decomposed into sub-services.

Application-level multicast schemes based on DHTs often send data along DHT routing hops. This has the advantage that the data flows benefit from the resilience and load-balancing properties of the DHT but it also incurs the penalty of more network traffic in the system. To evaluate this effect, the final placement scheme is DHTIntersection-Data, as shown in Figure 3, which in addition to using the DHT for service placement, also routes the data itself through the DHT. The last row in Table 1 suggests that the penalty is directly related to the key base, which determines the number of hops in the routing path. For the Bamboo DHT on PlanetLab, the penalty of routing data through the DHT compared to *All/Opt* placement is almost a factor of 3. We suggest that many applications would benefit from including their own resilience mechanisms at the application-level without paying the price for using the DHT for data routing.

4.3   Summary

Our experiments suggest that DHTs are less efficient than non-DHT alternatives, such as Relaxation placement, for service placement in SBONs. DHTs are designed for efficient key lookup, but this yields small candidate set sizes for service placement. Using a small key base increases the number of routing hops thus helping node discovery but also reduces the efficiency of key lookup for other applications sharing the DHT. A large key base, such as in one-hop routing, may not return enough useful nodes for service placement.

Another drawback is the low quality of the obtained candidate set from the DHT, which makes it necessary to perform a costly exhaustive search through all placement possibilities. Fundamentally, DHTs are not designed to optimize stream-based processing in the overlay network. A topology-aware DHT uses only latency to optimize its overlay routing paths. Since DHTs are connectionless by nature and thus unaware of the data streams in the SBON, they cannot

Table 2. SBONs classified by their placement techniques

| Node | | SBON Examples |
Discovery	Selection	
All	Random	PIER[3]
All	Relaxation	Hourglass[14]
All	Other (Human Decision)	GATES[15]
Consumer	—	Typ. Warehouse
Con. & Prod.	Varies (Random, Heuristic)	Typ. CQ System
DHTUnion	Greedy Heuristic on Opt	Borealis, SAND[2,16]
DHTIntersec.	—	Scribe[13], Bayeux[17]

easily optimize their routing tables for efficient service placement. Algorithms, such as Relaxation placement [5], designed specifically to minimize the amount of traffic in the SBON do not suffer from the same restrictions.

The intersection of DHT routing paths avoids the issue of a large, low-quality candidate set but has the problem that routing paths between pinned services may not converge. This is especially the case for services with a large number of incoming circuit links. Splitting services into sub-services addresses this problem but is not applicable in general. Routing data along DHT hops, as done by certain application-level multicast schemes, carries a large efficiency penalty.

5   Related Work

We suspect that the optimization of service placement decision in SBONs will be a growing research area, as can be seen from the wide-range of related work. New continuous query (CQ) work breathes life into questions that arose in distributed database optimization. Most related to our work is *SAND* [16] in the context of the stream-processing system *Borealis* [2]. In our terminology, they use DHTUnion to pick the candidate set, and a greedy heuristic on optimal for node selection. Their scheme can do no better than a *DHTUnion/Opt* placement.

The location of operators and corresponding relational tables in *PIER* [3], a distributed database built on top of a DHT, is determined through random hash selection from all overlay nodes and explicitly recognizes the possible inefficiency in such a service placement scheme, and is essentialy an *All/Random* placement.

Overlay routing and application level multicast systems consider where to place multicast services to best optimize an expanding array of metrics. For example, *Scribe* [13] uses a DHT to produce a multicast tree to connect publishers to subscribers. In our terminology, Scribe uses DHTIntersection-Split as its discovery mechanism and a "farthest common ancestor" heuristic as its selection mechanism. Grid users are recognizing the need to use in-network services to help process massive data streams. For instance, *GATES* [15] provides a way of introducing processing services but requires these services be pre-placed by a system administrator.

6   Conclusions

In this paper, we have shown that current DHTs do not produce a particularly good candidate set of nodes for service placement. DHT Union does not provide significant discovery value beyond that of selecting a random set of nodes from the overlay. If services cannot be split, DHT Intersection tends to reduce to Consumer placement, resulting in highly restricted and poor placement. If services can be split, we found that DHT Intersection still does not perform as well as a dedicated mechanism like Relaxation.

These results suggest a number of areas for further research. First, it remains an open question of whether it is possible to construct a DHT that is sufficiently network-aware such that it could be used to easily construct a good candidate set for node placement. How might we construct such a DHT? What does it mean for a DHT to be dynamically aware of network conditions? Second, should we declare that DHTs are not the correct abstraction on top of which to construct service placement algorithms? What alternative structures are possible? Third, is it necessary to globally optimize streaming applications? Do we believe that there will be sufficiently large amounts of streaming traffic to warrant building a system that does cross-circuit optimization instead of just local optimization? Answering these questions is crucial for successful deployment of stream-based applications.

References

1. Abadi, D., Carney, D., Cetintemel, U., et al.: Aurora: A New Model and Architecture for Data Stream Management. VLDB (2003)
2. Abadi, D., Ahmad, Y., Balakrishnan, H., et al.: The Design of the Borealis Stream Processing Engine. Technical Report CS-04-08, Brown University (2004)
3. Huebsch, R., Hellerstein, J.M., Lanham, N., et al.: Querying the Internet with PIER. In: VLDB, Berlin, Germany (2003)
4. Gibbons, P.B., Karp, B., Ke, Y., Nath, S., Seshan, S.: IrisNet: An Architecture for a World-Wide Sensor Web. IEEE Pervasive Computing 2 (2003)
5. Pietzuch, P., Shneidman, J., Welsh, M., Seltzer, M., Roussopoulos, M.: Path Optimization in Stream-Based Overlay Networks. Tr, Harvard University (2004)
6. Dabek, F., Cox, R., Kaashoek, F., Morris, R.: Vivaldi: A Decentralized Network Coordinate System. In: Proc. of ACM SIGCOMM'04, Portland, OR (2004)
7. The Planetlab Consortium. http://www.planet-lab.org (2004)
8. Stribling, J.: All-Pairs-Pings for PlanetLab (2004)
9. Zegura, E.W., Calvert, K.L., Bhattacharjee, S.: How to Model an Internetwork. In: Proc of IEEE Infocom'96. Volume 2., San Francisco, CA (1996) 594–602
10. Karp, B., Ratnasamy, S., Rhea, S., Shenker, S.: Spurring Adoption of DHTs with OpenHash, a Public DHT Service. In: Proc. of IPTPS'04, San Diego, CA (2004)
11. Rhea, S., Geels, D., Roscoe, T., Kubiatowicz, J.: Handling Churn in a DHT. In: USENIX '04, Boston, MA (2004)
12. Spring, N., Wetherall, D., Anderson, T.: Scriptroute. In: USITS'02. (2003)
13. Castro, M., Druschel, P., Kermarrec, A.M., Rowstron, A.: Scribe: A Large-scale and Decentralized Application-level Multicast Infrastructure. JSAC 20 (2002)
14. Shneidman, J., Pietzuch, P., Ledlie, J., Roussopoulos, M., Seltzer, M., Welsh, M.: Hourglass: An Infrastructure for Connecting Sensor Networks and Applications. Technical report, Harvard University (2004)
15. Chen, L., Reddy, K., Agrawal, G.: GATES: A Grid-Based Middleware for Processing Distributed Data Streams. In: HPDC-13, Honolulu, Hawaii (2004)
16. Ahmad, Y., Çetintemel, U.: Network-Aware Query Processing for Stream-based Applications. In: VLDB. (2004)
17. Zhuang, S.Q., Zhao, B.Y., Joseph, A.D., Katz, R.H., Kubiatowicz, J.: Bayeux: An Architecture for Scalable and Fault-tolerant Wide-Area Data Dissemination. In: NOSSDAV. (2002)

Author Index

Lecture Notes in Computer Science

For information about Vols. 1–3677

please contact your bookseller or Springer

Vol. 3721: A. Jorge, L. Torgo, P. Brazdil, R. Camacho, J. Gama (Eds.), Knowledge Discovery in Databases: PKDD 2005. XXIII, 719 pages. 2005. (Subseries LNAI).

Vol. 3720: J. Gama, R. Camacho, P. Brazdil, A. Jorge, L. Torgo (Eds.), Machine Learning: ECML 2005. XXIII, 769 pages. 2005. (Subseries LNAI).

Vol. 3719: M. Hobbs, A.M. Goscinski, W. Zhou (Eds.), Distributed and Parallel Computing. XI, 448 pages. 2005.

Vol. 3718: V.G. Ganzha, E.W. Mayr, E.V. Vorozhtsov (Eds.), Computer Algebra in Scientific Computing. XII, 502 pages. 2005.

Vol. 3717: B. Gramlich (Ed.), Frontiers of Combining Systems. X, 321 pages. 2005. (Subseries LNAI).

Vol. 3716: L. Delcambre, C. Kop, H.C. Mayr, J. Mylopoulos, O. Pastor (Eds.), Conceptual Modeling – ER 2005. XVI, 498 pages. 2005.

Vol. 3715: E. Dawson, S. Vaudenay (Eds.), Progress in Cryptology – Mycrypt 2005. XI, 329 pages. 2005.

Vol. 3714: H. Obbink, K. Pohl (Eds.), Software Product Lines. XIII, 235 pages. 2005.

Vol. 3713: L. Briand, C. Williams (Eds.), Model Driven Engineering Languages and Systems. XV, 722 pages. 2005.

Vol. 3712: R. Reussner, J. Mayer, J.A. Stafford, S. Overhage, S. Becker, P.J. Schroeder (Eds.), Quality of Software Architectures and Software Quality. XIII, 289 pages. 2005.

Vol. 3711: F. Kishino, Y. Kitamura, H. Kato, N. Nagata (Eds.), Entertainment Computing - ICEC 2005. XXIV, 540 pages. 2005.

Vol. 3710: M. Barni, I. Cox, T. Kalker, H.J. Kim (Eds.), Digital Watermarking. XII, 485 pages. 2005.

Vol. 3709: P. van Beek (Ed.), Principles and Practice of Constraint Programming - CP 2005. XX, 887 pages. 2005.

Vol. 3708: J. Blanc-Talon, W. Philips, D. Popescu, P. Scheunders (Eds.), Advanced Concepts for Intelligent Vision Systems. XXII, 725 pages. 2005.

Vol. 3707: D.A. Peled, Y.-K. Tsay (Eds.), Automated Technology for Verification and Analysis. XII, 506 pages. 2005.

Vol. 3706: H. Fuks, S. Lukosch, A.C. Salgado (Eds.), Groupware: Design, Implementation, and Use. XII, 378 pages. 2005.

Vol. 3704: M. De Gregorio, V. Di Maio, M. Frucci, C. Musio (Eds.), Brain, Vision, and Artificial Intelligence. XV, 556 pages. 2005.

Vol. 3703: F. Fages, S. Soliman (Eds.), Principles and Practice of Semantic Web Reasoning. VIII, 163 pages. 2005.

Vol. 3702: B. Beckert (Ed.), Automated Reasoning with Analytic Tableaux and Related Methods. XIII, 343 pages. 2005. (Subseries LNAI).

Vol. 3701: M. Coppo, E. Lodi, G. M. Pinna (Eds.), Theoretical Computer Science. XI, 411 pages. 2005.

Vol. 3699: C.S. Calude, M.J. Dinneen, G. Păun, M. J. Pérez-Jiménez, G. Rozenberg (Eds.), Unconventional Computation. XI, 267 pages. 2005.

Vol. 3698: U. Furbach (Ed.), KI 2005: Advances in Artificial Intelligence. XIII, 409 pages. 2005. (Subseries LNAI).

Vol. 3697: W. Duch, J. Kacprzyk, E. Oja, S. Zadrożny (Eds.), Artificial Neural Networks: Formal Models and Their Applications – ICANN 2005, Part II. XXXII, 1045 pages. 2005.

Vol. 3696: W. Duch, J. Kacprzyk, E. Oja, S. Zadrożny (Eds.), Artificial Neural Networks: Biological Inspirations – ICANN 2005, Part I. XXXI, 703 pages. 2005.

Vol. 3695: M.R. Berthold, R. Glen, K. Diederichs, O. Kohlbacher, I. Fischer (Eds.), Computational Life Sciences. XI, 277 pages. 2005. (Subseries LNBI).

Vol. 3694: M. Malek, E. Nett, N. Suri (Eds.), Service Availability. VIII, 213 pages. 2005.

Vol. 3693: A.G. Cohn, D.M. Mark (Eds.), Spatial Information Theory. XII, 493 pages. 2005.

Vol. 3692: R. Casadio, G. Myers (Eds.), Algorithms in Bioinformatics. X, 436 pages. 2005. (Subseries LNBI).

Vol. 3691: A. Gagalowicz, W. Philips (Eds.), Computer Analysis of Images and Patterns. XIX, 865 pages. 2005.

Vol. 3690: M. Pěchouček, P. Petta, L.Z. Varga (Eds.), Multi-Agent Systems and Applications IV. XVII, 667 pages. 2005. (Subseries LNAI).

Vol. 3689: G.G. Lee, A. Yamada, H. Meng, S.H. Myaeng (Eds.), Information Retrieval Technology. XVII, 735 pages. 2005.

Vol. 3688: R. Winther, B.A. Gran, G. Dahll (Eds.), Computer Safety, Reliability, and Security. XI, 405 pages. 2005.

Vol. 3687: S. Singh, M. Singh, C. Apte, P. Perner (Eds.), Pattern Recognition and Image Analysis, Part II. XXV, 809 pages. 2005.

Vol. 3686: S. Singh, M. Singh, C. Apte, P. Perner (Eds.), Pattern Recognition and Data Mining, Part I. XXVI, 689 pages. 2005.

Vol. 3685: V. Gorodetsky, I. Kotenko, V. Skormin (Eds.), Computer Network Security. XIV, 480 pages. 2005.

Vol. 3684: R. Khosla, R.J. Howlett, L.C. Jain (Eds.), Knowledge-Based Intelligent Information and Engineering Systems, Part IV. LXXIX, 933 pages. 2005. (Subseries LNAI).

Vol. 3683: R. Khosla, R.J. Howlett, L.C. Jain (Eds.), Knowledge-Based Intelligent Information and Engineering Systems, Part III. LXXX, 1397 pages. 2005. (Subseries LNAI).

Vol. 3682: R. Khosla, R.J. Howlett, L.C. Jain (Eds.), Knowledge-Based Intelligent Information and Engineering Systems, Part II. LXXIX, 1371 pages. 2005. (Subseries LNAI).

Vol. 3681: R. Khosla, R.J. Howlett, L.C. Jain (Eds.), Knowledge-Based Intelligent Information and Engineering Systems, Part I. LXXX, 1319 pages. 2005. (Subseries LNAI).

Vol. 3680: C. Priami, A. Zelikovsky (Eds.), Transactions on Computational Systems Biology II. IX, 153 pages. 2005. (Subseries LNBI).

Vol. 3679: S.d.C. di Vimercati, P. Syverson, D. Gollmann (Eds.), Computer Security – ESORICS 2005. XI, 509 pages. 2005.

Vol. 3678: A. McLysaght, D.H. Huson (Eds.), Comparative Genomics. VIII, 167 pages. 2005. (Subseries LNBI).